DEMOCRACY, ITALIAN STYLE

Battle of Ten Naked Men, engraving ca. 1465 by Antonio del Pollaiuolo.
Metropolitan Museum of Art, Purchase, 1917, Joseph Pulitzer Bequest (17.50.99)

DEMOCRACY
ITALIAN STYLE

JOSEPH LaPALOMBARA

YALE UNIVERSITY PRESS: NEW HAVEN AND LONDON

Designed by Sally Harris
and set in Galliard type by
Rainsford Type, Ridgefield, Conn.
Printed in the United States of America
by Vail-Ballou Press, Binghamton, New York.

Library of Congress Cataloging-in-Publication Data

LaPalombara, Joseph, 1925–
    Democracy, Italian style.

    Includes index.
    1. Italy—Politics and government—1976–
2. Democracy. I. Title.
JN5451.L36 1987   320.945   87–6124
ISBN 0–300–03913–1 (alk. paper)

10 9 8 7 6 5 4 3 2 1

To Constance

CONTENTS

PREFACE

Italy invites hyperbole. Almost everything about it appears monumental. This is not true just of the peninsula's physical beauty, its fabled history, or the treasures of antiquity it husbands. It is true as well of the ordinary pursuits and achievements, the pleasures and the passions that constitute daily life, at least as life is lived by the Italians.

Italy is also a place of nuance and illusion, of subtle and hidden meanings, not only in the fine arts but in the art of politics as well. At first glance, as in Pollaiuolo's famed *Battle of Ten Naked Men*, reproduced on this book's frontispiece, Italian politics seems a chaotic, unmitigated fight to the finish. Indeed, the picture we have of Italy is that of an ideologically polarized country engaged in an unremitting political war of all against all and on the verge of total disintegration.

But take a closer look at the Pollaiuolo engraving. The placement of the figures, their gestures, their relationship to each other and to the total space depicted makes this a composition that is in a state of both great tension but also almost perfect balance. The surface illusion of centrifugal conflict in effect obscures a much deeper harmony that is revealed to us by the artist only on further contemplation.

And so it is with Italian politics. On one level, we see in sharp focus little more than a long string of political excesses—inflated ideological warfare, cabinet crises without end, tax evasion, corruption, the Mafia, terrorism, and the like. It is easy to write the system off as impossibly polarized, and easier still to marvel that even a modicum of democracy is found there.

On closer inspection, the excesses turn out to be somewhat illusory and misleading. They may easily obscure, for example, the many stratagems that, over the centuries, the peninsula's residents have fashioned to

ix

keep excesses in check and to assure themselves relative freedom from political heavy-handedness. They may also cause us not to recognize the powerful impulses that send Italians in search of political harmony and lead them to manifest unusual levels of political toleration.

Above all, if we accept Italian politics at only face value, we will miss the basic point—namely, that Italy is fundamentally a healthy, dynamic, democratic country, with little chance of going over the brink and breaking to pieces. If some observers are coming slowly and reluctantly to that conclusion, many others, especially the Italians themselves, seem to have sensed it all along.

In my own case, I confess to having been a slow learner. Some of my earlier interpretations helped to establish certain images of the Italian polity, and of Italian political processes, that now strike me as inadequate—and very much in need of revision. This book is impelled by that conviction. Its central arguments are admittedly controversial. But I believe they will ultimately be judged a correct challenge to the now dominant views of Italian politics. I therefore ask of the reader not necessarily agreement regarding my formulations, but only an open mind.

These formulations will also have implications for theories about the conditions that bring democracy into being and encourage its longevity. Although Italy is far from a paragon of democracy, a democracy it certainly is—one that stands comparison to many others, including the much older ones of the United States and Great Britain. Italians participate in the political process differently; they have worked out their own ways of relating to and dealing with public officials and authorities, or, alternatively, with political terrorists; their political parties and the broad political subcultures of which the parties are expressions organize political life in ways that may strike us as unique, or even bizarre. But such things nourish Italian democracy. In the Italian context, even the most powerful non-ruling Communist party on earth has become a bulwark in support of liberal democratic institutions. This in itself is no mean achievement, but it is only one among many others we will note.

Mature, stable Italian democracy is largely the work of the much-maligned (but in my view secretly admired) "political class." Whatever their shortcomings, these political leaders have helped to mold an astonishingly solid democratic edifice from the ashes of fascism and war. Anyone who values pragmatism and finely honed political skills will have to admire the practical and often ingenious ways in which the Italians, led by their political class, have successfully attacked seemingly intractable problems. Democracy, Italian style, is above all else the art of permitting free government to endure under conditions that logically appear highly improbable.

This book is concocted of an unusual combination of ingredients. First, there is my personal scholarly and professional involvement with Italy, which now spans almost four decades. This experience has had its intimidating aspects: the more I sought to uncover the basic truths about Italian politics and democracy, the more complicated the search became. Despite such frustrations, I believe this volume will show that Italy has much to offer anyone who has ever wondered about politics, power, or people and their governors; the promotion and preservation of democratic institutions; the connection between political violence and political reform; or the borderline between freedom and license, liberty and anarchy.

A second ingredient was an unusual amount of moral and intellectual support. Much of both came from Constance LaPalombara, who more than anyone else has experienced the full range of my feelings about Italy, and about this book. Friends like Robert Dahl and David Apter prodded me to get on with a long overdue project. Both of them, as well as Kai Erikson and Ian Shapiro, were later to provide the kind of help with drafts of the manuscript that most authors can only dream about. I also benefited from Andrea Manzella's knowledge about Italy's governmental institutions and from Frederick Vreeland's experience in dealing with some of them as an outsider. Pendleton Herring reassured me that the Italian story could indeed illuminate our general knowledge about democracies.

There were others. Judy Harris Ajello, a journalist in Rome, read early drafts and critically reacted to the basic approach. Peter Sacks ran a poet's eye over those same pages with a view to the proper tone and cadence of the argument. Students like Sybil Fix, Eric Hepler, Nasser Hussain, Philip Klintner, and Alan Siaroff were also helpful critics, always ready to send me back to work armed with a fresh sense of what to discard or recast. David Hapgood, who writes for a living, read the bulk of the manuscript and sent it back relatively unscathed but nevertheless brimming over with suggested changes and corrections. On more than one occasion, E. A. Bayne, whose reports from Italy enlightened so many readers, provided valued support.

Two Italian colleagues, Giuliano Amato and Roberto D'Alimonte offered me pages of commentary as well as face-to-face arguments about difficult points in the manuscript. In the case of Amato, my gratitude is exceeded only by my admiration for his ability to manage the prime minister's office with one hand, complex political negotiations with the other, and still find the ways to alert me to innumerable pitfalls.

At Yale University Press, Laura Jones Dooley edited every line with impressive professional tact. And Marian Ash, whose editorial skills are well known to so many writers, did not deprive me on that score. She, like my friend Amato, wisely led me to make structural changes in the manuscript that I feel substantially improved it. John Nicoll added insights and strong advice that led to several late but necessary changes. Where imperfections persist, they have survived the best efforts of friends and colleagues to set things straight.

I composed this book on a word processor, about which apparatus I have mixed feelings. On one occasion, to my horror, I inadvertently sent a whole chapter into that black hole where electronic "bytes" go when they are not preventively "saved"—and printed! But word processors also release secretaries for more creative work. In my case, this meant that Sandra Rosen could turn her considerable talents to corrections of my manuscript as well as to the arcane ways of the personal computer itself.

Yale University's generous triennial leave program made it possible to produce a first draft of the manuscript at Rome. Thanks to my good friend and colleague Guglielmo Negri, I was able to use the facilities of the Chamber of Deputies library at Montecitorio.

By far my greatest debt is to the people of Italy. Over the years, many Italians, from every conceivable walk of life, have patiently offered me precious insights into the workings of their society, and particularly their political and economic institutions. Individually, the number who have gone out of their way on my behalf is much too large to enumerate here. Collectively, the Italians have made and reiterated one major point: to understand Italy, and especially its politics, requires a bit of *fantasia*. I hope the reader will find traces of that admirable and very Italian quality in the pages that follow.

1

A DEMOCRATIC PARADOX

Early in 1985, Ronald Reagan greeted Bettino Craxi, Italy's visiting prime minister, with the same question other U.S. presidents had put to Craxi's predecessors many times before. "How's your crisis going?" Reagan asked. "Very well, thank you," Craxi replied. It is doubtful that the prime minister's sardonic response succeeded in reassuring official Washington that, as Mark Twain once said of Richard Wagner's music, things are not really as bad as they sound.

"Things" in this case is the Italian political system. For forty years outsiders have thought about Italy, if at all, as a nation tottering at the brink of political disaster. That protracted balancing act should in itself have alerted us to the possibility that "things" in Italy are not necessarily as they appear on the surface. A country that seems to lean into the void but never really falls into it may actually be firmly anchored there, like the Tower of Pisa.

Italian commentary on political leaders and institutions is typically an off-key, atonal cacophony, not easy to comprehend. The fragments we hear suggest a dire situation. The clearest word filtering through the babble is *la crisi*, the crisis. One prime minister's visit will scarcely modify the common belief that Italian democracy lives by its wits alone, and on borrowed time.

During Easter Week that same year, NBC's "Today Show" transmitted from Rome by satellite. From the Spanish Steps, the Colosseum, and the Vatican, ten million viewers each day were served up with breakfast visual images of "modern" Italy. Most of what they saw and heard were clichés. Valentino was there, with some of his most dazzling creations. By now everyone knows that, when it comes to twenty-thousand-dollar items of high fashion, the Italians are unbeatable. Fiat's Gianni Agnelli appeared

on the video screen. We have all heard, many times, that he is Italy's
contemporary "Renaissance man." Peter Ustinov, appropriately dressed
in Roman toga as Nero, was there too—but in a Colosseum where the
most ferocious action these days is the clicking of high-speed camera
shutters.

About Italian democracy, NBC's overriding question was, "How come
it's still around?" There were predictable variations on this theme: Are
the Italian Communists really Communists? Are the labor unions too
strong? How do Italians feel about all of those changes in government?
Do the Italians really have confidence in their political leaders? Are they
too soft on terrorists? Is there too much corruption here? What about
all of that tax evasion? All in all, "How is your crisis going?"

Stereotypes of Italy invite such clichés. Italians themselves seem to work
hard to assure that they stay in place. When disaster fails to occur on
schedule it is easy to conclude that it's all play-acting. A *New York Times*
correspondent once lamented that, after more than twenty years of reporting from one or another of the world's hot-spots, he found his Italian
assignment utterly boring. "Nothing really happens here," he complained.
"It's only words, words, words." He was used to pitched military battles,
coups, and civil wars. Compared to where he had been, he may have
found prosaic such typical Italian events as political assassinations; bombs
in crowded piazzas or grenades in sidewalk cafés delivered by terrorists;
open warfare, from Sicily to Trento or Turin, between the police and
organized criminals; financial scandals that sometimes bring down governments; and so many other events that, politically speaking, look
pathological.

In a setting like Italy, where the tenth impression can be as deceptive
as the first, it is easy to confuse illusion with the real thing. True enough,
we should long since have realized that Italian Communists, who wear
splendidly tailored clothes and talk like your friendly loan officer down
at the bank, are really not plotting an Italian variation of the Bolshevik
revolution. Or we might have guessed that one reason why Italians create
the impression of crisis and chaos is that they want to be admired for
their ability to manage life despite such conditions. The point is that, to
get at reality, we need to overcome the clichés and, even more, to weigh
events in the Italian context.

This book is about Italian politics or, more precisely, about democratic
government as it is practiced in Italy. Its basic message is that, contrary
to appearances, and despite what so many Italians would have us believe,

Italian democracy is alive and thriving. If this statement seems unlikely, given what transpires in Italy, if the existence or survival of democratic government seems paradoxical, it will appear less so once we get the hang of how the system itself actually works.

A second message of the book refers to our theories of democracy. If Italy is a strong democracy but nevertheless fails to conform to what our theories specify as the requisite conditions of democracy, this is not necessarily a paradox. It may mean instead that we need to revise or expand our theories of the democratic state.

DISQUIETING SYMPTOMS

Italy abounds in symptoms that theorists and advocates of democratic government find disquieting. Political scandals are endemic. Officeholders and politicians, bankers and industrialists, military officers and members of the clergy, television personalities and magistrates themselves are hauled into court, and sometimes wind up behind bars, on charges of venality and corruption. Organized crime—the Mafia is only one of several major organizations—gains strangleholds, not just in Sicily or Naples but in cities like Milan and Turin and the places in between.

Terrorism has been part of the political landscape for fifteen years. Although domestic terrorists are not as virulent as earlier, they still managed in December 1984 to blow up a fast train headed from Florence to Bologna. The next spring, they murdered a professor of economics, in broad daylight, at the University of Rome. In March 1987 they shot and killed Gen. Licio Giorgieri in Rome. If this type of violence has been brought somewhat to heel, international terrorists have stepped in to keep nerves on edge.

Everyone agrees that the political management of the economy leaves much to be desired. Prime Minister Craxi himself publicly declared that as much as one-fourth of Italy's real gross national product might be in the "hidden"—that is, the cash and unreported—economy. At the 1987 exchange rate, this amounts to over sixty billion dollars! If this tells us that Italy is somewhat better off economically than the official statistics suggest, it also reveals that the government is not exactly on top of things. This is shown by such indicators as inflation rates, deficit levels, welfare expenditures, and the accumulated public debt of recent years.

To many, the institutions of Italian government seem weak and helpless to cope with such problems. To others, the overall picture looks so discouraging as to create doubts that the country is governable at all. The pollsters have reported for decades that citizens are disgusted with politics, scornful of political leaders, and downright hostile toward political parties. Mass attitudes seem to add up to the kind of "political alienation" that should spell trouble for a democratic society.

On close inspection, it can be shown that levels of governmental incompetence, of fierce ideological conflict, have been no greater in Italy than elsewhere among West European democracies. If Washington is nervous about Italy, and if others think that the survival of Italian democracy is paradoxical, this is so in part because Italians themselves have helped fashion these views. For decades now they have broadcast to the world that not only politics but every other conceivable aspect of their society is deeply in crisis. Where such litanies do not cause foreboding, they create the impression that it is indeed just words, words, words, spoken by a melodramatic people overinclined to see a wolf at the door.

As we will see, it is important not to take at face value the things Italians say about politics. If we do, then, like the pollsters, we will discover more paradoxes than the objective situation warrants. In a recent poll, for example, Italians in large numbers assured the interviewers that their neighborhoods, their towns and cities, and their country were all in dire decline. Yet when asked to comment on their material and economic conditions and their personal futures, these people just as overwhelmingly said that they were doing quite well, thank you, and expected to go right on in the same direction.

DEMOCRATIC BENCHMARKS

Even if we follow the stricture to be wary, the surface phenomena remain disquieting. The political scandals are real, and frequent enough to challenge credulity. The Mafia and Camorra are not perverse inventions of Mario Puzo, Hollywood, or the mass media but palpable, murderous organizations that wield economic and social, as well as political, power. Far from joining in any campaign to eradicate this problem, many enterprising members of the middle and upper classes invent scams of their own and thereby manage to bilk the state of hundreds of millions, even billions, of dollars. Furthermore, they often surpass the Mafiosi when it comes to the avoidance of prosecution and jail.

Italy also seems to fall short on other measures we use to gauge the health and stability of democratic governments. The language of politics, for example, is very intense: full of ideological assertions, sweeping condemnations of political opponents, and other expressions that suggest open warfare and irreconcilable conflict. Were one to read only the partisan press and to listen to speeches made in parliament or in the piazzas, one would quickly get the impression that, politically speaking, Italians are engaged in a war of all against all.

This image might easily be reinforced by some facts about government at every level. Cities can go for weeks, even months, without governments because the elected assembly members and their parties can't get together to form a working majority. In the republic's relatively short life there have already been forty-five national governments, or more than one per year. Any day of the week, it is a safe bet that one of the major regional or municipal governments will find itself in a state of apparent disintegration.[1] This has been the country's steady state for the past four decades. Isn't this evidence enough that the shortcomings Italians keep referring to are real?

Well, it depends. The shortcomings are almost always exaggerated and the crises invariably something less than that. In addition, certain aspects of Italian politics and government do not imply in Italy what such things might mean elsewhere. We all know that no democratic country will look entirely reassuring when measured against some abstract, idealized conception of the democratic state. It is not in this extremely demanding sense, therefore, that we should judge democracy, Italian style. This idea is difficult to sell, even in Italy, where, from the beginning of its history as a nation, intellectuals, journalists, and politicians have lamented the "revolutions," especially the democratic ones, that somehow managed to fail.

More typically, those who find Italian democracy weak, defective, and full of paradoxes make comparisons between Italy and such other democracies as Great Britain, France, the United States, or the Scandinavian countries. Although comparisons of this kind are sometimes useful, they can easily become arid, invidious, and misleading. They are arid because they invite endless, unproductive speculation as to what kind of a place Italy *might* be if only its leaders and its citizens were to behave differently: If there were fewer political parties, cabinet crises, or Communists; if the law governing elections were changed; if radical surgery were performed on the institutions of government; if the Catholic Church stayed out of politics; if Reaganomics replaced the welfare state; or if the Mafia were to disappear overnight. The wish list is open-ended, and speculation is limited only by the imagination. None of this helps us to understand how the political process actually works or how amenable a particular democratic system might be to change.

Comparisons with other countries are invidious because they imply, in some deep sense, that Italian democracy would be improved if Italy were more like Britain or the United States, if Italian citizens could emulate their counterparts elsewhere—in short, if Italians were less Italian. This sometimes leads us to the arrogant belief that American or some other brand of democracy is a template that can be stenciled onto almost any other country and produce similar effects there. We forget the spectacular failures that followed past efforts to export the American or British constitutional formula to Latin American, Asian, and African countries.

Comparisons of one democracy with another can also be misleading. For example, it is far from clear that Italian practice falls shorter of democratic norms than is true of other democracies in Europe or North America. Nor is it apparent why it makes sense to compare contemporary Italy with the Weimar Republic, a democracy that failed, or to insist, as so many Italians do, that the answer to what ails Italy is to make it, constitutionally speaking, more like the present Federal Republic of Germany. Prescriptions as to what changes are needed in Italy are also drawn from the French, British, or American models. The basic idea is that the ailing patient requires some combination of political amputation and grafts that will produce a sounder, healthier, longer-lasting democracy.

Most such thoughts are delusions. Political systems are highly complex, and for many reasons democracies qualify as the most complex of them all. This being so, most judgments as to what a particular symptom may mean, whether or not a given aspect of politics is or is not pathological, are little more than wild guesses. And when it comes to prescriptions, to suggestions as to what will correct the defects, the truth is that few of us would fare very well were there even mildly stringent laws against malpractice in the making and amendment of constitutions.

When it comes to political surgery, to radical intervention to remake political institutions, we know much less than we sometimes claim about what will cure or kill the patient. If the Italians change prime ministers more often than do the British, or than Americans change presidents, does this really mean that Italian democracy is more unstable than the others? If 90 percent of the Italians typically vote in national elections, as compared with just over half that number in American presidential elections, is it really the case, as some American scholars have claimed, that the Italian and not the American pattern is pathological? On reflection, which is the more serious weakness for democracy: the Italian government's apparent inability to bring the Mafia to heel in Sicily, or the failure of other democracies to deal with large-scale crime in their major cities? And which kind of corruption is more insidious: the headline-making scandals that fill Italy's daily newspapers, or the extensive "white-collar" crime in the United States, that rarely gets any public notice at all? [2]

The trouble with such comparisons is that they make it difficult to assess democracies in their own terms, within their particular social, economic, and historical contexts. The theorists of democracy are aware of this, and most of them therefore are careful to hedge what they say about the necessary and sufficient conditions for the birth, growth, maintenance, and breakdown of democracies. The typical hedge is to say that two or more factors will relate in a certain way if all other things are equal. But they rarely are. And so we are left in a terrible quandary when it comes to nailing down the factors inimical to democracy or to explaining why a particular condition will be fatal for one but not necessarily for another democratic system.

In discussing actual cases of breakdowns of democracies, we can and do attribute these to certain "excesses" of citizens, to certain failures of their representatives, to complex relations among social classes, perhaps to proclivities of the military, and even to complex events in international affairs. The richer the fabric of explanation, though, the more likely it will fit only one country or one situation. [3]

It would be nice to speak with confidence, to make accurate predictions, about the consequences for democracy of patterns or levels of economic mismanagement, tax evasion, political corruption, political meddling by the military, and even political violence like insurrection or civil war. However, people and institutions do not bend as readily as chemicals in test tubes to our efforts to discover the axioms of politics. A people's history and culture, its economic conditions and social norms, its aspirations and its workways and, yes, even its "national character" will affect the style and structure of government that develops in its midst. These same factors also limit the kinds of political engineering that can be performed in any given country.

As for democracy itself, it should now be obvious that it can flourish in remarkably different environments. This knowledge alone should alert us

to the possibility that something inconsistent with or inimical to democratic government in one place may be less so in another. In setting the
requisites or the benchmarks of democracy, therefore, we must be careful
not to limit these to certain institutions or certain ways of doing things
that are esoteric, anchored to one point, or descriptive of only one society.

In the Italian case, before leaping to the conclusion that democracy
there is ailing and in need of remedial intervention, we should try to gain
a better grasp of how the system works and with what effects on Italians.
Many persons who find Italian politics perversely awry and paradoxical
conclude that the Italians have the kind of government they deserve.
Judgments of this sort are invariably simplistic. A deeper, more interesting
truth may be another: that the Italians have the kind of government they
prefer. Furthermore, not only are political practice and the governmental
system essentially democratic, but they may also represent the only type
of democracy that is viable within the Italian context. This system, like
any other, is not without its imperfections. But it is highly unlikely that
Italian republican government can be transformed into something different, and perhaps better, without placing democracy itself at risk.

DEMOCRACY'S HISTORICAL ROOTS

The Italian republic is an accident of history. The *nation* of Italy is
barely beyond its first century.[+] Giuseppe Mazzini, early in the last century,
championed a united Italy, liberated from monarchies large and small,
foreign or indigenous, and from the Catholic church, which had for so
long dominated the peninsula. Another Giuseppe, the flamboyant Garibaldi, also wanted a united and republican Italy. To that end, he led his
glorious Thousand into Sicily and Naples to liberate both from an alien
Bourbon monarchy. The ubiquitous monuments to this republican-on-
horseback fail to convey that, as things worked out, Garibaldi, Mazzini,
and many who followed them fell short of their aspirations.

Count Camillo di Cavour, a contemporary of the Bismarck who united
Germany, was a more skillful and pragmatic founding father. He brought
the nation of Italy together under the aegis of the House of Savoy. And
so Italy's first steps in the direction of democracy were guided by aristocratic oligarchs who had a great fear of populism and who had no
intention at all of turning the national government over to the masses.

Contrary to the myths about the Risorgimento, this movement for

Italy's resurgence was anything but a popular ground swell—not in the north, certainly, but also not in the south. Tomaso de Lampedusa, in his wonderful novel, *The Leopard,* makes this point indelibly when he has his Sicilian aristocrat say that in order for everything to remain the same in Italy everything must change. In any event, all over the peninsula the peasants were either indifferent to the Risorgimento or, in many cases, readily joined forces with their betters, local power holders all, in taking up arms against the country's unification.

The Risorgimento may or may not be one of Italy's "failed revolutions," but it did leave many legacies. The most important of these is a widely shared belief about what makes the nation possible. The requirement is that as little as possible about the true nature of the national state—the compromises its existence requires, the price that its continuance extracts from classes, groups, and regions of the country—should be clearly defined or legislated. One of the strengths of the 1948 Italian constitution, for example, is vagueness on many issues that, if forthrightly treated, might seriously divide the country. Another merit of that document is that many of its more radical provisions are not, as the lawyers say, self-executing. This means that before they can go into effect additional laws must be passed, and Italians are masters at taking their sweet time on that score. The purists have found this foot-dragging outrageous and have scored the Christian Democrats for their failure to implement the constitution. The positive side of the practice is that the Republic of Italy is still around.

In Italy, the clarification of political problems and the establishment of clear-cut choices regarding them remains fundamentally erosive to national unity. Indeed, such practice is alien to the national character! The republic is still on its feet because, unlike the French who worship at the altar of Reason, the Italians have never believed that Reason, especially in politics, is anything more than a blunt tool. Italian national unity and indeed democracy itself have managed to sink roots in highly improbable soil because so much about power relationships—rights and privileges, duties and responsibilities—remains ambiguous. Unless this is understood, much of Italian national politics, from the 1860s to the present day, would defy comprehension.

Sometimes, as in love relationships, ambiguity seems to enrage Italians. Even in this delicate area, though, there exist modes and degrees of tolerance and accommodation that many outsiders might well find astounding. In politics, ambiguity enrages primarily the self-appointed intellectual vigilantes on the left and the terrorists. The others not only take ambiguity in stride; they openly admire those leaders who are skilled at its deliberate use in political negotiations and, more important, in finding workable, even if far from ideal, solutions to nagging problems.

Ambiguity also invites a muddling-through approach to the political management of the country. This implies a suspicion of well-made formulas and a preference for improvisation. When an Italian says, "Si tira avanti," this means that political or personal problems, and life itself, are faced one day and one issue at a time. In this context, the art of political improvisation, especially if it occasionally reaches virtuoso levels, assures its practitioners unabashed adulation.

Since the Italian nation-state was an unlikely prospect to begin with (some call it Italy's first "miracle"), its creation and survival have depended on a continuing, complex set of relationships and accommodations among the leaders of Italy's major regions, cities, economic classes, and principal political subcultures. The Fascists missed this point almost completely. They considered an abominable weakness what is really one of the country's major strengths. Even worse, the Blackshirts mistakenly blamed on Italy's flirtation with democracy every aspect of Italian society they found repugnant. Their effort to mold a single, highly disciplined national political system was doomed to failure, not because people preferred democracy but rather because ambiguously defined problems and suboptimal solutions to them are necessary conditions for the survival of the nation.

Another Risorgimento legacy is the Vatican, which furiously fought unification. Those imposing walls across the Tiber, the six-hundred-odd churches in Rome, the thousands of clergymen and nuns, and the millions of frontline militants in Catholic Action organizations are daily reminders that Rome is not one capital, but two. Joseph Stalin, who once derisively asked how many divisions the Pope commanded, never saw Saint Peter's Square on almost any Sunday morning.

Many of the Pope's "crack troops," the legions of Catholic Action militants, are headquartered in the opposing rows of ugly Fascist-era buildings that line the Via della Conciliazione, which begins on the west bank of the Tiber and then fans out into Saint Peter's Square. The "conciliation" for which the street is named refers to the agreement, reached by Benito Mussolini and Pope Pius XII in 1929, that ended, at a price, the Vatican's long hostility toward the Italian nation-state.

Official Catholicism's hostility to the Risorgimento is certainly understandable. Explicit in the idea of a single national government were the annexation of the Papal States and a severe reduction of the Pope's temporal powers. The Roman Curia therefore tried to torpedo unification by charging that the Risorgimento was a war against Catholicism itself. Millions of Italians believed the accusation, and they followed the Vatican's *Non Expedit*, an instruction to the faithful to boycott the new nation by not participating in national elections. They did so for several decades.

It took a far-sighted priest, Don Luigi Sturzo, to recognize that this strategy was, in the long run, an almost certain disaster for the Catholic church.[5] At the end of World War I, he created the Partito Popolare, the precursor of today's Christian Democratic party. Each party's intent was to assure that when the faithful did vote, they would be able to do so for candidates whose commitment to the church was at least as strong as their commitment to Italy as a nation. In particular, it was essential to give the masses options other than socialism.

Don Sturzo had to work against heavy odds and formidable opponents in the Vatican hierarchy to create the Partito Popolare. Alcide De Gasperi and other Catholic leaders who formed the Christian Democratic party after the fall of fascism found the high clergy more pliable. The latter now faced the grim prospect that, without a Catholic party alternative, voters would hand the Communist-dominated left a landslide victory.

De Gasperi and his collaborators, like Don Sturzo earlier, wished to create a "confessional" political party. Not in the slavish sense of a party directed by or from the Vatican and immediately at its disposal. But certainly "confessional" in the sense of providing the organized church with a direct instrument for its intervention in elections and in every other aspect of the political process.

Christian Democratic leaders deny that the party is confessional, and some of them are dead set against taking any kind of orders, direct or otherwise, from the Vatican or the clergy. But the cozy relationship between church and party is there, as obvious as the last meeting of a Catholic Action organization, or the more recent activities of the Communion and Liberation movement, or the latest exhortation from the pulpits that the faithful should cast their ballots for candidates and parties who favor "Christian unity."

The Concordat—the treaty the Vatican signed with Mussolini's Italy in 1929—was a one-sided bargain.[6] Not only did the church extract a large number of material privileges from the state; for all intents and purposes, Catholicism became the country's "established" religion. This situation remained intact until 1985, when Bettino Craxi and Pope John Paul II signed a new document that redefines, but does not abolish, rights, privileges, and obligations on both sides.

TRASFORMISMO

The Vatican was not the only powerful group that looked with disfavor on the New Italy. The *latifondisti*, large-scale landowners concentrated in the south, were hostile as well. With good reason, they feared that Cavour and the other liberals from the north would try to govern the new nation at their expense. If the House of Savoy and its exponents were to take control of the peninsula, they would have to find a way to placate and neutralize this southern opposition.

The solution they found is called *trasformismo*. This enduring practice blurs aspects of the political process that in other democracies may be much more limpid. For example, where trasformismo obtains, the distinction between majorities and minorities in the legislature will not be clear-cut; governmental coalitions will be loose, viscous, and shifting; and electoral outcomes will be, at best, only vaguely related to the formation of governments or the enactment of public policies. We will examine each of these matters in later chapters.

Following national unification, trasformismo made it possible for a small group of northern elites to manage the economy largely in their own interests. The long-term benefit to Italy of this greedy arrangement was the country's industrialization. In order to have a free hand in this process, though, the men from the north had to agree to leave the south in the hands of the reactionary latifondisti, whose interest it was to maintain the feudal system there largely intact. The cost to Italy of this aspect of the bargain was the permanent underdevelopment of the south, or Mezzogiorno.

Trasformismo has been an essential instrument of this historical understanding. For several decades after the country's unification, it permitted the shifts of power between the Historical Right and the Historical Left of the Liberal party to remain largely illusory, creating the impression but not the substance of alternation in government. Contemporary objections to the disjunction between electoral outcomes on one side and the formation of governments and enactment of public policies on the other trace back to this earliest practice.

For many Italians, trasformismo amounts to the type of political sleight-of-hand that makes a mockery of the democratic process. In earlier years, it was thought that trasformismo was the product of the small number of persons controlling the political process. Many find it amazing that the practice has persisted notwithstanding the extension of the suffrage, the development of political parties, and the emergence of a vast network of organized interest groups. In effect, if it is true that all democratic political systems are really oligarchies, run by a limited number of elites or highly influential persons, this pattern seems much more prominent in the Italian case.

No doubt it is. Nevertheless, the practice itself looks more objectionable in the Italian context because it has such an eye-catching label. For many decades, the critics of trasformismo have been able to claim that its existence continues to defeat the impulse toward liberal democracy that accompanied the Risorgimento. Such an indictment is not only erroneous; it obscures the more important aspect of trasformismo: that it represents in today's Italy, as in yesterday's, a necessary and not terribly high price that must be paid, given the structural constraints within which the Italian democratic system operates. This truth will become apparent as we move along.[7]

Bear in mind that Italy has had very little experience with alternations of governments, ruling majorities, or coalitions. The principle that from time to time the "ins" in politics will replace the "outs" is not well established there. The onset of mass parties late in the last century did not bring with it either a reduction of trasformismo or a strong demand for alternation.

As elsewhere in Europe, the first mass-based party was the Socialist party, and it too built its electoral support primarily on the urban working class created by industrialization. The rise of this party brought, at Don Sturzo's behest, a response from the country's Catholic subculture. For Sturzo, the real "opium of the masses" was Marxist doctrines and the political parties that mushroomed under its banner. As in Weimar Germany later, the most tragic upshot of this mutual hostility among the mass-based parties was the triumph of fascism. Despite facism's open threat to democracy, the Socialist, Popular, Liberal, and Communist parties created only opposition, and no government at all. Twenty years of dictatorship stepped in to fill this vacuum.[8]

REPUBLIC AND HEGEMONY

Political hegemony has been modern Italy's steady state. In its eleven-odd decades as a nation-state, there have been three dominant, hegemonic ruling political parties—the Liberals for the first half-century, the Fascists for two decades, and the Christian Democrats since World War II. It is true that beginning in 1980 smaller parties like the Republicans (with Giovanni Spadolini) and the Socialists (with Bettino Craxi) were able to name prime ministers. This change occurred, though, not in opposition to the Christian Democrats but at their suffrance.

Since its birth as a nation, Italy has experienced only one change of regime. This occurred when the monarchy was rejected by the voters in 1946 in favor of republican government. The fascist dictatorship, for all its undemocratic laws, was created "legally" without violence to the constitutional monarchy, which actually welcomed Mussolini's advent to power.

If we consider one regime change and three hegemonies in the past 117 years, Italy looks much less politically unstable than many people claim. Indeed, Italy's political system appears as one of the most stable in modern history. Furthermore, this stability has persisted notwithstanding a rash of conditions that in most other places would have led not only to constitutional and regime changes but also to revolution. We need mention only the enduring rivalry between church and state, the age-old antagonisms among the peninsula's major regions, the rise and fall of fascism and the civil war and bitterness it left in its wake, the occupation of the country by German and then Allied troops, two devastating wars, and class conflict that spawned the largest nonruling Communist party found anywhere, to say nothing of the economic disasters experienced along the way.

In more recent years, Italy has had to confront organized political violence on an unequaled scale. Internally, political terrorists on both the right and the left have taken dead aim at the liberal democratic state with the specific intention of bringing about its destruction. International terrorism also vents its anger and carries out some of its warfare on Italian territory. Nevertheless, the nation has held steady, refusing to react to organized terror with repressive measures.

The survival of a liberal, democratic, republican government in a place that had earlier known feudalism, oligarchy, monarchy, religious absolutism, and fascist dictatorship is noteworthy in its own right. It becomes even more so when we consider that the present republic was indeed a historical accident, unanticipated even by those who most ardently favored the abolition of the monarchy. As for the Christian Democrats and the Communists, who most wanted to be, and expected to become, the architects of Italy's postwar future, neither was a friend to republican government. For the Catholics, republicanism and anticlericalism are one and the same thing. For the Communists and Socialists, had the Soviet armies not been stopped at the Elbe, they would eagerly have expected Italy to become, to use a sardonic expression, a "people's republic."

As it turned out, and to everyone's surprise, the voters sent the monarchy packing and opted for republican government, though by only a small margin. To their credit, the Christian Democrats made a quick and then spectacularly successful adaptation to this turn of events. The Communists did this much later, in part because they thought that the republic would be transitory and that some sort of socialist, even Sovietlike, state would soon replace it.

Republican government is a historical accident also because Franklin Roosevelt and Winston Churchill were at odds over the future political shape of their defeated adversary. Churchill, more than Roosevelt, understood how unlimited were Stalin's territorial ambitions in Western Europe. For this reason, and perhaps because he was quite comfortable with the British monarchy, Churchill had no qualms about returning the House of Savoy to the Palazzo Quirinale. Roosevelt, for equally understandable reasons, was not enthusiastic about this idea. Neither of them, though, even remotely expected that Italy would evolve as a strong, democratic, republican government.

And with good reason. The auspices for Italian democracy were anything but promising. The fascist debacle had left the country in a state of chaos. The fall of the monarchy created a serious political vacuum. The strongest, most well organized postwar political groups and trade unions were those associated with the Communist party. The Socialists were hostages to this party, and it appeared relatively certain that the political left would look east, to Moscow, and not west for the model of government to be followed in Italy. It would take many Italian Communists years, even decades, to learn (or to acknowledge!) what political life is really like behind the Iron Curtain.

The problematical character of postwar Italy was well understood in Western capitals. As late as the onset of the Marshall Plan and the North

Atlantic Treaty Organization, there were many in Washington, London, and Paris who doubted that Italy could ever be constructively included in the Atlantic community. In Italy itself, particularly among leading Christian Democrats, there were deep reservations as to whether the country should line up with the West in postwar international politics. It required heroic efforts on the part of several leading Italian ambassadors to persuade the victorious allies, on the one hand, and leaders like Alcide De Gasperi, on the other, that Italy's proper destiny lay on the side of the Western bloc of democratic countries.[9]

Italian democracy, then, did not rise phoenixlike from the ashes of fascism and war; nor was it a governmental formula worked out and agreed to in advance by the country's major postwar political protagonists. Benito Mussolini had promised his countrymen a Third Rome, embellished by imperial splendors and in no way to be confused with the Western democracies Il Duce despised. His fear that Adolf Hitler alone might win the war and walk off with the spoils overshadowed his earlier insight that nazism represented the darkest and most degenerate moment in German history. So he attacked France and led his country not to new imperial glories but, rather, to the brink of disaster and beyond. Few who inherited this folly, including the most ardently antifascist among them, believed that a democratic system, tailored along liberal republican lines, should or could be erected in its wake.

PROBLEMATICAL DEMOCRACY

War left Italy in a state of extreme prostration. An estimated two-thirds of the country's economic capacity was destroyed. There were no Italian Dresdens, bombed beyond recognition by Allied aircraft, but key industrial centers were knocked out, and the railroad system was left a shambles. The vaunted fascist war machine not only turned out to be, like so much of the regime, a costly farce, but its quixotic deployment drained the country white and left industry in a state of obsolescence. By 1945 the country's productive capacity had fallen considerably below the level of 1938, a depression year.[10]

There was moral and psychological devastation as well, poignantly captured in great postwar films like *Rome, Open City,* and *The Bicycle Thief.* Most Italians had supported fascism, reluctantly at first but later with unabashed enthusiasm. The shameful conquest of Ethiopia, widely condemned in the West, was just as widely hailed in Italy as a first step toward a new Roman empire. Eventually, Fascist mythmakers persuaded most Italians that the famous March on Rome was a long, glorious column led by Mussolini rather than a ragtag band of political delinquents attracted to his cause. Above all, Italians came to value Il Duce's system of "law and order," and certainly preferred it to the chaos that preceded the advent of the fascist state.

Until disaster struck, Mussolini had gulled almost everyone into the belief that the regime's economic and military achievements were without parallel. We do not know for sure how many actually swallowed the propaganda that fascist science had invented a "death ray" that would stop enemy aircraft in midair. We do know that millions of Italian (and Italian-American) housewives responded at once to Mussolini's demand that they send him their wedding rings to help pay for what fascism wanted to erect.

It simply is not true that fascism was the madness of one man, forced on a reluctant people, just as it is not true that Italy under fascism was without anti-Semitism. Of course there was none of the mass murder of Jews that should forever mar the German psyche. But most Italians went meekly along with the fascist version of Jewish persecution that evolved under pressure from Hitler. Moreover, many in high places at Rome, including the Pope, were aware of Nazi depravity and did not utter a word in protest.

As the prospect of military defeat approached mathematical certainty, die-hard Fascists made a last-gasp effort to turn history around. In the north they formed, with Il Duce, the so-called Republic of Salò and thereby triggered a ferocious civil war. This war-within-the-war pitted neighbors against neighbors, brothers against brothers, sons against fathers. At one point, half of Italy had surrendered to the invading Allies, while the other half fought Allied troops in some sectors, Nazi troops in others, and each other in between. The climax of it all was, to say the least, as scarring as it was ignominious.

This was hardly solid ground on which to erect a democracy. And yet the democratic republic has already celebrated its fortieth anniversary. That republic is steady on its feet. Not only has it overcome the formidable handicaps that preceded and accompanied its birth; it has learned to walk and sometimes to run on its own. If there have been moments of regression, these seem to have encouraged an even greater resolve to make the republic work.

Many Cassandras are still inclined to bury the republic, but they are overwhelmingly outnumbered by Italians who must surely take perverse pleasure in confounding them. I suspect, too, that on the whole Italians are prouder of this extraordinary political achievement than they are willing to admit. The language of Italian politics is so inflated and so suggestive of unmitigated conflict and warfare, and Italians engage in such a degree of self-laceration in describing their politics—one has to get behind all of this in order to learn what is really going on.

By now, we are locked into the other image of Italy—the one that leads NBC reporters and others to wonder why the republic is still on its feet. All of that sound and fury, it seems, cannot be just that. The game of musical chairs that cabinet ministers play, the governmental crises, unreined terrorists in airports and train stations, double-digit inflation, and megascandals that reach even to the lofty heights of the Pope's favorite banker—these are a few of the symptoms that lead scholars to give their books such titles as *Italy: An Uncertain Republic, Does Government Exist in Italy?* or *Surviving without Governing.*

Some writers have made a virtual industry of depicting Italian democracy as headed if not toward oblivion then certainly toward some mortal encounter with its enemies. The country is described as dangerously "polarized," a word that easily produces images of two extreme groups, lethally armed and ready to mix it up in ways that assure that the first and principal victim will be the democratic system itself. An even more alarming picture depicts Italians as essentially anarchistic egoists, so selfish in their interests and so unalterably opposed to the interests of others as to create something like Hobbes's war of all against all. With images like these permeating one's consciousness, little wonder that Ronald Reagan, speaking for so many others, worries how Italy's "crisis" may be going.

If a democracy is launched in such problematical circumstances; if the structure of its basic institutions seems so fragile; if the climate of politics remains so stormy that the country seems to do little more than lurch from one crisis to another; and if Italians themselves keep warning that the shoals of complete disaster are nearby and inescapable, then the rest of us can be forgiven if we find its day-to-day and year-to-year survival paradoxical, even miraculous.

We will be rocked even more to discover the extent of Italy's economic and material well-being. This war-wracked country is today's fifth largest economy. Its people enjoy one of the highest living standards in the world. It serves as a magnet for millions of tourists each year who, beyond Italy's legendary artistic wealth and natural beauty, are able to sense, if they are at all awake, that something about the way the country is governed must be right. It is impossible to square today's Italy, in every sense, with the stereotypes that abound about that country.

A DEMOCRATIC POLYARCHY

In the pages ahead, we will see how and why Italy is less paradoxical than it appears. Several major themes run through this book. First, Italian society is permeated by politics and the democratic system itself is centered in the hands of political party elites. These leaders are much more skilled in the political management of the country than most persons, and especially the Italians themselves, are willing to acknowledge. Second, Italians, somewhat amazingly, given the monumental changes of recent decades, remain politically clustered into three major subcultures. Much of what occurs in Italian society, including politics, centers on these subcultures and the relationships among them. Third, Italy has a form of sub-rosa government that looks undemocratic but is not. In any case, it is the only viable democratic government there, given certain realities to be discussed later in detail. Fourth, historical events on the Italian peninsula, and especially the recent fascist interlude, have combined to create in Italy a deep-seated and widespread commitment to democratic government. Finally, Italian democracy is highly participatory, but not necessarily in the same ways as is characteristic of other democratic societies. If the Italian experience teaches anything about democracy, it is that there are myriad ways in which the ordinary citizen's actions involving politics will serve to reinforce his or her commitment to democracy.

To set the stage for what follows, we must note at the outset that we are in fact dealing with a democracy. The concept of course is slippery, not easy to define. We can easily agree that Italy, like all other representative democratic countries, does not resemble the classical democracies of ancient Greece.

Italian democracy does not fully satisfy the conditions of polyarchy either, although it comes much closer to doing so than many critics and detractors of the Italian system would have us believe. To qualify as a democratic polyarchy, certain conditions must be met." These include the rights of citizens to formulate their preferences; to form and join organizations; to become candidates for public office in pursuit of these preferences; to oppose peaceably the preferences of others, including those who constitute the government; to have access to information and to the instruments that produce and diffuse it; and to have preferences accepted or rejected as public policies both through free and open elections, and through procedures that ascribe essentially equal weight to all citizens, their preferences, and their votes.

This is a tall order, and no contemporary democratic state really fills it. One of the quarrels with Italian democracy is the allegation, already noted, that it is egregious in its failure to relate the formation of governments and the enactment of public policies to electoral outcomes. We assess this matter later in this book. At the moment, suffice it to repeat that, where the underlying issue is the form of political participation and the effects of participation on public policies, there are as many ways to it as there may be dead ends or blind alleys. We must be careful not to rule out the Italian way by mere fiat of definition.

On most of the other measures of polyarchy, Italy does not do badly at all. Universal suffrage is not only well established, but it is more assiduously indulged than almost anywhere else. Qualifications for public office are much like those of other democracies, and those who successfully run for office remain there only so long as the voters are willing, in subsequent elections, to leave them there. Furthermore, no one, not even the military, would think of opposing the outcome of elections, except on constitutional or legal grounds.

Italy is so even-handed toward those who seek public office that even jailed persons accused of serious crimes sometimes get on the ballot and are elected to high office. The Radical party has made this maneuver one of its specialties. The most arresting case to date occurred in 1983, when the Radicals nominated and then elected to the national legislature Toni Negri, who was then in jail awaiting trial on charges that he was one of the "brains" behind the Red Brigades. When it appeared that the lawmakers would vote to lift Negri's parliamentary immunity so he could stand trial, he took off for Paris, which has been a haven for Italian expatriates suspected or convicted of terrorism. Not long ago, Negri publicly complained that the Italian parliament, on the petty ground that he was not in regular attendance at Rome, was sending him only half of his parliamentarian's salary. On this occasion the government displayed a tin ear. But the fact that the government pays him anything at all says something about Italy's addiction to the rule of law and its political toleration. Toni Negri is, in writing, a sworn enemy of the Italian state.

By American, British, or German standards, the degree of freedom and liberty in Italy seems to border on license or anarchy. The press is certainly free, although its ownership structure would raise eyebrows in some other democracies. The Italian mass media also appear far more politicized than in other democracies, but this may mean no more than that the matter is more in the open there than elsewhere. On the other hand, the Italian mass media regularly publish material that in other democratic countries would be considered beyond the limits of "public decency" and, in many instances, libelous. In recent months, those who publish damaging statements about others have adopted the American-type defense that they are "investigative reporters" who need not divulge the sources of their incriminating claims. Such claims are hollow; genuine investigative Italian journalism is about as frequent as major snowstorms on the Isle of Capri.

On the other hand, unlike countries like the United States and Britain, Italy does not blandly accept the death of major newspapers as an inevitable outcome of the market's "hidden hand" at work. Instead, the government provides heavy subsidies to keep newspapers in print. This policy is even extended to radical papers like *Il Manifesto* that rarely have a kind word to say about the government. If, as some claim, Italians do not read very much—about politics or anything else—it is not because the print media are boring or conformist.

When it comes to political parties and pressure groups, Italians have shown no reluctance to further their proliferation. The best-known political parties number about six, although it is not uncommon for the voters to find three or four times that number on the ballot. These parties come into existence not just to participate in republican government; some of them openly intend to change the system radically if they attract enough votes. So far that has not happened, and it probably will not, but the basic freedom is there.

Italian democracy knows no alien and sedition laws. There are no witch hunts here of the kind that in the United States bear the names of the Salem Witch Hunts, Sacco and Vanzetti, or Sen. Joseph McCarthy. Even if Italian equivalents of Ethel and Julius Rosenberg were to be convicted of high treason, life imprisonment, and not the electric chair, would be their severest punishment. The worst one can say about Italy's treatment of political opponents of the republic who are arrested for terrorism is that they, like those arrested for other alleged crimes, may languish in prison for years before being tried.

On the other hand, terrorists not only survive in prison; they are notoriously well treated there. Unlike members of the Baader-Meinhof terrorist group in West Germany, they are not found dead in their cells, officially reported as cases of suicide committed in maximum-security prisons.

The Italian system of justice is certainly not without its faults, and some would argue that the most serious of these has been a gradual tendency of judges to become the willing tools of political groups and causes, including those of the terrorists. We will explore this issue later, when we face the question how much of the existing institutional state of things is in need of change.

The point here, at the beginning, is not to make invidious comparisons, not to believe that, when it comes to assessments of other political systems, we stand on Mount Olympus. From where the Italians stand, in any case, it is far from clear that the polyarchical or democratic conditions found elsewhere are superior. The fact that masses of Americans do not participate in elections strikes many Italians as strange and irresponsible. The British government's treatment of terrorists in Northern Ireland seems to many Italians to be dangerously beyond the limits that democratic norms would impose on government. The number of Americans below the so-called poverty line and the level of unemployment in Britain suggest to Italians that there are aspects of their democratic system working better than those of these much older democracies.

Italy not only meets the conditions of polyarchy; it manages to do so under a range of existential factors that, in many other places, would make democratic polyarchy highly improbable, or place it in jeopardy. This may very well mean that a polyarchy, once established, has more staying power than we imagined. Or it may suggest that a wider range of contextual factors, including some that may initially appear incompatible with a democratic system, may actually work to support democracy.

SOME APPARENT PARADOXES

Before we go on to explore this idea, we should enumerate a few of the specific aspects of Italian politics that make democracy there appear paradoxical to so many persons. Consider the following:

- Italy has the largest, strongest, and in many ways most able of Communist parties found among democracies. Nevertheless, that party has not only refrained from any subversive, to say nothing of revolutionary, assaults on democratic institutions and processes; at critical moments it has acted unambiguously to support and reinforce them.
- In much higher proportions than is true of other democracies (sometimes as many as eight or nine out of ten of those surveyed), Italians report that they are uninterested in politics, lack confidence in their political institutions, and never discuss politics with family members, friends, or neighbors. Yet they go to the polls—often, and in record numbers.
- The average life expectancy of a national government is around ten months, and since the late 1940s there have been forty-five of them. Some governmental crises lead to national elections in which voters can presumably reward and punish, modify the legislative majority, and thus produce the conditions for a new and different governmental coalition. Nevertheless, this never happens. From one election to another there are largely imperceptible changes in the proportion of the votes that go to parties of the left, center, and right wings of politics.
- Italians are acutely and unremittingly critical of government. They know where its weaknesses lie. With the help of the vigilant, and politically partisan, mass media, they can readily identify the miscreants, culprits, devils, and political machines and parties responsible for shortcomings, real or imagined. Nevertheless, no rascals are evicted from office here. There has never occurred the kind of alternation in office implied by the idea that once in a while the "ins" will be replaced by the "outs." As a matter of fact, a close look at the national legislature reveals that the Italian parliamentary system is without any opposition at all.

We could easily add more paradoxes. Outsiders find it strange, for example, that a country as Catholic as Italy is supposed to be reveals so much vehement anticlericalism. It is these same Catholics who, despite what the Vatican may say in the matter, award the Communist party about one-third of the vote. Furthermore, far from flourishing where poverty is rampant, the Communist party is strongest in some of the wealthiest regions of the peninsula and often weakest in the poorest regions.

Is it not paradoxical, as well as ironic, that the same national government that faces large-scale deficits in public spending fails to crack down on tax evaders, most of whom the government can readily identify if it is so inclined? And does one marvel or shudder over a government that first, and knowingly, permits millions of violations of building codes and city plans and then passes a law that "forgives" or grants amnesty to the violators in exchange for modest fines?

And how shall we judge growing unemployment in a country where those who work for the government grow in numbers, complete their day of public "service" by two o'clock, and then go on to fill second jobs in the hidden, or unreported (that is, untaxed) economy? All manner of projects that aim to reform some of these things either bog down in legislative committees or, if they ever pass, are quickly sabotaged by the bureaucrats themselves, working hand-in-glove with those who stand to lose if the rules are changed.

This situation, which some Italians certainly find intolerable, is supposed to result in "political alienation," in hostility toward the so-called "political class," and in a much-remarked lack of respect for political institutions and those elected or appointed to them. Were this the case, then the tremors in the political system would be of seismic proportions. And someday they may well be, but there is very little evidence thus far that this is the case or, for that matter, that Italian democracy is on such a course.

Instead, a nascent democracy that looked unlikely forty years ago is in good shape today, and on a relatively steady course. In many ways, democracy, Italian style, seems in better condition than many older democracies (Belgium, the Netherlands, even France and Britain might be examples) that seem unable to resolve their own problems.

Let's take a closer look at this peculiar and interesting political system.

2

WE, THE PEOPLE

Sixty million Italians make a fetish of appearing to be different from each other. It is not just that the haughty resident of Milan or Turin loathes being mistaken for a Neapolitan or a Sicilian—feelings that Sicilians and Neapolitans fully reciprocate. Residents of towns located within a few kilometers of each other also pride themselves on their cultural superiority over their neighbors.

Of course even Italians recognize that they resemble themselves more than they do outsiders, sharing not simply language, style of dress, and many other social preferences but also certain values, modes of behavior, and canons of public morality that are intimately related to politics. These may be assessed in terms of their negative, positive, mixed, or neutral consequences for democracy.

The stereotypes and dominant pictures we have of Italians are not entirely encouraging on this score. Giacomo Leopardi, a major nineteenth-century writer and poet, said that Italians not only lacked feelings for the nation as such; they were also devoid of any sense of society.[1] This being so, they were entirely without public morality, respect for others, and that minimum regard for public opinion that makes civilized living possible. Leopardi depicts Italians as rampant egoists, unremitting cynics, whose greatest and almost exclusive pleasure in life is to laugh derisively at humankind, beginning with themselves.

Leopardi goes on to say that Italians evince "a vivacity of character... that leads them to prefer the pleasures of *spettacolo*, and other delights of the senses, to other pleasures that are more appropriate to the spirit... and that impels them to entertainment, carelessness, and laziness." All they enjoy, he says, can be summed up in the *passeggiata*, or evening stroll, the spettacolo, and the church ceremony, which is of course just

25

another type of spettacolo. They prefer gala feasts, sacred or profane, to conversation. When they do converse, they do so primarily to heap derision on third persons, which they do "with a truer and more intimate and persuasive sense of scorn and cold-bloodedness than any other people." What little conversation there is, he adds, is "nothing other than a pure and continuous war without quarter; and, although only a war of words and style about things of little substance, it reveals how it must shatter and alienate everyone's soul."

Not a pretty picture. But if we look at Leopardi's famous essay more closely, we find that he is doing exactly what he excoriates, and for a good reason. He admires the very aspects of "national character" he purports to abhor. Why? Because, he says, Italians laugh at life, and they sense the vanity of things. The average Italian, he adds, is more philosophical than the professional philosophers outside Italy.

This is not exactly an indictment. It suggests that Italians will be more flexible and more tolerant than the inflated rhetoric of their political exchanges would lead one to believe. Indeed the level of toleration is sometimes so astonishing that the unwary observer may be misled to believe that the Italian citizen is without standards, or that he or she really does not care about whether the political system is working well or otherwise.

Perhaps the most damaging thing Leopardi has to say about Italians is that they are not, in his view, disposed to sacrifice anything, no matter how trivial, to public opinion. The Italian, he claims, lives only in the present. He has no sense of the future. He is therefore unconcerned with it. Because he arranges his life free of any future prospects, he incurs no obligations. For Leopardi, these characteristics are contrary to effective social organization. Insofar as any society exists at all, it is only an instrument of the overt expression of mutual aversion and disunion amongst men. It inflames the natural passions that men harbor toward each other, and especially toward their nearest neighbors. It leads, in the end, to a generalized condition of misanthropism.

In sum, Leopardi finds the peninsula overrun with customs and mores that are local and parochial, rather than national and universal, and with a type of individualism that borders on anarchism. As for public spirit, it is very rare, narrowly limited to what is explicitly prescribed by law. For the rest, one is free to do exactly as one's inclinations dictate, whether or not it may encumber the public. And if it does, the public itself will have a care not to pass judgment on this behavior. "Usages and customs in Italy," Leopardi concludes, "generally come down to this: that each follows his own, whatever they may be."

A CONTEMPORARY PORTRAIT

How does this unflattering picture compare with today's average citizens, with those protagonists of contemporary Italian democracy who are the principal objects of the public policy-making process? In some degree, the description fits perfectly, especially in the amount of time devoted to a derisive laying bare of the shortcomings and especially the pretentions of others. And there is little doubt that, especially among males, who are both the instruments and the victims of *machismo,* life is contestation: hand-to-hand combat in which the willful humiliation of adversaries is even more satisfying than their defeat.

From a political standpoint, though, are there any merits ascribable to these and to other characteristics noted by Leopardi? One advantage is that the average Italian is hardly likely to take any political leader, including those with dictatorial pretentions, too seriously. While this may not prevent a Mussolini from coming to power, it lowers the probability that the political regimes such men erect will resemble those of the likes of Stalin or Hitler.[2]

Second, as Leopardi was aware, Italians are far from indiscriminate or irresponsible in their attacks on third persons. At a minimum, they extend due and cautious regard to the potentially powerful and to the friends and potential friends of others. Italians display a sharply honed sense of the nature of power and of political struggle that, as noted earlier, goes back to Roman times. As the heirs of Machiavelli, they are keenly aware of the need to measure power with care and, even more important, not to exaggerate or to misuse it.

These characteristics may make Italians less idealistic and more cynical than the citizens of other democracies, even the French. But it also makes them notably more inclined to find some practical basis for keeping the war of all against all from getting out of hand. That is, side by side with the war itself go the beliefs that all conflict can be adjusted and that there is a solution, however temporary and imperfect, for every problem. Several important aspects of the political process to be noted in later chapters reflect this basic orientation. Suffice it for the moment to say that this attitude implies a pragmatism in Italians that tends to be obscured by the fiery ideological rhetoric spoken by politicians and intellectuals.

Furthermore, for all of his sharp insights, Leopardi seems to have greatly underestimated the importance of his own, correct, observation that for the most part the war itself is typically a war of words. The most ferocious language is applied to the most trivial as well as the most earthshaking matters. Indeed the war of words in Italian culture neutralizes sublimated and displaced deeper feelings of aggression that in other societies can lead to the taking of political prisoners, civil war, and genocide. If not all Italian politics is sound and fury, enough of it is to assure that less of both, and particularly the latter, will impair otherwise tolerant, accommodating approaches to political problem solving. In effect, Italians have known for centuries that politics is the art of compromise, an understanding without which no democracy is possible.

To be sure, today's Italy displays endless manifestations of the ego-centered individualism, the arrogant disregard for others, for society and its generalized norms, mentioned by Leopardi and many other writers. Traffic is chaotic, and pedestrians learn early on the distinction between the quick and the dead. Courtesy to third persons will vary, capriciously, between effusive proportions of it or none at all. The orderly queue is unknown, and no one expects to be treated on the basis of universally recognized norms of fairness or equity. Those who face life with the expectation that they will be treated evenhandedly in the private or public spheres are considered *fesso,* a condition of doltishness to be avoided at all cost.[3]

Paradoxically, this ego-centered individualism and struggle to avoid being considered fesso do not fan or reinforce conflict and aggression; rather, they modulate it. The truly untrammeled egoists and self-aggrandizing individualists, while not risk averse (they tend to be gamblers, and "high rollers" at that) are rarely in the true sense risk takers. They go to considerable pain to minimize risk. As a result, they work hard at developing a keen understanding of both the formal and the actual rules of the system. And they complain less than do the more idealistic or naive among men when they take note of this large gap. For example, Italian automobile drivers are highly skilled because they learn to expect all other drivers to behave in perverse and dangerous ways. No one needs to be reminded to drive defensively where sheer survival depends on that ability. Similar considerations apply to most of life's daily transactions, from the most banal, like shopping for groceries or getting to and from work, to the most portentous, like all forms of contact with public authority.

Ego-centered individualism also leads to the search for exceptions to and loopholes in regulations, and Italians from all walks of life expect to find them. They rarely believe that the system is in practice as democratic as the constitution prescribes or as the schoolbooks assert. Instead of raging over this disjunction, they learn to make do, and in the process they often work out quite creative accommodations.

This view of reality and the pattern of accommodation to it also engender a remarkable degree of tolerance, including official tolerance, toward transgressors. This is extended even to leaders of terrorist organizations who have committed murder. Outsiders mistake this for softness or moral laxity. Italians in turn consider many of the practices of older democracies little more than puritanical hypocrisy. In any case, this practice mediates potentially destabilizing confrontations.

Among the many stereotypes heaped on Italians by protagonists of "national character," one might note the following: Italians are highly emotional; they are entirely too dramatic about the ordinary in life. One image, no doubt born in Naples, depicts Italians as irrepressibly happy persons who break into song on any and every occasion, even one that elsewhere might bring forth tears. Parallel to this picture is its opposite—Italians who wallow in a life of *dolce far niente,* amiable idleness.

If this last image does not square with the individualism and propensity to anarchical behavior just described, or with the frenzy that accompanies so much of the country's everyday activities, so much the better. It shows up the ambiguity of such assertions. Italians may laugh at life; they also take it seriously enough to want to work very hard to find respite from its more nagging, boring, or threatening aspects. The above-ground economy may look like a shambles. But the underground economy could scarcely have reached its present magnitude were it not for the avidity of so many people to hold down two or three jobs.

As for singing, perhaps Italians do it more naturally than others, but they are no more inclined toward it, especially in the face of adversity or disaster. If so many of them sing, it is perhaps because they know that the official statistics on unemployment, inflation, fiscal drag, taxation, and per capita income are, like so much else about the country, a far from full account of what really goes on.

As for Leopardi's biting comment that Italians of his day lived in the present, with little or no regard for the future, one can just as easily argue today that the Italians' concern about the future is obsessive. For example, they save at much higher rates than the people of any other advanced industrial country except Japan. They husband the lira notwithstanding all the talk about the political mismanagement of the economy and the dire predictions as to what the future may have in store. This pattern is scarcely in keeping with live-today-cry-tomorrow images of the Italian people.

NEWER VALUES AND OLDER ONES

The trouble with the stereotypes is that they persist long after the bit of truth that encouraged their appearance has disappeared. Today the evidence is overwhelming that the large-scale demographic, economic, and social developments of the past forty years have also changed the people. In fact, many of the transformations in society have occurred *because* the Italians as individuals have changed.

Take for example the well-known Italian drive to become "fixed for life," or *sistemato*. This is a conservative impulse to find and keep a job, in a setting of poverty where jobs are very scarce. This was Italy's steady state, spanning centuries. In the underdeveloped south, a job in the public service, because it carried life tenure as well as high status, was considered the epitome of *sistemazione*. The scramble for these jobs sent many in search of political patrons who could deliver this form of economic salvation.

The *sistemarsi*, or get-fixed impulse, is not as strong as it once was, but it is still there. Its persistence both reflects and reinforces the patron and client aspect of politics that will be examined in the next chapter. Nevertheless, many studies of younger Italians show them to have much less economic anxiety about the future than was true of their parents. The newer generations are less inclined to consider a job with the government as the best of all possible careers. They are also not as ready to look to the state as the prime organization responsible for the satisfaction of their needs. In some ways, they resemble their American counterparts who, in contrast with their parents, did not experience the trauma and insecurity of the Great Depression.

This younger generation triggered the protests of the late 1960s and early 1970s, which represented, if nothing else, a ringing claim that the state was doing precious little to prepare younger people to work and live in better conditions of self-realization. Some detected in these collective action movements a newer system of values generated because families were more affluent and younger people did not have to work, as soon and as hard, to make their living. Those years created an impression not only of attenuated individualism and greater solidarity among the newer generations but also of a propensity to join with others, in voluntary organizations that were *not* tied to political parties, in pursuit of the common good.

How much change has occurred? One way to find an answer is to ask how important is today's family to younger Italians.[4] Newer attitudes toward life presumably should, sooner or later, affect their behavior and attitudes. We would expect them to save less of their income. They should be less inclined than their parents, or older persons in general, to value the nuclear family as the unit around which economic well-being and security, as well as political identities and loyalties, are organized.

The evidence is mixed. For example, if younger persons have more of a tendency to make purchases on the basis of time payments, it is also true that the strong propensity to save cuts across all age brackets and income categories.[5] Or take the salience of family. As elsewhere, parents are not quite the authority and security-giving figures of yesteryear: In 1969, when a national sample of Italians were asked in whom they would place faith and confidence, 72 percent of them mentioned personal family members, 21 percent mentioned friends, 5 percent indicated their spouse, and 14 percent said simply no one. More than a decade later, in 1983, in a similar sample of young Italians, only 59 percent mentioned their personal families, 33 percent mentioned friends, and 11 percent mentioned their spouse. Those who had faith in no one amounted to 12 percent, which suggests no change among the extreme cynics. The drop in the relative importance attributed to family members, although noteworthy, does not suggest a radical shift in values.

On matters of direct relevance to politics, the two surveys are more arresting. There is no question, for example, that younger Italians, much more than their elders, claim to be dubious about the value of political party affiliation and membership in ideological organizations. The authenticity of such attitudes is in turn supported by available information regarding the kinds of organizations these younger persons actually join.

They tend to shun political parties as well as such auxiliary political party organizations as youth groups. They also skirt the labor unions so important to several of the major parties.

On the other hand, youthful membership in religious, recreational, and sports associations is clearly up. Also, whereas in 1969 about three young Italians in ten would place their faith and confidence in the clergy, today that number has fallen well below one in ten. Teachers fare even worse; only one young Italian in a hundred considers them faith-worthy.

These statistics are difficult to interpret. The basic unit engaged in the savings behavior just noted is the nuclear family. So much of Italy's recent material progress turns on a cooperative effort by these units that writers now refer to each of them as "The Family, Inc."[6] The number of family enterprises in which two or more persons are gainfully employed is much higher today than ever before. These same families account for about 80 percent of all savings, a remarkable fact in itself.

In 1984, one-half of all families saved, and 30 percent of the families that did not save chose, and were not compelled, to spend what they earned. Not only is this form of capital accumulation astounding, but those who save have become much less conservative as to where they put their money. If nothing else, high rates of inflation in recent years have led them to shun savings accounts in favor of treasury bills indexed against inflation and to invest in securities and mutual funds, many of which are now peddled by door-to-door salesmen. In recent months, the explosive growth in the stock exchange at Milan implies that more of this huge mountain of family savings is finding its way into local capital markets.

In a country that was bogged down in poverty just a few decades ago, today only one Italian in four owns no real property. Sixty percent of homes are owned by private persons. Today more Italians than Americans are homeowners. In the last decade, the number of second homes, typically used for recreational purposes, has exploded. Rising income levels, the accumulation of savings, and the purchase of first and second homes not only imply that the nuclear family is in good health. They mean too that some of the bases for deep-seated political conflict that might erode democratic institutions and government have been greatly attenuated. The present condition of the Italian public is manifestly not one in which radical movements or ideologies will find great resonance.

Average prosperity is also aided by family size. Italy's birth rate, once among the highest in Europe, is now among the lowest—on a par with Denmark's and West Germany's—and is about one-half that of Catholic

Ireland. Today Italy's annual net growth in population is equal to that of the Low Countries, about one-third that of France, and only one-eighth that of Ireland. When it comes to the average age at which persons marry, only in Denmark among European countries are they older than in Italy. Demographers are worried that in 1987 Italy may not be able to maintain its current population.[7]

Postwar changes along these and other relevant dimensions are simply mind-boggling. If the Italian divorce rate remains lower than elsewhere in Europe, this may well reflect both the presence of Catholicism and the continuing importance placed on the nuclear family. Divorce is also a recently acquired right, and the trends since its legalization ten years ago indicate that the Italians will catch up with the rest of Europe here too.

Sociologists of the family claim that, by Western standards, the Italian variety remains highly authoritarian. Feminists complain that the much commented new equality between husband and wife is largely restricted to the family's economic affairs. Women still do the cooking and household chores, even if they are now, like American housewives, more "assisted" by electronic gadgets.

The residue of a male-centered, "macho" relationship between the sexes is hard to remove. Italy's feminist movements and organizations are pushing in this direction, but progress is slow. In Italy as elsewhere, women in the protest and revolutionary movements of recent vintage wound up cooking the meals and keeping house for their gun-carrying male counterparts. Some of them, though, also carried guns and numbered among the most fearsome terrorists. In any case, the condescension that American feminists often express toward their Italian sisters is misplaced in that it fails to appreciate, in relative terms, just how far Italian women—always the pivotal center of the nuclear family—have come in the last several decades.

THE FAMILY AND POLITICS

The question is whether the centrality of the family, its persistent authoritarian character, and its father- or husband-centered aspects, continue to have the political implications of years past. Do families still vote as a unit as much as they once did? The answer is probably no, although it is necessary to add that to some degree they never really did. For example, it is well known that women, in much larger proportions than men, support the Christian Democrats (DC). In fact, if universal suffrage had not been extended to women at war's end, the Communist and Socialist parties would have come immediately to power, and stayed there. As we will see in chapter 5, the fact that so much of the Christian Democratic vote comes from women has helped to slow the erosion of electoral support for the DC party that the turnover of generations is producing.

Changes in the role of women, in their family status and relationships, in their educational achievements and work opportunities, have no doubt freed many of them from the pervasive electoral influence of the pulpit. This is especially notable in the south and in the northeast, traditionally Catholic regions where the DC enjoyed until very recent years its most impressive bedrock strength. In these regions, electoral shifts away from the Christian Democrats could not have occurred, or would not have been as sharp, were it not for some radical changes in the voting patterns of women.

There are really two parallel changes with not necessarily similar consequences underway here. The newer values of the younger generation, including their attitudes toward parents and family, may well encourage more independent voting, based on issues or candidates as opposed to party identification, than in the past. If that is true, we should expect down the road to see less voting by Italians on the basis of the major political "families," or subcultures, to which they belong. As I will show later, however, all of this vaunted change in the values of the young seems to have had so far only a marginal impact on electoral politics.

The liberation of women may or may not lead in a similar direction. In the past, it seems clear that many Catholic wives supported the DC, although their husbands may have voted on the left. Will women's liberation then mean that in the future husbands and wives, each now freer to make individual electoral choices, will vote *more* compactly, as a family unit? It is too early to say. The point is that the political effects of certain changes in society are difficult to predict. Furthermore, the political subcultures of Italy have such astonishing staying power that we should be wary of the conclusion that the so-called postindustrial society will make them obsolete.[8]

The feminist movement, the student movements of the 1960s, the Workers' Statute enacted at the end of that decade, and higher levels of education and literacy not only brought about somewhat modified relationships between husbands and wives, parents and children; these events had the additional effect of leading Italians to an unprecedented level of private and public discussion regarding the rights granted to them under the republican constitution. It may be difficult to document how this process reinforces democracy, but it is certainly arguable that it does not hurt it. We know for certain, in any case, that public attitudes toward the institutions of government have greatly improved in recent years, and this change, too, may reflect a deeper and more widespread conviction that, with all of its faults, the existing system can be made to respond to individual demands.

POLITICAL SUBCULTURAL EFFECTS

Italy's three historical subcultures are the Catholic, the left (or Marxist), and the laical (or secular).[9] Each is deeply rooted in events that date back to the earliest conflicts between church and state, to the dynamics of the Risorgimento and the birth of the Italian nation, and to the left-wing ideologies and movements of the present century. Electorally symbolized by the political parties found at their apex, they have been characterized by networks of other organizations, from trade unions and student groups to consumer cooperatives, religious societies, and recreational associations—the day-to-day instruments through which the political party itself made its presence felt and thereby retained a firm hold on its electorate. On a continuing basis, such auxiliary organizations have expressed the values and the ideology of each subculture, thereby reinforcing them.

This pattern has changed as well, and, because this is so, many observers believe that it must inevitably have a major impact on electoral politics. Take, for example, the matter of membership in some of these subcultural groups. Once the Federation of Young Italian Communists (FGCI) was a formidable organization that numbered a half-million card carriers. This membership began to wane in the early seventies, but it received a shot in the arm in the mid-seventies, when the so-called Eurocommunist movement was nearing its peak. Then the bottom dropped out, in part because the earlier euphoria about Eurocommunism petered out as well. Today the FGCI counts less than fifty thousand members, who in their public meetings do not spare the Communist party (PCI) pointed, outspoken criticism. If FGCI membership figures are any indication of how the PCI is doing among the youth of the country, the party would do well to press the panic button. This crisis is real!

The Christian Democratic party's subculture hasn't fared much better.

The branches of Italian Catholic Action that recruit young men and women, and university students, have also declined. This erosion reflects considerable disaffection of younger Catholics from the authoritarian ways of Azione Cattolica Italiana, the umbrella organization at Rome under whose jurisdiction all branches of Catholic Action fall.[10] In addition, many younger Catholics are extremely critical of Catholic Action's associations with the more unsavory factions of the DC and of its failure to press more successfully for party reform. Like their counterparts in the FGCI, the younger Catholics are disenchanted with the political party that represents their subculture in elections and government.

Whereas the PCI has invented nothing to replace FGCI, younger Catholics have come together in a mass organization called Communion and Liberation. This organization is not formally tied to the DC and is, indeed, somewhat antagonistic toward it. However, the CL, as it is called, has explicit political aspirations and programmatic ideas, and it is prepared to take direct action to reform the party. It combines a commitment to high standards of public morality with equal suspicion of the pet solutions of left-wing ideologies. It appeals to hundreds of thousands of younger Catholics who believe that politics should more explicitly reflect religious values. They are ready to throw their support behind DC candidates who represent CL or are endorsed by it. There is every indication the CL is a force with which the DC and, indeed, the whole country will have to reckon.

Communione e Liberazione looks part of the worldwide resurgence of religious movements that attract primarily the young but also reflect a much broader revulsion with the older brand of politics and political organizations. Many who join CL no doubt have such considerations in mind. Given Italian history, however, members of the laical and leftist subcultures tend to see CL as little more than an updated version of many other church-related organizations that intend if they can to inflict *integralismo* on the country. The word translates badly as *integralism*. It refers to the age-old effort of the Catholic Church to mold Italy to its values and wishes and to use the state's apparatus to keep such a system in place after it is created. Millions of ardent Catholics, including those whose canons of public ethics and political morality are of the highest order, are committed to this view.

If Catholics worry about the undemocratic impulses of Communism, everyone else, including the Communists, fears that *integralismo*[11] has equally ominous implications. Integralismo casts the dark shadow of the Vatican across the peninsula. Many in Italy opposed Enrico Berlinguer's Eurocommunism and his Historic Compromise because they feared it would bring to power two partners, the DC and PCI, equally committed to a profoundly totalitarian view of society and its political management. Much of the current diffidence toward the CL rests on the assumption that it would favor Catholic political domination. Pope John Paul II's pronouncements of recent years about society and politics and the relationship of religion to both helps to fuel that suspicion. It also helps to keep the public grouped into these three political subcultures.

If people are less likely than in the past to join organizations that are expressions of these political subcultures; if, as many claim, they are now more inclined to form and join interest groups that resemble those of the United States, should this not have discernible consequences for the major political parties? In theory, yes; in practice, no—at least not yet. The decline of a major organization like the FGCI seems not to have hurt the Communist party at the polls. In the case of the DC, the Communion and Liberation movement may have brought it new votes from the younger generation; but it seems unable to reverse a generational decline of Christian Democratic electoral appeal.

Newer values and the relative decline of political subcultural organizations may not immediately affect the fortunes of political parties on election day. But they should certainly have an impact on the training of future political party and governmental leaders. This is obviously true of the Communist party, so many of whose leaders have always been expected to conduct their apprenticeship in a party auxiliary like the FGCI. It is almost as true of the DC, so many of whose older leaders today began their political activism in the ranks of Catholic Action organizations.

It may be that the effects of these changes are time-lagged, that they will be felt only after some years. It is also possible that, as the benefits brought by such organizations erode, other mechanisms become available that enable the political parties, as well as their subcultural identities, to survive. The mass media immediately come to mind; far from removing the boundaries between groups of people in mass society, they may actually help to reinforce these separate identities.

Another thought strikes me: the relationship of mass organizations to political parties is dynamic and cyclical. One organization may be critically important to a given party today, another organization tomorrow. Similarly, the way in which given organizations relate to the political parties can vary, even radically, over time. The labor unions would be a prime example.

THE TRADE UNION SPHERE

Italian trade unions, like those elsewhere in Europe, and unlike those of the United States, have always been deeply politicized. In the early postwar years, the two major labor confederations became deeply enmeshed in the struggle between the Christian Democrats and the Communists. Indeed, in microcosm, the Communist-dominated General Confederation of Italian Labor (CGIL) and the Christian Democratic-dominated Italian Confederation of Free Trade Unions (CISL) reproduced the broader international confrontation between East and West in the Cold War.[12]

Even if these major labor organizations could rightly claim that they were not the abject tools of the political parties with which they were identified, they were certainly major instruments through which these parties appealed to the voters. In more recent years, the Socialist party itself, under Bettino Craxi, has felt it necessary to assure that one of the confederations, the Italian Union of Labor (UIL), would be at its strategic disposal. By comparison, no American political party ever dreamed of making the kind of use of the trade unions that has been true of the left-wing and Christian Democratic parties in Italy.

Today the trade unions are in decline, the victims of recent transformations in the West that caught labor organizations flat-footed everywhere.[13] Statements of Italian union leaders ooze defensiveness and false confidence; brave words about a rosier future in the "postindustrial society" barely mask the underlying sense of anger and despair many of these leaders must feel. It is understandable; in the space of a decade, the trade union movement has gone from a condition of unimagined power to one of precipitous degeneration. Like unions elsewhere, those in Italy do not know what to make of, or how to adapt to, the economic and social transformations that have occurred during the so-called second industrial revolution.

Statistics tell some of the story about change and trade union decline. Currently the labor force numbers 23 million persons, of whom 6.7

million are women. About 36 percent of the employed are in industrial jobs, 52 percent are in the tertiary, or "service," sector, and the rest are in agriculture. Over 2 million persons were counted as unemployed in 1985, a high percentage even in a Europe that is still limping out of a worldwide recession. Of the unemployed, 129,000 persons, most of them young, were in search of their first jobs. In addition, there were 763,000 persons, not officially counted as unemployed, who would like to work if they could find jobs.

Among the unemployed young, university graduates are particularly hard hit, in part because Italian universities prepare them inadequately for available occupations. As ironic as it must surely appear to citizens who lament the country's awful health services, there is a gross oversupply of doctors, many of them of dubious training and skills. Equally ironic, for union leaders accustomed to assembly lines and the shop floor, must be the fact that, among the most radical and undisciplined of the unionized labor categories, the doctors' unions now occupy first place. In October 1986 the country's newspapers once again admonished everyone not to fall ill for five days because the medical profession was once more going on strike.

More than two hundred thousand aspirants enter the labor market each year. But the number of new jobs created remains largely at a standstill, which implies that the unemployment rolls will continue to grow. Italian newspapers are full of praise and awe over the explosion of new jobs in the United States in the early 1980s. They may wrongly attribute this "miracle" to Reaganomics. They may even fail to appreciate the extent to which those new American jobs involve persons who have returned to work at some fraction of what they were paid earlier. But they are rightly alarmed that Italy, like the rest of Western Europe, has registered a net loss in available jobs while the United States has moved in the opposite direction.

Adverse conditions of this kind do not bring new recruits to the labor unions. Membership in the trade unions peaked in the mid-1970s, when about twelve million workers, over half of the labor force, held union cards. The labor force has grown since then, but membership in the three major labor confederations has fallen officially to under nine million, and the real figure is probably lower than that. In 1984, just over half of these were in the CGIL, another three million were in the CISL, and just over one million were in the UIL. Tens of thousands of workers also belong either to smaller autonomous unions or to a confederation associated with the neofascist Italian Social Movement (MSI), but they do not count for much.

Trade union membership is down both in the largest factories and in the north, where large-scale industry is concentrated. The decline of the steel and shipbuilding industries and the fall in employment in publicly owned industries, also in trouble, are principal reasons for its erosion. Large-scale industry in general has also declined. Today over half of all workers are found in firms of under twenty employees, and such places are notoriously difficult to unionize. Also, the tertiary sector and the government now account for the employment of over half the labor force.[14]

With the exception of Turin and Taranto (a relatively new steel city in the south), the largest concentrations of employees are now found not in industry but rather in local public offices, universities, public transportation, banking, and other service sectors. At a minimum, these changes have disoriented the trade union movement; at most, they make it unlikely that the concept of the trade union itself, its role in society, and in particular its relationship to the political parties, can ever again be what they once were.

The unions also ran afoul of developments that go beyond recession or economic and social transformations. Their earlier, heady successes contributed to their undoing. By 1969 they had forced through the legislature the Workers' Statute, one of the most advanced and, as it was interpreted, radical industrial relations policies ever enacted in the West. Even before this law was passed, Italy provided typical levels of unemployment benefits and highly attractive compensation at the point of work severance. The statute came close to making the worker untouchable inside the work place or, for that matter, outside of it. With the help of politically radicalized judges, laborers could be absent from work with impunity and still claim their pay. Job transfers or reclassifications simply could not occur without the consent of the party involved. Any slight on the part of management was an almost certain invitation to a work stoppage. Side by side with these guarantees went improvements in fringe benefits that were as costly to employers as they were instrumental in changing the workers' standard of living. In these salad years, workers came to believe that a steep upward climb in their condition had become, retroactively, a birthright and that even dismissal from one's job for cause was nothing more than a quaint relic of bygone capitalism.[15]

A few years after the statute was passed, a second fateful step was taken:

an agreement of 1975 between organized labor and organized business (then led by Fiat's Gianni Agnelli) to make momentous changes in the famous escalator clause (the *scala mobile*) that governed wage increases. Under the agreement, the cost of living would be reviewed on a quarterly basis and wages adjusted upward to keep up with inflation. The technical basis for making these adjustments, however, was such that, whereas the highest wage earners would just barely stay even with inflation, the lowest wage earners would realize wage improvements slightly above the inflation rate. Without fully anticipating or desiring such an outcome, the parties to this agreement put in motion a policy that over time brought about an unprecedented redistribution of income.

WORKER REACTIONS

If these were conquests in favor of the working class, the workers failed to show their gratitude to the labor confederations that engineered them. Once rights of this kind become a matter of law, the felt need for trade union militancy, on the one hand, and disciplined behavior on the shop floor, on the other, evaporates. If the benefits normally associated with collective bargaining become a matter of official public policy, of law, why should a worker join a union and pay dues? The problem of the "free rider," who cannot be excluded from enjoying the public goods that others produce, rears its ugly head. In fact, the free rider psychology spread in Italy like news of a gold strike. Rather than stampede in the direction of union membership, the workers went in the other direction, in droves. Ironically, the successful unions lost members!

There were other deleterious effects. Because the scala mobile worked to "flatten" wage differentials, that is, to reduce the gap between the highest and lowest paid workers, under-the-table deals in full violation of national wage contracts occurred at the plant level. Either employers took the initiative to reintroduce greater de facto wage differentials or new "autonomous" or "wildcat" unions came into existence within the plants to push for special arrangements. Thus the older, more traditional unions not only lost membership; they encouraged competitors and lost their credibility as well. They were no longer able to assure anyone—employers or the government—that once they reached an agreement with the latter (for example, on incomes policies) they could deliver compliant behavior from workers within the workplace.[16]

Popular movements of the late 1960s and the 1970s brought more democracy into the workplace, and this did not help the unions either. For
example, the idea caught fire that workers, through the mechanism of
workers' councils and assemblies, should be directly involved in many
decisions having to do with the workplace. Council members were elected
at large without regard for their trade union membership status. Many
councils made more radical demands for workers' participation in management than had ever been voiced by the unions. Although government-
by-assembly (by all of the workers convened, as in a town meeting) turned
out to be an unworkable flash in the pan, the workers' councils managed
to hang on, and in some places to become very powerful. Indeed, in many
factories, managers preferred to deal with the councils, on the calculation
that they, more than the unions, controlled worker discipline.

The councils put the unions on the spot. Were the latter really in favor
of democratizing the workplace? If so, did it not make sense to give their
full support to the councils? Wasn't such a step well advised in view of
the number of council members who were also militant union leaders?
The unions openly supported the councils, but privately their more far-
thinking leaders understood that the councils would erode union authority in the workplace, especially when that authority was to be exercised
by union leaders outside the plant and, indeed, as far away as Rome.[17]

Council members did not easily accept orders from the outside. Moreover, they tended to believe, not without reason, that they knew more
about factory-centered problems and their solution than did union leaders
at the provincial, regional, or national headquarters. The latter found
their influence in the factories slipping away as the councils established
working relationships with plant-level management.

The situation took a bad turn in the late 1970s, when top union leaders
entered into close collaboration with the national government, then bent
on bringing inflation under control and on placing the economy on a
firmer footing. This implied wage restraint and other forms of austerity
that the unions, which had bargained with organized business and government to create an incomes policy, would try to enforce. It was at this
point that the above-mentioned problem of credibility emerged.[18]

The major leaders of the labor confederations made a unique contribution to their own crisis. Once the Workers' Statute was on the books
and the "escalator" began to work, national union leaders felt themselves
freer to engage the government in a broad debate about every conceivable
aspect of national policy. These were years when leading industrialists

and governmental officials, as well as the labor leaders, believed that a new era had dawned in which organized labor and business, together with the government, would make policy, thus making the political parties themselves obsolete.

It took only a few years and a world recession to show that these expectations were at least premature, perhaps even silly, and in any case potentially not in the interest of democracy. In the meantime, though, the unions had abandoned the factories to the councils and had brought about a de facto degree of decentralization of collective bargaining that eroded union strength. This would turn out more costly later, when the posture of organized business hardened.

There was an additional unanticipated cost in the shift of trade union leader attention away from the workplace and its bread-and-butter, worker-related concerns to the broader issues of public policy. The unions could hope to deal as a unified group with the government and the political parties only so long as there prevailed among these, and within organized business, a parallel agreement regarding the desirability of a common, consensual approach to policy matters. When in the late 1970s and the early 1980s this agreement evaporated and the parties took to quarreling with each other, the unions wound up doing the same. What little unity of action they had managed to forge disappeared. It was a retrograde step, back to the kind of politically based fragmentation that had been the prime cause of weakness in the labor movement in earlier years.

It was also a step that underscores what I suggested earlier: the relationship between political parties and the unions tends to be cyclical. There is no question today where the major parties stand on the question of trade union autonomy or independence. The parties—all of the major ones, and not just the Communist party—*need* the unions in the political struggle, and they will go to great pain to reenlist their assistance.

A NEW PLURALISM

Some will argue that, even if this last surmise is correct, other permanent changes in Italy will deeply affect the political process. Chief among these is the so-called New Pluralism—the new emphasis on voluntarism and the explosion in the number of interest groups and self-help associations.[19] Many of these are found at the regional and local levels. Almost all pursue interests that cut across the boundaries separating the political parties and subcultures.

The idea is that these groups do not have ideological hang-ups or commitments; their members presumably wish to make more "privatized" demands on the political system and, in pursuit of their satisfaction, are willing to join up with all others in a similar condition and frame of mind. The political parties of old, as well as the declining trade unions, are no longer seen as adequate competitors to this newer way of defining one's needs and of finding an acceptable mixture of private and public responses to them. Examples of such groups abound: The aged are interested in pensions irrespective of their individual political colorations. The same would be true of the handicapped, single-parent families, women, those in need of public health services, alcoholics and drug addicts, consumer advocates, environmentalists, and many others.

A Ministry of Labor survey early in the 1980s counted about seven thousand of these voluntary associations, four thousand of which were large national organizations. The rest were almost equally divided between "coordinated" associations, which operated in more or less broad regions of the country, and strictly local, autonomous organizations whose common interests were such things as drug control, pensions, recreational and cultural facilities, and so on.

The most remarkable aspect of these organizations is that although three-fourths of the *national* associations were around before 1976, about two-thirds of the others had come into existence since 1979. This is social pluralism with a vengeance! Never in its history has the country experienced anything like it. Everyone agrees that, sooner or later, this proliferation of local and regional groups must have an impact on politics.

Too many Italians, however, have leaped to the conclusion that these newer groups represent an "abandonment of politics" as practiced in the past.[20] They expect that the older, national groups will atrophy and that demands from below will no longer be limited to the channels once provided by political patrons for their clients, political parties or party factions for their adherents, and ancillary organizations associated with the parties for their members. People who think this way not only expect but demand that the national government accelerate the decentralization of authority to regional and local governments. The idea is that the New Pluralism should be given a helping hand.

These judgments seem dubious. If Italians have become "joiners" in unprecedented numbers, it does not follow that to join one organization implies that one will leave another. People can and do have multiple group affiliations. It is also doubtful that these new groups make more broadly "civic," as opposed to economic or otherwise self-interested, demands on governmental authorities.

The Italians I have been describing in this chapter are among the least likely persons anywhere to join organizations that seek to promote "public goods." Beyond individualism and other aspects of "national character," there are reasons for this surmise that will become clearer later, when we explore the meaning of politics in Italian life. It may be that the New Pluralism signals a greater predisposition toward self-help, as opposed to waiting around for the state to solve problems. My impression is that in Italy (and often elsewhere), such groups wind up addressing most of their demands to official bodies. And so the claim of commitment to self-help sounds hollow.

A more interesting side of the New Pluralism is the against-the-state attitude expressed by many of its exponents. Especially at the local level, groups have emerged because of the anger and frustration people share over the failure of the state, that is, of governmental authorities, to deal adequately with problems of health, drug addiction, recreational facilities, youth or the aged, schools or working mothers, and the environment.

Anger against the state sometimes brings on terrorism. Tumultuous events of the 1960s that fell short of terror were also intended to underscore that a business-as-usual approach to policy making was no longer acceptable to many. Even though the fervor of protest and the venom of political terror have abated, they have left a legacy not only of open defiance but also of open pursuit of narrow self-interest under the banner of the New Pluralism and self-help. On close inspection, it often turns out that most of these groups really want governmental authorities to do more, not less.

Typically, exponents of the New Pluralism also favor the devolution of governmental authority to regional and local bodies. The idea is that less remote governmental authorities will be more responsive and responsible. So far, there is scant evidence that the national government will go along with these pressures. This may not be so bad. In later chapters, I will show that advocates of the New Pluralism also favor certain other reforms, including a deliberate weakening of the role of political parties, whose potential impact on the democratic system would be pernicious.

PUBLIC MORALITY

Related to the above discussion is the question whether a new public morality is emerging among Italians. Especially when posed by an outsider, the question easily becomes gratuitous—for example in the sense of the invidious comparisons of Italian as opposed to other political practices among democracies. A better way to begin, therefore, is to note a few of the deep-seated Italian orientations both to the political process and to the roles of others as well as of themselves in that process.

Unsurprisingly, the picture Italy offers is complex, singular, shaded by nuance and contradiction. The same Italians supposed to be so distrustful and antagonistic toward government also expect government to solve most of their problems. This is as true of the self-styled free enterprisers, who typically milk the public treasury for all it is worth, as it is of ordinary citizens, who often feel they have nowhere else to turn. The political class unjustifiably gets only low grades from the citizenry, and especially from newspaper editors and intellectuals. Notwithstanding this apparent lack of confidence, these same critics demand that government solve for them and society an astounding variety of problems. It is not so much that modern democracies like Italy are increasingly "ungovernable." It is, rather, that even when much about society is governed well, there will be enough left over that remains unresolved to make it appear that there is close to no government at all. Such appearances are misleading. The remarkable achievement of a national government like Italy's is how many different demands it is able to handle, in circumstances that often appear impossibly beyond control.

The scope and magnitude of problems placed on the public agenda vary wildly. The government will be asked to restructure industry, to improve exports, to make Italy more competitive in world markets, to win it more prestige and respect in international politics, to close the amenities gap between the north and the south, to protect the lira and keep inflation within bounds, to reduce inequality, to reform education, to grant women equal rights, to provide cheaper energy and curb nuclear power, to guarantee everyone adequate housing and health care, to cope with terrorism and organized crime, to keep newspapers alive, to finance political parties, to take care of indigent poets, and so on. And if a citizen needs something very special from government, why this can be handled, quietly, by a *leggina,* a special "little law" enacted on his or her behalf in a unique way we will describe later.

Demands for state intervention are so varied and incessant that they might lead us to believe that Italians strongly favor modes of problem solving that are collective and based on a high degree of cooperation. We should not be so deceived. Measures enacted by the government in favor of the collectivity do not imply that the individual Italian will necessarily accept the solution as applying in his own case. Take the traffic nightmares we now find in most larger cities. One partial solution is the construction of multistoried parking facilities, below or above ground. In Italy, these typically remain half empty. People still prefer to park their cars everywhere else, including on sidewalks, in order to be within a few feet of where they work, or intend to dine or shop. For a while, the imperious Milanesi claimed that such uncivic behavior was limited to self-indulgent Romans and anarchistic Neapolitans. Today the sidewalks of Milan are also an extended parking lot.

Individual deviations from the collectivity's norms can reach ludicrous proportions and then emanate in remedies that look almost as ludicrous, but really are not. In the years since World War II, violations of the building codes have numbered in the millions. Much construction occurs after sundown not because traffic is lighter but because most of the municipal police go off duty and there are fewer prying eyes to detect these violations.

In order to put this matter straight, the national government enacted legislation that invited transgressors to come forward to confess the nature and magnitude of their violations, to ask that the deviation be accepted, and to learn what sort of penance, in the form of a fine, the state would extract. The time limit within which forgivable transactions were to have occurred *postdated* the promulgation of the law itself. There is something quintessentially Italian, as well as democratic, about this. It gave tens of thousands of citizens who had not transgressed an opportunity to do so within the deadline. In this way highly individualistic deviations from earlier norms are reintegrated into the collectivity.

These examples, among many that might be selected, underscore aspects of this culture that have profound political ramifications. Italians think of law as something that applies to third persons. In any event, they assume that law enforcement can be "negotiated." Slavish adherence to legal norms is widely considered to be evidence of a dull and unimaginative personality. This approach also suggests an unusual degree of tolerance that may be entirely compatible with, even essential to, democracy.

This is not a country of self-righteous vigilantes. News that in the American democracy there are about a half-billion pistols in circulation, most of them unregistered "Saturday night specials," leaves Italians gaping. Italian individualists who regularly skirt the law typically believe that others will do the same. But they rarely think of taking law into their own hands. Indeed quite the opposite is the case.

FISCAL SCAMS

The fiscal system and its tax laws are eye-opening on this score. Although it is probably a gross exaggeration to say that everyone in the country evades taxes, this is almost universally believed to be so. Wage earners whose tax contributions are deducted in advance might well protest that they do not fall into this category. Millions of them, nevertheless, are active in the underground economy, where little of the money that changes hands is recorded in the tax returns.

It may also be the case that widespread tax cheating results from a fiscal system that is too heavily based on the taxation of personal income.[21] One eminent economist identified with the political left recently claimed that this unbalanced system is so universally onerous it has turned Italy into a country of "cops and robbers," where the "cops" themselves, that is, the tax authorities, ape what the "robbers" do.

Thus, where the value-added tax is concerned, both sellers and buyers enter into unspoken agreements to evade it. In 1984, one research group estimated that as much as 45 percent of the value-added tax was evaded. This amounted to thirteen billion dollars, or more than one-fourth of the national government's deficit for that year. Other experts add that were all of the taxes legally owed to be collected they would fully cover the national deficit, which has hovered at an arresting 15 percent of the country's annual gross domestic product.

The blatancy, if not the pervasiveness, of tax evasion sometimes makes the headlines—as when the Ministry of Finance releases and the papers publish lists of prominent Italians who regularly report only fractions of what they receive in annual income. Think of Italian movie stars who claim to make less than your postal carrier, or industrial magnates who report little more than is now paid school administrators.

Just as frequently, professional categories, like doctors, lawyers, dentists, notaries, and accountants will be shown to be reporting, on average, less income than is paid to skilled industrial workers. The owners of leading restaurants and bars, which do land-office business in the tourist season or out, regularly report less income than they pay to the chefs, waiters, and dishwashers in their employ.

In 1984, Finance Minister Bruno Visentini unveiled his tax reform plan, designed to strike primarily at commercial establishments, well known as among the most unbridled of the tax dodgers. Needless to say, they set up a howl. In some cities, they went on strike. Throughout the country, they promised severe reprisals at the polls for all politicians and political parties that might support the plan. Visentini simply wanted more establishments to keep at least one set of books.

A few years earlier Franco Reviglio, another finance minister, compelled restaurants and other smaller establishments to install cash registers, certified by public authorities, that would provide a running account of sales. The anguished merchants claimed this to be an unjust infringement on their rights, as well as a dangerous precedent in policy making.

Sometimes the labor unions jump into this fray. In the mid-1980s, one of them took to publishing its own, often sensational, revelations about the tax returns of some of the "offended" fat-cat taxpayers. These stories make such good copy that newspapers themselves will conduct investigations and publish their findings. One of them in 1985 compared the average income of wage-rated workers (whose taxes are deducted) with the average income reported by pharmacies, car rental and travel agencies, supermarkets, jewelers, hotels, restaurants, bakeries, and other commercial categories, including delicatessens, butcher and grocery shops, tobacco shops, and so on. All but three of these categories reported less average income than their workers were paid.

The point to this recitation is not that tax evasion exists, that it is blatant, or that those who are finally stung (and only mildly, at that) will scream out in pain. It is, rather, that, like the rampant violation of traffic laws or building codes and zoning ordinances, the situation is tolerated and, indeed, accepted as quite normal. Furthermore, the prevailing mores have been around for a long time. If the game is really "cops and robbers," it is necessary to add that the distinction between the two categories is blurred. Because this is true, it would require an unusual degree of hypocrisy, as well as a form of self-righteousness alien to Italian culture, before anything like massive public pressure could be generated behind tax reform.

UNDERLYING IMPLICATIONS

A lot of implicit collusion is based on the assumption, no doubt, that if the tax laws are rigorously enforced against you today, they may be equally enforced against me tomorrow. Thus only an oafish stickler will insist on being provided with the "fiscal receipt" of commercial transactions, required by law, if he does not really need it. The underlying norm is that everyone benefits from evasion. As we will have more occasions to note in the pages ahead, this is one of the concrete ways in which democracy is made palpable, as well as attractive, to many Italian citizens.

And their votes count. They may not count enough to make and unmake governments. They do count in terms of bringing about at the polls minor shifts in popular support for parties, or among the factions within parties, that have more subtle but nevertheless powerful implications in Italy than they do anywhere else. When those merchants got rip-roaring mad at Minister of Finance Reviglio, he was not reappointed to that post. When owners of smaller commercial enterprises expressed rage at Minister Visentini's reforms, he experienced political quarantine. Not even the Communist party, which typically aligns itself on the side of public and civic morality, came out boldly, unequivocally in favor of squeezing those fiscal miscreants even harder.

A well-known Italian expression goes like this: *Fatta la legge, trovata l'inganno,* or, vulgarly translated, made the law, found the trick! Northerners like to say that this proverb is strictly Neapolitan. The theory is that the Neapolitans, widely recognized as the country's most gifted lawyers, are unsurpassed when it comes to inventing ways of defrauding the state or escaping its reach. But tax-evasion schemes travel up and down the peninsula on laser beams. Even were the Neapolitans to patent their fiscal magic, the adepts would emerge everywhere else, beginning in the north.

Another underlying reality is that, a good deal of the time, Italians are at war with the state. At the individual level, this attitude has deep historical roots. The recent emergence of groups with a distinctive against-the-state orientation, including the terroristic groups, simply gives more organizational coherence to this deeper frame of mind.

The attitude is rooted in Italian experience with arbitrary and capricious government for over a millenium. When the question of the creation of a nation-state arose just over a century ago, most Italians lacked any enthusiasm about the prospect, to say the least. In the south today, the idea dies hard that after unification the north was able to make progress largely at the former's enduring expense. The Fascists pretended that they could impose more authority and discipline on the citizenry than they were prepared to accept. Mussolini merely gave the people twenty years during which to hone to a keen edge their inventive ways to escape the state's heavy-handed regulations.

Even among those who strongly favor greater civic morality there is remarkable tolerance for the refusal of citizens to adhere to the country's laws. Many such Italians will argue that the state, in its imperious way, has so defrauded the ordinary taxpayer that it is entirely natural and acceptable that the latter should return the favor in kind.

Democracy's freedoms, the argument goes, should include the right of the individual to ignore those laws he or she considers unjust. In the Italian context, the argument makes sense. It might become erosive for democracy only if and when there occurred a head-on collision between those who follow the prevailing norm and large numbers of others who would like things to be different. There isn't much evidence that this will happen soon. In any case, it won't happen abruptly.

THE PEOPLE SPEAK

The people also have at their disposal formal mechanisms for expressing their refusal of law. The Italian constitution provides for the *referendum,* a system that permits the circulation of petitions, which, if signed by a sufficiently large number of qualified voters, bring the specific law in question before the electorate for approval or rejection. The referendum is much like similar arrangements found in Switzerland and in a number of American states.[22]

The first dramatic use of this instrument occurred in the early seventies, when Catholics opposed to divorce placed the new law authorizing it before the voters. A majority opted to keep it on the books. A few years later, Italy's unusually liberal law on abortion was also placed before the voters through the referendum procedure. Once again, but this time overwhelmingly, the voters supported the law. The outcome of these two referendums should remind us how misleading stereotypes can be. Almost 100 percent of Italians may be classified as Catholics. But in Italy, Catholicism, by a wide margin, does not mean what it may imply in the United States or Ireland. Italian Catholic voters openly defied the strongest pressures from the Vatican and the clergy against the laws on divorce and abortion.

Two other things might be said about the Italian voters, as evidenced by the outcomes of the many referendums submitted to their consideration. First, up to now, they have never overturned a law enacted by the national legislature. I underscore this point in order to help set the stage for a later discussion about the feelings of Italians toward their political institutions and leaders.

Second, Italian citizens have demonstrated a remarkable capacity to resist using the referendum in their narrow self-interest. No better demonstration of this is offered than their 1985 vote on a decree law that modified the scala mobile to the disadvantage of wage-rated workers. The Communist party sensed a major victory against the government and so forged ahead to gather over a million signatures in favor of placing the decree law before the voters. The government, headed by Bettino Craxi, took the view that the law was vital to a successful outcome of the war on inflation.

At the last minute, Craxi himself got cold feet and suggested, echoing the plea of Marco Pannella, the leader of the Radical party, that the voters might sit out the election and not vote at all. The point was that less than 50 percent participation by the qualified electorate would render the referendum null and void. Craxi met a barrage of criticism. Here was a head of government, the critics noted, so nervous about what the voters might do that he urged them to shun the polls. And this in a democracy whose constitution specifies that the vote is not merely a right of citizenship, but an obligation.

Despite efforts to avoid the confrontation, the election took place in June. Unabashed by his critics, the prime minister warned that, were the outcome to go against the government, he would resign two minutes after the result became apparent. Partly but not entirely for this reason, those who voted to sustain the government carried the day, and by a considerable margin.

The Communist party miscalculated that any attack on the scala mobile would create worker solidarity and mobilize them in opposition to efforts to modify it. Many experts who anticipated that the electorate would "vote its pocketbook" as opposed to the "general welfare" were equally in error. The most confused of all were those Italians who claimed that referendums on such issues should not be permitted, on the grounds that, where money is concerned, voters are unlikely to "rise above" their narrow self-interests. As if the issue of wages is more of a selfish interest than that of abortion or divorce!

The referendum is important because it gives concrete expression to the concept of "popular sovereignty." It permits the people to speak. It is true in theory that when the people speak in this way they may, through a numerical majority, behave irresponsibly or unjustly. Exactly such fears were expressed in the United States early in the century, when the referendum and other instruments of "direct legislation" like the initiative and the recall of public officials were incorporated into the constitutions of several American states. The specter was raised of frivolous or dangerous minorities who might gull electoral majorities into voting in populistic and undemocratic ways. Three-quarters of a century later, it turns out that most of these alarming predictions were the exaggerated fantasies of equally self-interested minorities who do not trust the masses.

The Italian experience so far has not been any different. There is little frivolity, and even less apparent danger, in the use Italian citizens and interested groups have made of their own system of direct legislation. Indeed, one would have to agree with the surveys that show Italians to be fundamentally quite conservative, in the specific sense that they are loath to reverse at the polls what their representatives have wrought through the law-making process.

Another objection to the use of the referendum in Italy is that the typical voter is especially uninformed and therefore not in a position to make either a careful evaluation of an issue or a rational choice regarding it in the polling place. Claims of this sort are based on surveys that, as we shall later see, leave something to be desired. These claims are dubious at best. At worst, they pretend to supply a logical basis for challenging the rationale for *any* form of universal suffrage in democracies. Indeed, such claims echo arguments of the Know-Nothing Movement in the United States, which was a thinly disguised strategem to disenfranchise lower-class voters, whose votes threatened to shift the balance of political power.

The truth is that the referendum simplifies matters. It may be overused, but objections to it cannot be grounded on the idea that the issues placed before the voters are beyond their abilities to comprehend. How much knowledge about the technicalities does a voter need in order to make a judgment for, or against, divorce, abortion, or cuts in the scala mobile!

EQUALITY AS A NORM

Some who feared that the voters would reverse the government on the scala mobile issue based this prediction on the average Italian's conception of equality. How much of what kind of equality do Italians really want? It is fair to say that they prefer equality of *results* to equality of *opportunity*. Thus, the system of tax evasion produces considerably more equality of income than we would find were we to look only at the official statistics on before- and after-taxes income. Similarly, the Workers' Statute and other social insurance laws bring about considerable equality of condition.

The same may be said for education. At first blush, it would appear that Italy's educational reforms of the past ten years or so were designed to make the *opportunity* for education, and especially of higher education, more universally available. Thus, much more than elsewhere in Europe, Italy, beginning in the late 1960s, opened the doors of its universities to essentially everyone who managed to get through the first thirteen years of school. Once enrolled, however, university students expected that they would graduate as a matter of right. Thus, great pressures were placed on professors to relax the stringency of the oral examination system that prevails in the universities.

Not only were admission and graduation made easier for the students. Those who taught in institutions of higher education moved politically to make their own jobs permanent as a matter of law. Several legislative reforms had the effect of granting tenure, in one fell swoop, to thousands of academics, irrespective of their qualifications as scholars and teachers. Not all of these would get to be full professors. But those in the lower ranks can now count on lifetime sinecures not unlike those that have long been available to millions of others in public-service jobs.

Equality of opportunity, especially in a market-oriented economy, not only implies considerable inequality of results or outcome; it also means that people must be willing to take certain risks. The welfare state typically provides some basic protection against the more severe consequences of failures in the market. This kind of protection against risk can easily degenerate to the point where not even the country's entrepreneurs, presumably the risk takers par excellence, are prepared to operate on this basis.

The tendency of Italians to turn to the institutions of government for help in so many areas reflects this preference for equality of outcome as opposed to equality of opportunity. This cultural dimension helps to account for not only the success of Christian Democracy in Italy but also for the remarkable staying power of the Italian Communist party. Italians tend to doubt that all men are created equal; but they know that the state can go a long way to assure equality of results, regardless of the structure of opportunity. Whether Christian Democrats or Communists, they take the view that the state has a moral obligation to do exactly this.

The characteristics of Italians reviewed here suggest that they are entirely compatible with democracy. Indeed, as we shall see, combined with attitudes Italians express toward politics and modes of political participation they pursue, these factors create a configuration of the political process that, although distinctively Italian, is no less democratic than political processes elsewhere.

It may be that certain generational changes are under way. Just as younger Italians, attracted by the New Pluralism, may not feel as closely tied to political parties or trade unions as were their elders, so may they be more willing than the latter to accept greater risks in life. This in turn might shift their preferences from equality of outcome to equality of opportunity. Such changes will be slow in coming. Their effect on democracy, should they materialize, is problematical. Such changes would require of Italians a fundamental rethinking of the nature of politics, not only as politics relates to society at large but, more immediately, as it impinges on one's personal life.

We must understand why this is so.

3

LIFE AS POLITICS

Let us assume that antipathy toward politics accurately describes the typical Italian's frame of mind. Why should this be so? Why, compared to citizens of other democracies, should Italians appear to be so politically "alienated," so lacking in "civic culture," so relentlessly inclined to give their political institutions and leaders failing grades?

One answer might be that Italians are well informed about their shortcomings and strongly inclined to condemn them. Another might be that politicians and governmental institutions are much as we find them elsewhere, but it is the Italians themselves who are much more demanding and difficult to satisfy. Whatever the reason, the torrent of criticism is steady and powerful, and at times reaches floodlike proportions. Members of the "political class" are derided for their inadequacies and run the risk of character assassination. Sometimes political assassination is literal, with leaders falling victim to organized crime or terrorism. When this occurs, even persons who were pilloried in life may achieve instant political sainthood, as did Aldo Moro. Even so, the halo quickly tarnishes. Italians are masterful at discovering that even their most revered political leaders have feet of clay.

In recent times, the only major figure spared the usual barrage of slings and arrows was former president Sandro Pertini, who occupied Palazzo Quirinale from 1978 to 1985. Pertini worked hard to burnish his charisma and keep his immunity intact. As an octogenarian, he impressed the public, and a cynical press, with his mental agility. As a grandfatherly figure, he made a point of personally greeting the thousands of schoolchildren who visited the presidential palace. As a studied humanitarian and man of great compassion, he was omnipresent at all forms of human disaster. He is said to hold the Italian record for appearances at funerals, and he once abruptly interrupted a state visit to Argentina in order to attend Konstantin Chernenko's at Moscow.

Above all, Pertini missed no opportunity to lash out at the foibles, and the more serious shortcomings of *la classe politica*. This ploy was a sure winner; millions of Italians who do the same thing, but less authoritatively, could reach a sublime identification with this man who symbolized for them a level of public morality that everyone else seemed to lack. Sandro Pertini, a Socialist, managed to fortify this image by establishing a close public friendship with Pope John Paul II. No other politician has been remotely as fortunate.

So much has been written about the problematical nature of the Italian Republic, about the venality and corruption of its leaders and the malfunctions and paralysis of its institutions, that the antagonism toward politics the citizenry ostensibly displays appears to be a reasonable, indeed the only rational, reaction. But we might consider an equally plausible, somewhat modifed proposition. It is, first, that Italians are critical of and antagonistic toward politics because they are uncommonly familiar with it; and, second, that things are not nearly as bad as they appear—and that most Italians really know this to be the case.

I offer this only as a working hypothesis, to set the background for the picture of Italy that will emerge along the way. That picture will not be one of a sick society that lacks a "civic culture," or of a political system that is weighted down by "political alienation." I will try to show, instead, that the extreme antipathy toward politics that outsiders, as well as many Italian observers, claim to see is not translated into behavior that is dangerous for democracy. More important, expressions of antipathy serve to reinforce, and not to undermine, democratic structures and practices.[1]

But let us pursue the thought that Italians know, or think they know, astonishingly much about their political institutions, processes, and leaders. One reason for this is simply the age of the peninsula. Politics there has been around, often in spectacular forms, for close to three millennia. Not all of this political experience has been edifying. In fact, a good deal of it has been, for most of those who experienced it or learned about it later, highly repulsive. But perhaps for that very reason politics remains fascinating to so many Italians.

Despite what they may say to the contrary, or rather precisely because what they do say about politics is so revealing, this fascination comes across vividly in almost any conversation. With the possible exception of gossip about the home soccer team or the clergy, there is little that Italians

more enjoy than to relate or hear about politics and its principal protagonists. The seamier and more graphic the stories, the more avid the
interest. Any story will do. Rumor is even better.

HISTORY AS TEACHER

This fascination has been machined, honed, and synchronized by well-
known historical events. The rise and fall of Rome, sometimes at the
expense of such highly developed civilizations as the Etruscan; the nu-
merous efforts to stave off, and later to civilize, conquering barbarian
hordes; the monumental collisions between the Catholic Church and
would-be challengers of the Pope's temporal powers: these are prime
examples. These "framing" events were accompanied by a procession of
intrigues, plots, counterplots, marriages, alliances, murders, and wars
among the rulers of myriad Italian principalities. With wave after wave
of incursions into the peninsula from elsewhere in Europe, and with the
simultaneous existence of monarchical, theocratic, republican, constitutional, and despotic governments, one can easily see why Italians remain
riveted in their attention to politics.

For centuries the peninsula was the battleground of both indigenous
and foreign political forces. The Pax Romana was established by force—
by Roman legions whose superior military technology enslaved peasants
from the Alps to and beyond the Straits of Messina. The south was invaded
by Greeks and Saracens, Normans and Bourbons. Once the barbarians
from the north shattered the Roman Empire, the peninsula became a
crazy quilt of warring states that persisted late into the last century. The
glorious city-states catch the historian's eye because they provided respites
of stability within warfare that brought a semblance of order to a generalized condition of turmoil and chaos.

Buffeted as they were by continual political conflict, hapless peasants,
as well as others, developed a keen sense of how to cope with and adapt
to abrupt, violent changes and the new waves of arbitrary government
that came with them. One was forever in search of political patrons who
might provide protection and livelihood. But always with an opportunistic
eye peeled for new changes in the political climate and the possible arrival
of a stronger, more reliable patron. The age-old peasant adage *Piove,
governo ladro!* (It's raining, thief of a government!) laconically captures

the belief that, for better but more often for worse, life is fundamentally political, and politics is fundamentally plundering.

Patrons and clients are still a prominent feature of the Italian political landscape. But it would be foolish to label this condition as "primitive" or "premodern," or to misjudge our own societies as relatively free from such relationships. In any case, those involved in such relationships *need* to be highly sensitive to the rules, and especially the nuances, of politics. Nor is it necessarily the case that where patron and client relationships define politics, democracy itself is unlikely or impossible.

Indeed, patrons in Italy weigh no more in the political process than do prominent, influential political elites in societies where personal political entourages are less obvious. Furthermore, in so far as the urban centers of other democracies still reveal the presence of the "big-city machines," these are highly similar in their operations to the generalized Italian condition. Like American-type "machine" politics, and unlike many other societies (Nigeria, for example), in Italy these patron and client relationships are located within the political party framework. They are, therefore, a critical part of the machinery that makes it possible for people to make their interests known and to work to aggrandize them. Clientelism is an efficient and effective way through which the political allegiances, preferences, and demands of citizens are brought to weigh on public policies— exactly as the spirit, if not the narrow definition, of polyarchy would require.[2]

A patronage system places a great premium on personal friendship and hierarchy. To operate within it well, the individual must be able to spread contacts far and wide and also to evaluate just how powerful, that is, how far up or down in the power hierarchy, each patron is located. The modern political party or interest group does not necessarily destroy or replace such relationships; instead, as is the case with Italy, it may incorporate them.

Two additional points are worth underscoring. First, a patron and client system inside the political party system encourages, indeed forces, people to become negotiators. Because everything is fluid, everything may also be considered negotiable. Second, because much that the individual may seek in life depends on how far up into this hierarchy of power he or she can reach, almost every aspect of relationships to other persons and organizations will tend to become both personalized and politicized. No wonder, then, that the average person has to pay considerable attention to politics and power hierarchies.

Familiarity may very well breed contempt. The system may easily impel those who know and use it to be openly critical, even disdainful, about the political process. Simultaneously, however, it sees to it that political events pertinent to individual interests are not restricted to occasional elections, rallies, or demonstrations. Above all, the system impels the citizen to seek information about who has how much power and how these power holders can most effectively be reached. This is no mean achievement in any context; but it is especially important in a country like Italy where many institutions of democracy do not operate as they do in other places.

RELIGION AND POLITICS

Some patrons are so big and powerful, so visibly and actively engaged in politics, that their clients can scarcely pretend to be unaware of or immune from the political activities in which their patrons—and by implication they themselves—are enmeshed. The Catholic church looms large as one of these. Ancient divisions of the peninsula's hamlets, towns, and cities and their residents into Guelfs and Ghibellines, into friends and enemies of the Vatican and its pontiff, continue to give religious practice profound political coloration.

The pope's secular and political arm, of course, has always extended beyond the Alps and across the Mediterranean. And even today a well-traveled Polish pope can make that power felt in Central and Eastern Europe, Latin America, or the United States. But Italy's experience with this powerful organization is qualitatively different, and not just because the seat of Catholicism is physically located in the middle of Rome. Unlike other parts of Europe, the peninsula experienced no breakup of the Catholic monolith, no wars of religion, no serious challenge to the Vatican's overweening authority. There was none of that conflict in Italy, within or about religion, that in other places created a stronger, neater, enduring separation between church and state.

The Italian response to the Protestant Reformation was reactionary. On the peninsula, the Vatican fought tenaciously not only for its religious integrity and authority but for its political power too. Thus, several centuries after Martin Luther and Henry VIII, we find millions of Italians who are unable or unwilling to draw a sharp line between Caesar and

God. Those Italians, now growing in numbers, who insist on such a separation find that the going is still sharply against the current.

The Vatican remains a formidable patron and a major factor in politics because of its capacity to adapt to regime changes. Yesterday the Vatican made its peace with fascism and managed to wring striking concessions from the fascist state. Today it has made the transition to democratic republican government relatively unscathed. Indeed, it is better off than ever. The Christian Democratic party, although it is not the Vatican's direct or abject instrument, has nevertheless used its forty-year political hegemony to fashion Italian democracy with a sharp view to the Vatican's preferences.

During the heyday of this hegemony, when the Vatican's influence within the DC was riding high, the patrons available to intercede on one's behalf might be as close as the local pastor or bishop, as distant as a cardinal in the powerful Curia at Rome. Alternatively, intercession with the party, and through it with the bureaucracy, might pass through the instrumentality of one of Catholic Action's organizational units. In effect, those associated with the Catholic church could "deliver" for their clients: jobs, pensions of several different descriptions, passports, public works contracts, access to the mass media, variances from the building codes, special permission to use sidewalks and other public facilities to one's private advantage, assistance with complex bureaucratic processes, and so on.[3]

Many Italians are unhappy about this "contamination" of politics by religion, and left-wing ideologues rage about this state of affairs. From their perspective, the church continues to have entirely too much influence over public education; the Vatican and its formidable group of Italian cardinals openly take partisan stands on issues of public policy and administration at all levels; and the church continues to extract special concessions from the state. Outside Italy, many would agree with Italians who find this situation repugnant. Whatever one's view in the matter, it is impossible not to recognize that politics and religion are highly interpenetrated.

Italy, or course, is not unique as a country where religion takes on political overtones. Political parties inspired by religious considerations, and in which church organizations may be enmeshed, are found in the Federal Republic of Germany, the Netherlands, and many Latin American countries. Indeed, in the latter, so-called liberation theology has brought the Catholic clergy so openly into politics Pope John Paul II has thought it best to urge them to pull in their horns. But with limited success.

The United States itself was founded by religious dissidents. The earliest governments these persons created in the New World were scarcely monuments to religious toleration. Furthermore, it would require deliberate opaqueness not to see the myriad ways in which the Anglican, the Catholic, the Baptist, the Mormon, the Jewish, and other churches are involved in the contemporary American political process. Thus far at least, Italy has nothing to compare with the political-evangelical religious sects that flourish in the United States and garner mass audiences on television and radio. Italians who know anything at all about American politics are by and large convinced that religion is a much more salient aspect of politics there than in their own country.

ITALY AS A SPECIAL CASE

If Italy is not unique on this score, it is a special case. Not only did the Catholic church actually govern the peninsula for several centuries; politically speaking, it occupied a significant part of the national territory until well into the last century. And although the constitution certainly would permit other religions to operate, the Catholic church has the field almost entirely to itself.[*] Thus, when religion speaks about politics, or intervenes in it, it does so as a single powerful organization that faces no other competition in its own realm.

From the nation's standpoint, the Catholic church is a theocratic government whose sovereign territory and capital are physically located in the middle of Italy's capital. From Rome, the Vatican State not only manages its global empire; it sees to its material, as well as spiritual, interests in Italy as well. The Vatican's radio station transmits to the Italian nation each day for hours on end. Its daily newspaper, *L'Osservatore Romano,* is on every newsstand. Ambassadors to the Vatican live in Rome, not behind the Vatican's walls. The millions of tourists and pilgrims from all over the world who visit the Vatican each year get there, by public transportation, through the city of Rome. Even without the several thousand churches and cathedrals that are spread throughout Italy, the Catholic church remains a more palpable and intrusive presence there than anywhere else.

Catholicism is not just churches and seminaries, nunneries, hospitals, and museums, in all of which Italy certainly abounds. It is also a vast, complex network of organizations, designed fundamentally to assure the presence of the church in the broadest possible spectrum of Italian life. In addition to the various branches of Catholic Action, there are organizations that prepare workers for membership in trade unions, bring together particularly devout practitioners, publish books and magazines, provide child care for working mothers, organize vacations and other leisure activities, and so on.

When necessary (for example in electoral or public relations campaigns or in political confrontations with left or laical parties), this organizational apparatus can and will be made available to the Christian Democratic party. This does not imply that the church runs the party or that the latter is necessarily and always its willing instrument. It does mean that the Vatican, through this highly organized system, has direct access to the party that for forty years has exercised almost uninterrupted political control over the country.

In addition, to anticipate a point to which we will return, we must stress that all of these organizations provide their Catholic members with a very important channel through which they can and do participate in the political process. As a major patron in this cliental system, the Catholic church has, within its own subcultural space, provided millions of its adherents with a variegated network through which they, as well as the church itself, can bring pressure to bear on the political process. As patron to so many clients, the church delivers palpable benefits such as those mentioned earlier. As a sponsor and collaborator of Christian Democracy, it uses its apparatus, including its pulpits, to bring millions of voters to the polls to support the DC.

SOME CONSEQUENCES

If religion is so deeply present in politics, and if religious life itself cannot proceed very far without taking politics into account, what difference does this make? Widespread anticlericalism is one answer. Except for a quite small minority of political leaders, however, it is rarely of the virulent kind found in other parts of Europe. For example, although many who vote for the Communist party would number among the fiercest critics of the church's political engagement, anticlericalism has never been the PCI's official stance. The PCI understands that, given the church's status and its appeal to the masses, anticlericalism represents potentially very dangerous waters. Rather than navigate these, the PCI has preferred higher ground.

The decision to give the church a wide berth, to avoid a head-on collision with it, was taken by Palmiro Togliatti just as World War II was ending in defeat for Italy. Much to everyone's surprise, he indicated that the PCI would accept the Concordat signed by Pope Pius XII and Mussolini in 1929. Since then the PCI has maintained an implicit agreement with the Vatican that it would not make religion one of its major political concerns. As a result, it was not the Communists who proposed the laws on divorce and on abortion that have so rankled the Vatican. Indeed, the PCI got behind the campaign to defeat church efforts to rescind these laws only after the Radicals, Socialists, and other laical parties had already acted.

Cynics might argue that the PCI avoids collision with the Vatican because it has its own political religion to propagate. Equally frequent is the argument that the PCI, in a Catholic country, must take pains not to create the impression that it is, as so many Catholics believe, the Antichrist. A better interpretation is that the Italian Communists, unlike many other Italians whose anticlericalism is visceral, are capable of making very sophisticated cost-and-benefit calculations before they make political moves, particularly against the Vatican!

To say that the Vatican, with its organizations, is deep into politics does not imply that it always has its way. For one thing, Italians are quite able to distinguish when the Vatican addresses matters of doctrine as opposed to matters of public policy, like social welfare, taxation, or public morality. Even when, as in the cases of divorce or abortion, the church tries to make burning political issues sound like matters of religious doctrine, millions of Catholics simply do not go along. Indeed, on the issues of divorce and abortion, the Italian Catholic voters have displayed a degree of sophistication and independence that their counterparts in other democracies would find incomprehensible. In the mid-1970s, the voters approved the divorce law by a margin of two-to-one. They did the same thing a few years later with the law on abortion.

This independence of mind is aided by the considerable leeway the Vatican allows each bishop, within his territorial jurisdiction, to intervene in the political process. Even the strongest pope knows that it is no simple matter to get bishops to march lockstep behind the pontiff as opposed to their own drum beat. The Vatican's political initiatives, and those of various cardinals and bishops, thus contribute to an overall lively political life within the religious community and the country at large.

As important as religion may be in a country like Italy, it is not to that aspect of society alone that the "life-as-politics" description of the country applies. It would be tedious to provide the complete bill of particulars on this score. But it will help to see how this matter relates to other important sectors: the artistic, intellectual, and educational communities, and, above all, the economy.

POLITICS AND THE ARTS

Even a moment's reflection will remind us that art is always intertwined with religion and politics. It would have to be so on a monumental scale in Italy, given the history of Christianity, the secular powers wielded by the Vatican for centuries, and the explosive flowering of the Renaissance on the peninsula. The patrons of the arts were not just the Medicis at Florence, or other secular princes or dukes scattered throughout Italy and Europe. Great popes and their lieutenants rivaled and often surpassed the former in this activity; magnificent cathedrals that reflect, and museums that husband, the Renaissance's patrimony provide the evidence.

The legacy of this patronage of the arts includes a conviction that the contemporary state should be directly involved in the provision of financial support for the arts. This may be an admirable concept, but it also opens the door to the politicization of the arts. Let us see why.

In today's Italy, the state is the only significant patron of the arts. Private philanthropy is essentially unknown and, in fact, the tax laws discourage it. If the arts survive at all, it is because the state provides them with public subsidies.[5] Thus, for every theater ticket purchased in Italy, the state puts up, at the 1987 exchange rate, about thirty dollars! Milan's famous La Scala is a vast, featherbedded public enterprise, whose on-stage performers are a small fraction of the more than twelve hundred persons on its payroll. Not surprisingly, the cost of any La Scala production is several times greater than a similar production by New York's Metropolitan Opera. Those who have visited Italy might find incredible the assertion that the arts are heavily subsidized by the state. Given the abysmal condition of so many public museums, the deteriorating condition of some of the most important monuments and works of art, one might well believe that the Italian state is frivolous and even mocking toward its unique artistic heritage. The more simple point is that the power to allocate public funds is no guarantee that they will be wisely used.

In practice, funds are allocated on the basis of crass, straightforward political criteria. Theatrical companies make it to the stage, even smaller provincial stages, only if they are recommended by one or more of the political parties. Visual artists, too, are unlikely to go far unless they are taken under the protective wing of a political party, trade union, organized business, or other interest group associated with a political party. It is not just who you know that counts in Italy; it is whom you know in politics with direct access to the major political parties.

Far from shunning such patronage, artists go avidly in search of it. At the same time, many of them make the somewhat contradictory demand that the state extend to them both complete artistic freedom and the economic status of public servants. Few, however, escape a simple reality: those in the public sector who supply the oxygen will favor others toward whom they feel ideological kinship and with whom they maintain the strongest political ties. In any case, none will be favored who fail to demonstrate some sort of political connection.

Such connections really mean the political parties, which are at the center of this politicized system of artistic patronage. Just as the Medicis and the ancient popes had their favorites, so do those who now channel public support to particular painters, sculptors, filmmakers, writers, poets, dance groups, musicians, art galleries, photographic studios, and the like.

The relationship is symbiotic; the parties get something out of it too. In Italy politics permeates the arts also because, at least since the Renaissance but actually much longer, Culture, writ large, is very much a public issue.[6] People value it somewhat more than elsewhere. They go to great pains to avoid being labeled as someone *senza cultura*, without culture. Parties seek out these symbols of culture in order to demonstrate that leading exponents of the fine and visual arts are located in their ranks or approve their programs.

It has always been a matter of great moment to the Communist party, and of chagrin to its opponents, that so many of the most prominent painters, sculptors, architects, filmmakers, musicians, writers, actors, and actresses have been party members or supporters. Names come to mind: Visconti, Pasolini, Fellini, Rossellini, Silone, Manzu, De Sica, Zeffirelli, Cardinale, and Mastroianni. Vittorio Gassman and Giorgio Strehler are identified with the Socialist party, as is Lina Wertmüller somewhat more loosely.

Some of those once close to the PCI, like Ignazio Silone, later broke with it and moved closer to the Socialists. Whenever shifts of this kind occur they elicit remarkable attention from the mass media. Years ago, Curzio Malaparte, a well-known novelist and member of the PCI, was reported by nuns to have called for the last sacraments, which were duly (and triumphantly) administered. This set off a minor uproar. The death of Renato Guttuso early in 1987 had an even stormier effect. Evidently the renowned painter, once a member of the PCI's central committee, died in the presence of a clergyman who had counseled him for several months.

The fact that no level of government in Italy is controlled exclusively by a single party, or by the same coalition of parties, introduces some democracy into the prevailing system of patronage. Far from implying winner-take-all, the norms suggest and indeed require that some of these highly sought-after forms of support go to persons and groups that are not necessarily close to the government. Moreover, because so many of the most obviously outstanding artists have long been associated with the Communist party, it, and the left in general, can count on a good slice of available patronage where the fine arts are concerned.

If not obviously democratic or based on universal criteria of merit, the spoils system described is much more nuanced and civilized than the American type that we associate with Andrew Jackson and the political machines that developed later. The American approach to patronage does not require that crumbs, to say nothing of juicy morsels or sumptuous feasts, be left to political opponents. Where the arts are concerned, the Italian spirit is more magnanimous. Even there, however, the patronage game can turn ugly where the spoils in question are, for example, control of the mass media, newspaper ownership or editorships, or major industrial and financial empires in the public sector.

In the arts the basic understanding is that for any creative person in search of support, the right political party connection is as important as, and perhaps more important than, sheer talent. As in other areas of work and life, it would be considered the height of folly were a person to make career plans largely on the basis of personal talent and promise.

These impulses toward nepotism and political favoritism are universal, and some democratic societies take trouble to encourage a minimum level of objectivity in the selection of the recipients of public support. Private foundations can sometimes create at least the impression that awards are made without regard to the recipient's ideological or political coloration. In Italy, the private foundations are largely an extension of the interests, and egos, of those who fund them.

In short, Italians are less squeamish about mingling art and politics. If their practices seem unusually blatant, they are also less hypocritical. Not only is it relatively easy to pin a political label on leading artists, who will wear it with pride. Party leaders themselves are genuinely proud of this identification and are ready to extend themselves to further artistic careers.

POLITICIZED INTELLECTUALS

Where intellectuals are concerned (I do not mean to exclude artists from this category!), we expect them to be much concerned with politics and to find many of them openly lined up with political parties. Despite arguments about how important it is in democratic society that its intellectuals remain somewhat aloof from the political parties or that they keep politics at a distance and in perspective, not many of them anywhere succeed in bringing off this difficult maneuver. In the United States since the New Deal and in Western Europe over a much longer period, intellectuals have held prominent roles in all levels of government.

Nevertheless, the intellectual as a relatively autonomous, demanding, honest critic of social, political, and economic arrangements remains a vital ingredient of a free society. The politicization of the intellectual community is not entirely compatible with this function. It is therefore fair to say that the role of a somewhat removed, unbiased critic of society and its institutions is an ideal to which intellectuals should aspire. If they do not, it is unlikely that anyone else will.

By and large, Italian intellectuals of every variety and in every sphere not only shun any such effort; they tend to be skeptical and often scathingly incredulous toward those who believe it should be pursued. As a group, they are engulfed by politics and happily wallow in it. Far from being the critics of political parties and party factions, they are often the latter's major spokesmen. Far from seeking a modicum of space, in a politicized society that admittedly offers very little of it to anyone, they hanker after the rewards, including public offices, that the parties can distribute to the faithful.

The major newspapers and publishing houses do not provide them refuge. They, too, either are owned by the parties and their major supporters or exist as instruments of industrialists, financiers, or other private interests intent on promoting a particular set of public policies.[7] In effect, most intellectuals are found in one political stable or another. A few manage to display notable independence of mind, but they appear as aberrations.

To be intellectually independent is also risky. In journalism, for example, reporters will sometimes write articles that do not conform to the editorial line a newspaper or magazine represents. Under existing labor laws, it may be difficult or impossible for the editors or owners to fire such persons. But they can easily be relegated to a limbo that keeps what they write from appearing in print.

The occasional daily newspaper that tries its hand at objective, critical reporting, or that publishes writers who may represent contrasting points of view on matters of public policy, will easily be condemned on grounds that it "lacks coherence." In effect, the print media and the broadcast media are markedly different from their counterparts in the United States.[8]

Not that the latter are unconcerned with politics or never follow a "political line." The difference lies in the fact that, once a newspaper, magazine, or radio or television station has established its political ties and identification, it loses any semblance of independent judgment whenever issues have political implications. In a deeply politicized society, even the most innocuous "human interest" news item can be turned to political use, and often is. In this context it is easy for the newspapers to become the uncritical instrument of the political party or faction whose mouthpiece it is, and is widely known to be.

It is customary in Italy to think of intellectuals as heavily lined up on the political left. Although this is a conceit of the left itself, the general skew is in that direction. For one thing, left-wing parties like the Communists and the Socialists (PSI) court the intellectuals. As in the case of creative artists, the Communist party excels at this practice and has often turned it to its advantage. Indeed, for many years the PCI was able to boast, with good reason, a remarkable proportion of the leading intellectuals. Today the situation has changed; one certain sign that the PCI is in serious trouble lies in the sizeable number of intellectuals who have abandoned it.

Some of these political apostates have gone over to the Socialists, but there has been no stampede of intellectuals to the PSI. Under Bettino

Craxi, that party has openly used its still growing control over patronage to offer intellectuals the kinds of material and power inducements many of them find hard to turn down. Nevertheless, the same intellectuals who may leave the PCI for political or ideological reasons may find it difficult to join a PSI whose propensity toward patronage is already legendary and whose record of political morality is anything but unblemished.

The Christian Democrats have also made efforts to improve their standing within the intellectual community. This is an uphill, although far from hopeless, struggle. The DC must overcome the ancient and widely held prejudice, rooted in the Catholic world's hostile, obscurantist reactions to the Enlightenment, that Catholics themselves are without culture. The obverse of this judgment is the immodest claim, made by Communist intellectuals and contested by the laical community, that something called the "Communist culture" is superior to all others.

Despite this handicap, the DC has managed to develop its own stable of intellectuals. That group looked pitiably small a generation ago; it is much more impressive today. It has been augmented and fortified not only by transformations within the Catholic church and its auxiliary organizations. A Catholic presence in the universities, well-known Catholic research organizations, and the emergence of important writers, philosophers, poets, scientists, and social scientists of Catholic persuasion have contributed as well.

So much does politics permeate intellectual life that any intellectual without a political party identity or affiliation may well find him or herself wandering in the material and emotional wilderness. In the case of those who were close to the PCI and are now estranged from it, the sense of social and emotional isolation can be profound. Some of these former PCI advocates try to deal with this malaise by arrogating to themselves the role of severest critics of the party. As if their earlier obtuseness about the "true nature" of communism gives them unusually attractive credentials as the PCI's critics.

There is a not-so-subtle form of anticommunism that goes with this kind of sublimation. Some leading intellectuals, at one time among the most articulate and effective spokesmen for the PCI, have remained just as prominent as they find unlimited opportunities to write, to speak, to appear on radio and television to explain in detail the Communist party's alleged misdeeds, failures, blind spots, wrongheadedness and other shortcomings.

As with the arts, intellectual life is also politicized because of the material

rewards that political parties and their leaders can provide. Because intellectuals deal with ideas, however, we must not underestimate the seductive appeal of power, which is often the necessary condition for
translating ideas into public policies. Along with power, of course, goes
status, another nonmaterial reward that intellectuals, especially those on
the left, are supposed to consider ephemeral and pernicious. In practice,
they display a gargantuan and insatiable appetite for status. Italy is a
perfect place for them: not only are Italians tolerant of jealous preening
of every conceivable variety; they esteem elegance of language and assign
a special place to those whose craft it is to use language with skill.

The politicians and the intellectuals of Italy live in a state of near-perfect
symbiosis. In their glosses of what the politicians say, the latter bring
some semblance of coherence to discourses that typically defy
comprehension.

THE POLITICAL GROVES OF ACADEME

In a society permeated by politics, one might think that the academic
community would offer refuge for those, intellectuals or others, who
might prefer to remain aloof from political conflict. But politics seeps into
this sector as well—not only in the universities but in the educational
system from bottom to top, from nursery and elementary schools to the
high schools and *licei* that prepare students (relatively few of them) for
university training. The schools have always been a major arena of struggle
between the Catholic church and the laical forces. Teachers are notoriously
committed to one political party or another. The schools produce in some
students and reinforce in others clear-cut political predispositions. Not
necessarily in everyone. But it is not uncommon to find one liceo identified
as "Communist" or "left," another as "Catholic," a third as "neofascist,"
and so on.

The universities stand at the apex of this system. Despite several reforms
of recent decades, higher education remains elitist. Some of the universities are among the oldest and most distinguished in the West. Many
boast centuries of humanistic and scientific achievements. Even today,
despite the intrusion of politics into this realm, several of the universities
remain islands of intellectual rigor and innovation that rival similar institutions anywhere else.

Even these islands, though, are firmly in the hands of autocratic senior professors, unfondly called "the barons," who constitute as powerful an interest group as one can find in the country. Despite the university reforms of the last two decades, many of which were designed to democratize the university system, these life-tenured educators maintain a stranglehold over higher education.[9] In particular, through a system of written rules and unspoken norms that are reminiscent of the novels of C. P. Snow, they exercise iron-clad control over promotions to their ranks. They may not have kept the masses from gaining footholds in the universities, but they will certainly use their considerable knowledge of Byzantine political maneuvering to assure that those who gain the highest ranks will do so strictly through a system of cooptation.

My purpose here is neither to discuss the structure of power within higher education nor to assess the extent to which it has been democratized or otherwise modified by reforms of recent years. It is, rather, to underscore that in Italian higher education the "barons" are not just playing academic politics; they are intricately a part of the bigger political game as well.

In the bargains the "barons" strike, in the trade-offs they concoct, and in the "balance" they seek to establish within the university community, political and ideological considerations that reflect the politics of the nation play a central part. The political coloration of the competing candidates weighs at least as heavily as their professional qualifications, and sometimes more. The system is rarely blatant. One does not ask, directly, whether the candidate is a Christian Democrat or Communist, a Socialist, Republican, or Liberal. One asks, or notes, instead that one particular candidate is from the Catholic "area," another from the left or laical "area," and so on. Italian academics, too, are word masters, experts in the refined use of the subjunctive and triple conditional, couched in long, interminable, elegantly constructed sentences. Code words abound, and they often convey reams of unspoken information and understandings.

Despite appearances to the contrary, the professors, too, become involved in a system of allocating desired positions on the basis of a rough balance among the three subcultures: left, laical, and Catholic. The pattern resembles the system of *proporz* that in Austria governs the distribution of almost everything of value there between Catholics and Socialists. In practice, the Italian system is more complicated, not just because there are more political parties and subcultures there than in Austria, but also because Italy, as we shall see later, does not qualify as a consociational democracy.

The intrusion of politics into the university system is most dramatically apparent whenever elections are held to name the *magnifici rettori*, the rectors, or presidents, of the universities. There being only one rector per university, this coveted position of power, influence, and prestige cannot be divided. Because rectors are chosen by election of the professoriate, all of the maneuvers associated with coalition building go into operation. Competition can be fierce; around the campaign itself will revolve the burning question whether the university will remain or fall into the hands of the Communists, the Catholics, or the laical forces. For any of these groups, a rectorship remains an important instrument for the exercise of cultural, and by implication political, power.

Needless to add, university student bodies are highly politicized as well. In the late 1960s and early 1970s they represented the prime recruiting ground for political terrorist organizations, particularly those on the left. Several founding members of the Red Brigades, for example, were contemporary students of sociology at the University of Trento. And Toni Negri, considered by many to be the intellectual nerve center of the most extreme leftist terrorist groups, was himself a university professor who in the classroom openly condoned political violence.

But even the more normal, essentially peaceful, and law-abiding student organizations are typically organized along the same lines that define the country's political parties. These are very European and are not like those anemic groups one finds in American universities. They are often vigorous, active bodies with formal ties to the political parties within which many of the students will pursue political careers or on which they intend to call for support when they go out to look for jobs.

PUBLIC AND PRIVATE ECONOMICS

Up to this point we have seen that politics intrudes into religion, the arts, the mass media, education, and intellectual life. What about industry and commerce? Can one escape politics there? Not likely. To begin with, without even a tip of the hat to Karl Marx, the Italian economy is one of the most "socialist" we find among democracies. The Italian state owns a striking proportion of the country's banking and industrial capacity. This is so not because Italian political leaders wanted to create socialism. It is true because from its birth as a nation some eleven decades ago, Italy developed the coziest of relationships between capitalists and political leaders.

Because Italy, like Germany, became a nation later than other European countries, its aspiring industrializers were in a hurry to make up for lost time. In order to move along, to catch up with the more industrialized nations, they required two things. One was the help, financial and legal, of the state itself. The other, a condition of the first, was to keep the southern landowners off their backs. They satisfied this last condition through the system of trasformismo discussed in the last chapter. The latifondisti got a free hand in the south, in exchange for which the northern industrialists were at liberty to use and to milk the state to their own purposes.[10]

The steel industry is a prime example of this arrangement. That sector took off, at the city of Terni, late in the nineteenth century. Its development was financed not by private capital but rather by the taxpayers whose money the state funneled to aspiring steel magnates. As with the canals and railroads in the United States in the last century, and with the later development of some of the basic industries there, this kind of economic transformation would not have occurred or proceeded as rapidly without legal and material assistance from the state. The Italian state gave similar assistance in other sectors as well. Indeed, it remains available today, permitting private entrepreneurs to find capital when they need it; to extract certain material incentives from the public sector, which lower the risk level of enterprise; and to turn to the state for bail-out assistance whenever investments sour. Few so-called free enterprisers have been more coddled and cushioned by the state.

But for some exceptions in northern Italy, it would be a mistake to think of those who industrialized the country as risk-taking entrepreneurs or swashbuckling captains of industry. Whenever they could, which was often, they shifted the high risk from themselves to the state, that is, to the general public and taxpayers. This tradition is so deeply ingrained that even today the most eloquent defenders of the merits of "free enterprise" will, without blushing, demand that the state acquire, at premium prices, industries that are colossal failures. When it comes to the systematic use of state power for the benefit of a handful of powerful familes in the private sector, Italy looks more like a Third World country than a modern industrial democracy.

State or public ownership of large-scale industrial enterprise was a spontaneous, accidental occurrence that began with the stock market crash of 1929 and the Great Depression that followed.[11] Under Italian law, banks could own stocks and bonds in industrial corporations, and they took full advantage of this privilege. In the heyday of the 1920s it looked in Italy, as it did everywhere else in market economies, that investors of every variety would go on forever, adding riches to riches.

Black Thursday's seismic wave hit Wall Street first, then crossed the ocean and leveled European economies too. Italy's economy was a house of cards, built on no foundation. The threat there was not just the failure of some corporations and the banks that had invested in them; the danger was of complete chaos that might endanger even the dictatorship that Mussolini was then hard at work to solidify. Indeed, the frail condition of the Italian economy had been telegraphed to London and Washington three years earlier, when a major effort was required to keep it from collapsing.

With the crash, all of the leading economies were in dire straits, and in Italy the fascist state came to the rescue. It saved the banks by acquiring from them the more or less worthless securities they held in bankrupted corporations. Through this salvage operation, the state became either the sole or partial owner of the industries involved, depending on what proportion of the stock of these companies the banks held at the time the latter were rescued at public expense.

There was no Marxist or other socialist ideology at work here that argued that the state *should* be the owner of the instruments of production. No one welcomed the move on the basis of any ideological principle. In effect, the state backed into public ownership, and apologized for doing so. If this was socialism, it anticipated the postwar British Labour party approach to it. There, in the eyes of many left-wing ideologues, the Labour government produced a form of "ashcan socialism," by nationalizing obsolete and failing coal mines and industries, and then paying private stockholders handsome prices for their nearly worthless securities.

In order to bring some semblance of orderliness to these new holdings, the state created, in the early 1930s, the Institute for Industrial Reconstruction (IRI).[12] It was designed to be a temporary public corporation. The idea was that as soon as the economy turned around, the acquired industries would be turned back to private ownership. It never happened. Not only is IRI still very much around; it is immensely larger. Indeed, it is one of the world's largest industrial holding companies, whose various branches do tens of billions of dollars of business each year.

IRI grew larger not for ideological reasons, and certainly not because the Italian state felt any need to use public corporations as "yard sticks" designed to keep rapacious private corporations in line. It grew because other capitalists who fell on bad times found it irresistible to dump into the lap of an accommodating government their sick or dying industries.

These days, this cynical practice masquerades behind the demand for "deregulation." At one level, demands for deregulation reflect the genuine conviction (among many Socialists, for example) that bureaucratic intrusions, as well as ownership, by the state amounts to enormous waste in the production and delivery of goods and services. At another level, and shorn of precious ideological camouflage, deregulation demands that emanate from the industrial community amount to this: the state should acquire, at premium prices, the real "dogs," the megalosers in the private sector. In exchange, the state should sell to the private sector, at bargain-basement prices, the industrial "jewels," the big winners, held by public corporations like IRI. These entirely cynical demands are, of course, carefully wrapped in the mantle of democracy, liberal economics, and the market's beneficent hand. Or they may be hidden behind a smokescreen that suggests that only if the government sells off industrial enterprise to the Italian private sector can Italy remain competitive in world markets. The rationales are infinite when it comes to making it appear that selfish interests and the public welfare are one and the same thing.

Even if state ownership of industry proceeded willy-nilly, it has reached vast proportions. Today IRI owns 100 percent of the shipbuilding industry, all of the airlines, four-fifths of the steel and metal-working sectors, almost all of telecommunications, a good chunk of the automobile industry, and a lot more. Nor is this the whole story. Ente Nazionale Idrocarburi (ENI), a giant holding company in the energy sector, is also state-owned. Last year, its companies did about twenty billion dollars worth of business. Through another state-owned company, electric power is nationalized.

The ENI story is even more interesting than the IRI's.[13] It is a descendent of AGIP, a petroleum company created by the fascist government in the 1920s. At war's end, the government appointed Enrico Mattei, one of the few genuine entrepreneurs in Italy's history, to liquidate AGIP by turning it over to private interests. This is what the major petroleum companies outside Italy, the so-called Seven Sisters, wanted, and the postwar Italian government appeared disposed to accommodate them.

Not Enrico Mattei.[14] He found some highly promising geological surveys in the bowels of AGIP and set his people to drilling holes in Sicily and the Po Valley. The Seven Sisters set up an incredible din against this blatantly "socialist" ploy. They spent a lot of money and lobbied against Mattei in Italy. They importuned their own national governments, for example, in London and Washington, to bring pressure on Rome to get on with AGIP's liquidation. Mattei countered by spending AGIP money to buy support among Italy's politicians, irrespective of their political party identity. About the time it looked like he would be compelled to throw in the towel, Mattei made his first important strike at Cortemaggiore and became a national hero.

The rest is history. AGIP today is only one of eleven industrial groups that fall under the umbrella of the state-owned ENI. In order to set this train in motion, though, Enrico Mattei had to use not just industrial, financial, and commercial power, but political power as well. Furthermore, when one adds to the alphabet soup a number of other state institutions that own or direct industrial and commercial enterprise, we get a picture of a mixed economy in which the presence of the state is so massively palpable it would be a miracle if Italian economic life escaped the entanglements of politics.

POLITICS IN THE ECONOMY

Of course it does not. Those who work for, and especially those who manage, state-owned industries are deeply conscious of politics. For one thing, those who manage state enterprises near or at the top are quintessential political appointees. They owe their jobs to *lottizzazione*. This is an endemic, much-maligned patronage system whereby jobs and other valued things are apportioned among the leading political parties roughly in proportion to their electoral strength. For a long time, this economic patronage was divided largely among the internal factions of the DC. This was so because the Christian Democrats, as the hegemonic party, held a near monopoly of these highly coveted positions. Although they are anything but Leninists, the Christian Democrats certainly take quite literally Lenin's adage that those who control the "commanding heights" of the economic system actually control the country. If the power of the DC is anchored on one side in the Catholic church and its subcultural organizational apparatus; on the other side that anchorage is located in the state-owned industrial and banking sectors.

As the DC's electoral preponderance eroded, however, it was forced to form coalitions, and the price it had to pay for this support was to share some of these industrial plums with other political parties. The Socialists in particular display an insatiable appetite for these lucrative patronage jobs—lucrative, we might add, not just for those who are named to manage industrial firms but for the political parties they represent, to which, one way or another, they manage to funnel money.

The more pivotal the Socialists became in the more recent national coalition governments, the greater their propensity to extract from the DC direct control of patronage jobs in the public industrial sector, as well as in the state-owned banking and telecommunications spheres. These positions were then awarded to Socialists, or to Italians the Socialists wished to favor. However great may be the PSI's appetite, though, it will take years to reduce the DC's proportionate weight. In the banking sector, for example, the ratio of Christian Democratic to Socialist managers is today about eight-to-one. In the mass media, the Socialists seem to have reduced considerably Christian Democratic domination of the RAI radio and television networks, but recent inroads represent only the top of that deep iceberg.

On the other hand, with the advent in the early eighties of the first Socialist prime minister, the broader patronage power of the PSI was accelerated and consolidated. Indeed, in their hunger for patronage, in their blatant use of it for their own narrow party purposes, and in their willingness (in the use of public funds) to walk the razor's edge of legality, often without success, the Socialists have by now proved beyond any doubt that they require no instruction at all from their much maligned Christian Democratic coalition partners. In the public industrial sphere, each of these parties now has a major stronghold: the IRI is the unquestioned domain of the DC, and the ENI has become the fiefdom of the PSI. In practice, there is a wider mix of political party affiliations among the managers of these enterprises, but it is orchestrated by the dominant party in each sector.

As with the naming of university professors, then, it is not just the professional qualifications of an industrial manager that will land him or her a top-level position in state-owned industry. It is also, and above all, that person's political party association and sponsorship. When the parties fail to agree as to how these juicy plums are to be distributed, the positions can go unfilled for months or even years. This happened recently in the banking sector, as well as within the RAI Corporation mentioned a moment ago. There, it is openly understood that Channel One belongs to the DC, Channel Two to the Socialists, and the relatively small Channel Three more or less to the Communists. The smaller parties get the crumbs of this allocative process.[15]

It goes without saying that this form of patronage translates not only into high-income jobs for the party favorites, but also into the political management of the news. In the mid-1980s the process of lottizzazione regarding RAI positions had become so protracted, so scandalous in the open revelation of what was at stake, and so cynical and arrogant regarding the public itself, the cry went up that the RAI should be sold off to private interests. As if this step would imply the RAI's removal from the influence of politics!

Once managers are appointed to industries or mass communications systems on the basis of political considerations, they must keep a sharp eye out for what their sponsors want, what will please or enrage them. Sometimes these sponsors are not political parties as a whole but warring factions within them. Thus, a small shift in the balance of power within the governmental coalition, or within a single party, can and does mean that some managers will lose their jobs and other aspirants will find new ones.

Even if they experience impressive longevity, these managers are subject to continual political pressures in connection with the decisions they take. Where to invest, which plants to expand or close down, where and when to make acquisitions, what kinds of deals to strike with other companies, how to handle the company's debt structure—all of these as well as other management issues may well find powerful figures in parliament, the cabinet, or the office of the prime minister disposed to intervene. There is some irony here in that, whereas the politicians provide very little *general policy direction* for the state-owned industries, they offer no end of *interference* with the day-to-day operations of the state-owned firms.

The picture is only slightly overdrawn. Quantitatively speaking, most of the decisions that public-sector managers take can and do proceed without the interfering presence of persons on the political side. Indeed, the truly skilled manager is one who worries about the political implications of his work in advance, takes these into account, and thereby also optimizes the degree of actual independence he can exercise in his job. Accountability, formal or informal, to many different "constituencies" tends to make the public-sector managers who survive the process persons of unusual knowledge, experience, and know-how, and in many ways superior to their private-sector counterparts.

Is it any different in the private sector? Yes and no. Gianni Agnelli of Fiat, Leopoldo Pirelli of the company that bears his name, and other major private-sector industrialists do not have to check with Rome when they name senior managers. However, it is worth noting that there are relatively few large-scale private financial and industrial organizations in the country. Most of these are associated with a single man or family, or with several of these, and operate through well-known financial corsortia. It is typical of the major industries in the private sector that a single person speaks authoritatively, often autocratically, for each of them.

These industrial leaders are deeply enmeshed in the political process. They carry on their own negotiations with the national and regional governments, as well as with the trade unions. They intervene openly and directly in political matters of every conceivable variety. They engage in maneuvers—for example, the acquisition of major newspapers or private television stations—that cannot proceed unless they manage to put together a political coalition in Rome.

These men may pay lip service to free enterprise and other canons of liberal economics. But what they practice is certainly not what they preach. Behind the facade of their words, behind their pious claims about how much better the economy would proceed if only the government and the politicians left business to the business community, the reality is that the cozy relationships between government and business mentioned earlier remain very much in place.

Italy's leading industrialists, their minions or members of their families, are not as openly involved in politics as are members of the American business community. Italian businessmen do not as readily hold public office or cabinet positions, nor are they as visibly active as American businessmen in the channeling of financial support to the candidates and political parties they favor. They share with businessmen everywhere great antipathy toward politics. Unlike some industrial elites, however, the Italians still believe that the most effective way to intervene in the political process is to corrupt it.

Italian industrialists are powerful forces to be reckoned with. They own significant pieces of the print and broadcast media. They create the most intricate interlocking directorates and financial holding companies. They manipulate the still underdeveloped stock market at Milan and manage to keep the government from passing regulations that would make financial and stock transactions more transparent. Their sense of encouraging "publicly held" companies, in which the "little guy" should be encouraged to invest, is that the latter should remain the prey of a few manipulators who, operating away from public scrutiny, can orchestrate markets to their hearts' content. Through "secret" arrangements, they gain de facto control of major commercial banks that ostensibly belong to the state and the public.

These maneuvers require, at a minimum, tacit support and, at a maximum, overt assistance from the government. Rarely can they proceed unless key persons in the business community have lined up powerful allies in the political sphere. And as for the so-called bottom line, the profitability of enterprise, industrialists seek and get from the government fail-safe policies, iron-clad insurance against their incompetency and potential failures as managers. Those few Italian entrepreneurs who prefer rugged individualism, relatively free from political and governmental assistance, are a disappearing breed.

Do the industrialists express any public gratitude for such an accommodating posture by the politicians? Not in the slightest! When the industrialists' top organization, Confindustria, holds its annual meetings, a stream of the country's leading political party and governmental leaders, including the prime minister, will appear there. Far from hearing words of thanks for all their material help to the business community, they may have to listen and later reply to industrial spokespersons who claim to find the government wanting on many dimensions. Newspapers will then announce that the businessmen have "given the government failing grades" or otherwise taken it to task.[16] The American National Association of Manufacturers and even the formidable Business Round Table would gasp at this open display of the political muscle of business.

What about the workers? Are they aware of the politicization of the economy? In a labor force of about twenty million, three million work for governmental authorities and an additional two million are unemployed. It is inevitable that this 25 percent are acutely aware of politics. Indeed, on a day-to-day basis, they loom as major protagonists in the political process.

Workers who hold jobs in the private sector are members of trade unions that boast over eight million members. These unions, like employers' associations, carry on continual negotiations with the government. In fact, there is scarcely any major issue of industrial relations that proceeds to a resolution without the intervention of one branch of government or another. This might mean a committee of parliament, the ministries of labor and social security, finance, or treasury, state industrial holdings, or the ministry for the development of the south. Regional or local governments or the office of the prime minister may also become involved. These procedures, which receive extensive coverage by the mass media, remind the workers that the calculus they use in problem-solving requires the inclusion of the political system and process as a major factor.

If the unions do not take the initiative in making contact with government, the latter will pick up the slack. The political management of the economy, so far at least, proceeds on the expectation that the government will consult the so-called "social partners," that is, organized labor and business. In fact, the national government is scarcely inclined to believe that it can carry out any public policy affecting organized labor without bringing the trade unions materially into the governmental process.

The unions themselves remind their members that the economy is snarled in politics. Each of the major trade union confederations has a distinctive political identity. The General Confederation of Italian Labor is dominated by the Communist party, with a minority group associated with the Socialists. The Italian Confederation of Free Trade Unions has always had more or less strong ties to the Christian Democrats. The Italian Union of Labor, the smallest of the major confederations, is an admixture of Socialist, Social Democratic, and Republican workers and leaders, although the Socialist segment predominates. Even the neofascists have their own national labor confederation. In short, it is next to impossible to think of work and workers without addressing the question of how they and their organizations relate to and are affected by politics.

Italy's complex economic mosaic also includes the "second" or "hidden" economy, where small- and medium-scale entrepreneurs operate with a minimum of scrutiny from government, and even less reporting by these economic actors to governmental authorities. For some years now the message has been: leave these economic operators alone, because they seem to represent the only truly dynamic sector of the economy.

In their own way, of course, these entrepreneurs, and those workers in the unreported economy whom they employ, are also acting "against the state," but only ostensibly so. These widely admired "self-made men," have in effect entered into a form of more or less open collusion with public authorities at both the regional and national levels. Beyond being left alone when it comes to careful fiscal reporting or strict adherence to the country's social insurance laws, these operators also require, and increasingly get, other forms of direct assistance from public authorities.

For example, because these smaller industries are so important as exporters who affect Italy's balance of payments, governmental officials at every level are at pains to lend them a hand in holding on to and expanding their overseas market shares. The notion that these entrepreneurs are moving forward strictly under their own power, outside the realm of politics and despite the dead hand of the bureaucracy, is pure fiction.

POLITICAL SATURATION

Bear in mind that we have been proceeding by illustration. It is not just religion and the arts, mass education and the mass media, public employment and the economy that are permeated by politics.[17] Society reeks of politics. Those who really hate politics cannot escape it. It is not just the likes of the tax collectors or the traffic cops who creep into one's consciousness. The former are evaded with impunity; and those designated to regulate traffic would easily qualify as card-carrying anarchists. It is not even the legions of public servants, and the shabby treatment they heap on citizens, that make the latter hyperconscious about politics. It is, rather, that all of these things combined with much more make politics something that reaches and then, like an oil slick on water, clings to each citizen. The presence of politics may be intrusive or subtle, but it is unmistakably there. This being so, it would be astounding were Italians without strong feelings about politics.

What we have here, then, is a society saturated by politics. In one's place of worship or work, education or enterprise, pursuit of pleasure or privacy, politics intrudes and makes its presence felt. To be oblivious to this condition, or able to ignore it, would require that a person be deaf, dumb, and blind. No degree of resolution would suffice to keep politics muffled and relegated to the background.

There are also factors outside Italy that force Italians to pay attention to politics and to dramatize certain aspects of it. Take Catholicism and communism. Although these movements tend to clash on a worldwide basis, the tension and conflict come to a sharp focus in Italy for reasons already noted. Beginning with the Cold War, Western governments, chief among them the one in Washington, have intervened in Italian electoral politics. It is safe to say that no democratic electorate in history has had as many "pen pals" as the Italian. No other has experienced the deluge of letters, containing exhortations, instructions, and dire threats regarding how the Italians should vote, sent to them in years past by family members, friends, or total strangers in the United States.

The "problem of communism" has greatly intensified the political awareness of millions of Italians. In foreign affairs it has induced Italy to become not only a loyal ally of the United States but also a country almost abjectly inclined to follow American leadership in international politics, no matter where it might lead. In domestic politics, the problem is not only central to the confrontation between church and state; it has been at the center of some of the most dramatic postwar political events, such as the assassination of Aldo Moro, murdered by the Red Brigades precisely because he favored bringing the PCI back into the national government. Terrorism itself, as we shall see, is intimately related to the communist question. The hundreds of victims terrorism has claimed are a sure-fire bet to raise everyone's political consciousness.

So is the threat of a communist "take-over." In the early 1980s the DC began to slide electorally, and in 1984, in elections for the European parliament, the PCI for the first time in history edged out the DC. This created another sharp jump in the political Richter scale. The shock brought the Vatican back to its old tricks of mobilizing the clergy against the PCI and, by implication, in favor of the DC. Several archbishops issued scathing denunciations of the sorry plight of cities administered by the Communists. As local elections approached in the spring of 1985, the Episcopal Council reminded voters that "not all choices are compatible with the Christian faith." Archbishop Motelese of Taranto had earlier been less oblique; with Ciriaco De Mita, the DC secretary general, at his side, he warned that the voters' choice would be "with God or without God." No one could mistake his meaning.

It is not just these confrontations at election time that call the omnipresence of politics to the attention of citizens. Patron-client politics goes on all the time. The Mafia, the Camorra, and other elements of organized crime carry on daily warfare against the state. So do the political terrorists. When public officials are not killed or wounded in their warfare against these organizations, they are hauled into court and jailed on charges of collusion with them.

Moreover, leading industrialists and bankers provide a continuing stream of evidence that they too are mired down, if not in political scandals, then certainly in the kinds of eye-catching maneuvers mentioned above. It is not that one is surprised to find that industrialists intervene in the political process, that some of them run for office and then become public officials and cabinet members. Nor is it that, from time to time, industrialists are prominent in political scandals or found in organizations with hostile intentions toward the democratic state. It is, rather, that Italy's private-sector economic power is concentrated in a very few hands; that these individuals and families are more or less openly, but always intimately, involved in the political process; and that this involvement is well known to the country's elites, and to the masses as well.

Indeed, one way or another, directly or indirectly, citizens are inundated with information through which they learn, or reconfirm, that society and life are steeped in patron-client politics, and that there exist no hermetically sealed compartments that are beyond its presence and influence. It is worth repeating that for anyone who hates politics, or wants refuge or immunity from it, or prefers a life where political considerations have relatively low salience, Italy is definitely the wrong place to be.

A SMALL-SCALE SOCIETY

Life is also deeply politicized in that way because Italy, relatively speaking, is a society of very small "scale."[18] Anthropologists and others may find this assertion stretched, perhaps absurd. For the anthropologist a small-scale society is one whose inhabitants display a restricted sense of time and space. Little written history exists in such places, and knowledge of the past is transmitted largely through story-telling. In addition, people there rarely travel more than a few miles from home, and there is scant knowledge of the larger world outside.

It is also true of small-scale societies that those who live there have almost total information about what everyone else does in waking or sleeping hours. Italy is small-scale primarily in this last sense, but it displays aspects of the other features as well.

For example, by comparison with other industrial democracies, Italians are relative stay-at-homes. Of course they travel to the mountains and seashores on vacation. But they rarely willingly move beyond their hometowns. Millions of southerners did travel north, and beyond the borders, in the 1960s in search of better economic conditions. Such population movements come in waves, as they did following World War I, when millions of southerners sailed from Naples to Ellis Island, and those American streets "paved with gold."

Despite such evidence, it is well known that Italians move reluctantly.

Italy has the devil's time dealing with unemployment in part because Italian workers refuse to travel to where the jobs are located. Even when they do move, for example to cities like Turin or Milan, they often encounter "racism" and, in any event, are unhappy in these new places and plan eventually to return "home."

Home is the place of one's birth and early years. A resident of Milan whose *grandparents* may have migrated there from Palermo will still consider himself, and be identified by the Milanese, as a Sicilian. Even today, in a world presumably shrunk by the mass media, the typical Italian man has a distinctive way of identifying himself. Say he was born in Lucca and now lives in Milan. He will say, first, that he is Luccan, then that he is a Tuscan, the region in which Lucca is located. He will then announce, with additional pride, that he is a northerner and definitely not from the south. Finally, and only if pressed, he will concede that he is Italian, in the sense of belonging, as a citizen, to this ephemeral thing called Italy or the Italian republic.

This attitude is often called *campanilismo*. The idea is that one's basic territorial, ethnic, social, cultural, and political identities center on the bell tower of the church that a person and his family members have attended, or shunned, for generations or even centuries. Given the circumscribed space this implies, it is easy to understand why the people involved assume the existence of a seamless web between politics and everything else that makes up society and life.

Italy's physical size, its systems of formal and informal communication, the content of its newspapers and magazines, the formats of its broadcast media, its local dialects and rich variegation of local cultures reinforce the sense of small scale. In this context there emerges the belief, valid or not, that everyone possesses, or can obtain, near-total information about what everyone else, and particularly the great and near great, may be up to.

Gossip about the president and prime minister, about academic politics or trade union affairs, about who attends private meetings and dinners of industrialists and what is said there, moves up and down the peninsula without need of assistance from the mass media. Information about cardinals and soccer heroes, bankers and television personalities, or about "secret" meetings among ministers of government or political party leaders springs up everywhere to become everyone's daily fare. Even the Vatican, behind its formidable walls, and the Communist party headquarters, almost as well protected, often appear to be glass houses, wired for sound.

Does this smaller scale of society, this political saturation of life, this real or imagined familiarity with la classe politica breed contempt toward politics or political alienation of the masses? At best, it does so only some of the time, and under special circumstances we will look at later.

Most of the time, the political permeation of life seems to feed a special kind of political involvement in the political process. Inflated political rhetoric is one aspect of this process. Remarkable levels of participation in elections is another. Certain very Italian ways of discussing politics and of expressing attitudes toward political leaders and institutions are also important dimensions of this system. These attitudes are mistakenly labeled by some as "political alienation" or as evidence that Italian democracy is fragile. Taken at face value or interpreted in this way, the attitudes and behavior of Italian citizens often leave us baffled, and, because we are baffled, we speak about the paradoxes of Italian democracy.

It may be that some of these attitudes and behaviors are, if not immediately inimical to democracy, incompatible with it in the long term. We must leave that an open question that can perhaps be addressed with greater confidence later in this book. At this point, though, a tentative answer to the question raised early in this chapter would go like this: Italy is a small-scale society in which we can say about its political side that it is pervasive and omnipresent, that citizens are aware of this, and that, at least at the verbal level, they are much inclined to be hypercritical of the persons and institutions directly involved in the political process. That is, familiarity with politics, where politics affects so much of life, often arbitrarily, does seem to breed contempt.

It is nevertheless plausible that these same conditions represent something additional and perhaps quite different. That is, in the type of society Italy is, familiarity with politics, the political saturation of life, and citizen reactions to all of this may very well produce in Italians a special orientation toward politics. What if politics, like so many other aspects of Italy, is to a considerable extent a form of spettacolo?

4

POLITICS AS SPETTACOLO

In English, *spettacolo* might be said to mean performance, scene, view, sight, or spectacle. On the whole, the word carries a negative connotation—as in, "Don't make a spectacle of yourself." In Italian, the expression "Che spettacolo!" might carry either negative or positive meaning, depending on which of the two words is stressed. The expression itself might be used to register one's reactions to a prize fight or soccer match, a circus or theatrical performance, a fireworks display, or a person's behavior at the dinner table. It is also used to convey feelings—often negative ones—about politics. The public opinion pollsters run into many reactions of this kind. This leads them to conclude that Italian democracy is in a jam, and headed for even deeper trouble.

This is a misreading of the situation. There is no doubt that politics in Italy is a form of spettacolo, by which I mean not entertainment but certainly an ongoing drama, something out of the ordinary, that pervades life and demands attention. Spettacolo unfolds when events and language associated with them are perceived, reported, and to some extent evaluated as if they were staged. For political events to take on the trappings and the aura of spettacolo, it is helpful if politics is omnipresent, if it is believed to affect the most mundane as well as the most extraordinary aspects of life, and if it permits people from all walks of life to feel that they are part of the process, of the bigger picture.

Note that more is involved here than the opportunity to participate in the political process in the ways—like voting or contacting public officials—that are common to many democracies. I have in mind, in addition, a political environment or context within which the individual, alone or with others, believes that what he or she does has a discernable effect on the political process.

Italy's political framework not only permits such participation; it impels it. Where politics permeates so much of life, some sort of participation turns out to be a "coerced" choice. In effect, the omnipresence of politics suggests that few Italians can afford to be passive toward it. And indeed most are not. As the pollsters know, they tend instead to be unusually articulate, as well as passionate, in the views they express about politics. This is so even when, by the measures pollsters use, they are badly informed about political events and institutions.

Two points relevant to democratic theory are worth noting here. First, attitudes about politics expressed by citizens who are ill informed as to the "facts" are not necessarily unhealthy for democracy. Second, the language or rhetoric used in politics or adopted by citizens to express their evaluations of political leaders, institutions, and policies must be assessed, carefully, within its own national setting.

It is possible, for example, that, despite what the language or tone of voice may suggest, Italians are no more passionate about politics, or feel politics no more intensely, than others. Alternatively, even if they are more passionate or intense than others, it does not follow that the consequences of these feelings will be the same in Italy as they might be in some other democratic country like the United States, Great Britain, or even France.

Many of us have failed to make this distinction in the past. The attitudes Italians expressed about their political institutions and leaders appeared so severe, so unremittingly negative, it seemed only a matter of time before the fledgling democracy would disintegrate into something else. These judgments and predictions were simply wrong.[1]

In the spettacolo of politics, as I see it, Italians are not only spectators but also avid participants, not only severe critics but also active and satisfied appreciators. Indeed, the act of criticism itself must be understood, in the Italian context, to be a significant form of democratic political participation, with positive and not negative implications for the system. As perverse as it may appear, the Italian citizen's articulate, often excoriating, commentary on his political system may actually reveal considerable underlying satisfaction with it.

To repeat, context is important. A taciturn Dane who quietly expresses negative feelings about the polity may be prepared to overthrow it. A wildly gesticulating Italian who shouts obscenities about politics may actually like the polity very much, particularly if he can attack it openly with impunity.

Attention to context will also show us that passionate involvement with politics, as well as the fiery outbursts, are of short duration, without long-term negative consequences. Thus, even when Italian political events are at their most spectacular, the citizens' attention span remains relatively short. They are easily bored, often despite ingenious schemes of the mass media to keep indignation and blood pressure at high levels.

Impassioned expressions, even highly negative ones, about the polity tell us only one thing without equivocation: they are not uttered by "outsiders." The true outsiders are persons who see themselves as little more than the inert objects of political decisions taken by others. Italian citizens also are, and know themselves to be, performers in the ongoing political spettacolo. This being the case, the Italian is deeply "inside" the political system, and hardly as "alienated" from it as so many have claimed.[2]

A spettacolo dimension that blurs the line between players and spectators can be detected in many other aspects of Italian culture, such as soccer games or grand opera. Sophisticated New Yorkers, for example (to say nothing of the British) would rarely offer more than an occasional "boo" at a very bad peformance at the Metropolitan (or Covent Gardens). In fact, by Italian standards New Yorkers are much too free with their applause and much too reticent to raise their voices against mediocrity.

At Milan's La Scala, seemingly enraged audiences will literally whistle down a botched performance and even drive the offenders off stage— only to applaud even louder if the hapless tenor or diva makes a virtuoso recovery in the second or third act. Italian operagoers (and it is true of soccer fans and political observers as well) believe that such treatment not only spurs the professionals to greater levels of achievement; they also expect this behavior to bring about a special type of rapport between performers and audiences, elites and masses.

Take the national game of soccer. Like rabid sports fans everywhere, the Italians prefer their teams to win. But they also want them to play well, not sloppily, to make strategic moves elegantly, to execute with precision. If, in this context, they also are treated to a virtuoso performance, so much the better. It is surely uncommon in the United States to find spectators who cry out derisively at inelegant play by the home team, even if it is winning. This happens all the time in Italy's stadiums on Sunday afternoons. It is followed on Monday mornings by reams of newspaper commentary that readily misleads the unwary to believe that sportswriters despise athletes, particularly those on the home team, who fall short of perfection. In effect, what looks like "alienation" from the game of soccer and those who play it simply is not. Instead, it is the way participation takes place and affection is expressed.

A NATIONAL GLOBE THEATRE

It may help to drive home the basic point here if we think of Italian politics as unfolding, like Shakespearean drama, in a nation-sized Globe Theatre of Elizabethan times. The Globe's multitiered stage not only permitted instantaneous scene changes; it also made possible the simultaneous occurrence of separated, but interconnected, action. The king of Denmark's castle would be a good example. On stage you might see, at the same time, Hamlet and his murdered father's ghost on the ramparts; Laertes in quiet conversation with his father, Polonius; Ophelia brushing her hair in her bedroom; and Hamlet's mother in bed with the villainous new king—all of them doomed to expire before the final curtain.

Quick scene changes, simultaneous and often confusing action, tragedy on one occasion and comedy on another, unexpected ironic twists of fate, many layers of meaning: all of this and more is the stuff of Italian political drama. Shakespeare, who was so often inspired by Italian political tales, understood and captured this important aspect of the culture better than have contemporary analysts of the Italian political system. Italians themselves, however, remain more self-conscious, and more willing to accept, than others that politics is the main stage on which the spettacolo of life unfolds.

There were no "orchestra" seats at the Globe. Instead, the space immediately in front of the main stage was reserved for the masses, who crowded and milled around it. These were the groundlings, who came to participate in the Elizabethan theater in a very special way. The theatrical asides, for example, were typically addressed to the groundlings, who were expected to react spontaneously to them. This they did, with relish, ad-libbing responses, sometimes comical, sometimes angry, often boisterous and, of course, always adding variation, and a good deal of spice, to individual performances. Brooklyn's Living Theater tried to recreate this dynamic in the 1960s, but with limited success in the United States. The experiment went much more successfully in Italy.

Groundling participation at the Globe may have introduced some variations, and even a few surprises; but it never changed the overall structure of the performance or the drama's outcome. Nor did anyone expect this. No Juliet ever awakened in the nick of time to avert tragedy. No deus ex machina ever managed to rewrite, on the spot, the last few lines of Shakespeare or any other dramatist. Nevertheless, this did not inhibit repeated groundling participation in tomorrow's replays.

That is how it is with Italian politics. The "theater" is very much alive, and highly democratic. Everyone is or can become involved in its ongoing performances—as actor and audience, as cause and object, all at once, of political drama and melodrama. At some level, most Italians know this to be the case. We in turn must try to understand it as a particular and important aspect of the kind and style of democracy they have evolved. This may not be the American or British type of polyarchy, but it is, along the important dimension of citizen involvement and participation, a polyarchy par excellence.

DRAMATIC REPERTOIRE

Italy's political theater offers as wide and imaginative a repertoire as one will find among contemporary democracies. Offerings range from standard comedies like "Tax Evasion Dragnet" or "Reducing the Budget Deficit," to the kinds of tragic drama that national and international political terror introduce. The Mafia, Camorra, and other elements of organized crime also produce staple fare. Even here, as with terrorism, the dramas are played out in ways that bring a great many persons, including ordinary citizens, into the process in unusual, and sometimes spectacular, ways.

Take "War on the Mafia" as a theme that in the last year or so has attracted much critical attention. In its efforts to bring this ancient, powerful Sicilian organization to heel, the national government has mounted a major, well-advertised campaign in which assistance has been enlisted from the Vatican and the United States government. In 1983, the Mafia's response to this dramatic shift in public policy was the broad-daylight murder of Gen. Carlo Alberto Dalla Chiesa, the outstanding man named to spearhead and coordinate the government's attack.

This move may have been a serious Mafia error. Not only an anti-Mafia parliamentary committee but also leading prelates, chief among them Cardinal Pappalardo of Palermo and Pope John Paul II himself, urged the general public as well as governmental authorities to step up the effort against the so-called Honored Society. One Mafioso, captured in Rio de Janeiro and loaned to American authorities in connection with a major drug case to be tried in New York, decided to talk, and he implicated literally hundreds of his former associates in Sicily.

The upshot of this were over seven hundred arrest warrants and, beginning in February 1986, the prosecution of almost five hundred persons in a much ballyhooed "maxitrial" in Palermo. Thirty cages (where prisoners are kept during trial proceedings) were constructed to accommodate the accused in the courtroom. The defendants amassed almost three hundred defense attorneys against a tiny fraction of that number who would represent the state. Family members of persons the Mafia was accused of maiming or murdering searched, largely in vain, for lawyers in Palermo who might represent their interests. Prominent lawyers from as far away as Milan volunteered their services. A well-known criminal lawyer of Palermo, and leader of the Communist party there, was found to be defending one of the accused, and this triggered a national debate about the propriety of this act. Evidence and depositions prepared for the trial itself totaled seven hundred thousand pages, and defense attorneys threatened to have all of them read in open court. This would have consumed a full year.

Needless to say, the trial was ideally suited to mass-media exploitation.[3] Indeed, it came at a most opportune moment, at the tail end of the so-called trial of the century—that is, the trial of persons alleged by the Turk Ali Agca to have been the "Bulgarian connection," or coconspirators, in his attempted assassination of Pope John Paul II in Saint Peter's Square. Although Italy has had a surfeit of "trials of the century," this one against so many Mafiosi, including one of the most notorious, Michele Greco, who was captured a few days after the trial began, promised to rival all others in the amount of riveted public attention it would elicit.

To the average observer, the courtroom looked like a zoo, and the trial itself resembled a three-ring circus. The cynics would claim that the haste with which the prosecution moved, and the massive trial itself, were prima facie evidence if not of collusion with the Mafia then of a lack of seriousness of purpose in the method of carrying the campaign forward. To others as well, pitting the state against so many Mafiosi did not appear the optimal way to make real inroads against such a formidable organization. Although the newspapers reflected some of this skepticism, their objections were muted. The symbolic value of the state, aided by the Vatican, taking on the Mafia in such a massive way was not lost on anyone.

Furthermore, if earlier mass trials of terrorists were any test, many of the Mafiosi would certainly wind up serving long jail sentences.

Rome and Italy, of course, bow to no other place when it comes to providing circuses of this kind. In recent years there have been other "maxitrials"—for example, of terrorists—and these too drew considerable skepticism and criticism. Nevertheless, many terrorists were duly convicted, as have been members of the Mafia and other underworld groups who were similarly treated by the judicial system.

These trials, and the process that leads up to them, raise some important questions about due process of law that we will come back to. But the mere fact that the judicial process is so theatrical, that it partakes so openly of aspects of spettacolo, should not lead automatically to the conclusion that it is ineffectual or, what would be worse, undemocratic.

The dramatic repertoire covers the widest variety of topics and situations. A recurring tragicomedy is *"Franchi Tiratori* (sharpshooters) at Montecitorio." The basic plot is simple, but its possible nuances and permutations are infinite: A coalition government, even one with a very comfortable majority in the national legislature, discovers, in a secret balloting, that its majority has evaporated. At a minimum, these defeats cause the government considerable embarrassment; on occasion they lead to cabinet crises, and even national elections.

Obviously, these shocks are administered by defecting lawmakers who are members of the governing coalition. For different reasons, they lie in ambush and then unexpectedly, in a secret ballot, "shoot down" their own governments. It goes without saying that the prime ministers and cabinet members who fall prey to these sharpshooters are not enthusiastic about the practice and would like to correct it. But the political groundlings of every ideological description delight in it. The practice introduces a degree of uncertainty into the policy-making process that constitutional purists find horrendous. The lawmakers themselves, though, have shown a remarkable capacity to work within these constraints without inducing disaster or, for that matter, actual paralysis.

Political dramas whose billings include the word *crisis* will likely draw an indifferent reaction from the public. Nevertheless, they appear with solar regularity: crises about inflation, public deficits, balance of payments, exchange rates, industrial production, and innovation are couched in the arcane language of economics and easily lead to boredom. The so-called crises of basic values, the family, the fine arts, the university, or post-industrial society bring into play the even more abstruse language of sociology, toward which Italians display an astonishing tolerance.

When *scandolo,* or scandal, breaks out, which is almost daily, it is a sure winner in drawing public attention. Scandals typically involve the underworld, leading political parties, major industries and banks, and even the Vatican. The spotlight focuses not on abstractions like the working class, civil society, or the youth or women of the country but rather on real people, on well-known bankers, prelates, politicians, athletes, television personalities, moguls of the underworld, industrial magnates, and even miscreant judges who jail their political opponents on trumped-up charges and leave them to languish in jail, before trial, sometimes for years.

Scandolo also calls attention to money, which in Italy often changes hands, in questionable circumstances, in unbelievably large amounts. On rarer occasions, considerations of money are overshadowed by apparent plots to overthrow the democratic state. This was the case with Propaganda 2, the secret masonic lodge that was uncovered in 1981. It appeared that this subversive organization had recruited several hundred members, many of them highly prominent, who were only ostensibly committed to "defending the integrity of the republic" against any possible coming to power by the left. Scandals of this kind are certain to capture public attention, especially if, as sometimes now occurs, the culprits are actually forced to resign their jobs, or wind up in jail as opposed to Miami, the Bahamas, or Latin America.

When internal conditions turn humdrum, Italians become inventive about keeping political issues before the public. A few years ago, when much of the world became highly critical about the overseas operations of the multinational corporations, the Italians came up with an entirely different twist. Rather than blast the corporations for alleged misbehavior, they created a crisis atmosphere around the possibility—largely fantasy— that these corporations might divest their Italian holdings. "Are the Multinationals Abandoning Us?" or "Is There a Multinational Exodus?" the newspapers asked. Even the Communists got into the act, to assure everyone that they certainly were not unfriendly toward the multinational corporations, American or otherwise.

In the 1980s, "King Dollar" grabbed the limelight. The story line, until the dollar began to slide, was that Italy's economy was hobbled or strangled by an artificially overvalued American dollar. Eye-catching headlines in the leading newspapers included: "The Dollar to the Stars," "King Dollar Suffocates Us," and, more recently and triumphantly, "King Dollar

Is Dead." Before long, of course, the headlines will complain that the dollar is artificially undervalued, with untold nefarious consequences for Italy.

These political dramas and melodramas play themselves out in a very special way, given the small scale of Italian society discussed in the previous chapter. Such events are by and large assured a national audience, and they involve characters who are relatively well known to everyone on the peninsula. Far from bringing about negative consequences for the polity, they actually have the effect of integrating it around commonly shared experiences. In this sense, it is important for Italy's national political integrity that a major scandal like Propaganda 2 and a number of minor ones involving political parties involved persons and cities in the north.

IS IT REALLY THEATER?

Is there evidence, of the kind that social scientists call "hard" or "systematic," to support the idea that Italians think about politics as spettacolo? Hardly any at all. But this may be so only because those who study Italy have never given this possibility any serious consideration. The right questions have not been asked. Even if they were, the risk would be great that spettacolo would be misunderstood as *merely theater*, that is, something not substantially part of life and therefore not to be taken seriously. Because this is Italy, the imagery drawn from the theater also degenerates into the stereotype of a people too much inclined to emote about those things in life that others take more stoically or casually.[4]

My present usage of spettacolo refers to the ongoing scene, in which a political dimension is not only always present but, more often than not, often the most intrusive or subtle, the most simple or complex, the most welcome or repugnant, and always the most fascinating aspect. As a practical matter, the political dimension is not restricted to the formal institutions of government or politics, or to those who are officially associated with them. As we saw in the last chapter, the political dimension is present essentially everywhere.

In a country where politics is omnipresent and citizens are incorporated as both participants and performers, many of the questions the pollsters typically ask either are out of place or will produce highly misleading replies. Italians are often asked, for example, whether they have problems that relate to government (and who does not!) and, if they do, whether they ever bother to contact some government official about them. This query makes sense in North America or northern Europe. But it may be completely off the mark in the kind of patron and client society, and system of "making contact" with public officials, that prevails in Italy. Furthermore, such questions almost invariably carry the hidden or open assumption that the British or American way is "normal," that it produces results that make citizens feel more efficacious, and that, even on more objective examination, it provides the citizen with better control over government and governors than is true of other modes of behavior.

Questions of this kind, more often than not, startle Italians. In overwhelming numbers they reply that, of course, they never, but never, contact public officials. They then go on to say, with great relish, that they never discuss politics with anyone, that they distrust and hate politicians, and that Italy would be much better off if it did not have any government at all. When asked about their political institutions, they almost never have a generous word to spare for them.

It looks like a grim picture. If you take the replies at face value, if you fail to understand that there are other more Italian ways to intervene in the political process, and if you miss the extent to which the replies themselves are "automatic," it will be easy to conclude that Italians lack something called "civic culture" and that Italian democracy is immature or in a parlous state. It is a short step from this reaction to another: amazement over the seeming paradox that a democracy whose citizens think about politics and their political institutions in this way can survive at all.

But what if many of these responses are essentially rote, automatically delivered on cue, like memorized lines from Shakespeare or Pirandello? What if the replies represent little beyond what is expected of citizens in the Italian context? That context, let me stress, is one in which it is considered unusual, fawning, or cause for suspicion if someone says something upbeat or positive about political leaders or institutions. It is simply not done. The citizen performs his or her role well when the replies are downbeat, and the more creatively so the better.

As for citizen contacts with public officials, we have already noted that where a patron and client structure is as powerfully implanted as in Italy, and where subcultural organizations are so strong, Italians can and will reach governmental authorities in ways that may not be American or

British. However, a "made in USA" or equivalent trademark on a given political practice does not make it exportable or endow it with more democratic authenticity.

KEEPING ONE'S DISTANCE

It would be difficult to summarize Italians' orientations toward government. We can depict them best by noting a few of the guidelines or rules the streetwise citizen tries to follow:

Distrust Government, Especially at Rome!
Resist Taxation, and Other Official Constraints!
Avoid Direct Contacts with Governmental Authorities!
Make Demands on Government, Preferably Impossible Ones!
Attack the Failure of Government To Satisfy Demands!
Keep the Politicians and Public Officials Off Balance!

Some of these guidelines have more immediate operational implications than others. The first, for example, is essentially a state of mind. Although it is not unique to Italians, they acquire it at birth, along with other inherited characteristics. The left, especially the Communists, hate this attitude and call it *qualunquista*, an untranslatable word that means, roughly, a person without clear ideological principles or commitments. The PCI's objections notwithstanding, the attitude is ubiquitous among Italians.

By now, Italians are masters at piling up demands on government, followed by a good deal of carping when they are not met. Sometimes these demands are spontaneous occurrences; more often they are generated by political parties and organized interest groups. There is little question that the government at Rome is overloaded with demands it cannot easily satisfy.

When it comes to resistance against taxes, the evasion of other laws or regulations considered unacceptable, or the shunning of contacts with public authorities, Italians are prepared to devote a good deal of energy to these imperatives. As a fundamental operational rule, they consider it highly preferable to keep encounters with officialdom to the barest possible minimum.

This principle was once suggested to me by a Roman friend who picked me up in his dilapidated Volkswagen van. The van lacked a front bumper;

one headlight did not work; the taillight was missing; the door on the driver's side was partly ripped off; and the windshield gave no evidence at all, in the form of stickers, that the road tax had been paid or that the vehicle and owner were insured. In addition, the German license plate at the rear of the van had long since expired. When I remarked about all of these violations, my friend added that he did not have, nor had he ever applied for, a driver's license.

I was mildly apprehensive about this. "Listen," he said, "if we are stopped by the police, they will find me with at least fourteen different violations, some of them serious. This means (it was then late spring) that they will have to spend at least three months with me in court if they write tickets. Instead they will give me a lecture and then let me go. Stay calm!" He then added the basic rule: "In this country, we all try to have as little contact as possible with the state. Less is better. I'm among those who have no contact at all. That's almost perfect."

Italians shun governmental contacts for all sorts of reasons. A trip to the post office would quickly reveal some of them. Public servants are completely misnamed. They serve essentially their own interests and convenience. Their demeanor toward the public varies between annoyance and arrogance. As a matter of fact, in comparison with other governmental agencies, the post office looks like a paragon of civic virtue. War veterans and retired people can spend years in their efforts to receive the pensions they are owed. Those who call to make appointments with doctors in publicly run clinics are often told that they will have to wait from six months to over a year. If they wind up in a public or private hospital, the doctors and nurses are almost certain to go on strike during part of their stay. It crosses no one's mind to file a complaint about this kind of treatment; it would only make things worse. Franz Kafka would understand.

Years ago, an American social scientist went to Italy to study a small town in the south.[5] He was so amazed by what he found there that he coined the term *amoral familism* to describe the behavior of its residents. He meant by this that the southern peasants care for and pursue the interests of only their immediate, or nuclear, families. As for everyone else, including other relatives, why they could simply go to the devil. This reading of southern Italy, as Italians themselves were later to complain, was somewhat gratuitous and reeked of stereotypes.

Nevertheless, there were aspects of the town and its inhabitants that reflected the simultaneous operation of the above guidelines, and often in apparently contradictory fashion. For example, the investigator found it baffling that the town's citizens failed to chip in to buy an ambulance— to transport the very ill to the nearest hospital, some miles away. As he saw it, the town lacked a civic spirit, a better balance between self reliance and collective responsibility. He found it curious that the same citizens who shunned and distrusted government would also criticize its failure to provide either local health care or the ambulance in question.

The investigator's real puzzlement was that these southern Italians had not behaved as would Kansas farmers, with whom he actually compared them. He recognized that much of the fatalism was produced by centuries of poverty and unhappy experiences with public authority. But he some-how assumed that where there occurs government indifference or inca-pacity, and particularly where citizens are inclined to place most of their ills at the feet of a "thief of a government," something like a pioneer spirit will intervene to take up the slack.

That is not how the process and the drama of politics are played out in Italy. Where hospitals are not at a stone's throw from the ill and infirm, people improvise. Where health services are as poor as they remain in Italy (but not only there!), it is clear that the rich will be better served and that many of the poor will prefer to die at home as opposed to in hospitals. In any event, not long after this early study Italy exploded into an orgy of self-government, including in the organization and delivery of health services, that the author would have found as baffling as was his failure to sense that Italy is less destructively anarchistic than his book suggests.

POLITICAL ROLES

Compared to citizens of other democracies, Italians are much less in-clined to contact public officials (or to chip in to buy an ambulance). On the other hand, they far outdistance the others when it comes to partic-ipating in national, regional, and local elections.[6] In all cases, it is an open question how much of political participation is motivated by "civic" con-siderations, that is, by concern for the collective good as opposed to the narrower interests of the individual.

It is fair to say that when Italians participate, for example when they join political parties, trade unions, or other interest groups, they do so primarily for selfish reasons. That is, they expect to get something in return. If persons elsewhere do these things for reasons of civic pride, or primarily in order to enhance the general welfare, Italians would find such motivations curious, naive and, above all, doubtful.

However, there is in the Italian posture an element of reciprocity whose importance should not be underestimated. The *raccomandazione*, the recommendation or favor, is something exchanged—between patrons and their clients as well as among equals. The raccomandazione will readily be provided for a total stranger, provided that the one who wants or needs it finds the appropriate person to make the request of the recommender. No one is surprised or offended by this common practice. No one passes moral judgment on others because acts are selfishly motivated or, as in the raccomandazione, because someone may commend to favorable consideration a third person actually unknown to him or her. The system has a logic of its own, and it works quite well. "Free riders" may not be considered heroes in Italy, but they are secretly admired. In any event, selfless citizens who work essentially for the common good are not considered one of democracy's necessary conditions.

Often Italians have no choice in the matter of joining politically relevant organizations. Their friends and neighbors, their agricultural or consumer cooperatives, their trade unions, or their political patrons may compel them to sign up. There are few "volunteer" or "public interest" groups here—no leagues of women voters, gray ladies, candy stripers, or museum docents who offer their time freely. Among other things, Italians believe that middle-class persons who provide such free services deprive others of gainful employment. This attitude may be changing in some parts of Italy, as persons combine in movements and organizations dedicated to environmental protection and to various forms of self-help, but the transformation is quite slow. The "what's in it for me" approach may not be any stronger or widespread in Italy than elsewhere, but it is patently more open.

The underlying idea in efforts to avoid contacts with government is to spare oneself frustration or trouble. This is an entirely rational impulse; it does not imply that those who act on it lack "civic culture" or a sense of "political efficacy," or that they are indifferent to their own condition.

The imperious and stultifying nature of the public bureaucracy is quickly learned by the youngest schoolchildren. Schoolteachers themselves inadvertently get the first messages across. The way the schools are run and the state examinations are administered by the Ministry of Education drives home for all except the extreme dullards the capriciousness of the bureaucratic state. Parliamentarians make ringing speeches on the shortcomings of the bureaucracy, and journalists and editorial writers fill columns with the minutest details about the abysmal condition of public services. The clergy itself excoriates governmental lapses, not just from the pulpit but in pastoral letters as well. Letters to the editor from ordinary citizens are superfluous in this setting.

The Italian who wants real help in this Kafkaesque world will, more often than not, go to his "patron," that is, to a person, trade union, political party, or church group that knows the ropes and that can bring real pressure to bear on the public officials. Unlike what citizens elsewhere might do, the approach is indirect. It is also based on the knowledge, not uncommon in Western democracies, that some citizens count or weigh more than others.[7] People in Italy who fail to understand this, who behave as if public authorities will treat any citizen like every other, are very rare. They are also considered doltish, or fesso.

Many years ago, in a Neapolitan bar, I eavesdropped on a conversation between two natives of that city. One of them had just returned from a frustrating week in Rome, where he had gone in a vain effort to extract from the appropriate ministry his veteran's pension, already some years overdue. At the end of his tirade, his friend replied: "You are really fesso, maybe even crazy. You know how they are in the ministries. Tomorrow, buy yourself a piece of *carta bollata* [lined paper, highly taxed, on which official requests must be made] and send your petition directly to Alcide De Gasperi. You know, just like we used to do with the king."

In the spring of 1985, Riccardo Bacchelli, one of Italy's most distinguished novelists of this century (the author, for example, of *The Mill on the Po*), was found to be living out his last years in a state of destitution. The press went all out on his behalf and created an uproar of public indignation. In response, the national government passed a law to guarantee a decent living, at public expense, to "Italian citizens of clear renown who have honored *la Patria* through the merit they have gained in the fields of science, letters, the arts, the economy, sports, and in the conduct of their public responsibilities; or in activities pursued in the interest of social, philanthropic, or humanitarian objectives."

Several aspects of this anecdote are noteworthy. First, members of parliament worried that the law might open the floodgates to a deluge of petitioners, or even legal claimants. The government made it clear that it did not want too many postulants, but that remains to be seen. Second, the law specifies that all such petitions must go directly to the prime minister, who, after examining the validity of the claim and after consulting with other governmental authorities, is empowered to assign the lucky person up to the equivalent of seventy thousand dollars a year. Bacchelli was evidently the first beneficiary of this new law during the last year of his life, but, given predictable bureaucratic delays, it is doubtful that he ever saw a lira of public funds.

The man in the Neapolitan bar obviously had a point. This relatively minor drama might not play well on Broadway or in London's West End, but it was a smash hit in Italy, where it produced several million words, debates in the legislature and in family and social circles, and the kind of overall participation that is entirely germane to the idea of politics as spettacolo. The point is that, on a wide spectrum of public issues, and even more seemingly private ones, many citizens can and do get into the act—but in an Italian and not necessarily in a universally recognized way.

THE LANGUAGE OF POLITICS

The words and language of politics also make it plain that we are dealing with spettacolo. We think about politicians everywhere as users of inflated language. When it comes to rotund oratory, hyperbole, wrapping oneself in the flag, or just plain demagoguery, Italian politicians are certainly among the frontrunners. The bombastic Mussolini was not a caricature of the Italian species; he was just your ordinary political speechifier raised to a power.

In Italy there is much more to notice about the language of politics. To begin with, it is curial, as in *curia,* a word that means either a bishop's see or the bar association. The language, that is, derives from the Catholic Church, an organization that for centuries has been running one of the most successful spettacolos in history. Curial language is highly nuanced, which in English suggests something subtle or refined. The Italian word for nuanced, however, is *sfumato*, which the dictionary warns us means something shaded, vague, trimmed, even vanished, or not there. Think of a mirage!

Curial language is not only sfumato, it is also coded and indirect. Like the Latin from which its political version derives, the language is not intended to be fully understood by the ordinary layperson. Rather, it is designed as a means of arcane communication among adepts. These experts are aware of the infinity of meanings, loopholes, escape hatches, and trapdoors that are built into this language. Anglo-American lawyers and businesspeople go crazy when they encounter phraseology of this kind in their Italian dealings. Their Japanese counterparts, who understand that real agreements are often unspoken, based on faith in bows or handshakes, are entirely at ease with it.

Although political discourse of this kind is daily fare, much more of it occurs on weekends. These are times when the country's major and minor politicians scatter throughout the peninsula to deliver speeches to the party faithful—in rented theaters (where else!) usually, but often in the open piazzas when larger crowds can be drummed up. Some of what is spoken is directed to the immediate audiences. Most of it, though, is meant for the consumption of political allies or opponents, members of the political class who are engaged in the same weekend activity. Sometimes these other actors are named; most of the time they are only alluded to. It takes practice to detect with any kind of accuracy not only the meaning of what is spoken, or left unspoken, but also the specific persons, political parties, or party factions to which messages are directed.

On occasion, the objects or targets of political communication are easily understood, but not so the meaning of what is said. If a couple of Communist party leaders describe some new twist in their party's approach as "Copernican," we can be sure that the word will subsequently be picked up in dozens of other speeches. It would take a while to establish that the expression implied that in future the PCI's friends and enemies, as well as potential coalition partners, would no longer be identified on the basis of ideological coloration and affinity. Central attention would focus on the policy and programmatic commitments of each party.

Needless to say, the mass media are an essential part of this scenario.[8] The politicians count on the editorial and journalistic community to provide not just commentary but also interpretation of what is said on weekends. In fact, it might be said that all of the weekend speeches are directed primarily to the mass media, which will serve as the first-level filters and interpreters. The masses—all those who were not in the theater or the piazza to hear it firsthand—will have reality served up by their favorite journalist or commentator, much like illiterate peasants would turn to scribes as their instruments of written communication. This type of help from the media is obviously not unique to Italy, but it looms as distinctively important there because the language of politics is as many layered as I have suggested.

Some years ago, the ill-fated Aldo Moro, a master of impenetrable political prose, described what he thought was in progress on the main political stage as a movement toward "converging parallels." Aside from the predictable fun-poking these words provoked, reams of additional words were spent in efforts to divine what he really had in mind. This was no joking matter either, in that Moro's basic reference was to the evolving relationship between his Christian Democratic and Berlinguer's Communist parties, and the prospect that the latter would be welcomed back into the national governmental coalition.

To come back to the weekends, efforts to decipher the principal speeches begin with the late newscasts on Sunday night. The really in-depth analyses, though, are found on the front pages of the Monday morning newspapers. Was the prime minister's speech really an attempt to make peace with the president of the republic? Or was it rather a subtle torpedo, directed at the foreign minister? Perhaps the prime minister is running for the presidency himself? If Communist leaders use a term like "Copernican revolution" to downgrade their earlier approach to making deals with allies, does this mean that they hope to improve their relationships with the Christian Democrats, the Socialists, or with neither? If a Christian Democrat who is a deputy prime minister asks his party not to be so regretful about its having turned over the prime ministership to a Socialist, does this mean that he is running for that office, wants to be the next president of the republic, or both or neither of these things?

By midweek, those whose speeches have been dissected and put under the microscope will be hard at work to confirm or deny the dominant interpretations, but always in language that will encourage even more dissection and speculation. Aldo Moro was peerless when it came to the use of clarification as a generator of even more confusion. The process inevitably turns into VIPs journalists who are highly skilled at deciphering these signals. As for the consumers, those who really want to be on top of things typically read at least six newspapers each day.

A cardinal rule of Italian political communication is that the speaker should not appear *sbilanciato*, a difficult word to translate. It means that, given the context, the circumstances, the nature of the problem addressed, the possible solutions to it, and the pitfalls and opportunities that may lie down the road, there was something out of kilter in what was said or in the tone that was used. In a curial language where most of the meaning is actually located between the lines, words must be selected with the greatest care, and their delivery must be finely tuned to achieve the desired effect.

The language politicians use is not just arcane or incomprehensible. It is also "democratic." There is something in it for everyone. To come back for a moment to Shakespeare and the Globe, recall that the Bard's high-flown language was written in iambic pentameter, an elegant form of poetic expression. But the "asides," directed at the groundlings, were spoken in plain, everyday language the latter understood. The groundlings had to work harder to get a clearer sense of the rest of the meter. But even if they failed to grasp the full meaning of Shakespeare's words, loaded as they were with so many different and remarkable allusions, they had a fairly good idea about the overall meaning of the play and its action.

The more often one participated at the Globe, the more readily one came to understand and to appreciate the Bard's allusions, his ironies, his indirect praises or assaults, many of them aimed at the great and near great of Elizabethan times. There was something fundamentally unifying, something that gave everyone a shared identity, in all of this.

This is a useful way to think about the language of Italian politics. It too is complex, rich with allusions, but not beyond the ken of those who use or make an effort to understand it at some level. For those of us on the outside, it is vital to see the language of politics in this perspective. We will otherwise misinterpret Italian political rhetoric not only as inflated but also as ominously full of conflict. Indeed, heavy ideological content of the language will easily lead to the conclusion that political warfare is without quarter and potentially lethal to democracy.[9]

Nothing can be farther from the truth. To be sure, words are important. They raise or lower temperatures; they inflame or soothe, wound or heal; they narrow or expand the space within which compromise, the essence of politics, is possible. Words, in fact, may be the only aspect of politics that has any substance. They certainly represent the only solid evidence we have that man is different from all other animal species. If this makes sense, it should drive home to each of us that language should not, indeed cannot, be interpreted except within the cultural framework in which it occurs.

Whatever may be the level of complexity of what is written or spoken, it is essential to establish exactly how words—the language of politics—affect the relationships among citizens, between citizens and their leaders, and, above all, among the political leaders themselves. Members of the Italian political class are masterful manipulators of words; they rarely talk or write themselves into blind alleys; they make of wisdom and the instinct to survive instruments that keep in check a more primeval urge to humiliate one's opponents. Most of them practice, to wholesome effect, what Machiavelli preached: a defeated political enemy must be either utterly destroyed or (cautiously!) turned into an ally.

No one can doubt that language is a vital, indeed *the* vital, ingredient in a system of politics that partakes so much of spettacolo. The visual media, such as television, may have added some new settings to these dramas, created illusions about space and time, and perhaps induced a strong sense of common participation in single events by tens of millions of adults. But the visual images are, at bottom, only props; they would quickly degenerate into meaninglessness were it not for the language— the words and their nuances—that accompanies them. The language of politics will also reveal the extent to which both leaders and citizens recognize that they are essentially role-players in a particular type of spettacolo.

THE PIAZZA AS STAGE

As I have already noted, much of the language of politics is spoken in the piazzas, not just during electoral campaigns but throughout the year. These are the public places, the hustings, where leaders and their followers, political friends and foes, have met for centuries to play out important political scenes. In this century, we have sometimes come to associate this aspect of European and Latin American politics with demagoguery and dictatorship. One thinks of the "Heil Hitler!" frenzies orchestrated by Joseph Goebbels at the Brandenburg Gate and elsewhere. Or one remembers a half-million Italians, in Piazza Venezia or Piazza del Popolo, chanting " . . . ce-Du, ce-Du, ce-Du-ce" in equal adulation of their leader. Juan Perón brought this extravaganza to Argentina. But, like the Hitler and Mussolini he emulated, he was only exploiting to the hilt a form of political life that Plato and Aristotle had also witnessed and that Mark Antony mastered in his famous oration to the Roman plebes on the heels of Caesar's assassination.

The English, and Americans even more, tend to be nervous about mass meetings in public squares. The United States, of course, has relatively few of the latter, which means that whenever a mere handful of citizens gather on the streets it tends to look like a mass demonstration. The Italian piazza, like its counterparts around the world, was created to be a focal point of public activities, including mass gatherings of the citizenry.

Unlike Rome or Milan, or such smaller cities as Bologna, Florence, or Catania, there are few American cities where up to a million or so persons can easily assemble.

Mass meetings in piazzas, in large and small towns and in every season of the year, represent an important piece of the democratic process in Italy. Small meetings, casual or formal, take place in the piazzas as well. If freedom of assembly is a critically important ingredient of a democratic polyarchy, the Italian setup and practice seem far superior to situations in other democracies where either climate or public architecture make such outdoor meetings more improbable.

On occasion the mass meetings can degenerate into riots, and because this is so, the larger or more provocative a particular political gathering, the larger will be the forces of public order that also gather there. The latter, under orders from officials, may actually initiate violence, and the history of Italy is littered with unhappy, sometimes tragic, examples of such provocations.

On the Continent, nevertheless, the freedom of the people to "go down to the piazza" for political and other reasons of common concern is the essence of the constitutional right of peaceable assembly. Indeed, those large public squares in the major cities make it possible to think about a "town meeting" on a gigantic scale. Italians exercise this right hungrily. They gather often, sometimes at a moment's notice, by the tens and hundreds of thousands, and for reasons that might on some occasions appear trivial or perhaps bizarre to those on the outside. On the whole, however, no one can doubt that this aspect of the political process reinforces its quality of spettacolo.

Consider the following examples:

In June 1984, as he spoke in an overflowing piazza at Verona, Enrico Berlinguer, the Communist leader, became visibly ill. Notwithstanding his obvious agony, he continued to speak—until the crowd itself set up a roar of protest, imploring him to stop. He had suffered a stroke, of which he died a few days later.

Lying in a coma, Berlinguer was visited at his bedside by the then prime minister and members of the cabinet (of which Berlinguer's PCI was certainly not a member), by the leaders of other political parties, and by Sandro Pertini, then president of the republic. Pertini had Berlinguer's body flown back to Rome on the presidential plane. During the four days that preceded his death, Berlinguer was the object of exhaustive attention from the mass media. Few heads of state elsewhere have been accorded similar attention in comparable circumstances. Yet this was only a prelude.

Berlinguer's funeral ceremonies took place in Piazza San Giovanni in Laterano, the principal locus in Rome for the PCI's mass meetings. Two million people from all over Italy and many parts of the globe showed up. In the piazza, the white flags of Christian Democracy mingled with the red ones of Italian communism and of Italian socialism. The standards of other political parties, of the trade unions, and of many Italian cities were there too. Those who were not present in the immense square saw it all on television or read about it in the additional saturation coverage provided by the print media.

A few days after Berlinguer's funeral, the Communist party, for the first time in history, outdistanced all other competitors, in national elections for Italy's representation in the European parliament. Many ascribed this unprecedented event to a "sympathy vote" connected with the stricken leader's death. More than one editor regretted in print that the country had turned the tragedy itself into a spectacular event that produced unexpected and somewhat alarming electoral consequences.

Nine months later, in another electoral campaign (for regional and local legislative assemblies), the piazzas were filled again—this time with the partisans of one political party or another. The Christian Democrats were back to raising for the voters the specter of the "Communist menace." The Communists in turn howled, as often in the past, about the "unconstitutional" interference of the Catholic church in the country's political affairs. These imprecations and exhortations were typically delivered from a high dais draped in bunting and surrounded by flags and emblems of whatever red, white, or other color that are the parties' trappings. Without any radical change in the setting or its props, yesterday's stage for the expression of political solidarity and ecumenism became today's arena for political warfare.

It is not just electoral campaigns that bring the masses into the piazzas. Shortly before Christmas 1984, a time bomb placed by terrorists on an express train exploded as the train raced through a long tunnel between Florence and Bologna. Miraculously, only about twenty persons were killed, while several hundred more were injured. The next day, crowds filled piazzas all over the country. They were there not just to express their human solidarity with the victims or to direct their indignation toward the terrorists; they had gathered as well to reaffirm their commitment to the democratic state, the real target of the terrorists. They had done it many times before in recent years as an unequivocal symbol of their rejection of violence as an instrument of politics.

On Christmas Day in many of the same piazzas, thousands again assembled, this time to mark their concern for those millions in Africa and elsewhere who are ravaged by starvation. It was not just symbolic support. Manifestations of this kind led the government to allocate the equivalent of one billion dollars in relief for the stricken.

Two months later, on a rainy February day, traffic in Rome was snarled for hours. Tens of thousands of women, from all over the country, had come to the city to assemble, parade, and protest against rape and to urge the government to be more vigilant in the protection of women's rights. Some taxi drivers snarled that the women should be home, minding the kids and preparing lunch. But Italians are remarkably tolerant of these frequent inconveniences, in part no doubt because most of them know that, sooner of later, they too will march and assemble for a cause that will paralyze traffic for a little while.

In mid-March, at Milan, fifty thousand workers gathered in another piazza to express their indignation against the government, which had, by decree, modified the scala mobile to labor's disadvantage. This meeting took place three months before the referendum election that was eventually held on this issue and before anyone was certain that the election would take place at all. Considerations of this kind, though, rarely dampen enthusiasm for meetings in the public squares. Indeed, in the interest of gaining public attention and governmental approval of their causes, all manner of taxi drivers, students, garbage collectors, doctors and nurses, wounded war veterans, old age pensioners, postal employees, lawyers, bank clerks, agricultural workers, squatters in public and private housing, and you-name-the-category will take to the streets and use the piazza as a dramatic means of political communication.

The next month (skipping over dozens of other examples), on Palm Sunday, about two hundred thousand people assembled in Saint Peter's Square. They were there at the pope's invitation—not to hear mass but simply to underscore that the year 1985 had been declared by the United Nations to be International Youth Year. A week later, of course, the same piazza was again mobbed even more, by the faithful and the curious who gather in that place each Easter Sunday morning.

If piazzas dense with people are as common as pizza, it is also true that this form of mass political participation is in decline. The automobile and television are the reason. The ubiquitous Fiats make it possible for millions of Italians to find their weekend recreation away from the piazzas. And television, when it covers the major events in the public squares, brings the speakers, by zoom lens, into one's living room and onto one's lap. As with the movie houses, though, television has not yet dealt the harangue-in-the-piazza a death blow. There are still many who want their political spettacolo to be three-dimensional and palpable.

On the other hand, the mass media remain a major instrument for the transformation of all manner of "human interest" events into political spettacolo. Where the fusion of ordinary life with politics is as relentless as I have suggested, all manner of events lend themselves to this reconversion. In Rome a few years ago, a young boy fell into an abandoned well shaft, and this impending tragedy immediately produced, as it would have anywhere else in the West, media attention on a national scale. In Rome it also produced, roughly in this order, a chaotic circuslike atmosphere at the wellhead; President Sandro Pertini, who spent hours before the television cameras, competing with others for media attention; and, once the unfortunate little Alfredo died, a wave of politically motivated recriminations about the gross mishandling of the rescue operation.

With the sometimes mirthful collaboration of the media, art and the weather will sometimes turn political as well. In the summer of 1984, officials at Livorno, the birthplace of Amadeo Modigliani, claimed to have dredged up from the local canal three sculpted heads the artist was rumored to have dumped there seventy years earlier in a fit of pique over the cool reception accorded the works by his townspeople. The marble heads were quickly authenticated by several critics and historians of art.

Several of the latter were well-known sympathizers or members of the Communist party, as was the mayor of Livorno and his sister, who directed the local museum and who presumably had importuned the mayor to authorize the search. Everything seemed to be in order, however, and there was great rejoicing about the find.

Suddenly, three, then four, university students volunteered that they had sculpted the heads and dumped them into the canal as a prank. The mayor and his sister cried foul. The left-wing press noted that one of the students was the son of a well-known member of the local fascist party. The experts held their ground, and the claim was voiced that it was really a political plot to embarrass the Communist administration. Then the Christian-Democratic-controlled national television network challenged the young men to prove their claim by sculpting another head, on camera. This they did, and the finished product was indistinguishable from the other three.

Mass media coverage of this human-interest-story-turned-political occurred in proportions that Americans would consider inconceivable. For several days, the country's leading newspapers devoted from three to six full pages to the raging fracas. On this occasion, the prize for timely exploitation of the event went to the Black and Decker Company, one of whose drills was a major tool used by the miscreant students. The company flooded the country with posters depicting a somewhat fuzzy but clearly recognizable "Modigliani" head. Below it, in very sharp focus, lay a drill of the kind used. The caption read: "It's a cinch with a Black and Decker!"

A few months later, in January 1985, Rome experienced one of its worst snowfalls in modern history. It happened on a Sunday, and this brought into the streets thousands of cross-country skiers and dare-devil drivers who challenged the local hills. Predictably, cities to the north treated the Romans with levels of derision that sometimes reached "racist" tones. Milan's newspapers in particular ridiculed the administrative ineptness and "Mediterranean" approach to the problem. The then mayor of Rome, a Communist, claimed that the criticisms were politically motivated (the mayor of Milan was a Socialist) and that, indeed, they represented a danger to democracy! This triggered a nationwide polemic. One of Milan's journalists, who had been among the first to politicize the issue, tried, unsuccessfully, to calm things down by remarking that, alas, in Italy even snowfalls take on left-wing or right-wing political coloration. Your average Italian citizen would reply, "Is there any other kind of snowfall?"

LEGISLATIVE DRAMA

Frequent gatherings in the public squares and everyday happenings that tend to become politicized on a national scale and highlighted in the mass media are single pieces in a much larger mosaic that brings politics across as a form of spettacolo. Within this framework, we come to recognize that persons from all walks of life are continually, and willingly, drawn into the spettacolo itself, as participants and performers. Those who are inside this system do not ask whether the mundane or the esoteric might turn political; they simply wonder when, how, and in what more or less distressing or entertaining fashion this will occur.

The key branches of government operate within this same framework. Although each governmental institution is drawn into the drama from time to time, most of the attention focuses on Montecitorio, the Roman hill of that name on which the lower house of the national legislature is perched. Next door to it is Palazzo Chigi, the headquarters of the prime minister and his staff. Not far down the hill, toward Piazza Navona, is located the senate, housed in Palazzo Madama. The president of the republic is also a short distance away, in the Palazzo Quirinale, located on another of Rome's seven hills, where the mighty have built their seats of power for centuries. These are the main stages where the more spectacular aspects of politics are played out.

Montecitorio, where governments are made and unmade, gets the lion's share of public attention, much like the House of Commons does in the United Kingdom.[10] By comparison with Montecitorio, though, the latter chamber is a paragon of decorum and discipline. It could not be otherwise when one considers that Montecitorio generally hosts four times the number of political parties; that, with the exception of the Communists, these are remarkably undisciplined; and that secret balloting makes it impossible to determine who actually supports the governmental coalition and who does not. Even the United States Congress, where each representative or senator votes as he or she chooses, appears orderly and predictable by comparison.

All legislative bodies of course have their norms, and all of them will sometimes provide attention-catching drama. The "style" of House of Commons performance may be different from Montecitorio's. But the valued norms of the British parliamentary game certainly include such things as wit, polite but stinging insults of one's opponents, elegance of expression, and bravura performance in debate. The American Senate's fillibuster, although often dramatic, pales by comparison.

Montecitorio gets the lion's share of attention not just because it is the place where, in formal terms, governments are made and unmade or because it has primary responsibility for legislative policy. It draws media and public attention because this is where governments will be struck down in ambush; where political parties will be continually tested in their skills at negotiation, parliamentary manipulation, and exploitation of public relations opportunities. It is here that over the years the Communist party, although almost always in opposition, has managed to exercise a remarkable influence over public policies. Its parliamentary astuteness has gained the limelight so often that most Italians, including the PCI's most implacable opponents, are forced to grant that it is peerless when it comes to exploiting Montecitorio as a stage.

Where legislative votes proceed by secret balloting and roll-call votes are rare, the potential for arresting political drama is at its maximum. Even after governments fall to the "sharpshooters" who are defectors from the ruling parties, political leaders and pundits will spend days in efforts to sort out who the "traitors" may have been. Far from reacting to episodes of this kind with horror or disgust, it is clear that the man on the street finds much of it highly entertaining. And those who are not avid readers of the print media are provided with daily in-depth television coverage of parliamentary events.

Not everyone involved in political drama of this kind is happy with the arrangements. It is no small matter in a democracy that each prime minister, including those with majorities of fifty or sixty members in the lower house, lives with the certain knowledge that he and his government are likely to be defeated on important issues, and when least expected. A number of the institutional reforms discussed in a later chapter are intended to curtail this particular form of spettacolo.

EMPTY SPETTACOLO?

Is this system an empty one, with ominous implications for democracy? Well, it depends—and each reader will eventually draw some conclusions of his or her own on this score. Those who urge change, of course, tend toward the blackest kinds of interpretations and the most dire predictions about the eventual breakdown of what little democracy there is. The idea is that too much spettacolo degenerates into a three-ring circus and that little that citizens of a free society can actually respect will emerge from political scenarios of this kind. Furthermore, even if there is frequent and varied participation by the "political groundlings," the suspicion is great that they have precious little opportunity to affect which policy drama will be offered, and what direction it will take.

All such observations have a grain of truth, tend to be exaggerated, and carry the obvious but simplistic assumption that the democratic process could be improved. Nevertheless, closer inspection will almost always reveal that surface phenomena obscure very interesting and often ingenious ways in which Italians have managed to cope with the problems of governance. It is simply false to say that the masses are, relatively speaking, without effective voice. There is immensely less paralysis in government than may appear, or than many claim. Neither protracted legislative debates nor sharpshooters-in-ambush can keep the cabinet from enacting legislation by executive decree. Although constitutionally authorized, the procedure is meant to be limited to rare emergency situations. Its escalated use represents a pragmatic answer to serious bottlenecks in the representative system. Because some Italians believe this to be an abuse of power and a disquieting symptom for democracy, proposals to curb the use of the decree are being considered.

Another very Italian answer to the threat of legislative stagnation is to provide two levels of lawmaking, one of them very visible, and sometimes spectacular, the other much less visible, and highly efficient. The constitution authorizes two methods for enacting legislation. The first is very much as we find it in all democratic legislatures. Bills are introduced; they are reviewed, debated, and perhaps amended in committee; they are then placed on the "calendar" for debate and disposition by vote of the legislature as a whole. All of Italy's most important pieces of legislation, if they are not enacted by decree, go this route.

The second method permits individual committees of the legislature to enact laws, by vote of a simple majority of the committee's membership. In practice, a very large proportion of all the laws passed in Italy—and they run into several thousand in each legislative session—are enacted in this way. In fact, they are often passed by unanimous vote of the committee members, which means, among other things, that members of the government and of the so-called opposition collaborate in ways that almost never occur when the first method is used."

What better evidence than this of politics-as-spettacolo! Flowery speeches, bitter debates, principled "position-taking" by members of parliament for all that regards the most visible and public aspects of the lawmaking process. Then, secret ballots, and surprising defeats of governments with strong majorities. These events create dramatic moments in political life that might lead the untrained observer to conclude that the system is falling apart. And below the surface, business as usual that produces a continuous flow of legislation. Not many democracies around can claim this degree of refinement in the operation of their major institutions.

Far from supporting the conclusion that Italian democracy is weak, arrangements of this kind may well suggest exactly the opposite. There is an underlying pragmatism at work here, an understanding and a general consensus that, despite the inevitable snags in the democratic process, the show must go on. And it does. We think about Italian politics as being so dominated by ideological conflict and so deeply characterized by inflated rhetoric, we fail to observe exactly how pragmatic, how prone to compromise, and how ingenious at the discovery of the instruments that facilitate compromise itself the Italians really are.

Similarly, we should not confuse spettacolo with the idea that this particular democratic process is a sham or that what it produces by way of public policies is lacking in substance. Were that actually the case, republican Italy would long since have withered away and, one way or another, been transformed into something else. Perhaps it would be better were Montecitorio to resemble more its British or American counterparts. But as I warned in the opening pages of this book, judgments of this kind may overlook the extent to which the Italian arrangement is not just a matter of choice but the only one possible. From a democratic standpoint, it also seems to work reasonably well. That seems to be the case not just with the national legislature but also with the electoral system, which is the first place we look when we seek to establish whether, and to what extent, a government is democratic.

5

PARTIES AND ELECTIONS: THE RASHOMON SYNDROME

Constitutions provide the framework for democracy, but political parties and elections are its lifeblood. Dictators know this. When they take over, they quickly outlaw the competition. Elections, if held at all, turn into hollow rituals in which near-unanimous votes are cast, under duress, for the "leader" and his party. The Italians experienced almost two decades of this under Mussolini's fascist regime.

In republican Italy, elections occur regularly, and without duress. One finds there no more stuffed ballot boxes, or other forms of political chicanery, than in other democracies. And when electoral irregularities do occur, the miscreants often wind up behind bars.

By American or British standards, though, the number of political parties is excessive. Italians are as unabashed as their Israeli neighbors across the Mediterranean in the proliferation of political parties. In some regions, voters find upwards of fifteen parties on the ballot, most of them flashes in the pan. In national politics, the major and minor parties number about ten, of which seven have been around at least since 1946.

It is also the case that political parties in Italy enjoy a dubious reputation. In fact, as we will see later in more detail, growing numbers of Italians have fallen into thinking that the country is ruled by a "partyocracy" and that this is not a good thing. This mistaken idea is potentially dangerous; it can lead to attempts at "reform" that, ironically, may themselves upset the delicate balance that underlies any successful democracy. Furthermore, attacks on political parties, even when well motivated, frequently degenerate into attacks on democracy itself.

THE PARTY SPECTRUM

The parties vary considerably in age, size of membership, ideology, and attractiveness at the polls.[1] The extreme left is from time to time occupied by smaller splinter parties that come into existence because some Communist party leaders accuse the party of betraying the revolution or working class, or of making too many compromises in the interest of gaining respectability with the voters and, especially, with the other parties—a much more pertinent consideration in Italy. One of these, the party of Proletarian Unity (PDUP), settled its differences with the PCI and rejoined it in 1983. The other, Proletarian Democracy (DP), now numbers seven deputies in the lower house, all of them prepared to remind the PCI of its Marxist origins.

The PCI itself is the strongest in the Western world. It boasts more than a million card-carrying members, and, more important, it attracts the electoral support of about one out of every three adults. Despite a declining membership and a mild electoral slide since 1979, it remains the only viable alternative to the Christian Democratic party.

Many but obviously not all Italians find this a worrisome possibility. Some of them are visceral or knee-jerk anticommunists of the kind found in the United States. Others have narrow material interests to defend and believe, rightly or wrongly, that these would be placed in jeopardy were the PCI to come to power. For most, though, the main reason for diffidence and suspicion turns on the fear that the Communists remain entirely too uncritical of and tied to the Soviet Union.

The PCI's political opponents exploit this fear to their advantage whenever they can. If more Italians than ever before agree that the PCI is willing to play by the democratic rules of the game, the PCI's competitors reply, "So what?" when the democratic game is the only one in town. As for international affairs, it takes no effort at all to show that, for all of its sometimes courageous criticisms of the Soviet Union's excesses (for example, in Afghanistan), it always manages to excuse Soviet behavior and never finds saving graces for the acts of the United States and other Western countries.

The PCI aids and abets these attacks because it wallows in a crisis of ambiguity. It has talked about a "third way" different from capitalism and democratic socialism, without providing even the dimmest description of what the alternative society its "way" would foster might look like. Its efforts to explain itself, to justify its failures to render internal party procedures more open and democratic, and to clarify its orientation toward the Soviet Union are swollen with language that makes ordinarily abstruse political discourse look like a paragon of clarity. Thus, sincere or cynical, principled or opportunistic, anti-Communists find their task child's play.

The Socialist party has also had its share of identity problems, some severe enough to suggest political schizophrenia. Should the party remain committed to socialism, or should it follow in the footsteps of other Socialist parties, like those of France or Spain, that have become the darlings of capitalists? Should the PSI be fundamentally allied with the Communists or the Christian Democrats, and with what protections against errors of the past? How should the party relate to the labor movement, to organized business, to the Catholic Church? What should be its international posture, especially on basic issues pertaining to East-West and North-South relations?

Bettino Craxi, with consummate skill, has put distance between the PSI and the Communist party, but without bringing about a complete rupture between them. He has stolen the initiative from the Communists, in the sense of compelling them to worry about what to do about the Socialists, and not vice-versa. In international politics, Craxi has made it plain that he stands with the West, although he has also sought, gingerly, to make Italy more autonomous in the Middle East and on north-south issues.

In times past, when the PSI was closely allied with the PCI, both parties seemed committed to the creation of a socialist society. Today, neither of them really is, but only the Socialists, under Craxi's impetus, have been able to say so openly. The PSI, far from causing any consternation among the owning classes, provides assurance and tranquility. If the Communists really wish to avoid being relegated to political limbo, they will have to be more assiduous in the clarification of their ideological and program-matic identity.

The secular or laical parties number four. The oldest are the Liberals (PLI) and Republicans (PRI), closely associated with the Risorgimento. Two parties that were born after the war are the Social Democrats (PSDI) and the Radicals (PR). As a group, these parties rarely get more than 13 percent of the vote, which places them, collectively, at about the level of the PSI. Aside from their support for the republic and for liberal demo-cratic institutions, their antipathy toward Christian Democracy, and their even stronger dislike of the Soviet Union, the four parties have little in common.

The Republicans, as their name suggests, are fierce opponents of the monarchy and its trappings and of any inkling of church interference in politics. They are also strong advocates of "rigor" in public spending, which now means curtailed outlays for welfare-state programs. The Liberals, threatened by electoral extinction, have tried in recent years to develop a somewhat less conservative posture than has been true of that party during this century. The PRI and PLI are important symbolically to Italian democracy far beyond their puny electoral performances.

As for the Social Democrats, the only remotely left-wing aspect of the PSDI is its propensity to favor populist policies. The PSDI is better understood as decisively opportunistic, ready to move right or left in search of votes but, even more important, in a hungry quest of cabinet seats and anything else that might give the party's leaders access to patronage. Its new leadership may try to change that image, but it has been etched very deeply right from the beginning.

The Radical party is difficult to place ideologically, largely because it appears as little more than the extension of the ego of one man, Marco Pannella, its founder and guru. The PR has also attracted other mavericks who share highly libertarian views, dissatisfaction with the country's political institutions, and opposition to the domination of politics by the old-style parties. Despite their somtimes zany and often irresponsible antics, the Radicals have been at the forefront of certain reform campaigns and are implacable opponents of corruption. On balance, though, Marco Pannella, for all of his charm and partly for that very reason, comes off looking more like a P. T. Barnum than a serious democratic statesman.

Pannella sets a standard that makes of the PR the quintessential example of politics-as-spettacolo. It was the radicals who pioneered the use of the referendum, an important step they later managed to trivialize by their overuse of that instrument. It is they who use the fillibuster—by offering thousands of amendments to proposed laws—primarily to demonstrate the ludicrousness of certain institutions and procedures. It is they who make principled debate look like demagoguery, which on closer inspection turns out to be even more so. The Radicals claim it is democracy's good health they wish to promote, and many younger voters who support the PR at the polls believe this is so.

Smaller parties are also found on the right. Until recently, the two major conservative parties were the Monarchist and the neo-Fascist. Those who harbor nostalgia for the monarchy or believe it can come back are a disappearing breed, but others who favor some sort of fascist state in exchange for a democratic one are not. These persons are now found in the Italian Social Movement (MSI), which constitutes the country's fourth largest vote-getter.

This leaves Christian Democracy, Italy's catch-all and hegemonic party par excellence. Because it has averaged almost 40 percent of the vote, it has accounted for all but two of the postwar prime ministers. When Giovanni Spadolini, a Republican, and Bettino Craxi, a Socialist, gained that coveted office in the early 1980s, it was at the sufferance of the DC. Until Craxi, no one doubted the DC's ability to orchestrate politics pretty much as it might desire.

Although the DC appears to occupy the center of the left-right spectrum, it is not, strictly speaking, a center party. For one thing, many of the policies it has enacted would certainly qualify as left of center. For another, within the party's ranks there coexist all manner of ideological preferences. In fact, the DC's internal groups often differ so fundamentally that they could easily split off and form separate, more ideologically coherent, parties.

What holds such a party together? To some extent, confessionalism— that shared, deeply felt identification with Catholicism that helps to bring together under one roof Christian Democrats of markedly different and even antagonistic ideological persuasions. But there is also power, for which the Christian Democrats have an uncommon appetite and an even more unusual capacity to hold on to once they acquire it. By itself, the cement of common religious identity, as strong as it is, would not suffice to bind together these strangest of bedfellows. Religious conviction combined with secular power turn out to be sufficient conditions for profitable, even if sometimes uncomfortable and acrimonious, cohabitation.

To hang on to power, Christian Democrats have employed unexcelled electoral and patronage skills. Any other party with a similar record of scandal, corrupt behavior, collusion with the underworld, and other blemishes would long since have been catapulted from office. Instead, the DC has made it almost axiomatic that morality in public office and success at the polls are, if anything, inversely related to each other. Their shared religious convictions have not led many Christian Democrats to imagine that the earth will someday belong to the meek or that the more important rewards will be found in the afterlife.

It must be added, though, that the DC is everyone's favorite target. Everything in Italy considered unsavory or evil is laid at the DC's doorstep. Everything commendable about the country, all that it has achieved in the last forty years, is attributed to others. The left, above all the intel-lectuals of that persuasion, believe that anything good registered in Italy occurs despite the monopoly of power the DC has enjoyed.

If the DC opportunistically raises the specter of the Communist menace, the Communists rave on about the danger of Christian Democratic he-gemony. For the PCI, the DC is the hallmark of political immorality against which it measures and displays its own superiority. But with little effect: not even in times of egregious scandal and corruption in which the DC was clearly implicated have the Communists managed to turn this to their own advantage on election day.

PARTIES TIMES FACTIONS

Like everything else about Italian politics, there is more to these parties than their number and labels suggest. For example, the parties are, to put it mildly, faction ridden. A faction, or *corrente* in the Italian lexicon, is a group of party leaders and militants who agree to work together to control the party itself. This means that they will, as a group, compete for leadership positions within the party at the local, regional, and national levels and then use these positions to name party candidates (mostly their own faction members) for elective and appointive office, coveted jobs in the public and private sectors, positions of great influence in the print and visual media—in short, for the range of patronage discussed in an earlier chapter.[2]

Not only are there many factions, but they are often formally recog-nized, in the sense that the parties' internal rules permit them to present formal motions about platforms and programs, to organize formal slates for election to internal governing bodies, and to obtain guaranteed mi-nority representation on these same bodies. These factions may be based on ideological affinity and agreement as to public policies, on the geo-graphic origins and location of those who make them up, or on major personalities in the system of patron and client that guides politics. More often than not, they are based on a combination of all of these things— but driven by the overarching, opportunistic quest for power.[3]

Only the PCI claims to be without factions, and the party's by-laws prohibit them. Bettino Craxi, too, as well as the DC leader, Ciriaco De Mita, went through the motions of having their respective parties agree to abolish factions. This happens from time to time, especially in the DC, which, as an openly catch-all party, has given factions the freest reign. But neither the PCI's authoritarian ways nor the efforts of Craxi or De Mita to emulate them ever succeed in abolishing these groups. If, as is true, one can identify right, center, and left factions within the PCI, why would they not persist in political parties that are internally much less self-disciplined?

The PCI leaders nevertheless still go to great pains to deny this. For example, before the 1986 PCI Congress, no formal votes were cast against the theses, or party positions, approved by the PCI Central Committee for the congress, even though it was a matter of public record that disagreements on many of the theses were extreme and uncompromising. This became clear in the debates and votes of the local and regional party meetings that led up to the congress. Some amendments to the theses were openly pro-Soviet, while some leaders on the right were identified by the press as the "American party." Thus, one good reason for the PCI's identity crisis is that its leaders go to such extremes to paper over these differences and to mask the fact that the party's consensus is bogus. In this way, too, the colorless bureaucrats who run the PCI succeed in denying the party even the faintest glimmer of a personality.

What about the Socialists? Under Bettino Craxi, who has tried to reorganize the PSI along monarchical lines, with himself as absolute monarch, the factional structure of old is supposed to have disappeared. And well it might. Even when it got under 10 percent of the national vote, the PSI still managed to spawn five different factions! But even Craxi's magic is limited. The old left wing of the PSI is still there, perhaps as strong as 30 percent of the party. The factions will reemerge, full blown, as soon as Craxi shows signs of weakening or moves on to higher office, like the republic's presidency.

Even the smallest parties, like the Liberals and the Republicans, have their identifiable factions, headed by single leaders. A leading journalist identified with the PLI lamented in 1986 that a party whose electoral appeal varied between 1 and 2.5 percent could still produce four internal factions!

As I suggested a moment ago, the quintessential factional structure is found, not surprisingly, in the Christian Democratic party. This is so not just because the DC is the largest party. As a catch-all party that contains so many ideological groups, and as a confederation of party "notables" who control their own local or regional political machines, the party cannot escape—indeed, it could scarcely do without—factional structure. Efforts to overcome this reality are doomed to fail.

Factions carry some costs. They make it improbable that one person or, for that matter, one faction will for long succeed in giving a party central direction. Needless to add, it is from these same factions that are drawn the sharpshooters who bring down their own governments.

Factions, obviously, exist wherever there are political parties.[+] They may be more visible in Italy, but this alone does not establish that they weigh more there. It is, in any case, wrong to ignore the inner workings of parties and to treat them instead as if it were a single living person who walks on two feet, faces options, and chooses, more or less rationally, among them. We should try not to gloss over what may be one of the most interesting and important aspects of any democracy: the nature of political struggle within, and not just between and among, parties. A great merit of Italy's political parties is that their factional structure is so blatant it makes unlikely the fiction that the parties are single, coherent entities, easily placed on a left-to-right ideological scale.

In Italy, it seems plausible that the benefits deriving from party factions outweigh their demerits. Factions, and not the parties as such, constitute the bridges between and among parties. Not only do factions constitute the major network of interparty communication; they also make it possible for like-minded persons from several different parties to act in collaboration with each other. For example, clearly identifiable left-wing factions within the DC and PSI have more in common with the right wing of the PCI than they have with the other factions of their own parties.

Factions also constitute effective channels for the representation of interests, not only within specific political parties but in legislative bodies and the bureaucracy as well. As in the case of lottizzazione, it is really through the factions—at least the more important ones within each party—that most of the valued things the government controls are distributed. This makes factions prime political brokers through which individuals, organizations, patrons, and clients operate. They keep the system running. Without them, it would probably fall apart.

Thus, as perverse as it may seem, factions in Italy are a vital piece of the mechanism that makes the system a successful polyarchy. If like-minded persons can find appropriate factions in several *different* political parties, then, for example, society's cleavages and conflicts will not degenerate into a hopelessly polarized situation, inimical to democracy.

Finally, to anticipate a subject that will come up more than once as we move along, factions tend to correct what many claim to be one of Italian democracy's more serious defects. I refer to the alleged malfunctioning of representative institutions like the legislature and to the lack of a strong connection between electoral outcomes and the formation of government and the enactment of public policy. Italian democracy, and especially the representative aspects of it, operate overwhelmingly through the political parties. This being so, the division of these parties into subdivisions called factions is not only quite logical, it is a godsend.

ELECTIONS AND VOTERS

Because political parties and elections are vital to democracy, they get a lot of attention—from pollsters, journalists, scholars, and just ordinary citizens. If there is any meaning at all to the democratic idea "rule by the people," it is in elections and what results from them that we would expect to learn whether the idea itself is valid or vacuous.

Italian evidence on this point is fuzzy. Italy holds many elections, although those caused by national cabinet crises are still rare. As a rule voters are called to the polls at least once a year to elect members to a variety of deliberative bodies. These include the schools and neighborhood councils and extend through cities, communes, provinces, regions, and the national government.

There is also the referendum. As we saw in chapter 2, it definitely gives the people an opportunity to vote their minds on laws the national legislature has enacted. Only rarely has a democratic state ever extended this type of power to its national electorate.

Italians spend much time preparing for, voting in, and then talking about the results of elections. In fact, political life might be described as one of elections occasionally interrupted by politically quiescent periods in August and around the Christmas holidays. For many years, no one dared call a national election in summer, but even that norm was broken in 1983.[5]

Elections point up a number of Italian political characteristics that are worth underscoring.

- If turnout at the polls is one sign of civic-mindedness, Italians walk away with the honors on this score. They vote in astonishingly large numbers. Politicians and the experts become perplexed when partici-

when participation falls below 90 percent. This figure refers not just to "registered" voters in the American sense. Italians, like Europeans in general, need take no special steps to register; their names are automatically maintained on the electoral registries. Failure to vote, even in several consecutive elections, does not result in the citizen being dropped from the electoral lists. A 90 percent turnout in Italy means that nine of every ten adult citizens have gone to the polls.

• For a variety of reasons, Italians maintain their place of official residence where they were born and not where they may actually be living today. However, except for those who live abroad and a few others, absentee voting is not permitted. Thus, in order to vote, one must travel back to one's hometown. Several million do this, typically by public transportation provided at cut-rate prices to encourage fuller electoral participation. There is also moral pressure to do this: the constitution makes it the citizen's civic duty to vote, and official notice is taken of those who fail to do so.

• Inside the polling booth, voters have the option of marking their ballots for one party or another or leaving them blank. They can also deliberately invalidate the ballot by writing messages on it or otherwise defacing it. The number of blank, or spoiled, ballots can run into two or three million, and the trend of recent years has seen that number edge upward. I once asked a friend why he would travel four hundred miles to write on his ballot, "This government stinks." He said he went home, at the special travel rate, primarily to see his family and to visit with friends. But he voted, too! It would not have occurred to him to do otherwise.

• If you look at electoral outcomes, at the votes for each party, and, even more important, at the proportions of the total vote that go to clusters of left-, center-, and right-wing parties, Italians for four decades have seemed to vote in a monotonously similar way. This remarkably persistent pattern will require a closer look in a moment.

• There is little apparent connection between what happens at the polls and what follows, for example, in the selection of a prime minister, the formation of a cabinet, the naming of cabinet members, to say nothing about the content of public policies. Trasformismo is obviously at work here. But there is more to be explored. The nagging question, the apparent paradox, is this: Why do Italians continue to vote in such record-breaking proportions if they know in advance that elections themselves will change very little, or nothing, about the politics of the country?

• Italy has held ten national parliamentary elections in forty years, eleven if we count the 1984 elections to the European parliament. This is average among democracies. In that same period, however, Italy has actually had forty-five governments, and that number is way over par! Prime ministers come into office knowing that by and large they will not remain there for as long as a year. If, as in the case of Aldo Moro, tenure exceeds two years, and, in the Bettino Craxi case, an unprecedented almost four years, these exceptions not only raise the average; they imply that some governments last only a few weeks, or days. As soon as a new government is installed, speculation begins as to whether the prime minister will be in Palazzo Chigi long enough to learn its floor plan.

• On no occasion in these past forty years has a national election resulted directly in the defeat of the previous government and its replacement by an opposition. As a matter of fact, "government and opposition" is simply not an appropriate description of national politics. Think of national government instead as an umbrella under which, depending on circumstances, as few as one party and as many as six may find shelter.

THE ELECTORAL CONNECTION

We now turn to the results of these ten elections to discover, if possible, what they might mean.[6] Bear in mind that what we say regarding them depends in part on where we stand, what we see, and how we count. We "see" at best imperfectly; our preferences and prejudices not only direct our vision, they also obscure it. We wear lenses through which the so-called facts are filtered, and in this way we create our private reality. The lenses reflect our individual wishes or needs, our beliefs about society and politics, our ideologies, and even our fantasies. We do not wish to be disappointed, upset, or frightened by the "facts" of political life. Above all, we do not wish to be surprised by them.

Pirandello, that ironic Sicilian playwright, exploited this human condition by placing it dead center in more than one of his works. Akira Kurosawa, the distinguished Japanese film director, has done much the same. The action in his outstanding film *Rashomon* opens with a scene of sexual violence and death. There then follow descriptions and interpretations of what happened from each of the major protagonists and a witness to the opening scene. The viewer, of course, "sees" it all and is able to appreciate not just the subtlety of Kurosawa's direction but also the plausibility of each interpretation.

The messages of Pirandello and Kurosawa are one and the same: the "reality" of things is not something objective out there, waiting to be discovered. It is at its core a construction of our own minds and an extension of our personalities. Trial lawyers are acutely aware of this. They are more prepared than the rest of us for the fantastic variations in the accounts of events provided by two or more eyewitnesses.

Politicians "see" in this specialized way deliberately, as a matter of practice. The lenses they wear come with their job descriptions. Reporters and editorial writers, and scholars themselves, are not much better off. The so-called conceptual frameworks the scholars boast are little more than another device for filtering reality.

Italian elections are ideally suited to produce a Rashomon Syndrome. To begin with, there is no direct election of a president, no single contest that might permit us to identify which party has won and which has lost. National elections are held to name over six hundred members for the lower chamber and about half that number for the senate. In these contests, no single party has ever reached 50 percent of the votes cast.

When citizens vote, they are better able to predict which parties will not be part of the government than which will. Even if they guess the basic makeup of a coalition, they would not come close to predicting which party factions would be represented in the cabinet.

Typically, the losses or gains registered by individual political parties from one election to another tend to be quite slight, sometimes infinitesimal. Irrespective of the outcome, the general assumption remains that neither the Communists nor the neo-Fascists will be invited to join a governmental coalition. This means that somewhere between 35 and 40 percent of the electorate regularly go to the polls without any expectation whatever that they can "win," as that term is usually intended.

It is also understood that everyone, with the possible exception of the very extreme parties on the left and right, will somehow get a piece of the action once a government is formed. That is, regardless of what may happen at the polls, party leaders know that they will rarely be completely cut out of the system that distributes things people value. The two-tiered, visible versus invisible, aspect of the national legislature described in the last chapter would be an example of what this assumption means in practice. The allocation of coveted jobs on the basis of lottizzazione would be another example. In this basic sense, everybody "wins" in Italian elections.

On the other hand, since coalitions are typically based on the lowest common denominator approach to public policy; because no single party can expect its own programs to prevail; and because even coalitions with strong legislative majorities can readily be ambushed and shot down by the snipers, nobody really "wins." Indeed, Italians who detest this system complain that everybody, and particularly the country itself, "loses."

THE RASHOMON SYNDROME

Let us see how the Rashomon Syndrome might work out in practice. As soon as the results of the June 1983 national elections were known, television screens and newspapers produced a table that looked more or less like this one:

Votes and Seats, by Party,
Chamber of Deputies, 1979 and 1983

Party	1979			1983		
	Votes	%	Seats	Votes	%	Seats
DC	14,046,290	38.3	262	12,145,800	32.9	225
PCI	11,139,231	30.4	201	11,028,158	29.9	198
PSI	3,596,802	9.8	57	4,222,487	11.4	73
PSDI	1,407,535	3.8	20	1,507,431	4.1	23
PRI	1,110,209	3.0	16	1,872,536	5.1	29
PLI	712,646	1.9	9	1,065,833	2.9	16
PR	1,264,870	3.5	18	809,672	2.2	11
DP	294,462	0.8	—	541,493	1.5	7
PDUP[a]	502,247	1.4	6	—	—	—
MSI	1,930,693	6.1	35	2,511,722	6.8	42
Others	666,377	1.8	6	1,185,157	3.2	6

[a]In 1983 the PDUP rejoined the PCI.

Who "won" this election? Obviously it depends.[7] If the test is which party received more votes than any other, then the DC won, as it has won, in this sense, every election since 1946. But in 1983 everyone agreed that the DC had taken quite a beating, evidenced by the downward slide that is apparent between 1979 and 1983. Indeed, the newspapers described this slide as an "earthquake." It was not that at all, but it looked that way in a country where small shifts are rare and where even these tend to be blown up out of proportion.

Ciriaco De Mita, the DC's secretary general, did not equivocate. He said to the press: "Who says that Victory has a hundred fathers and that Defeat is always an orphan? This time, Defeat's father is right here, with first and last name, address, and telephone number. It is I." Then he added, "The other parties hope they can govern without us. Just let them try!" He was right, of course. The DC went right back into office, not with the prime ministership, but with most of the cabinet seats, as befits the largest party by far within the government coalition. From that vantage point, the DC went right on winning.

What about the Communists; did they win or lose? Again it depends. In past years, if the PCI failed to get as many votes as predicted or if it fell back even .1 percent, not only its Italian opponents but also foreign newspapers like the *New York Times* would editorialize about the party's "setback." The Communists, on the other hand, took the view in 1983 that since they had declined only .5 percent when everyone thought their losses would be much greater, they had actually "won."

Did the Socialists "win"? You would have to stretch to believe it. Whereas in 1979, 98 of every 1,000 voters who cast valid ballots voted for the PSI, in 1983 that number had risen to only 114. Furthermore, since the polls predicted that the PSI would do much better, many concluded that the Socialists had actually "lost." Bettino Craxi, however, took a different view of it. A journalist asked him, "Really now, do you actually believe you have won?" Craxi replied, "We won. It's the first time in twenty years that the PSI moves ahead in this way in national elections ... the first time. We've gone through a ring of fire. Think of it. Everyone was on our backs, parties and newspapers. And we held our own and made gains. We didn't expect much more." In the most dramatic sense, Craxi was right: a few weeks later he moved into Palazzo Chigi as the first Socialist prime minister in Italy's history.[8]

In the Italian context, the clearest "winner" in 1983 was the Republican party. From the scant 3 percent of the vote it received in 1979, the PRI jumped 60 percent in 1983 and came close to doubling its representation in the legislature. Yet, whereas its paltry showing in 1979 brought the party the prime ministership, in 1983 it was awarded only three seats in the five-party cabinet headed by Bettino Craxi.

Not to be outdone by these esoteric interpretations, one of the country's leading newspaper editors provided his own unique reading of the 1983 results. With only a mild apology to his readers, he added together blank and invalid ballots (5.6 percent), those who did not vote (11 percent), and the votes cast for the MSI (6.8 percent), Radicals (2.2 percent), DP (1.5 percent), and a few minor parties (2.0 percent) for a total of 29 percent. He then concluded that well over one-fourth of the electorate had voted "against the republic."

This argument is the Rashomon Syndrome run wild. Among other things, it ascribes to the nonvoters a very specific and antagonistic attitude toward the existing political system. Imagine how this would sound in the United States, where half the electorate typically fails to vote in presidential elections. Italians really worry about electoral abstainers, and think about them and those who cast blank and defaced ballots as the third largest "party."

Another leading journalist, without benefit of even a small survey of voters leaving the polling place, claimed, reasonably enough, that the most unambiguous aspect of the 1983 outcome was the sharp drop in the DC vote. But he added: "The DC was punished, in a delayed reaction, for the prolonged laxity of some of its governments in the face of disorder, waste, corruption, crime, inflation, and other types of crises, and for the wicked operation of the bureaucracy and other public services."[9]

POLLSTERS AND PUNDITS

Everyone speculates—more often than not guided by the same factors that encourage Rashomon Syndrome interpretations of political events. The evidential basis for speculation inevitably varies, and there is no special demerit that goes to those who fail to consult what the public opinion polls may have to say about politics. This is particularly the case with Italy, where although many polls are conducted they are, on the whole, less reliable than in other democracies.

A major reason why the 1983 electoral results were so surprising is the pollsters themselves. They and other pundits predicted that the DC would hold its own or improve its electoral standing, that the PCI would continue its decline since 1979, and that the PSI would do considerably better than turned out to be the case. Ciriaco De Mita was so gulled by these reports that, during a televised debate with the PCI's Enrico Berlinguer, he made the remarkable statement that there no longer existed any prejudice against the Communists forming a government, were the electoral results to justify such a step. As it turned out, the PCI came astonishingly close to cashing in on De Mita's unprecedented concession.

Polls often go wrong for technical reasons.[10] The sample may be too small. It may be difficult to reach certain people, and so the sample used, even if large enough, may not be truly representative of the population. Or the polls conducted before election day may fail to pick up last-minute shifts in voter opinions. Other technical difficulties abound.

Polls go wrong for political reasons, too. Italy is not the only country where political parties use their own polls, and their own esoteric interpretations of them, not as a means of getting objective information but rather as just another weapon in the political campaign. Polling "results" can be reported to create a bandwagon effect, or to scare voters about unhappy or dangerous outcomes if they fail to vote, or if they vote for one party as against another. The mass media, too, highly politicized as they are, conduct their own polls, as they do in other countries. This means that, far beyond locating and reporting the news that's fit to print, the mass media actually manufacture the "news" itself, on which they then comment, often with their own political ends in view.

Even in the best of circumstances, Italy confronts the pollsters with a nightmarish problem. Normally, upwards of 20 percent of those who are interviewed refuse to reveal how they have voted in the past or to give any indication whatever of which party they intend to support in an oncoming election. Ingenious questions devised by the pollsters have failed to solve this problem. This means that predictions about how the elections will turn out are, to say the least, extremely problematical.

Nor is this the only ingredient in the nightmare. Italians greatly enjoy confounding the experts. They are highly skeptical of claims that human behavior can be studied "scientifically." The social sciences, particularly those that boast refined empirical theories and methods of conducting research, have had very tough sledding in this country. The Marxists, with their ready-made "scientific" explanations of history and everything else in society, are instinctively hostile to modern social science. So are those millions of others who, consciously or otherwise, share the reservations about social science engendered earlier in this century by Benedetto Croce, a gifted and domineering Italian philosopher.

It may be that this diffidence toward social science is eroding. Italians, who are peerless when it comes to fascination with electronic gadgetry, have fallen head over heels for computers and computer software. Totocalcio, the national weekly gambling pool based on soccer matches, for example, was once a real game of chance that provided fabulous winnings for those rare persons who guessed the outcomes of thirteen out of thirteen Sunday afternoon matches. Computerized betting "systems" are now so sophisticated that there are now dozens and even hundreds of "thirteens" each week.

It will nevertheless be some time before this fascination with "science" helps the political pollsters. The reason is—privacy. Unlike many other peoples, Italians are avid about guarding their private affairs from public, and especially governmental, scrutiny. They find it incredible, for example, that Americans, in exchange for a paltry credit card, will reveal to total strangers information about their income, savings, and ownership of property. This kind of information is in Italy as tightly guarded as are secrets of state—often against one's own family members, to say nothing of outsiders.

Remarkable bookkeeping practices, ingenious tax-evasion schemes, solutions to marital problems that, until recently, had to exclude divorce, and even the Italian's so-called addiction for *la bella figura* signal the same warning: what you claim to see or to understand about this country and its inhabitants may not be even remotely related to things as they actually are. Why should this change when a pollster arrives to ask questions about one's past, present, and future political preferences or affiliations—in a country, we might add, where for better or for worse every aspect of life itself is permeated by politics. Viewed from this perspective, the remarkable achievement of the pollsters is that their error margins are not larger.

Over the years, the Rashomon Syndrome has been most apparent regarding the electoral performance of the Communist party. For one thing, it is the members and the supporters of this party who are the most reluctant, and perhaps the most perverse, when it comes to telling the pollsters a straight story. For decades, the polls showed that under 10 percent of those sampled supported the PCI. Just as monotonously, the party received from twice to more than three times that number of votes in elections.

Wishful thinking has also been at work here. Despite years of research that shows it to be inaccurate, many still believe a very early American interpretation of the Communist vote as "negative," or as representing "protest." This simplistic view of politics would have the Communist vote decline as the basic material needs of the population are satisfied.

It has not happened. Americans in particular keep scratching their heads about the persistent strength of the PCI, long after Italy has become the world's fifth leading economy and Italians themselves have experienced unimagined improvements in their standard of living. This does not make the Italians odd. It means only that outside observers have failed to capture as well as they might the implications of Italy's political religions and political subcultures, or its political families."

Bad predictions of the PCI's electoral performance, surprise over the failure of the PCI to fade away, and stubborn insistence that sooner or later the PCI *must* decline, are also based on the thought that what goes on inside a political party will make a difference to the voters. The idea is that if the party is not internally democratic, if its leaders cannot make up their minds what to do about "democratic centralism," or if they are forever at odds over the correct reading of Karl Marx, this will cost them dearly on election day. This is nonsense.

To begin with, no one bothers to explain why, if there is some sort of axiom here, it should apply to the PCI and not to other parties. That party is certainly tightly controlled at the center. But so is the PSI under Bettino Craxi. In the PSI's case, however, centralized control is supposedly beneficial and not harmful. How come? The answer lies in part in the kind of anticommunism discussed earlier, in part in the genuine fear that the PCI's disciplined internal structure gives it a lopsided advantage against other parties.

Looked at internally, though, few political parties in the history of democracy would qualify as anything better than oligarchies. In any case, it is unlikely that the average voter either notices or cares about their internal workings. It would be astonishing if more than a tiny fraction of any electorate voted for or against a given party on this basis. In Italy, there is no evidence at all that this has ever been a salient electoral issue. A stronger prediction is that, despite what may transpire within the parties or within the country, citizens will vote tomorrow as they voted yesterday.

THE VOTING HABIT

We can now turn to some of the perplexing questions raised earlier in this chapter. Why do Italians vote in droves if they know in advance that the ritual is an empty one? Why have there not occurred, if not radical shifts in the vote for each party, at least enough changes to force one group from power and to open the door to an alternative group? If people are as disgruntled, or as "alienated," about politics as many claim, why have they not used their ballots to do something about this? After all, no legal bars stand in the way. Nothing in the constitution requires that the same hegemonic party, and three or four of its satellites, should control the national government eternally.

Following the local and regional elections of 1985, a leading journalist put the matter as follows:

> *The family portrait is the same as that taken forty years ago. . . . There have been some changes in proportions, but it's the same thing. Very much like the arrow of Zeno of Elea—in flight but actually standing still. . . . In effect, Italy is a masterpiece of movement without motion, a trajectory without an arrow, an arrow without a trajectory. . . . This static quality is forty years old and nothing in Europe compares with it. . . . We are the only Europeans who run en masse to the polls, establishing records that vary between 89 and 93 percent. We vote with passion, massively, repeatedly, always more in love with a democracy in which nothing changes. . . . It is true that we are a truly exceptional "case": On one side, the most vital, frenetic, epileptic society, full of rousings. On the other side, the most static, the most petrified of political structures. . . . Blocked democracy is not a sickness, it is a physiological condition. If people thought of it as sickness, they would have removed the condition long ago.*[12]

These words capture not only the most striking quality of electoral outcomes but also the frustration that many Italians experience over their apparently static quality. To get a better handle on their meaning, we need to look at elections from other angles, and within the Italian context.[13]

To begin with high turnouts, recall that politics not only permeates life; it is also the Big Spettacolo. Not just the politicians but almost everyone else (certainly everyone else who counts) is "on stage" almost all of the time. Political roles differ. Some persons give speeches while others listen. Some are active in the trade unions, the industrial organizations, or Catholic Action, while countless others will go on strike or engage in political demonstrations. Every day, in some palpable way, millions of Italians are arrayed on one side or another of many, many public issues.

And everybody votes. Not only is this expected of everyone; everyone expects to do it—as an integral part of his or her own role as citizen. Furthermore, to vote is one of the relatively few things, like written (not spoken!) Italian and the Fiat automobile, that residents of the peninsula really have in common. Pasta, after all, is a staple food largely in the south; in the north, it is rice.

Participation in national elections is symbolically important in any democracy. It is particularly so with an Italy that experienced twenty years of dictatorship and is a still-young nation, striving on a peninsula where diversity and conflict have been the rule for centuries. To vote in national elections reaffirms the nation; it also sublimates deadlier forms of political participation that are also Italy's political heritage.

Italians not only vote in record numbers; they also take their elections in stride. Voting is a habit. School children watch their parents vie and vote for offices that relate to the governance of their schools. Residents of given *quartieri* vote for representatives to neighborhood councils. Workers elect members to factory councils. In the high schools and universities, elections take on the same political coloration (Communist, Socialist, Christian Democratic, and so on) that one finds in local and national elections for public office.

Elections are so routine and ubiquitous they do not, as in other democracies, appear to interrupt the more "normal" aspects of daily living. For most Italian citizens, to vote is as natural as it is to get up in the morning and go to school or work. Citizens may arrive at the polling place to cast a blank or invalid ballot, but they participate nevertheless.

To my mind, the act of voting does not mean in Italy what it does elsewhere. It is not just the urge to win or the fear of defeat that brings out the voters. Nor is it, as some Italians claim, the fear of communism. Of course, some vote for this reason, just as others do so out of a sense of civic duty. As I see it, the Italian citizen goes to the polls primarily to "give testimony." The difference is enormous.

When the average citizen votes here, it is "to witness," as this term is understood, for example, in fundamentalist religious groups. The polling booth is a place where the average Italian is able to assert, to reaffirm—to give testimony—as to his or her "political identity." The act of voting is not as public as the evening stroll, the ubiquitous passeggiata, but it serves a similar purpose. Both acts are intended to establish or to reconfirm, for oneself as well as for others, who one is.

This identity—who and what one is, politically speaking—extends far beyond one's membership in or support for a given political party. It is associated with the "political subculture" to which each person belongs. This act of reaffirming one's political identity (Communist, Socialist, or just plain left; Catholic or Christian Democratic; Republican, Liberal, or just plain laical) occurs without any expectation that it will bear directly on the formation of government and the selection of a prime minister. Had voters, particularly those on the left, ever entertained any such thought, they would have abandoned the voting booth decades ago.

Something else is afoot here. The impulse to vote transcends and therefore is not dampened by the knowledge that votes rarely have more than a marginal effect on government or that, whatever the outcome, it is unlikely that certain parties will be included in a governmental coalition. One welcomes the opportunity to give "public" expression to personal political identity. One prefers company in doing so; but the mere fact of being small, or outside the majority, does not lead to political apathy and absenteeism. Indeed, it may well lead in the opposite direction, especially in a setting where no one expects the next government to survive more than a few months anyway.

High tension levels can distort this pattern of giving testimony on behalf of one's party. The best postwar example would be the elections of 1948, which took place on the heels of the Communist takeover in Czechoslovakia. As a result, the Italian elections degenerated into a forced choice between "Christ or communism." Millions voted "against their own identity" for the Christian Democrats in order to prevent the Communists and Socialists from winning. Later, most of these would return to "witness" their truer political identities.

A generation later, when it appeared that the PCI might become the main party and form a government, the distortion occurred again. Indro Montanelli, the distinguished editor of *Il giornale nuovo,* keenly aware that Italians prefer to "witness" and not necessarily to win, urged the voters to "hold their noses" and to vote for the Christian Democrats. Enough of them did to muffle the PCI's knock on the door of national government. As we will see in a moment, that tactic is a wasting asset.

The political identity discussed here should not be confused with what in the United States is called "party identification."[14] We are not talking about Italian equivalents of weak, strong, or die-hard Republicans or Democrats. We are not thinking of a special category of voters who have never supported but a single party and would not think of supporting any other. Nor is there any room, in this explanation of Italian political identity, for voters called Independents, who pridefully disclaim affiliation with any party.

We refer instead to those broad, but essentially separate, divisions of Italian society that are generally described as left, secular or laical, and

Catholic. Between and among these categories there is very little overlap. In any case, the typical Italian has no trouble at all specifying in which of these he or she belongs.

With the exception of the American South, and perhaps a few large cities earlier in this century, the United States has not had any noteworthy political subcultures. Furthermore, Americans somehow prize the so-called independent voters, whereas Europeans often see them either as spineless persons who cannot make choices or as fickle ones whose choices are ephemeral. In Italy, one gains a subcultural identity at birth. To lose it, or to be without one, may well imply that one lacks culture in the larger sense.

STABILITY AND CHANGE

Much has been written about Italy's political subcultures, and especially about how fragmented and mutually exclusive they are. For each of the major subcultures—the Marxist, Catholic, and laical—the political parties in these areas presumably represented only the tip of the iceberg. Below the surface, one expected to find families, work groups, friends and neighbors, school teachers, political patrons, and especially a large network of organizations that are integral parts of the subculture and work to reinforce it. In particular, organized groups like trade unions, religious organizations, producer and consumer cooperatives, and recreational and athletic associations were expected to provide daily reminders of the existence of each subculture. They also made it possible for members to live isolated from other subcultures.

It was a mistake to think that as Italy became more "modern," as the mass media served to shrink the size of the community and to homogenize values and tastes, as people became less isolated and more inclined to make contact across existing subcultures, the latter would gradually disappear. Today's Italians are clearly less isolated and parochial than in the past. They are more inclined to establish a wider range of social relationships with persons from different subcultures. The nature of the workplace; higher levels of education; greater travel to distant places; modified norms that apply to friendship and marriage: all of these things and more signal that once mutually exclusive subcultural compartments are today less so.

But political subcultures have remarkable staying power. This is so in part because, as noted earlier, the Catholic and Communist subcultures are "religiously" based. It is so, above all, because membership in one of the subcultures is a state of mind, a way of thinking about oneself, that makes it highly unlikely, for example, that a Christian Democrat can imagine that he or she would vote for a Communist or Socialist, and vice versa. The very high stability of Italian voting patterns, the relatively low proportion of "floating voters" who move about from one party to another, find their explanations here. It is in this setting that to "witness" in an election is more important than to "win" it.

In recent years, some scholars have challenged the idea that Italians do not change their political stripes, or that few of them shop around among parties at election time.[15] It is true, for example, that outcomes that look almost static from one election to another may hide a good deal of shifting on the part of voters. For example, in a two-party race in two consecutive elections, almost all of the voters might switch parties the second time and the latter outcome would look like the first. The new Italian information suggests that, far from marching monotonously lockstep with the same party time after time, perhaps as many as a quarter of the voters actually shift their votes from one party to another, but in complementary ways that bring about similar outcomes.

Even if this is so, it is equally clear that shifts rarely bring voters to cross subcultural boundaries. That is, voters disgruntled with the PCI may vote farther to the left, or cast blank or invalid ballots, or perhaps support the PSI. But they will not be found in the ranks of the parties of the center or the right. The same reasoning would apply to voters in the Catholic subculture who are loath to support left-wing parties. And, even among those parties that constitute the center, their supporters sometimes have to "hold their noses," when they shift to the DC. The center, after all, includes the laical parties that have their own ancient quarrels with organized Catholicism.

If the postwar vote has been cast primarily within these subcultures, it has not been entirely static. Beginning in the mid-1950s and for twenty years thereafter, the electoral ratio between parties of the center-right and those on the left was about five-to-four. From the mid-1970s to the present that ratio has shifted to one-to-one. Today, both the center-right and the left-wing groups of parties get about 45 percent of the total vote, and the remaining 10 percent goes to the right and to some minor parties.[16]

The DC remains the pivot of this system despite this shift and despite its own gradual decline. This has been made possible because, as noted earlier, the Socialist party under Craxi decided to move right, away from the PCI, leaving the latter high and dry. Thus, whereas the electorate seems to have moved left, governments have moved in the opposite direction. Pirandello would understand.

No matter how infected one may be by the Rashomon Syndrome, certain of the changes of the past four decades are impossible to deny. In the early 1950s for example, the PCI got about 23 percent of the vote; in more recent years, it reached almost 35 percent and now hovers at about 30 percent. During this same period, the DC went from a high of 48 percent to a more recent average of under 40 percent.

Several interesting phenomena are at work here. First, on average and between any two elections during the past four decades, the net shift in the vote among parties has been an amazingly low 1.6 percent. Second, except for the relatively mild shifts already noted, party results look astonishingly static. Third, this stability persists notwithstanding monumental changes in Italian society as well as equally remarkable changes in the electoral body itself.

In 1948, there were 29 million qualified voters, of which 27 million turned up at the polls that April. Almost 13 million of these citizens voted for the DC. In 1983, the number of qualified voters had climbed to 44 million, and in June of that year 38.5 million of them voted. The DC received just over 12 million of these votes. But the broad distribution of votes into right, center, and left clusters were about the same as in earlier elections.

Quite obviously, these two electorates, separated by thirty-five years, were radically different from each other. For example, the *youngest* of the 1983 voters who also voted in 1948 would have to have been at least fifty-six years old. Also, since in the mid-1970s the minimum voting age for the Chamber of Deputies was reduced from twenty-one to eighteen years, in 1983, unlike in 1948, there were several million persons from the eighteen-to-twenty-year age group whose 1948 counterparts could not legally vote.

The point is that a majority of those who voted in the late 1940s are no longer on the electoral roles. Some may have migrated out of Italy; others may now be members of the larger pool of nonvoters. But most were removed from the electoral rolls by death. We tend to overlook this last important fact when we compare outcomes of two or more elections. In these comparisons, we are never talking about the same electoral body.

That some voters die and new ones reach minimum voting age makes the near-static nature of electoral outcomes look that much more impressive. One reason for the persistence of older patterns is the existence of the subcultures and the propensity of the voters to "witness." It would be different if Italians treated the polling place as a supermarket where they might shop around for the political party that best suits today's taste or whim.

The so-called models of electoral choice and voting behavior that treat votes as money, and parties and candidates as purchases that the voters make, are inappropriate for Italy. Supermarkets exist in the Italian world of commerce, too. Even so, Italian consumers show that, regardless of price, they prefer the small boutiques downtown and the "ma-and-pa" stores in their own neighborhoods.

The gradual change in voting patterns and electoral outcomes that has occurred is therefore best explained by the slow, generational transformation of the electorate itself. The newest and youngest voters are quite different from the oldest voters and from former voters who have died. Since 1948, the electoral body has grown by about .5 million people each year. But this is the net figure; that is, it represents the difference between those who reach the minimum voting age (about 1.5 million annually) and those others (about 1 million) who have dropped out because of death or other reasons.

Looking back on the past forty years, we know that the newer generations of voters have tended to be somewhat more left-wing than earlier generations. An important consequence of this has been, on one side, the gradual erosion in the vote for the Christian Democrats and, on the other, an equally gradual gain in the vote for the left, particularly for the PCI.

The existence of this pattern refutes the old saw that as people age they also grow more conservative. Were this the case in Italy, in view of marked increases in longevity, we would expect to see a conservative drift in the electorate. But, as we have seen, the opposite is the case. A much more powerful idea is that people tend to vote for the party, or among the parties, that are represented by one's particular political subculture.

It is primarily the younger voters who have brought about some of the interesting electoral transformations of recent years. For example, they account for the reemergence of the Radical party in the 1970s, just as it is they who will determine whether a strong Green, or ecological, party finds roots in Italy. It is also these younger voters who may someday be more inclined than their predecessors to vote on the basis of issues, as opposed to parties. They have already demonstrated less tolerance than their elders for high-flown and vacuous political rhetoric and more openness toward those outside their individual subcultures.

This does not imply that the younger voters will be less partisan or less likely to develop political subcultural identities and political party choices that endure throughout life. We find, in this regard, that today's younger Italians are entirely and even fiercely clear about who they are and where they stand politically. This seems to be truer of younger Italians than of their counterparts in most other democracies. Thus all of the factors we have touched upon that contribute to distinctive subcultural identities and lifelong identification with parties of the left, center, or right remain quite prominent.

This being so, we should expect the overall results of Italian elections to change quite slowly, and only at the margins. Even if the latest group of newest and youngest voters turns out to be much more radical—to the left or right—than is true of the rest of the electorate, their impact would be minimal at first. It would become more prominent over time, but only if additional new voters were to share similar radical views. Barring catastrophic economic or military events, it would require a generation to feel the full effects of a radical shift in the electorate.

I am aware that this particular way of looking at things may also suffer from the Rashomon Syndrome. For example, it may imply the dubious assumptions that only the young get radical ideas or that their views will not infect their elders. However, I intend here only to stress that the sharp increase in the PCI vote in the mid-1970s was the direct and apparently one-time-only effect of a drop in minimum voting age that brought over three million new voters into the electorate at the same time. Most electoral changes move much more slowly.

What of the sharp drop in the DC vote in 1983? It may be that among those older voters who died between 1979 and 1983, there were disproportionate numbers of lifelong supporters of the DC. It may also be the case, as some DC leaders themselves claim, that the increase in both the number of nonvoters and of blank and invalid ballots hurt the DC more than others. It is also apparent that when newer small parties recruit primarily among those persons who are retired from work and/or on pensions, the votes they attract are disproportionately at the DC's expense.

Whatever the reasons for the sharp drop, the DC's decline should level off. Even more than the Communist party, the DC has a hard core of "true believers" who have never voted for any other party and probably never will. A recent upsurge in Catholic mass movements and organizations among the young suggests that this hard core is getting a new infusion. A burning question for the PCI is whether it can do as well with younger voters. The evidence so far is not very impressive on that score.

More than is true of most other democracies, then, we can anticipate that Italian elections will continue to produce relatively static results. Italians know this, and I believe that deep down they do not mind it. Is this a sign of weakness or instability in Italian democracy? Is the country really paralyzed, frozen into a pattern of politics labeled "polarized pluralism" that is dangerous for democracy?[17]

I don't think so. The polarization is more apparent than real; much of it is largely rhetorical—entirely in keeping with the model of Italian politics that I have been describing. Words and rhetoric are of course also the stuff of politics, and it would be silly not to pay attention to them. But we need to go behind the words as well, and especially behind those fire-eating ideological phrases that are the staple of political discourse. Behind them, at the operating level, we find much more collaboration among the politicians and political parties than anyone looking only at surface behavior might imagine.

In the Big Spettacolo of Italian politics, communication is marked by inflated rhetoric. When the words turn virulent, many of them are directed at the institutions of government and, above all, at la classe politica. Were we to accept the words at face value, this class would appear to be the main problem, indeed the bane, of Italian politics.

As a matter of fact, it is nothing of the kind. A closer look will tell us why.

6

CRISIS AND LA CLASSE POLITICA

The word *la crisi*, crisis, is heard in Italy almost as frequently as ciao or pasta. You will not find it on the menu of your favorite trattoria; but when the waiter explains why the pasta is overcooked, the service is so bad, or your favorite dish is not available, he will almost certainly refer to la crisi. He might intend by this the chef's state of mind, the low wages the restaurant pays, or the fact that the truck farmers are on strike. Or he might mean that he himself is in crisis. If he talks long enough, he will almost certainly claim that the government is in crisis and, for this reason, is the root cause of whatever is not working well at the moment.

Italians are expert at using a vague and general reference to la crisi to explain everything from a late arrival at dinner to runaway inflation or the aftermath of a major earthquake. The approach makes sense. Even when we discount for hyperbole, there are still enough crises around to make any farfetched explanation sound entirely reasonable. Travelers find evidence of crisis in unkept train schedules, in canceled airline flights, and in singular baggage-handling procedures in the major airports. Open any daily newspaper at random and you are certain to find several crises reported there. The government is always in trouble, stumbling from one crisis to another. The public services are massively in crisis. Where health is concerned, only the most destitute will, with great fear and reluctance, seek assistance in public hospitals. They know that doctors and nurses may go on strike, leaving even the seriously ill to fend for themselves. Their family members often wind up as nurses or caterers of food to and from hospital wards.

Despite the abysmal quality of public services, Italians are careful to complain, if at all, from a distance. As we saw earlier, common prudence dictates avoidance of any direct contact with governmental officials. One tries to operate through intermediating patrons and organizations. Physical contact with the bureaucracy means entering the world of Franz Kafka, peopled by officials who are unrivaled in the number of diabolical indignities they can heap on hapless citizens. Visitors to Italy are enraged when they are the victims of such experiences. Italians display a cynical but nevertheless remarkable patience about them.

On the heels of President Reagan's Star Wars defense proposals, the French countered with the idea that European countries themselves should build supercomputers that would make possible strategic defense decisions in billionths of a second. An Italian editorial writer responded that this would be great, even fantastic, but in the year 2000, how many days will it take to move a letter from Aosta to Potenza; how many months before an Italian citizen receives his or her pension or renewed driver's license? "What good are the stars," he asked, "if the postal system isn't working? While people hear the year 2000 ballyhooed, they live their daily lives with services that remain eighteenth-century."

Traffic snarls, crowded beaches, polluted waters no one should swim in but many do, public museums that close down for years on end, wildcat strikes ingeniously timed to coincide with peak Italian or tourist demands for goods and services—these and many other occurrences underscore that things could be much better than they are. It takes a good deal of courage to argue that things are better than they seem.

CRISIS, CRISIS EVERYWHERE

As Italians themselves would have it, essentially everything is in crisis.[1] From the balance of payments to the Italian lira, from basic industries to agricultural production. The whole south is said to have been languishing in crisis for well over a century. Religion is in crisis, too, as evidenced by a decline in church attendance and other religious practices. Youth is in crisis, largely, but not exclusively, because it is unable to find work. Women are in crisis, because the country has not yet managed to assure them full equality with the other gender. So many of the institutions of government are said to be in crisis that the republic itself seems headed toward a permanent sunset.

Name the category, and almost anyone will volunteer to provide, in minute detail, evidence that it, too, is in crisis. The schools and the arts, housing and the retail trade, the labor unions and the tax system, the aged, lawyers and architects, the theater and textiles, the soccer teams and the national lottery, the secret services and the prisons, university research, the system of justice, and the Italian language itself—all are said to be in crisis. Even Italy's system of values, infected by consumerism and other signs of decadence, is supposed to be in crisis. High fashion and the Fiat Company for the moment are said not to be in crisis, but wiser heads know that this is only a temporary state, to be followed later by even more dire trouble.

These claims easily give one the impression that the country is poised, unsteadily, at the brink of chaos. If disaster fails to materialize, many are ready to explain that the country is somehow under the tutelage of *lo stellone*, that large guiding star that prevents it from going over the precipice.

This catastrophic orientation to life is leavened by last-minute remissions reminiscent of *The Perils of Pauline*. This does not mean that Italians are perverse or that they forever cry wolf in order to demonstrate how clever and resourceful they are in overcoming adversity. By now, enough real disasters have afflicted the peninsula to make any alleged crisis appear entirely credible. Not only Italians believe that the country's last-minute escapes are evidence of lucky stars and virtuoso performances. The years since World War II abound in examples of lifesaving measures taken at exactly those moments when things looked beyond repair. If nothing else, this way of life is free of tedium.

LA CLASSE POLITICA AS CULPRIT

Ask any Italian about the cause of any particular crisis, and the words *la classe politica* will appear in the reply.[2] This is one of the reasons why the pollsters believe that Italian democracy and its institutions are on shaky footing. By and large, the citizenry does think of this class as the "heavies" in the dramas played out in almost every walk of life. As heavies, members of the political class also tend to be the fall guys for anything that displeases or goes wrong. In the unlikely event a kind word has ever been spoken about la classe politica, there is no trace of it.

Who constitute this much-maligned group, and why are they the objects of so much hostility?

Italians commonly distinguish between la classe politica, or the political class, and *la classe dirigente*, or the ruling class.[3] The two are obviously related, in the sense that the political class—those who control the political apparatuses and processes of the country—are largely drawn from the other, broader category.

The ruling class are the elites or recognized leaders of one or more sectors of society. The leading industrialists, landowners, bankers, educators, newspaper owners and editors, trade unionists, motion picture producers, book publishers, writers, owners and managers of professional athletic teams, clergymen, lawyers, doctors, architects, engineers and other professionals, owners and managers of the broadcast media, and other categories we might add, as well as the persons who hold major political and bureaucratic positions are members of the ruling class.

These elite categories exist everywhere and are found in regional and local as well as national communities. The elite of a small town or city, of course, may not qualify as members of the ruling class of the whole nation. When we think "ruling class," we are really thinking about persons we know as VIPs at their respective levels of influence and power.

Italians mean by la classe politica a specific subset of such elites: those persons who occupy key positions in political parties and in elective and appointive public office. This does not seem to make complete sense; it creates the erroneous impression that public policies and the political management of the country are largely in the hands of such persons. We know that reality is quite different, not only in Italy but in all democracies. Some persons and organizations, without the slightest trace of public status or governmental authority, nevertheless exercise enormous influence over public policies, from their enactment through their administration.

Italy's leading capitalists, often referred to as the *razza padrona*, or master race, fall into this category.[4] As a group, intellectuals—the prime opinion makers—are in it. University students are in it, too, along with trade union leaders, professors, fashion designers, clergymen, and members of the liberal professions. Art critics, too, and scientists, leading soccer players as well as distinguished actors, actresses, journalists, magistrates, military officers, and television personalities.

The category is like an accordian; it can be expanded or contracted, depending on who is using it and on whether we are talking about a city or province or the whole nation, and so on. Above all, the political patrons, whether or not they have official status as party leaders or public officials, fall into the category of those who count. So, when we encounter

Italian references to the political class, we should be aware that they refer to a relatively small and specialized segment of those who really run the country.

SINNERS OR SCAPEGOATS?

It takes a thick skin to become and remain a member of the political class. Attacks come from every conceivable sector of society. To some extent, the political parties try to blunt these attacks by going out of their way to recruit candidates to public office who are prominent members of some of the other elite categories. The Communist party pioneered this approach and made much of the fact that leading scientists, intellectuals, artists, writers, and other professionals were willing to run as Independents under the PCI label. Other parties quickly followed suit with distinguished candidates of their own. Under Bettino Craxi, the PSI created a national council consisting largely of several hundred elites from nonpolitical walks of life. This organization is devoid of effective power; but it provides the PSI with some patina and perhaps with some protection against criticism over the depths of scandal to which some members of the Socialist political class have fallen.

One of the country's favorite pastimes, then, is to take the name of la classe politica in vain. When someone makes a scathing remark of this kind, however, personal friends, neighbors, and members of one's political party, trade union, or professional association may well be exempted. La classe politica then becomes "they," those other people, those incompetents and mischief-makers. Certainly not "we," I or my close friends, but those others, known and unknown members of la classe politica who are at the bottom of the worst crises that beset Italy.

It can be confusing to hear a perfectly obvious, prominent, powerful member of Italy's ruling class excoriate la classe politica as if he or she were in no way responsible for the political or economic condition of the country. Newspaper editors and political journalists, intellectuals, and university professors are especially prone to this sort of confusion. Leading industrialists do the same thing, but often with tones of self-righteousness that quickly give the game away. There is much unintended irony and self-deception in all of this. It also looks disingenuous when the same persons who push public policies in one direction or another nevertheless pile the blame for failures of policy on the political class.

Is la classe politica, then, just a scapegoat? Do the frequent references to it mean only that Italians have found an all too convenient way of denying, or escaping from, their own responsibilities in a democratic society? Do the frequent, ubiquitous negative references to this group establish that Italians are indeed politically alienated and that they lack civic culture? Does it really make sense to argue, as many do, that the "real" country is sound, while the "legal" country, which includes the political class, is wallowing in decadence? In short, how much of what the Italians say about la classe politica should we take at face value?

Frankly, I am not sure. It depends. Everyone scapegoats at one time or another. We all tend to look elsewhere for the causes of those aspects of society, and of our own lives within it, that we find unpalatable or worse. Furthermore, it is typical of democracies, and not a sign of pathology, that citizens within them believe, at some level, that they are better, sounder, less open to moral and other forms of corruption than the politicians and officeholders who govern them. Walter Bagehot, a famous nineteenth-century commentator on British politics, once wrote that British citizens preferred to be governed by their "betters." This statement was largely a figment of Bagehot's aristocratic imagination. He confused his wish with reality. If he ever did eavesdrop on the British common man's (or woman's) evaluation of the British ruling or political class, he either misunderstood or repressed what he heard.

Nevertheless, Italy does appear different, not only in the frequency of hostile references to la classe politica but also in the vehemence with which each condemnation is expressed. Even so, in view of what I have said in preceding pages, it would not seem a good idea to accept all of this at face value. By now, criticism is so ritualized, so well integrated into the citizen's role, we cannot be sure how much of it is deeply felt. More to the point, we lack anything like persuasive evidence that these hostile expressions have negative or erosive implications for democracy.[5]

MEASURING EFFECTS

How would we measure such consequences? We know that the test of participation in elections will not take us very far. This would be so even were we to accept the argument that all of those who abstain from going to the polls or who vote blank or invalid ballots there constitute a "third

party," arrayed against the republic. In fact, most forms of political participation suggest that the democratic fabric is very strong.

The presence of the Mafia will not do either as a measure. That
organization has been around for centuries; it has always been able to
count on the more or less willing "collaboration" of a small fraction of
the population, and some public officials under every Italian regime,
including the fascist, have fallen into corrupt relationships with it. If
anything, in recent years the national government, with the collaboration
of the Vatican and the United States government, has shown an uncommon resolution to take on the Mafia, in Sicily and elsewhere. This campaign could not proceed were it not for widespread support among the
citizenry.

What about political terrorism? Is not its appearance and explosive
growth in the 1970s pretty good evidence that some of the condemnation
of la classe politica is in dead earnest, and has deadly consequences for
the system? Yes, and no. Terrorism, after all, emerged elsewhere in Europe
at the same time. It was not a reflection, therefore, of something uniquely
awry with Italian democracy. Indeed, we have since come to realize that
terrorism of one type or another is now, alas, a normal aspect of the
political process. In addition, terrorism is not necessarily an indication of
the widespread antagonism of citizens toward the political class that governs them.

Terrorism in Italy is so striking and important a political development
that we will treat it separately in the next chapter. We can acknowledge
here that it could not have mushroomed as it did were it not for tens of
thousands of Italians, many of them disgusted and angry with the state,
who gave terrorists aid and comfort. Equally striking, terrorism also served
to demonstrate that la classe politica was not without quite obvious merit
and that millions of others were willing to support its struggle to bring
the terrorists to heel. During the worst of the "leaden years," thoughtful
Italians discovered that, all things considered, they didn't find la classe
politica all that bad. In this sense, terrorism did not weaken Italian democracy; it strengthened it.

We might try tax evasion as evidence that Italians in large numbers
disdain the political class and, partly as a consequence, choose this dramatic way of expressing their rejection of civic virtue. There is, no doubt,
some truth to that, too. But tax evasion is another of those gray areas
where it is not easy to say whether the act itself is considered condem-

natory by those who commit it or, for that matter, by others who do not.

My sense is that the Italian national state is probably collecting all of the taxes it can, or dares, without introducing very serious instability into the system. This is so because tax evasion is really an unspoken understanding, a contract, among millions of Italians. It is a form of collusion, of live and let live, whereby everyone assumes that he or she will be left alone, within reason, if others are treated similarly. Italy is not the kind of culture that produces bounty hunters, in the shape of informers to the tax authorities, who get a percentage of what the latter may extract from tax delinquents.

Furthermore, like so many aspects of this political system the outsider may find anomalous, there is something fundamentally democratic about tax evasion; one way or another, the practice is open to a very large proportion of the adult population. It is true, of course, that those on fixed wages and salaries cannot evade, but this applies only to one's first— and not second or third—job. Those who are working in the second and unreported economy include hundreds of thousands of blue-collar workers or members of their families. As for fiscal reform and better methods for collecting the actual taxes owed, entirely respectable economists, including those on the political left, have urged the government to go slow lest it introduce unwanted disequilibrium into both the economy and the political system.

What about the Communist party? Time was when the existence of the PCI, its two million members and its attractiveness to almost one of every three voters, were taken as strong indicators of widespread alienation among citizens or as evidence of popular disgust with the political class. Americans in particular tend to believe that a vote for a Communist party, anywhere, is a sure sign of political pathology. One of the first postwar American books on Italian communism argued that Italians who supported it at the polls were expressing desperate political feelings. Another early American analysis of the appeals of communism treated both Communist leaders and those who were attracted to them and the PCI as a form of neurosis.

Interpretations of this kind emerged in the heat and smoke of the Cold War, when vision on both sides was blurred by ideology and each side used oversimplification as a means of making highly nuanced parts of the picture appear artificially sharper. We now know better. It may be that some small minority of the PCI leaders, and of those who vote for that party, remain die-hard Stalinists and, in any case, enemies of the democratic republic. As for the rest, it requires equally rigid and unmitigated anticommunism not to acknowledge that the PCI, its leaders as well as its followers and voters, represent not just adherents but also mainstays of Italian democracy.

One problem with measuring the meaning and the consequences of attacks on the political class is that these attacks are almost exclusively verbal. They involve expressions of attitude or opinion and not the actual behavior of the citizens. We hear these attitudes, often very heated, voiced in conversations about politics; we read about them in editorials and other political commentary; the pollsters learn about them when they conduct public opinion surveys.[6]

Rarely, if ever, has the Italian citizen been asked by anyone, "Well, if you think that the political class is so rotten, what have you done or what will you do about it?" Whenever I have asked this question, the typical response has been either a vague "Bisogna rinnovarla" (We have to renew or replace it) or a deceptively fatalistic "Pazienza. Non c'e niente da fare" (Never mind. Nothing can be done). We are left with the suspicion that here, too, as in so many other aspects of politics, we should be asking what it is, other than what appears to be most obvious, that the attacks on the political class might signify.

ANOTHER INTERPRETATION

My view of the relationship between crises, real or imagined, the widespread condemnation of la classe politica, and the failure of this presumed alienation of the citizenry to show itself in demonstrable pathologies, is that this aspect of politics has positive, not negative, implications for democratic stability. Beyond the need to find a scapegoat, to point the finger of accusation elsewhere, and beyond the simple idea of the utility of a verbal escape valve, Italians seem to require in political discourse, and to enjoy using, very abstract categories. The country's two political religions, Catholicism and Marxism, abound in these. Catholic intellectuals typically produce the most abstruse writings about politics and society. They are rivaled by those on the left who have long since come to believe that politics is almost entirely about the words that intellectuals speak and write for each other. Italians in the so-called laical tradition are scarcely better off, mesmerized and cowed as they are by Benedetto Croce's imperious way of laying down the laws and interpretations of politics and history. In the curial, nuanced, coded language of politics discussed earlier, abstract categories enjoy special prominence.

La classe politica is an abstraction of an abstraction; it is more serviceable than the bourgeoisie or the ruling or working class, because it creates the illusion of concreteness. It is similar to words like state, civil society, *congiuntura* (a truly untranslatable word), historical moment, *integralismo* (another untranslatable word), praxis, and many others that could be added. Unlike many of these terms, however, la classe politica is doubly useful: it not only creates the illusion of concreteness; it can often be used to allude to specific, but nevertheless unnamed, persons.

In this last sense, la classe politica is a safe term. It permits the most ferocious, outspoken attacks on political miscreants without having to name any of them, and therefore without creating any serious threat of reprisal. This is no mean advantage in a country where political reprisals directed against individuals are a well-understood aspect of the political process. One can assault la classe politica with impunity; it is quite another kind of game when the target has a first and last name and turns out to be a powerful member of the political class. Even journalists, who have a professional and moral responsibility to name names (which many of them certainly do, sometimes with astonishing abandon), learn to be circumspect in this regard.

Frequent references to the political class are also a consequence of the absence in Italy of *government* and *opposition* as these terms are commonly understood in other democracies. The closest thing to government would be the Christian Democratic party, because of the hegemonic control of major institutions it has so far maintained. For this reason, the DC often stands as a surrogate for la classe politica. Italians who complain about the shortcomings of the political class will often specify that they mean to refer to the DC and its political mismanagement. Even so, when something does go wrong, it is extremely difficult to nail down exactly who, or which party, is responsible. In this circumstance, la classe politica serves as a convenient object or reference point for the citizen's ire.

Recall, for example, that under the system of rules and the practice that prevails in the national legislature, well over four-fifths of the laws passed are fully enacted in legislative committees. Not only is this form of lawmaking largely hidden from public view; it proceeds on the basis of a high degree of collaboration among the parties that compose the gov-

ernmental coalition and other parties that are supposed to be the opposition, loyal or otherwise, but in fact are not either. Even those
committee hearings on bills that will eventually go before the full legislature for debate are rarely open to the public. And in most instances
only a minimal official record is kept of what transpires in committee. If
the system of trasformismo is really to work, not much of it can be open
to public scrutiny.

This is an extraordinary, syncretistic form of passing laws and making
public policy. When these laws displease some segment of the public, or
are badly made, or have unintended negative consequences, it is natural
that dissatisfaction should be expressed not toward the government, or
the "ins," but, rather, toward la classe politica, as a broad category that
encompasses essentially everyone in public office. It could not be otherwise where it is next to impossible to determine who actually favored,
opposed, and then wound up passing so many different laws. It is worth
repeating that this system, far from encouraging political polarization,
has the effect of dampening centrifugal forces in the polity.

Attacks on the political class may also represent a variation on "failed
opportunities," an idea that is deeply imbedded in the Italian psyche. For
generations the intellectuals have hammered away at this theme and, in
the process, have instilled in the country a widespread sense of incompetency and guilt. Italy, after all, produced the Counter-Reformation.
The peninsula, led by the Vatican, became a bulwark against the Enlightenment. The French Revolution may have sent tremors around Europe,
but these petered out at the Italian Alps. Napoleon may have crossed the
latter, but the liberal revolutionary waves that followed in his wake barely
touched the shores of Piedmont and Lombardy. The Industrial Revolution, which triggered radical changes on the Continent, left most of
the peninsula relatively unscathed for almost two centuries.

Nationhood itself, around which so many of the above historical dramas
unfolded, came very late to Italy. Even here, those who united the
country—the political class—botched the job, and left the enduring legacy
of the great gap between north and south. In the two major wars of this
century, that same group reached the limits of incompetence: it demonstrated that Italy could diminish its international stature regardless of
the side on which it fought or how the war came out. As a result, the
feeling is widespread that Italy should shun foreign affairs, or risk yet
another ludicrous fiasco. As for political innovation, fascism seems to
many to have been Italy's sole and lamentable contribution.

Considerations and recitals of this kind require some convenient way of expressing the deep feelings of inadequacy that underlie them. On occasion, the comment will be self-lacerating: "noi italiani siamo fatti così" (that's the way we Italians are). Much more often, the reference will be to the political class as the group that has led itself, and with it the rest of the country, in the wrong direction. There is more than scapegoating to this form of expression, and it does not signal only a cynical passivity, or fatalism, about life and politics. It tells us, rather, that the Italians have developed a highly refined sense of understanding both the possibilities and the limits of politics. One way to remind the political elite of this is to keep it under a constant, sobering stream of highly articulate criticism. Democracy is vouchsafed by following a two-pronged strategy. First, do not demand too much of democracy itself. Second, do not encourage the political class to believe that the people will give them the credit they may rightly deserve for the country's political or other achievements.

POLITICS AS A PROFESSION

A further important aspect of the political class, and Italian reactions to it, is that many of its members who hold public office or who are political militants constitute a "professional" group. I mean by this that many Italians opt early in their adult lives for politics as a profession.[7]

These career choices have several implications for the people involved, as well as for society at large. For example, the political parties loom as very important in society; they are the key mechanisms through which the aspiring "pros" pursue and develop their careers. For a while after the birth of the republic, the labor unions represented a second important channel through which a political career might be developed. But the political party leaders took care of that competition a few years ago when they made it officially impossible for a person to hold simultaneously an elective office and a leadership position of consequence in one of the trade unions.

The present system gives the political party leaders, including the leaders of party factions, striking power over the aspiring political professionals. These latter must learn the rules of the system. Those rules are not written in black and white, but they are as clearly understood as are the norms that govern the modern corporation or the academic community.

Unlike almost every other career, though, politics and political parties do not offer "tenure." In fact, the political parties may well be the only organizations in Italy where professionals, even at fairly high levels, can be abruptly sacked, without notice, without specified cause, and without unemployment compensation.

Nevertheless, a politicized society implies that one or more political parties constitute its nerve center. Close association with the political party is a highly effective way to obtain high status and respect, as well as very high income, in other than political pursuits. Lottizzazione, that system for awarding highly sought after positions in industry, the mass media, the banks, the universities, and everywhere else except perhaps the clergy, hinges on the political parties. They are the filters through which the key members of the political class are sorted out and distributed among the most desirable occupations, the "gatekeepers" who control access to those things in life for which people compete. For this reason they are resented by some, feared by others, but respected by everyone as the crucial power brokers. Resentment, appropriately rendered prudent by fear, will be vented against the political class as an abstract category; but it is also to members of the same political class that the aspiring upwardly mobile, in and out of politics and government, will turn for assistance.

STABILITY GENERATOR

There is another important implication in this pattern. It is that members of the political class in this small-scale society are well-known personalities who are going to be around for a long time, and people know this. The early choices of party membership the professional and near-professional members of the political class make tend to be permanent. There may be a bit of horizontal movement, back and forth, from one party faction to another. There may even be schisms that lead some persons to form new parties. But there is almost zero movement out of one existing party into another, unless, as in the striking case of the postwar Action party, the organization itself dissolves.

This rigidity, this lack of occupational and career mobility, is true of society at large. By comparison with the United States, for example, there is infinitely less mobility among industrial managers who move from one company to another in search of rapid promotion or more interesting

work. Even in large-scale corporations with many operating divisions this
type of mobility is relatively rare. The same thing is true of ordinary
workers, who, for example, are not inclined to leave their hometowns or
places of residence in order to go where the jobs may be. As for those
who are forced to migrate, they do so with great reluctance and almost
always with the intention of returning "home" someday.

Almost everywhere, in private as well as in public employment, the
Italian tends to "sign on" for life. This is the essence of what the Italian
means by the expression *essere sistemato*, literally, to be "fixed up" for the
long pull. And preferably in one's hometown, close to one's own political
subculture, and in a government job that gives lifetime tenure. This profoundly conservative spirit may be changing with the newer generations,
but only very slowly. Attitudes of this kind also help to explain the lack
of electoral mobility discussed in an earlier chapter.

The political class reflects the same pattern. Those who get into it do
not expect to be transients, even if some of them do fall by the wayside.
Its more enduring members, particularly the most prominent, are well
known to everyone. Political cartoonists can caricature literally hundreds
of them without name tags and without fear that they will be unrecognized
by the public. The term political class is thus abstract and concrete at the
same time, and one has considerable leeway in imagining who represents
its incarnation.

Over the past forty years, the political class has expanded considerably.
A conservative estimate today would place it at several hundred thousand
persons, most of whom are in fact "pros," who spend their lives doing
politics. Independents, those interlopers who come into politics late, who
crash the political stage, or who make cameo appearances there, are relatively unknown. The political pros begin as ingenues; they typically tie
themselves to one or more of the seasoned performers; they pass through
very typical career stages, even though some of the more talented may
well skip over a few of these. The nerve center of this system, the main
stage, is located at Rome, much to the chagrin of cities like Turin or
Milan.

We are back to the Globe Theatre. La classe politica are the professional
performers. The groundlings, those citizens out there who are spectator-
performers themselves, seem to be saying that the pros have not performed
very well. They do not fully mean this. Indeed, as we shall see in a moment,
there is a lot of evidence that the professionals have done quite well, and
that this is widely recognized, even by their fiercest critics.

More important, the political class as just described, with its well-understood rules and norms and with its much increased number of lifetime professionals, has brought the peninsula a degree of homogeniety that is without precedent. The national bureaucracy certainly never served this purpose. Today, more than ever in the past, it is a bureaucracy overwhelmingly peopled by southerners. This makes public administration internally homogeneous, but it is scarcely the way to promote the greater amalgamation of the nation as a whole. Southern domination of the bureaucracy is one of the prime reasons for the unqualified hostility that northerners express toward "the government at Rome."

It is different with the postwar classe politica. Whether they originate from Milan or Naples, Turin or Palermo, Bologna or Reggio Calabria, Trento or Taormina, its members learn and live by the same norms. This is true regardless of what may be the ideological or other differences among its members. In their day-to-day dealings with each other, they have set rules and standards that, all things considered, add up to a polyarchical democratic system, but with specific characteristics that are found in Italy and not necessarily anywhere else.

A CONSOCIATIONAL DEMOCRACY?

The system I am describing should not be confused with what some writers call "consociational democracy."[8] It is true that, on the surface, Italy seems to meet some of the conditions of consociationalism. For a few years after the war, the national government was, in fact, a "grand coalition" that included all of the major parties except the neofascist. But since 1947 the Communists have been formally excluded from the cabinet; although they certainly have an influence over public policy, they do not enjoy a veto over it.

Elections based on proportional representation and coveted positions awarded on the basis of lottizzazione might suggest that the principle of "proportionality," another of the necessary ingredients of consociational democracy, is also found in Italy. Again, this is deceptive. No principle of proportionality applies to the allocation of senior positions in the public service, and there are segments of the bureaucracy, and of the state-owned banking and industrial sectors, from which exponents of certain political parties are systematically excluded.

Autonomy for geographic regions or groups, which a democracy built along consociational lines would require, is also missing. Italy is not a federal system like Canada or the United States, where states or provinces have a considerable amount of independent authority. The decentralization of certain powers to the regions has proceeded at a snail's pace, and the bureaucrats at Rome do everything in their power to slow down the process. Even regions like Sicily and Sardinia, granted autonomy under the constitution, scarcely elude the heavy bureaucratic hand of Rome.

Consociational democracy requires not only a lot of collaboration among a country's political elites; it implies that, in some basic sense, there exists a rule for making decisions that clearly protects the vital interests of all significant minorities. The essence of the Italian democratic system, however, lies in its fuzziness, in its avoidance of clear-cut distributions or delegations of power and authority, and, indeed, in its ability to function politically without benefit of any single decision rule. Italy is a far cry from a parliamentary system of the British variety, where majority and minority are unmistakable and where decision rules are clear-cut. But it is not a consociational democracy either.

Perhaps the strongest reason for not mistaking the system for consociational democracy is that Italian society does not consist of "pillars" that are fundamentally at war with each other. The country's political arrangements and norms of politics are responses to the unresolved problems of the Mezzogiorno, the gap between north and south; to "the problem of communism"; to the physical presence at Rome of the world center of Catholicism; to the recent experience with a fascist regime; and, of course, to the fact that, more than a century after unification, the state exists but not yet Italians, in the sense intended by the founding fathers.

The fact is that, unlike some countries described as consociational democracies, Italy does not require that its political elites collaborate in order to keep the system from blowing apart. Indeed, for all of the differences—of religious belief and practice, of ideology, of social class, of regional culture, of economics, or even of language—Italians remain among the least sectarian and most tolerant of people one will find anywhere. Historically they have lacked experience, as well as institutions, with which to give concrete meaning to the nation-state, to a *national* political system in which those who man the apparatus of the state understand, and are willing to operate by, a common set of norms.

POLITICAL CLASS ACHIEVEMENTS

During its first decades as a nation-state, the country was governed by two sets of norms, which, for want of another term, we will call northern and southern. In addition, some fundamental differences were apparent over conceptions of government and of the proper relationship between the state and religious organizations. The fascist regime tried to impose a new, national, set of rules (including new modes of salutation and verbal address among its subjects), but with farcical and then tragic outcomes. Furthermore, neither the Fascists nor the Historical Liberals before them succeeded in the creation of an integrated national system based on the existence of mass political parties and universal suffrage. The laical, Catholic, and Socialist subcultures were there. Indeed, they were increasingly well organized. Nevertheless, the peninsula still lacked a real nation-state, democratic or otherwise.

The postwar political class has clearly succeeded where the others failed. It is a remarkable achievement, given the conditions, already described, under which the republic began its journey four decades ago. Its mission is far from complete; witness the many problems, some severe, that still bedevil the country. Nevertheless, the transformation of a large-scale Communist party into an entirely valid and dependable element in a pluralist democratic system is an extraordinary achievement, as is the fact that, among West European democracies, Italy today is least harassed by a powerful, antidemocratic right-wing party.

Accomplishments of the political class have not been without costs, or without aspects that citizens of other democracies might well find unappetizing or disconcerting. To a great extent, as we have seen, la classe politica is relatively immune from outside checks of the kind that elections can provide. It is also a closed, tightly held group into which membership is obtained largely through the machinery of cooptation that is almost exclusively in the hands of the political parties. The parties have in turn colonized most of the other sectors of society, deeply politicizing them in the process. Without doubt, as I will later detail, so much of Italian society is now in the hands of the political parties that many critics believe that, perversely, they represent a threat to democracy rather than its mainstay. Some reform proposals, discussed in a later chapter, are explicitly designed to reduce party domination. But they will not be easy to enact.

It may well be that la classe politica comes under fire, and is blamed for almost any real or imagined ill, because it is so salient to whatever happens in the country. For exactly this same reason, though, it is doubtful—indeed, it is highly irrational to believe—that this same class is responsible for all of the negative and none of the positive side of the republic's postwar development. One way or another, openly or otherwise, grudgingly or not, it must also be given credit for many of the achievements that have been chalked up since the fall of fascism.[9]

Many other gains are noteworthy, sometimes breathtaking. A few will be mentioned here, if only to keep the overall picture in balance. Consider that this relatively young democratic state has been almost universally viewed as bogged down in permanent crisis. Words and phrases used to describe it include, but are not limited to, these: fragmentation, helplessness, paralysis, immobilism, confusion, lack of direction, polarization, indecision, scandal, corruption, apathy, alienation, venality, bad judgment, incapacity. Nevertheless, regarding this same political system, the following things are also true, and might provoke some thought.

From the state of economic and psychological collapse that afflicted the country at war's end, Italy has become the world's fifth-largest economy. This relative standing is not based on the official statistics, which would place Italy one or more places lower. But we saw much earlier, official estimates place at least a quarter of the country's real domestic product in the hidden, or unreported, economy.

Forty years ago, among the countries of Western Europe, Italian per capita income was right at the bottom, little better than one would find in much less developed countries like Spain, Portugal, Ireland, or Greece. On this measure today, Italians are immensely better off—about on a par with France and Belgium and, since 1986, ahead of the British. In terms of life's amenities, Italians are not pipe-dreaming when they boast of reaching and passing Scandinavian standards by the turn of the century.

This quantum leap forward in the standard of living is more apparent in the north than in the central or southern regions. But it is evident everywhere: in the still-growing number of automobiles that glut city streets and, on weekends and at vacation times, the country's outstanding system of superhighways. In what the consumer sees, and can afford to buy, in the markets and shops. In what the average Italian man eats, how he dresses, how much he saves, how many homes he owns, where and how often he vacations, and so on. A 1986 survey of thirty thousand families, conducted by the Central Institute of Statistics, led the major newspapers to conclude that if Italians are not living richer lives than those of people elsewhere in Western Europe or North America, the difference is only a hair's width.

Forty years ago, the country was overwhelmingly agricultural, and illiteracy levels were remarkably high, especially in the underdeveloped south, in sections of which more than 90 percent of adults qualified as illiterate. Today illiteracy is largely a thing of the past. Not only does a compulsory school system assure literacy to the newer generations; a massive program to remove illiteracy among older members of the population has worked.

Today Italy is an advanced industrial country, where the number of persons who work in agriculture has been drastically reduced, and where, as in many other democracies, the so-called tertiary employment sector is in rapid expansion. This radical transformation could not occur without equally major changes in older ways of doing things. Thus, the average size of the family has fallen, and industrial centers have emerged in places where only farmers and artisans were once employed. Indeed, despite the Vatican's unbending campaign on issues like birth control and abortion, Italy by 1986 was no longer replacing its population and had a birthrate lower than all other countries in Europe except Denmark and West Germany.

Furthermore, beginning in the late 1950s, Italy experienced one of the most remarkable population movements ever registered anywhere. I refer not just to the several million Italians who moved abroad in search of new work opportunities. This had happened before, and countries of the New World, like Brazil and Argentina but particularly the United States, were the clear beneficiaries of this outward flow of cheap labor. I refer instead to the several million Italians, often entire families, who pulled up their roots in the Mezzogiorno and transferred to northern cities and industrial centers to begin life anew there—often in circumstances of local hostility toward these *terroni*, or clodhoppers, unmatched in foreign countries that received immigrants.

With these economic and demographic transformations occurred, inevitably, changes in religious practice, basic values, and life-style. In less than three decades, Italy became not just a richer, less agricultural, more industrial society; it became a more urban and secular one as well. To be *secular* means to shed, or radically to change, older, well-established ideas about compulsory public education, marriage, procreation, abortion, divorce, exposure to the views and life-styles of others, separation of church and state, the relative responsibilities of spouses and their children, the nature of work and leisure, and so on.

Not only was illiteracy largely eradicated during these years; Italian universities opened up to more students at a pace that surpasses that of any other European country. In less than a decade, the number of students enrolled in higher education increased more than twelve times. This was, no doubt, much too rapid a rate of expansion, and it brought with it a rash of problems, some of them old ones blown out of proportion, others quite new. In retrospect, it is far from the case that mushrooming enrollments were either well managed by governmental and university authorities or beneficial for the students themselves. Nevertheless, this explosive change forever transformed one aspect of Italy—higher education—that once worked to assure that only the tiniest fraction of the population could aspire to be upwardly mobile.

In the past forty years, Italy not only caught up with other democracies that were hard at work creating, or "perfecting," the welfare state; in many ways it far surpassed most of them. The welfare state is now under attack, not only by Ronald Reagan or Margaret Thatcher but generally within those democracies where, until recently, it did not have a bad name at all. It has come in for criticism in Italy, too. Some critics claim that once the architects of welfare belatedly got underway there, they created a monstrosity.

Defects there certainly are, and some of them (for example, in public health services) are truly staggering. Nevertheless, during the 1960s and 1970s Italy put a floor under poverty, greatly improved opportunities for higher education, provided a vast network of health and other forms of social insurance, rendered unemployment immensely less traumatic than it once was, and provided millions of Italians with protections and benefits that put some real meaning into sections of the republic's constitution that, in very specific and unprecedented terms as far as such documents go, call for exactly such results.

In the matter of housing, for those who do not own their own homes, Italy has had for many years now a fair-rent law that must surely be unique and is, in any case, the kind of legislation that drives landlords to distraction. Under this law, not only do rents increase only very gradually; once installed, tenants are next to impossible to evict even if they fail to pay rent.

These protections are available to foreigners as well, including those who, like thousands of reasonably well fixed Italians, could (and on moral grounds should) pay more rent than they do. Many Americans who are longtime residents in Rome occupy spacious apartments that fifteen years ago cost them $150 per month, say, and now cost them double, maybe triple, that amount. At going rates, however, these apartments would easily rent at $1,500 or $2,000 per month were it not for rent controls. Along with Italian renters, these Americans complain bitterly about avaricious landlords who are bent on having them evicted.

Where wages are concerned, Italy in the mid-1970s redesigned its scala mobile, or escalator clause on automatic wage increases, so that its effects turned out to be surprisingly perverse. That is, as inflation forced up prices, wages at some levels climbed at even faster rates, setting a vicious circle in motion. As a result, and whether intended or not, the scala mobile turned out to be one of the most effective, and radical, instruments for the redistribution of income!

This occurred for reasons well known to economists. For example, the method adopted for assigning increases resulted in higher rates of increase at the lower than at the upper end of the wage scales. The effect of this was to narrow or to "flatten" the differentials between the highest- and lowest-paid workers. Thus, whereas in 1975 the wage differential between a skilled and a manual industrial worker may have been 3-to-1, by 1985 that differential had fallen to about 1.8-to-1. This happened in salaried jobs, too. In 1975 a full professor was paid about four times as much as a beedle or a secretary; ten years later they were all being paid about the same thing. How you felt about this depended, of course, on where you were at the beginning. The time within which this occurred was accelerated because the inflation rate and increases were calculated four times each year.

Another factor, strictly speaking not a formal part of the escalator clause, was "fiscal drag." This problem is also found in other countries where the income tax is "progressive" and where inflation has the effect of pushing up wages and salaries. As nominal wages increase, people tend to get pushed into new and higher tax brackets. They earn more but, because of inflation and the higher tax brackets they get into, their real wages actually go down. In Italy these two factors working in tandem produced the most unexpected effects.

The upshot of the changes and policies I have just described is that Italy in recent years has experienced a marked increase in economic and material equality. In fact, close examination of the dimensions of equality would almost certainly show that there is more of it in Italy than one will find in other democracies, like those of the United States, France, West Germany, or Great Britain, and perhaps as much of it as one finds in Scandinavia, where, presumably, the welfare state, guided by democratic socialism, has reached its apogee. The Italians did not get there by a slavish adherence to someone else's formula or road map, but get there they did, even though not everyone in Italy enjoyed the trip.

The point of this recitation, of course, is that it did not just happen by chance in this land of miracles that keep everyone gasping. Modern Italy, democratic Italy, well-off Italy, did not emerge, like Minerva, from the brow of Jove. Someone had an idea or concocted a formula, someone else drew a road map, others volunteered, or were impressed, to do the driving. Along the way there were surprises and adventures, road blocks and detours, failures of will, as well as moments of great courage and inventiveness. There were also failures of specific plans that had to be redrawn again, from scratch.

The Italians who engineered all of this were, largely even if not exclusively, members of la classe politica. If whatever was, is, or will remain wrong with the country is to be laid at the feet of the political class, it is contrary to fact, mean, and the height of disingenuousness to insist that whatever is right happened without the political class's participation and, perhaps, in spite of it. The truth is that, in addition to its already considerable achievement of making the Italian democratic state a reality, la classe politica has shown how primary political rights and the democratic process can be used to improve the material and, in my view, the moral condition of the peninsula's inhabitants.

If there ever occurs a real crisis for Italian democracy, it will grow out of the failure of the Italians themselves to recognize how far the country has come and how important has been the much-maligned political class in this transformation. I see relatively little chance of any such occurrence, though. This is so not just because so much of politics is, in fact, spettacolo. It is so because Italian citizens, singly and in groups, display a number of characteristics that make the Italian brand of the democratic state entirely viable, enduring, and even enviable.

If this judgment is even moderately persuasive, it makes all the more puzzling the violent assaults on the Italian state carried out by the Revolutionary Armed Nuclei, the Red Brigades, and several other terroristic groups.

7

POLITICAL TERROR

Aldo Moro may have believed it was time to bring the Communists back under the umbrella of national government. But his commitment to the "historic compromise," as the operation was called, was not so strong that he was prepared to die for it. This reluctance is apparent in the letters he wrote from the still-unidentified place of his imprisonment—letters he addressed to his wife, Eleanora; to his political protégé and friend, Francesco Cossiga, now president of the republic; and to members of his party, Christian Democracy.

Moro's abduction on March 16, 1978, plunged the country into a worldwide drama. This was no ordinary crisis, nor the kind of hyped-up political melodrama Italians have come to experience to the point of bored indifference; the Red Brigades (BR) had managed to abduct the then most important figure in Italian politics. Despite the efforts of five bodyguards who died in the ambush and shootout, the operation was executed with military precision. Right to the end of the fifty-four-day confrontation, the BR claimed the right to "execute" their prisoner if the state refused to negotiate with this most feared of the country's terrorist organizations.[1]

The BR sees a state of war between themselves and the republic. In their eyes, Moro was nothing more than one of the most prominent "enemies of the people," a tool of the imperialistic American multinationals, captured in mortal combat. Having "tried" and found him guilty of the most unspeakable crimes, the BR notified the political class that the only remaining question was whether the sentence of death would be carried out.

Seen in this light, Moro was only a tragic symbol around whom this political drama was played out. During the agonizing weeks of his captivity, the spotlight focused on many others: on the political parties and their leaders, compelled to decide whether the state should refuse to negotiate with an enemy simply on the grounds that he carried the label terrorist, rather than soldier or something else; on members of the Moro family, engaged in a desperate, lonely struggle to save Moro's life; on an errant president of the republic, so weighted down by the Lockheed Scandal that he must already have been preparing his letter of resignation; and on many others, well meaning or goulishly self-serving, who got into the act.

As we shall see, the mass media played a key role in this affair, not just as vehicles for the gathering and diffusion of information but rather as first-person protagonists who, wilfully or otherwise, managed to instrumentalize this tragedy to their own purpose. Much of the press, and especially the print media, sought to use Moro's abduction and protracted imprisonment, his searing and often pathetic letters, his "trial," and finally his "execution" to political advantage. Furthermore, without the cooperation of the mass media, the Moro case might not have become such a memorable example of politics-as-spettacolo. No one understood this better than Mario Moretti, one of the BR's founding leaders. Moretti was the real director of events—from the bloody, expertly executed abduction in Via Fani, up to the point where, perhaps, he lost control to those among Moro's BR jailers who opted for political murder.

VARIETIES OF TERROR

To regard political terror as mere theater is to remain indifferent to those who are its victims and to ignore its potentially disintegrative implications, especially for a democratic state. In the years since the mindless bombing in Milan's Piazza Fontana in December 1969, hundreds of Italians have been kidnapped, "kneecapped" or otherwise maimed or wounded, and many have been killed by terrorist organizations of the extreme left or right.[2] Thousands of Italians looked the other way in the face of terroristic acts, and some citizens gave terrorists other forms of aid and comfort. Many more were intimidated in subtle ways—reflected, for example, in the deserted streets of the major cities at hours when they ordinarily teem with human activity.

Terrorism peaked during the late 1970s, when the Italian government launched a remarkably successful campaign to bring the terrorists to heel. If nothing else, Moro's martyrdom warned the republic just how potentially lethal the terrorists' war against the state had become. It should have underscored as well that democracy's most pernicious enemies are often those who wear their "democratic" credentials on their sleeves.

Now that most of the older generation of terrorist leaders are behind bars or living in Paris, where they enjoy a benign and perplexing asylum courtesy of the French government, it would be a mistake to think that the problem is entirely under control. Just as Italy began to relax, and even to congratulate itself on this score, a time bomb went off on a fast train moving through a tunnel between Florence and Bologna. Scores of passengers were killed or injured. This massacre, typical of right-wing terrorism, occurred just before Christmas 1984. Three months later, in broad daylight on the campus of the University of Rome, left-wing terrorism struck. Two members of the BR's Roman Column fired a spurt of fifteen rounds into the body of Ezio Tarantelli, a professor of economics.

From the BR's standpoint, Tarantelli was an obvious target. He was the author of modifications in the scala mobile that the Craxi government eventually adopted as official policy. The "freeze" Tarantelli's plan placed on wage increases was easily defined by the BR as an act against the working class. Similarly, Gen. Licio Giorgieri, assassinated in March 1987, was singled out because of his responsibilities in the North Atlantic Treaty Organization and the space defense program. But the Red Brigades also strike for no apparent reason, as in early 1986 when they struck down Lando Conti, a former deputy mayor of Florence.

Italy has also drawn worldwide attention in connection with international terrorism. Italy in general, and the city of Rome in particular, have more than their share of terrorists associated with the Middle East. These killers have claimed lives in the international airport at Rome, murdered each other on the Via Veneto, and used Italy as a staging area or safe haven for their operations in the Mediterranean Basin. When Arab terrorists hijacked the Italian cruise ship *Achille Lauro* in October 1985, they caused a major confrontation between Italy and the United States and Egypt. American overreaction to Italian handling of this case was so severe that it nearly brought down the Italian government. The episode also demonstrated how radically democracies can differ in the delicate matter of selecting the weapons to use against terrorists.[3]

No one knows better than the Italians that terrorism confronts the democratic state with a fundamental challenge—not to its physical integrity but rather to the strength of its moral commitment to democratic institutions and processes. It may be that all terrorists intend to destroy the fundamental underpinnings of the political systems that are their targets. Few of them can believe that this will ever be achieved by a direct violent confrontation between themselves and the state's police and military apparatus. Their basic aim, therefore, is to defeat democracy by demoralizing it.

If right-wing terrorists murder indiscriminately, and those on the left handpick their targets, the international terrorists make no such distinctions. Furthermore, whereas most of the international terrorists found in Italy are basically concerned with Israel, Libya, and the Middle East and have no particular Italy-directed axe to grind, the internal terrorists are almost exclusively preoccupied with the Italian state. Whether fascist or communist, the domestic terrorists share the hope that their acts will lead the democratic state to destroy itself.

There are two styles of internal violence.[+] The neofascists place bombs in piazzas, on trains or aircraft, or in railroad stations. This indiscriminate violence is designed to create the maximum possible fear, intimidation, and panic among the general public. Their aim is to prove that the state is weak. Their hope is that the inability of the democratic state to cope with violence will bring on demands for The Dictator.

The Red Brigades and other terrorist groups on the extreme left provoke not so much to show that the state is weak but to goad the state into taking repressive action. Their fear is that citizens, and especially leaders on the left, who should favor revolutionary change, are too complacent toward the existing state—willing to accept half a loaf now in the insidious belief that the other half will be forthcoming in due time. Thus, if the state, in its reactions to terror, does turn repressive, this will lead the oppressed workers and other classes to revolt.

Although it was unclear at the time, Aldo Moro's abduction and murder helped to bring both streams of terrorism to a peak from which it then subsided. Terrorism reached its high point in part because the terrorists could count on a certain amount of understanding and indeed collusion on the part of some persons. Segments of the public favored the terrorists with the kind of tacit support the Mafia and other forms of banditry have long enjoyed. Terrorism created for a time a certain effervescence, a sense of energy and enthusiasm, a youthful outburst in favor of more social justice. This reaction occurred because, in its earliest phases, terrorism appeared as little more than an extension of the protest movements and the hundreds of more or less revolutionary groups that mushroomed in the universities in the late 1960s. Initially these groups talked and talked. Some then turned to kidnapping and kneecapping. Murder came later.

Political murder, particularly in Aldo Moro's case, rocked the country. Up to that point, though, the explosion of terrorist acts produced two arresting effects. First, political party leaders and intellectuals on the left for some time refused to acknowledge that at least a segment of the terrorist groups represented the political left. Second, scores of intellectuals and social scientists provided reams of interpretation and explanation that turned out to be not-so-subtle apologies for violence itself.

During the heaviest of the so-called leaden years, the ubiquitous and unremitting hostility of this group toward the nation's political class and institutions took on ominous implications. This experience suggests, therefore, that attacks on the political class are not always innocuous in their consequences. In more ways than Italians themselves may have anticipated, terrorism brutally tested the proposition that Italy's is at bottom a strong, healthy democracy.

TAPROOTS OF VIOLENCE

Political violence has a long Italian heritage. The Mafia in Sicily, and similar underworld organizations like the 'Ndrangetta and Camorra that operate on the mainland, have been around for centuries. Members of these groups, when they are not making war on each other or attacking innocent victims, have not hesitated to target public officials. General Carlo Alberto Dalla Chiesa, whose successful antiterrorist exploits in the north won him national recognition, was brutally killed in Palermo a few years ago, shortly after he arrived there to do battle against the Mafia. His murder was only one among many.

The Mafia's often violent assault on the state has a long history of more-or-less willing collusion from the Sicilian population. From its origins in the seventeenth century to the present day, the Honored Society has been able to exploit the myth that it stands for the people as against the state, ready to alleviate the latter's arbitrary behavior through violence if necessary. The Mafia is also able to exploit *omertà*, that conspiracy of silence, based on custom and fear, that makes its members relatively immune from public prosecution.[5]

Like most societies that have their roots in antiquity, the peninsula has also been much exposed to the violence we associate with banditry—against the powerful, including the state and its representatives, in favor or in the name of the general populace.[6] This form of violence is grist refined into legend by the mythmakers. The world-famous bandit Giuliano, killed in ambush by a small army of Italian law enforcers, is a modern exemplar. He remains for many Italians not a miscreant but a folk hero of the Robin Hood or Jesse James stripe.

Latter-day terrorists appear less unusual in Italy than they might in countries whose national histories are freer of the forms of violence just described. That is, the type of political violence perpetrated is just as important as the violence itself. In this sense, the kidnappings and kneecappings of individuals by the Red Brigades did not appear so unusual. Given Italy's familiarity with traditional forms of violence it was several years before terroristic acts reached a level of spectacularity that produced headlines worthy of the Mafia or Camorra. On the other hand, Italians are probably less prepared than Americans to expect that their president or chief executive may be assassinated. The Aldo Moro case was all the more gripping for this reason.

It is now apparent that local terrorist groups have established certain linkages, or agreements of convenience, not only with international terrorism but, even more immediately, with organized crime. Some of the latter collaboration is no doubt the product of contacts made behind prison walls. And, although its magnitude is not known, it appears that jailed terrorists, and particularly those of the Red Brigades, were able to make new converts to their violent political cause among inmates who did not have previous records of political activism.

In fact, imprisonment has produced a remarkable reciprocity of benefits between the underworld and terrorists. Mario Moretti, for example, learned while imprisoned that, like so many jailed Mafiosi, he could more efficiently direct the command structure of the Red Brigades from behind bars. Among other things, prison greatly diminished the problems of finding security from provocateurs, police, and other enemies. It also made it easier to carry on "dialogues" with members of the press and public officials, many of whom treated the jailed terrorists as VIPs.

The taproots of violence are also distinctly political. Like other countries of Southern Europe, Italy's history is rich in anarchistic acts. The Russian anarchist Bakunin moved to Naples in the middle of the last century, where he found hundreds of acolytes. Karl Marx derided his revolutionary rival as a "lawyer without clients, or doctor without patients," but, for the victims of these "well-meaning" anarchists, their acts of terror were real enough.

Bakunin was but one of many leaders associated with political violence on the peninsula. Georges Sorel, the French thinker, who had a large following among Italians, favored the use of violence in a general strike. Anarchosyndicalism also found fertile soil in Italy, and several leaders of this European movement were among the first to be attracted to fascism. Mussolini mesmerized them with bombastic promises that blood would be spilled to bring about radical change in favor of the working class.

Futurism, that broad twentieth-century movement whose political aspects easily turned malign, is also an important piece of the Italian landscape and found its most dynamic and enduring moment there. It fell into a symbiotic relationship with fascism because both tended to make of violence a morally justifiable tool of politics. And Marxism-Leninism itself, in so far as it is a call to violence, is anything but alien to the peninsula's political experiences. Well aware of this, Antonio Gramsci worked hard to convince Italian Communists that, in part for this very reason, violent revolution would *not* be an efficacious road to power in Italy.

Political violence can also be traced to peasants who in the past used force to occupy and claim the lands they worked and who were routinely and even more violently evicted by landowners and public authorities. The Risorgimento, of which the ubiquitous statues of Garibaldi on horseback are the most palpable symbols, was a very bloody affair, and armed resistance, official or otherwise, against the unification of Italy was for decades the order of the day. Fascism itself pitted Mussolini's *squadristi* against armed opponents from the other parties who despaired over the democratic state's inability or unwillingness to defend itself against violent attacks.

Fascism fell, let us remember, not just to the allied armies but also to the Armed Resistance, whose fighters handed over to the liberators the keys to northern cities that they had wrested from the Fascists and Nazis. Mussolini's Republic of Salò, that last-gasp effort to save his toppling regime, produced in the north a fratricidal civil war, more angry and without quarter in its violence than any battle the Italian army fought during World War II. The immediate postwar years were pockmarked by additional violence between and among warring political factions, or the trade unions, or those who wanted to settle scores associated with the fascist regime.

This bloody political history of course extends much farther back, to the wars between Guelfs and Ghibellines, between and among city-states and other principalities, and to the waves and swarms of invaders from the outside. Those massive walls and medieval towers one finds everywhere today were not built for the edification of twentieth-century tourists to Italy. The historians show us, as do the collections of art and artifacts in the museums, that more often than not the hallmark of politics was violence.

We naturally expect to find less violence once a nation-state has emerged in a given territory. Nationhood and civilization, if that is the appropriate word, imply that violence will be placed under wraps, to be used by the state only when the need arises. Indeed, the essence of the stable polity, whether or not democratic, is generally understood to be the absence of violence.

In a democracy, the trouble with terrorism lies neither in its violence per se nor in the fact that its occurrence may be unexpected. The trouble is that acts of terror, on the part of the state or any of its citizens, are unqualifiedly excluded from the "rules of the game." Terrorism is simply not accepted as a legitimate form of political expression on anyone's part. Terrorism manifestly threatens the democratic order. It is for this political reason that the Italian state fears the Red Brigades more than it does organized crime, which everywhere among democracies manages to enjoy a certain "legitimacy."

There is an even deeper disquieting dimension to political violence. Technological progress may have brought us many desirable material benefits, but it has also greatly enhanced the ease and the sophistication with which warfare is conducted. In the form of modern arms and explosives, surveillance and communications devices, jet travel and logistical management, this technology is also available to terrorist organizations. It makes the latter immensely more difficult to control today than in the past. It means, as one high Italian official once assured me, that the Red Brigades and Italy are indeed at war, in the sense that war means nothing more than the absence of peace and the presence of politically motivated violence.

TERRORISM AND THE LEFT

In view of the historical antecedents just recited, why should the Italian left have resisted the idea that some of the violent acts produced by persons at their end of the political spectrum were anything other than terrorism?

One reason is that in the past some acts of violence officially attributed to the left were in reality "provocations" committed by the state or by right-wingers who acted with the state's acquiescence and blessing. It appears, for example, that the secret services and other authorities conspired to pin the responsibility for the bombing in Piazza Fontana on "anarchists" who were innocent of this act. In view of such precedents, many on the left might have initially believed that even the Red Brigades were nothing other than "official" provocateurs.

It is also the case that, whereas hundreds of left-wing terrorists have by now been arrested, tried, and convicted, most of the terrorist acts of acknowledged right-wing stamp remain unexplained, their perpetrators still at large. True, some right-wing terrorists have wound up behind bars. But they represent a drop in the bucket compared with the others. One does not have to be a paranoid to reach the conclusion that there is something suspicious about this imbalance.

In the second place, though, for a good many years after Piazza Fontana, and in the teeth of impressive evidence that those on the left could also make time bombs and fire automatic weapons, the Communist party and a fair chunk of the Italian intellectual establishment refused to believe or to grant that this was indeed the case.[7] In 1972, for example, Giangiacomo Feltrinelli, a wealthy and eccentric publisher identified with the left, blew himself up outside Milan, when the bomb he was setting to destroy a power line inadvertently exploded. Leftist intellectuals and the friendly news media performed somersaults looking for an alternative explanation. In those days, the left directed its attacks not against the terrorists but rather against those, especially reporters and other intellectuals, who dared to speak about left-wing terrorism.[8]

Guido Viola, an enterprising judge-investigator, was put on the Feltrinelli case. His work turned up the first of the Red Brigades *covi*, or hideouts. His evidence seemed to establish very close connections between the BR and Potere Operaio, a farflung radical left-wing organization with considerable influence in the factories, the schools, and the universities of the country. It was later to become Autonomia Operaia Organizzata and a major bridge between radicalized university students and full-scale terrorist groups like the BR.

As far as the left establishment was concerned, the real enemy was Viola. He was ridiculed and vilified by the press. Some time later, similar treatment was meted out to Judge Pietro Calogero, the investigating magistrate who indicted Professor Antonio Negri on grounds that the latter was implicated in the Moro abduction and murder. In Viola's case, the other judges in the left-wing organization of magistrates (all professions being politicized) to which Viola himself belonged tried to ride him out on a rail. In their eyes, Viola, knowingly or otherwise, had become a tool of right-wing reactionary forces.

In orthodox left-wing circles, the line that the Red Brigades were essentially hired provocateurs whose mission it was to create mischief for the "forces of democracy" persisted until 1974. As for Potere Operaio, Autonomia Operaia Organizzata, and a host of other left-wing groups openly committed to the destruction of the democratic state, the left-wing parties and intellectuals displayed toward them what can only appear in retrospect (to many of them, too!) as an inexplicable degree of understanding, tolerance, sympathy, and support. The most generous interpretation of this myopia is that those who shared it thought it inconceivable that left-wing forces would ever use terror as a political weapon.

The Communist party's posture is perhaps the easiest to understand. As suggested above, it is well aware that agencies of the bourgeois, liberal, democratic state will not flinch to use provocateurs against the left. Furthermore, although Marx and Lenin, and Palmiro Togliatti himself disdained the use of terror and cautioned against it, the PCI, like its counterparts elsewhere, is saddled with two serious handicaps. The first is that Marxism-Leninism is, after all, a theory of violent revolution in which the Communist party is charged with the major responsibility for bringing it about. The second is the deeply ingrained Communist adage: No Enemies to the Left!

Taken together, these two handicaps make it extremely difficult for any Communist party, including the PCI, to engage in anything like "loyal opposition" to the liberal democratic state. On the one hand, No Enemies to the Left! implies not only that the Communists will try to avoid being outflanked on the left. They will also go to great pains to find excuses for the behavior of the extreme left, no matter how much such behavior may violate the normal canons of democracy. On the other hand, the tradition of Marxist-Leninist thought cannot help but leave a residue of hope, a glimmer of a once-burning conviction, that the bourgeois state can, after all, be destroyed by violence. Thus, as terrorism developed, the PCI was torn between the above impulses and the felt need to demonstrate that its commitment to democracy was unequivocal.

During the first half of the 1970s, the pages of leading PCI publications like *L'Unità* and *Rinascita* were a study in schizophrenia. One side of the party voiced disdain for the terrorists. Among other things, these party leaders understood that the terrorists had not only infiltrated the factories and the labor movement; they were equally aware that the key hope of the terrorists was to goad the state into adopting antidemocratic measures. They recognized that terrorism was more than an assault on the state; it was also a movement that would, in the eyes of many, discredit the PCI itself. The urge was strong to undercut this basis for establishing guilt-by-association.

The other side of the party looked everywhere for the terrorists except within its own ranks. There it would have found younger comrades who once may have displayed deeply felt left-wing but nevertheless democratic ideals but who were now brandishing automatic weapons placed on the open market by Czechoslovakia, Israel, the Soviet Union, the United States, France, and other manufacturing countries. When these weapons could not be purchased in Eastern Europe or off the shelves at Beirut, they were willingly supplied by Libya's Colonel Qaddafi. Only slowly and with embarrassment did the PCI acknowledge that some of those terrorists had come from, or were still located in, its own backyard.

It is no wonder then that in the earliest years the PCI displayed first a certain amount of evasiveness, then double-talk, and later just an apology for some "comrades gone wrong." When the chips really came down in the Moro case, however, the PCI was literally at the forefront of those who opted for a "hard line" against Moro's abductors. The cynics would say that, given all of the rhetoric about revolution the PCI had turned out over the years, and in view of the fact that the Red Brigades, as well as other smaller but no less violent groups, called themselves the "real" Marxist-Leninists and the only "genuine" communists, the PCI had no other choice.

The Italian left, we must add, is not made up only of those of communist or socialist persuasion. Organized Catholicism, as in the case of certain units of Italian Catholic Action, has its share of left-wing adherents. The Christian Democratic party, too, has a left wing whose members are often as critical of the bourgeois capitalist state as any Marxist-Leninist could ever be. By and large, even these Christian Democrats unqualifiedly condemned acts of violence, but the same was not the case with many of the more ardent Catholics, especially the younger persons among them.

The "true believers" among Catholics are as capable as anyone else of an angry, armed assault on the existing order. At a minimum, as the

Liberation Theology movement in Latin America attests, this branch of Catholicism, including the clergy, will openly support guerrilla and similar movements. At most, as in the case of Italian terrorism, persons active in Catholic organizations can become major figures in the recesses of political terroristic movements.

The world press, and particularly its American branch, which rarely writes about Italy except in clichés, reported on the Red Brigades as if these men and women were essentially left-wing extremists who had come from the Communist party. The press made little of the fact that several of the founding members of the BR, like Renato Curcio, Alberto Franceschini, and Mario Moretti had been militant Catholics.[9] The deeper truth is that Italian terrorism shook the democratic state at its foundations precisely because membership in terrorist organizations and open or tacit support for the terrorist groups, at least up to the Moro affair, was widespread.

VICARIOUS PLEASURES

This being so, the role of the intellectuals during the heyday of terrorism was more than subtle; it was morally ambiguous. It is arguable, for example, that university students would scarcely have turned violent were it not for professors and writers who egged them on. This seemingly ungenerous view is difficult to document. Furthermore, it predictably leads intellectuals themselves to outraged proclamations in their own defense.

Nevertheless, during the heaviest of the leaden years, when terrorism managed to empty the country's streets after dark, Italian intellectuals were much more equivocal about these groups than were their German counterparts in response to the acts of terror committed by the Baader-Meinhof organization. To be sure, many Germans equivocated as well. And, just as certainly, some intellectuals in Italy did sound the alarm; but they were a tiny minority. Furthermore, the dissenters from the prevailing intellectual posture were rarely prominent members of the left establishment, and this made it easy for the rest to treat the former with condescension or suspicion. The orthodox line required studied intellectual hostility toward the state and almost benign tolerance toward "errant youngsters" who behaved like gangsters and were not so young at that.[10]

Gangsters is what they really were—gangsters recruited not among office workers or in the factories, and not among the small-fry of the underworld, but in the universities, in the intellectual community of which the terrorists were an integral part. In fact, left-wing terrorists became in the 1970s that group's most dramatic, as well as most virulent, expression. Their ultimate weapon was not the Sterling, the Skorpion, the Kalecnikof, or equivalent that anyone who set his or her mind to it could buy; it was instead their intellectual approach to their work. This being so, it was perhaps inevitable that much of the intellectual world would wind up making excuses for mayhem.

There is more. Italy is a country that wallows in words, in forensic exchanges, and in other forms of showmanship that strive for the virtuoso effect that will be widely admired. Intellectuals are word merchants whose "battles of ideas" are won or lost not on the battlefield or in armed combat but rather in the classroom, in the print and broadcast media, or in the endless public and private meetings and conferences at which they are the center of attention. With the possible exception of the struggle with Catholicism, or the question of the south, no theme outdistances terrorism in its seductive appeal to intellectuals.

Intellectuals also tend to turn, in their search for groups to support, to those that mount violent protests and even assaults against the bourgeois state, especially their own. In Britain, this inclination could easily be played out in episodes as early as Suez or as recent as the Falklands, with the ongoing violent confrontations in Northern Ireland in between. France faced similar problems in Vietnam and in Algeria and other parts of Africa, and French intellectuals were not miserly with their attacks against the state. Indeed, they prepared the way for the explosive events of the late 1960s. The disastrous American entanglement in Vietnam provided the intellectuals of that country with an unsurpassed opportunity (emulated by intellectuals worldwide) to identify with the oppressed and the underdog against the military-industrial complex centered in Washington.

Similar episodes and opportunities did not materialize as readily (for obvious reasons) in Italy, West Germany, and Japan. The governments of these countries had gone for more than three decades without major violent encounters outside their borders. Is it entirely fortuitous that these postwar democracies have experienced by far the greatest incidence of internal terroristic violence and that the intellectuals of all three provided the local terrorists with varying but significant degrees of moral succor?

If intellectuals, as seems possible, derive some vicarious pleasure from acts of political violence, particularly when these are directed against the state, postwar Italy would be unusually well suited for them. First, two of the country's three major political subcultures, the Marxist and the Catholic, not only have deep-seated antagonisms toward capitalism; they also find it relatively easy to mount philosophical justifications for political violence. One of Italy's lingering problems on this score is that neither subculture really shares the laical subculture's deep "sense of the state" and the need to protect the state's integrity against violent assaults from its internal enemies.

Second, Italy is the seat of two powers toward which Italian intellectuals entertain hostility. The first of these, the Vatican, is both a world power and a symbol, in the eyes of many, of halfhearted approaches to the alleviation of human injustice. The second power, the Italian liberal democratic state, is in the hands of the Christian Democrats. The DC is widely identified as an expression of the Vatican's interests. As the party that has held Italy in its hegemonic grip for decades, it has become the more or less direct object of the widespread attacks on la classe politica. As we know, in the minds of most critics, all that is wrong, immoral, or unacceptable in the country can be laid at the doorstep of this party. If the DC somehow escaped retribution for this at the hands of the electorate, the terrorists were now available to redress that oversight. The underlying idea was that terrorists like the Red Brigades, who made the DC itself their major target, were not, after all, without redeeming social value. No one said this in so many words, but the feeling itself was definitely in the air, even after Moro's murder.

Underlying smugness about terrorism, or self-righteous approval of terrorist acts, was perhaps more apparent at the beginning, when the principal targets were members of the razza padrona, or capitalist class, and others close to the DC. Faced with having to comment on the kidnappings and kneecappings of such persons, intellectuals and journalists succeeded only partially in masking their belief that these victims got little more than they deserved. The Red Brigades and other left-wing terrorist groups were careful not only to select individual victims from categories that have always been the intellectuals' major targets; they also provided voluminous, provocative "briefs" in defense of their acts of violence. Many intellectuals found this somewhat macabre dialogue and logic irresistible, and they wallowed in it. So did the press, which went out of its way to diffuse these terrorist tracts.

AGAINST THE STATE

It is important to recall that, as a group, Italy's intellectuals are arrayed "against the state." This antagonism has many dimensions. One is that the state is capitalistic. Intellectuals argue, not entirely without reason, that for all of its recent economic progress Italy remains a striking example of "primitive capitalism," with power in the hands of a small number of rapacious individuals and their families, many of them allied with American multinational corporations. Even today, many intellectuals will insist that much of the terrorism in the country is an emanation of the multinationals, often aided by intelligence services like the CIA.

Books on the Moro case continue to appear, full of insinuations that the whole thing was engineered by the BR with the complicity of American and Israeli secret services in favor of American oil interests, and of those in the United States who were determined to keep the PCI from joining the Christian Democrats in the governmental coalition." Needless to add, the alleged conspiracy could not have been executed with such precision without the collusion of those Christian Democrats and other Italian state authorities who opposed this move. In a country that feeds itself a very heavy diet of devil's theories, this one is among the easiest to digest. Swallowing it will be greatly facilitated by revelations about the United States's "behavior" produced by the "Irangate" scandal.

On the occasion of Aldo Moro's kidnapping, when it became apparent that everyone must take a stand, Leonardo Sciascia, a leading intellectual and ex-Communist-turned-Radical, declared that he was "neither with the state nor with the Red Brigades." This chilling abdication of responsibility was nothing more than a public expression of the private view that the intellectual community had entertained all along. Others might be less openly candid or laconic than Sciascia. They might wrap their moral indifference in more abstract phraseology. But their underlying antagonism toward the contemporary state is not hard to detect.

The intellectual community could indulge in this more or less open justification of terrorism in part because it remains so deeply addicted to abstract discourse and argumentation. There is no empirical tradition in Italian philosophy worthy of the name. The pretentions of logical positivism were demolished by the towering philosopher Benedetto Croce early in this century. Although Croce had turned his guns on Marxism as well, his philosophical idealism made it all too easy for intellectuals to conclude that terrorism made its appearance in Italy because the combination of social, economic, and political factors—the congiuntura—were right for it. In effect, many viewed terrorism as an ineluctable aspect of a given "historical moment."

Italian Marxists themselves are unexcelled in pretending that their avid discussions of "Italy's problems" have some minimal correspondence to the realities of the country. They too have been deeply influenced by Croce and share the fundamental prejudice that the elegance of an intellectual formulation or argument should not be marred by excessive concern with the facts. In the case of terrorism, the facts were ignored, reinterpreted, forced into procrustean conceptual schemes, and brutally sacrificed in favor of maintaining an ideological, moral, or expediential justification for the onset of violent attacks against the democratic state.

This is exactly what transpired—in the senior high schools and universities, in the factories and public bureaucratic agencies, in political party and trade union circles, and on the pages of the newspapers and magazines. Beginning in the 1960s, and in the name of freedom of thought and a better future world, intellectuals engaged in an orgiastic attack on the democratic state and its institutions. Some of them, including many of unmistakable intellectual power and charisma, made and wrote statements that nudged others in the direction of armed political confrontation.

A considerable number of university professors, by their own later admission, watched quite dispassionately on the sidelines as their students left the "occupied" universities in disgust and sought more immediate revolutionary gratifications in organizations like Potere Operaio, Autonomia Operaia Organizzata, Gruppi Armati Proletari, Prima Linea, and, of course, the Brigate Rosse. Several of the latter's "historical chiefs" were student contemporaries in the late 1960s in the University of Trento's Department of Sociology. Others were either students of Toni Negri at the University of Padua or were deeply influenced by his subversive writings. One way or another, middle-class professors in the classrooms provided philosophical justifications for middle-class students inclined to take up arms—from Nietzsche's idea that the creation of anything worthwhile requires destruction as a precondition, to Foucault's potentially murderous distinction between "constructive" and "destructive" violence.[12]

As I suggested earlier, terrorism would not have proceeded as far as it did were it not for a certain amount of legitimacy it extracted not only from intellectuals but, through them, from the broader community as well. This type of legitimacy does not come in one fell swoop but is formed gradually, like the concentric circles that follow a stone's fall into a pond. Like those same circles, though, legitimacy and the support that goes with it are impermanent. Whatever may have been, or remain, the causes of the intellectual community's dissatisfaction with the state, however strongly, subtly, or otherwise they may have sought to provide a moral gloss for those who took dead aim at the state's vital parts, the general population soon shied away from these heady but deeply disquieting vicarious experiences.

EXPLANATIONS GALORE

If some intellectuals welcome terrorism or aid and abet it and others condemn it unqualifiedly, almost all share the belief that terrorism must and can be explained. The impulse is as generous and human as it is often self-serving. All manner of phenomena pique our curiosity. But none fascinate us more than the underlying reasons for violent human behavior directed against something as powerful as the state. Regicide, as a theatrical theme that spans the centuries and cultures, is proof enough of this fascination.

Explanations and the theories on which they are based may be sociological, psychological, anthropological, historical, or a combination of any or all of these and more. Most explanations of political terrorism, in Italy or elsewhere, provided thus far are disappointing. This is so because they have in common two arresting and disconcerting features. First, there is ultimately very little that nails down what it really is that brings some people, but not others, to engage in political terror. Second, these explanations are rarely of the kind that might emerge if the investigator had posed, as a first question, the following test: What sort of information or evidence should I look for that would *refute* my hunch, belief, or theory about the causes of terrorism.[13]

This demanding approach to the demonstration of proof is associated with the philosopher Karl Popper, who currently enjoys an unlikely popularity in Italy. Karl Marx and Benedetto Croce are deeply implanted in the spirit and the psyches of Italy's intellectuals, and the back-the-argument-with-facts approach is still very suspect, if not entirely disdained. Also, those others in the West who have used more rigorous or "scientific" methods in their efforts to lay bare the origins or causes of terrorism have scarcely done much better. Whatever the approach, most of us sift the facts at our disposal not to refute but rather to confirm our pet ideas about human events.

What we have, then, are literally mountains of purported explanations that are either abstract or based on evidence that is anything but exhaustive and is more commonly nothing more than illustration and anecdote. Unfortunately, almost any of these will sound reasonable or convincing without close inspection. More often than not, the case for any one explanation will often rest on forensic skill and force of argument. This leaves us with little more than our own prejudices to guide us to the explanation we will accept as valid.

Let us glance at just a few of the major explanations of terrorism Italians themselves have offered along the way. It will be helpful as you read to ask yourself which of these sound reasonable, which do not, why this is so, and how you would feel if life itself depended on even a minimal demonstration that one explanation is superior to another. Bear in mind, too, that public officials who have to deal with the terrorists on a day-to-day basis face this issue not in the abstract but as part of their jobs.[14]

We have been told that political terror broke out, spread, and to some extent persists, in Italy because:

Society is unjust.

The political system is a fraud; nothing ever really changes in Italy.

The school system, especially at the university level, is dreadful.

The Communist party has preached revolution for years.

The intellectuals provided a philosophical justification for terror, and even fomented it.

The things people value are changing.

Neither the church nor the family provides the kind of education or control it once did.

Capitalism is the opiate of the masses.

Marxism is the opiate of the intellectuals.

Forces outside Italy are orchestrating terror.

The growth of the tertiary, or service, sector in the economy has weakened the control the unions have over workers.

People have improved their economic condition too fast, and so they have "rising expectations" and want even more.

Italy's governmental institutions do not function as they should.

There is too much trasformismo, and the voters want a more direct say about what happens in government.

A new sense of individuality and freedom among the young leads them toward acts of "self-realization."

The state is impotent against organized crime and political corruption, against the rape of the environment and rampant tax evasion.

There is a single "brain," or a Great Old Man who is behind it all.

The "true believers" of the Catholic and Marxist "churches" are angry because first principles of these organizations have been neglected or abandoned.

Modern industrial society produces "alienated" persons.

Liberal democracies are a disillusionment.

The state itself is essentially violent, and its laws inflict injustice, pain, suffering, and death on others.

We could easily add again as many more explanations to this list, but that is not the point of the exercise. Nor is it the point, or my intention, to show that some of the above explanations are more persuasive than others. Obviously, I do have a point of view, one that places more responsibility at the feet of intellectuals than the latter would ever be willing to accept. I have also suggested that, given the forms of violence the peninsula has experienced through the centuries, recent acts of terror are not as surprising (or for that matter as destabilizing) as similar acts might be, say, in Switzerland or Scandinavia.

It is also my conviction that not just the intellectual community but also the mass media tend in general to encourage rather than to discourage terrorism. This tendency is intensified in a country like Italy, where so much of politics is not only transformed into spettacolo but is spettacolo by its very nature. To some extent, terrorism escalated in Italy because there occurred such a mad rush to gain center stage.

The western world of the 1970s provided a perfect backdrop for this particular Italian drama. Kids were loading bombs in Greenwich Village; the Black Panthers were being entertained by famous Americans in Westchester County and Connecticut; Dutch youngsters were bombing royal corteges; the IRA was outgunning Her Majesty's Government in London; Portugal seemed on the verge of revolution; and students from

Berkeley to Nanterre, from the Sorbonne in Paris to the Free University of Berlin seemed of a mind to reproduce the wave of revulsion against the powers-that-be that had occurred on the Continent in 1848. This is the stuff that spurs Italians to outdo everyone else, beginning with themselves.

In Italy, all manner of leading personages made headlines. Gianni Agnelli, in an apparent love feast with organized labor, engineered changes in the scala mobile he was later to regret. Aldo Moro and other leading Christian Democrats seemed determined to translate Eurocommunism into a complete rehabilitation of the Italian Communist party that would return it to national government after a forty-year diaspora. Early signals from the Carter administration indicated that such a step might not sit badly with Washington. Enrico Berlinguer was lionized in Paris and Bonn, while cautious Italians began to send their capital abroad.

Needless to say, the intellectuals not only jumped on this bandwagon, they invented it, enlarged it, urged others to climb on, ridiculed or excoriated those who did not, and then spurred, pushed, and pulled it along its "historically ineluctable" path. Terrorism became an inevitable part of this excited process. It had to fight with others for the spotlight. When its more mundane methods of getting attention failed or began to fade, it escalated to acts like the Moro affair.

If this sounds farfetched, consider again the list of "explanations" suggested a moment ago, or add some others of your own. Most of the sociological or psychological factors offered will not lay the matter to rest. For example, all societies are unjust in some measure, but Italian society is considerably less so than many—such as the United States or France. Why then should there have been more terrorism in Italy than in other countries?

People's values are in transition everywhere, educational systems are far from perfect, the nuclear family has more or less disintegrated, churches no longer provide the anchorage and direction they once did, and the expectations of citizens tend to outrun the ability of the state to satisfy them. Where? Well, not just in Italy, and not just in those places where terrorism reached its more intensive levels. The truth is that we are all groping in the dark for a modicum of understanding of what it is that leads a small number of similarly situated persons to take up arms against the state, to maim and kill, sometimes indiscriminately, to risk their own lives in mortal combat—all in the belief that these acts of terror will destroy one political system and erect a better one in its place.

In the spirit of Pirandello, we might say that all points of view or explanations are equally valid or invalid, right or wrong. Perhaps the only relevant aspect of this discussion would be to acknowledge this, although it would scarcely bring any comfort to those officials who are forced to face the terrorists and to make risky and painful decisions regarding them. Italy was forced to do exactly this on several occasions: when it passed emergency legislation that increased police powers against suspected terrorists, when it had to decide whether the state would negotiate with the Red Brigades, and later when it faced the prospect of enacting into law a policy of leniency toward terrorists who turned state's evidence.[15]

Like other forms of deviant behavior, terrorism draws many explanations that shift blame from those who violate society's norms to society itself. The terrorists, of course, love this. If there is any doubt on this score, it would be erased by even a superficial reading of what it is the terrorists, especially those on the left, offer by way of self-justification. The widely reported "communiqués" of the Red Brigades read like a random intellectual mosaic formed of Marx, Engels, Lenin, Gramsci, Mao, Fanon, Che, the Frankfurt School, Freud, Neitzsche, Hegel, Sartre, and any other theorists of the social sciences or history who may be convenient. Much of wl at is offered is badly woven together, and it is delivered in dense, near-incomprehensible prose. The man-on-the-street understands only so much of these messages as the intellectual community and the mass media render less obscure. It is the sort of "society is guilty" approach that appeals to the tender-minded.

MULTIMEDIA SPETTACOLO

This brings us to look at the role of the mass media, and particularly of the press. To be optimally successful, modern terrorism requires a great deal of publicity, and Italy's mass media have been remarkably accommodating. Indeed, the media helped to domesticate terroristic violence, just as their American counterparts did with the Vietnam War, bringing it into their homes at dinner time or offering it up for bedtime contemplation with the "Eleven O'Clock News."

The Red Brigades took careful photographs of their victims—posed before a dark cloth backdrop and wearing as a sardonic necklace the five-pointed star within a circle that became the BR's logo. No one who has seen the polaroid snapshot of Aldo Moro in that pose—pained, remorseful, and accusatory at the same time—will soon forget it, or doubt the impact of such images.

The BR regularly delivered such photographs to the press, and they were dutifully published. The BR sent forth a stream of communiqués, carefully numbered, like executive orders or bulletins from the front lines. These were deposited in trash cans or other public places, and it was the press, not the authorities, that were notified and invited to retrieve and publicize these messages. The press cooperated. There were other channels of communication as well, but these rarely eluded the journalists. Aldo Moro thought the first three letters he sent from his place of confinement were highly personal documents, to be read only by their recipients. The BR, however, made copies available to the newspapers, which were only too willing to share their contents with their readers.[16]

The terrorist's need for publicity easily establishes a symbiotic relationship with the mass media's need—indeed, their responsibility in a free society—to gather and disseminate information. This prospect raises delicate questions in a democracy. Should there be a total news black out of the kind that military commanders sometimes impose at the front lines? Who is to decide when this will happen? If the black out is to be only partial, how is one to determine, on the spot, which news items will be released and which not? If the newspapers are the first to receive a communication from terrorist organizations, should they be free to publish before they have discussed, or even consigned, the material to public authorities? If the terrorists invite representatives of the press to serve as messengers or mediators between themselves and "the state," is this acceptable, and, if so, under what circumstances? Is it acceptable for reporters or editors to hold back from public authorities information they may have on terrorists or their organizations? If journalists actually meet with terrorists, is this "privileged" information that they are free to deny to governmental officials? In short, exactly where does one draw the line between the state's war on terrorism and the public's right to know what is going on? And where do freedom of the press and the limits of investigative journalism fit into this puzzle?

These and related questions were searingly on the agenda during the leaden years, and particularly during the Moro affair.[17] As we have seen, the Italian press is as free as in any other democratic country. By comparison, it is also much more politicized. By conservative estimates, three of every four journalists either have backgrounds in or maintain close relationships with one or more political parties. This being so, the straightforward news story is relatively unknown. So is investigative news gathering, except of the most superficial kind that reflects a very blunt axe to grind. Any two newspapers or television stations, chosen at random, are likely to produce disquietingly different versions of the same story, particularly if it has political implications. Even if it does not, the more enterprising journalist will turn a story in that direction.

Acts of terrorism place these and related aspects of the mass media in bold relief. One senses, for example, that the papers and magazines vie with each other for the "honor" of being the first point of contact made by the terrorists. Interviews are held with terrorists, in undisclosed places, in open violation of the law that makes such acts a crime for ordinary citizens. During the Moro affair, even the country's leading newspapers easily lent themselves to the diffusion of "disinformation" generated by the terrorists. In some instances, the most elementary effort to verify information supplied by the terrorists would have shown it to be false. The media's claim that in the midst of crisis there is little time for verification has a hollow ring.

The impulse to "scoop" the competition is as old as the town crier. So is sensationalistic journalism, of which Italy has considerably more than its fair share. Combined with the underlying political mission of so many newspapers and television stations, it adds up to a structural condition the terrorists can readily exploit. The relative handful of Italian writers who have broached this problem have been either ignored by the press or shot down by it in self-righteous outrage.[18] Indeed, those who would curb some of the press's excesses in the treatment of terrorism fall prey to the daunting accusation that they reveal "fascistic" mentalities.

But here is a view of the role of the press expressed by Alberto Franceschini, one of the BR's founding fathers: "The more we grew militarily," he says, "the more we were living in the mass media, in the giant headlines of the newspapers. At a certain point, we began to measure our initiatives more against the space the media gave us than against society's approval. Without our catching on, the society of the spettacolo was using us as elements of the spettacolo itself. In this way we, the enemies of the state, the 'terrorists,' became the favorite actors of the state."[19] Another terrorist adds that once this transformation had occurred, once the BR had been "legitimated" in this way, they received an avalanche of requests for membership and affiliation from all over the country.

Because so many aspects of terrorism are, potentially at least, pure spettacolo, the media would need to work doubly hard not to become the vital linkage that guarantees that outcome. One step in that direction would be to avoid syntony, or that degree of harmony that turns on the element of timing. Timing is essential to create tension, to maintain audience interest, to rekindle it when it flags, to bring drama to an optimal climax, and to assure that the denouement will produce both the immediate and more enduring effects desired. Even a modest interruption of the timing element would represent a gain for society at terrorism's expense.

The careful timing of the letters from Aldo Moro, the telephone calls to members of his family, the go-betweens selected by the BR to deliver messages from themselves or their prisoner, the announcement of the date of Moro's "trial," the deliberately garbled nature of the "sentence" pronounced against him, the initially false communiqué that he had been "executed" and his body dumped into an icy lake in the region of the Abruzzi, the eleventh-hour warning that he might still be spared if his family or friends managed to persuade the state to release some imprisoned terrorists, and finally the cryptic, double-edged message, "The Mandarin [meaning tangerine or mandarin!] Is Rotten," that announced Moro's death, and the placement of his riddled corpse halfway between the headquarters of the Christian Democratic and Communist parties—all of this conveyed one stark and overwhelming message: Mario Moretti and his BR cohorts were consummately skilled in the art of stage direction.

The most striking aspect of the role of the press was its failure (to this day) to turn a critical analytical eye in the direction of terrorism, particularly that aspect of it that sought to provide social, political, and moral justification for its criminal acts. Instead, the press, when it did not exploit terror for its own political purposes, became a passive, uncritical instrument through which the terrorists, the rumormongers, the speculators, and the sensation seekers could easily communicate to the country at large. Little wonder, then, that some Italians believed that the mass media had taken to winking at terrorism itself. It is this that led some to suggest that Italians might actually be fond of their terrorists; why else would the mass media appear to be so uncritically at its service?

POLITICAL RESPONSE

Terrorism has also forced the political parties to react, especially to decide how they wish to treat this form of political participation and opposition. Party responses have not been uniform. The Radical party's position, for example, is at least ambiguous and potentially dangerous. Members of the party have willingly served as communications links between jailed terrorists and the rest of the world, including the government. The Radicals pretend to write their own rules about what is or is not compatible with the democratic process. The party's secretary, Marco Pannella, once falsified his identity in order to enter a prison to talk with some terrorists, oblivious to the howl that this behavior by a prominent member of parliament caused in some quarters. A few years later these same Radicals nominated and elected Toni Negri to parliament, thus permitting this accused "brain" of the Red Brigades to leave jail under parliamentary immunity. They did the same thing again, a few years later, in favor of Enzo Tortora, a major television personality accused (and later absolved) of more ordinary crimes. The Radicals are unparalleled impresarios when it comes to turning serious matters into pure theater.

The Moro kidnapping forced the parties to say whether the state should negotiate with terrorists who, almost literally speaking, were holding a gun at its temple. In the last decade, other governments and their leading political parties have faced the same dilemma. And it turns out that even as powerful a state as the United States will find it necessary or convenient to equivocate, as it did in 1984 when it used Syria to negotiate with PLO terrorists who hijacked a TWA airliner, killed one American, and threatened to blow up the aircraft and hostages held at Beirut. Ronald Reagan himself, after many ringing declarations about the need to avoid even the slightest evidence of weakness in the face of terrorist extortions over hostages, wound up shocking the world by his "secret" dealings with Iran late in 1986 to gain the release of a handful of Americans.

Italian intellectuals and the press were less split on the question of negotiations than their past behavior might have led one to expect. The Moro abduction, and the five cold-blooded murders that accompanied it, was a *doccia scozzese*—a cold shower, or moment of truth, for everyone. It raised the question whether those who must officially react to terrorist demands were guided by what the constitutional lawyers and political philosophers call "the sense of the state." In ordinary language the question is whether the state should ever permit outlaws to dictate terms— even when the lives of hostages may be the price of obstinacy.

Although there were differences of opinion within the DC, Moro's party—despite Moro's own desperate pleas that they negotiate—refused to bargain. So did the Communist party, in the most unmitigated terms. The laical parties—Republicans and Liberals—were equally steadfast. No one had the slightest doubt that these two exponents of liberal democracy would be guided by "the sense of the state." Many were amazed, on the other hand, that the DC and PCI would come down on the same side. This seemed to indicate that Italian democracy would indeed pass one of its most severe postwar challenges.

The chink in this armor was the Socialist party, which had only recently come under the leadership and control of Bettino Craxi. The PSI was in search of a place in the sun, and it believed it could achieve this quickly by taking stands that were quite different from those assumed by other parties, and particularly by the Communists. This impulse was a major reason why the PSI urged accommodation with the BR in exchange for Moro's life and to that end took its own initiative.

With Bettino Craxi's authorization, the PSI, through intermediaries, sought to establish negotiations with the BR.[20] Craxi later confirmed this to the parliamentary committee named to investigate the Moro case. He told the committee that in order to satisfy himself that Moro was still alive, he sent the BR the request that a photograph of Moro be provided on which the words "Measure for Measure" were to appear. If Mario Moretti had doubted it earlier, this reference to Shakespeare assured him that the Socialists at least were willing to play out the spettacolo under his direction.

Another Socialist leader, Claudio Signorile, reinforced the widespread thought that the Socialists were grandstanding. Beyond any humanitarian considerations, he told the parliamentary committee, the PSI felt that "going against the current, we also hoped to gain some political space. Our choice was simultaneously both instinctive and meditated. Going against the current in the Moro case, we were not only committing a sacrosanct act; we could also create, in very short time, the image of an autonomous party, which was our intention."

Historians will never sort out all of the motivations for this serious lapse, nor will they (or, for that matter, will we) be able to show whether the behavior of the Radicals or Socialists toward the terrorists made things worse. Many in Italy have no doubt whatsoever on the last score, just as any suggestion to that effect immediately makes the PSI's leaders extraordinarily defensive. An irony here is that a Communist party, whose democratic credentials many distrust, should have been so unqualifiedly "hard" on terrorism, whereas the Socialist party, under the tutelage of Bettino Craxi, who has taken the PSI so far over to the right, should have been so "soft."

The committee of parliament charged with the investigation has yet to file its final report. Its sessions frequently reopen old wounds and bring forth a good deal of venom that still festers there. There are feelings of guilt and remorse all around, as well as ruminations about why it took so long before the country woke up to the need to go all out against terrorism. Even here, though, it is instructive that the Italian democratic state was able to respond to this mortal threat without, on the whole, placing in additional jeopardy the same democratic institutions the terrorists hoped to destroy.

DEMOCRATIC RESPONSE

Because so many aspects of terrorism are incipiently pure spettacolo, it is easy to look into its recent Italian history to aspects of it that border on sheer slapstick. Renato Curcio, a founding father of the Red Brigades, was once arrested and, for inexplicable reasons, confined in a minimum-security prison. Two journalists who investigated the Moro affair assert that Curcio behaved in prison like "a terrorist on sabbatical." In any event, Mara Cagol, Curcio's wife and a founding "mother" of the BR, managed to spring him from confinement by the simple act of walking into the prison, where she is quoted as having shouted, "Renato, where are you?" "I'm right here," replied the bearded Curcio, as he left his unlocked cell and walked out of jail arm in arm with Cagol. The day before, prison authorities had delivered to Curcio a telegram that read, "Bacchus arrives tomorrow."

As we know, West German terrorists in maximum-security prisons there mysteriously commit suicide. In Italy, terrorists get married in prison. Indeed, some of them apparently manage to get pregnant in open court—in those steel-barred cages where the accused are kept. There, in addition to making love, they can also smoke, chat among themselves, hurl invectives at judges and lawyers, threaten prospective jurors with death, hold press conferences, make impassioned speeches against the hated bourgeois state, and bar from their own cages those among their comrades with whom they are quarreling or who have turned state's evidence. Little in the Globe Theatre came close to scenarios of this kind.

The state, though, is not indiscriminately permissive or accommodating. Following the Moro affair, for example, it enacted a somewhat draconian measure that gives investigating magistrates and the police extensive powers to jail "preventively" persons who are suspected of terroristic acts or of providing terrorists with aid and comfort. There is little question that these powers have been misused by some officials, sometimes for heavy-handed political reasons. Abuses have led to demands that the authority to arrest and detain on the basis of suspicion or flimsy evidence be radically curtailed.

Those who favor easy arrest argue that it has been a relatively small price to pay for the successes registered against the terrorists. It may be true that terrorism has its sequels, and that new "columns" of the Red Brigades replace those that have been decimated through arrests, detention, and convictions. For example, the terrorists who kidnapped the American general James Dozier were not the same men who carried off the Moro abduction several years earlier. On the other hand, Dozier's spectacular rescue by the leathernecks would not have occurred but for a modified legal framework that readily brought suspects into jail, where authorities could tempt them with leniency in exchange for useful information.

It turns out that several of the Italian police officials involved in Dozier's rescue also used third-degree methods with some jailed terrorists in order to compel their collaboration. Those accused of torture have since been tried and convicted.

It also turns out that the general public is not of one mind regarding the Law of the Repented, under which leniency is extended to those who turn state's evidence. The law was carefully drafted. If, on the one hand, the "repented" have openly rejected armed conflict against the state, they do not, on the other hand, have to "rat" on their former comrades in arms by identifying any of them by name. There is a nice Italian touch to this.

Leniency, of course, is not guaranteed, even if the terrorists and their lawyers ask for it and the prosecutors recommend it. The presiding judges make the final determination. Recent practice has shown that some jailed terrorists will talk and that the judges will indeed reduce the severity of their sentences. On the other hand, the organizational and command structures of the Red Brigades were so ingeniously constructed that relatively little useful information has been turned up from interrogation of the "repented."

In a Catholic country, it is perhaps inevitable, and even charming, that those who turn state's evidence are called by this term. This allusion to salvation, to penance and absolution, to forgiveness in exchange for genuine remorse, is deeply rooted in the culture. In this setting, even the Marxists are entirely open to this manner of dealing with deviants. Furthermore, as we have seen, for many on the left, terrorists of the same ideological persuasion are considered well-meaning "comrades" who had gone wrong.

The Law of the Repented has produced further drama in the jails and courtrooms, reams of newspaper coverage, and no end of additional debate and conversation. For example, some of those who favor the law as it applies to terrorists do not support its application to members of the Mafia or other elements of organized crime who turn state's evidence. The suspicion is also afoot that the "repented" have introduced a pernicious new twist in a system of justice already overburdened with questionable practices. It is all too easy, the argument goes, for those who claim to recant to falsely accuse innocent persons, and in this way damage the democratic system even more.

As a result of this law, the jailed terrorists are now divided into not two but three groups. The first are the ultras, or die-hards, those who show no remorse at all and who continue to mouth stale attacks on the state. A second group would be the repented. As you might imagine, they are not very popular with the die-hards, and it has been necessary to isolate and protect them, not only in prison but in open court as well. In between these two categories there is a third: the self-styled detached, or disaffiliated. These are persons who have broken with their former comrades but who do not wish to be mistaken as having abandoned the terrorists' indictment against the state or the goal of a better society. The disaffiliated have taken to writing books with such titles as these: *Do I Really Need to Be a Lifetime Terrorist? I, The Infamous One,* and *Living with Terrorism.*

The newspapers' and intellectuals' reactions to all of this is instructive.[21] To begin with, many of them consider the repented to be self-serving stool pigeons who have betrayed their comrades-in-arms and the "cause" as well. Thus, because the penitents are considered morally suspect opportunists, statements and accusations they make against others are automatically placed in doubt.

Secondly and not surprisingly, the disaffiliated get a better press than do the penitents. Intellectuals are generous in their admiration of these persons. In effect, these wrongdoers may regret the dismal climate they helped to create, and the kneecappings and murders, but they have not abandoned their underlying principles—and they are not ready to bow out with their tails between their legs. This piece of the spettacolo continues to produce a remarkable amount of applause.

One might easily turn cynical or pessimistic about this scenario. The Red Brigades, after all, have always included in their theoretical baggage the importance to their mission of the "propaganda of the deed." Understanding, as they most certainly do, the importance of the mass media, they have exploited with remarkable skill the instrumental use of the media to bring their acts to national and, indeed, worldwide attention. Furthermore, coming, as so many of them do, from the country's intellectual circles, they have also managed to exploit the underlying guildlike sense of solidarity of that group.

It is apparent that the terrorists do manage to reconstitute themselves. It is likely that there will be sequels to the leaden years of the 1970s. In the cauldron that is the Middle East and in the Mediterranean Basin that is the major theater of operations of so many different conflicting political interests, terrorism has now taken on new ominous proportions. The hijacking of the luxury liner *Achille Lauro*, hand grenades tossed at crowded open-air cafes, and the wanton murder of innocent travelers at Rome's major airport are unequivocal signals that terrorism remains part of life.

The latter development, however, is not an Italian but, rather, a much broader problem that many nations working in collaboration will have to face. The more encouraging side of the domestic scenario is that over a period of several years Italian authorities managed to bring domestic terrorism largely under control.

Other democratic governments can learn much from the Italian experience. Two lessons seem of particular importance. First, democracy too requires, on the part of those in charge of law and order, the "propaganda of the deed." The Italians have insisted that terrorism can and must be defeated without resort to patently undemocratic means. That commitment alone has served to reinforce democratic institutions.

Second, it now seems apparent that terrorism cannot be defeated without unqualified help from the intellectual community and the mass media. Whatever may be its causes, terrorism will not long survive disapproval and antagonism that reflects the broadest public consensus. Insofar as this is not forthcoming from major sectors of society, like the intellectual community and the mass media, this may be as threatening to democracy as anything else the terrorists themselves are able to do.

8

WHO GOVERNS ITALY?

Terrorism, as well as other aspects of politics so far described, makes one wonder whether there is anyone really in charge of this interesting country. To hear many Italians tell it, the answer is emphatically no. And some would add *meno male,* or, and it's a good thing, or thank goodness. The idea persists that la classe politica produces mischief or worse, and that whatever is praiseworthy about Italy, whatever is working well, is the merit of ordinary citizens, of the "real" as opposed to the "legal" country.

We now recognize that comments of this sort should not be taken at face value. It is nevertheless understandable that many Italians feel that even their most prominent political leaders are irrelevant to the country's governance. A cabinet crisis, for example, may leave the country, strictly speaking, without a government for weeks on end, but this would not cause things to fall apart. Government offices would continue to provide citizens with the same indifferent or terrible services to which they are inured. From the standpoint of the ordinary Italian's day-to-day contacts with government, the bureaucracy is obviously in charge.

When we ask who governs a democracy, we naturally have much more in mind. We want to know not only who makes public policies or administers them but also whether the people who are the objects of these policies have anything to say about which are rejected, which chosen, and how the latter are interpreted and carried out. That is, we wish to establish the extent to which it is the people themselves who govern.

We are concerned, too, about the transparency of the policy process. Bureaucrats, even those in free societies, loathe transparency. They know that the control of information is a prime ingredient of power. They will find no end of excuses to deny citizens access to information. Left to their own devices, the bureaucrats will in short order create a world of nightmares. Their way of doing things can become so entrenched that it requires an ombudsman, Nader's Raiders, parliamentary oversight, or a freedom of information act to reassert the right of citizens to know what transpires in places where governmental power is exercised.

The question, Who governs? is especially appropriate for those democracies, like Italy's, where no one seems in charge and where the remoteness, insensitivity, and arrogance of public servants reach extremes. Italians themselves often shrug off these conditions. After all, they say, the country is essentially ungovernable and even borders on anarchy. The more authoritarian among them, if they are old enough, will make nostalgic reference to the law and order fascism brought. Others will voice laments about "crisis" and warn that the country is ready to fall into the abyss. The same Italians, who somewhere in their psyches recognize that they are today among the freest people on earth, nevertheless believe that freedom itself will eventually turn out to be their political undoing.

Hyperbole of this sort may well obscure some basic realities. The first is that power vacuums are largely mythical. If they exist, it is only for a moment. Anarchy itself is a system of power; some persons turn out to be stronger than others. Those who score the country as "ungovernable" have something else in mind: they wish that public policies were closer to their own preferences.

Claims of ungovernability may also refer to trasformismo or, alternatively, to the singular meaning that government and opposition take on in the Italian context. The first, as we have seen, is that sleight of hand that seems to make a mockery of the electoral process. The second implies that government is really a club whose elite members pay only lip service to the idea that the people should have something to say about who governs them, and in what way. Together these conditions appear to make the political process entirely too arcane.[1]

Were this a complete description of that process, we would expect to find anarchy part of the time and largely invisible government the rest of it. In practice neither condition prevails, but it is still difficult to nail down exactly how to describe the system. The pattern shifts, depending on the issues involved, the magnitude of the interests affected, and the level of government called upon to intervene.

If government means the systematic exercise of legitimate power over a designated territory, there is no question whatever that Italy is both governable and governed. Moreover, the process of government is much more open to observation than first impressions might suggest. On close examination, we will easily discern a system in which political elites play a special role, in which the political parties are present even if in ways that many claim are highly unacceptable, and in which the people themselves have a variety of channels and opportunities through which to make their preferences known.

Let us provide some details for this broad sketch.

BIG GOVERNMENT

Italian government is not just omnipresent, it is also very big.[2] As in other welfare states, government is big in scope—in the sweep of social life and organization that comes within its domain. Big government sometimes implies Big Brother, that looming Orwellian figure who made his appearance in Italy in the form of Il Duce. Most Italians do not want to be big in that way again, and this may well be fascism's most precious political legacy to Italy.

Another common indicator of bigness is the proportion of the goods and services produced each year that the government, one way or another, appropriates and then spends. In the United States, a relatively modest one-third of the gross domestic product passes through the government. In Italy, the proportion exceeds 50 percent. The figure is even higher in the Scandinavian countries, but they have somehow managed to escape the political saturation of society that seems to go with it in Italy.

Italian government is also quite large when measured by how much of the economy is socialized, or owned by the state. Indeed, until the recent spate of nationalizations of banks and industries that France experienced at the hands of its socialist government, Italy's economy was the most socialist in the West after that of Austria.[3]

Italy's socialism was and remains of the "ash can" variety described earlier. Except for the nationalization of the electrical industry in the early 1960s, state ownership of industries and banks has been inspired not by any intention of destroying capitalism but, rather, of keeping capitalism alive. Under fascism the state saved the banks by taking over the worthless investments they had made in many industries. Ever since, Italy's capitalists have unloaded their "losers" on the state. The unions have gone along with these salvage operations in order to protect jobs. The upshot is that much of the economy is in the hands of the extensive system of public corporations described earlier. Thus, government looms large also because it is a major factor in industry and banking, in the labor and capital markets, in manufacturing, and in foreign trade.

With so much of the economy within its domain, you might think the government would opt for economic planning, in which case we might well expect that those responsible for this activity would be very much in charge of the country. Nothing of the kind has occurred so far, and it is highly unlikely that it ever will. The only political party with anything like a commitment to some form of centralized planning of the economy is the PCI, and the prospect that it would ever be in a position to further such an aim is, at best, remote.

ECONOMIC PROGRAMMING

A halfhearted step toward economic planning was taken in the mid-1960s, not at the PCI's behest but under the impetus of the Socialists, who were brought into the national government with the so-called opening to the left. A few PSI leaders, as well as a small segment of the DC, believed that the nationalization of electricity, coupled with the vast empires of the IRI (Institute for Industrial Reconstruction) and the ENI (National Hydrocarbons Entity), and with the government's control of credit and finance, provided it with an unexcelled opportunity to engage in "economic planning by inducement."

This was a time of similar experiments in democratic planning in countries like France and Britain.[*] Compared to them, many thought, Italy could not fail. After all, the IRI controlled all or most of such key industrial sectors as steel, shipbuilding, banking, air transportation, metal-mechanical industries, and food processing; the ENI was a worldscale petrochemical holding company operating in diversified energy sectors; utilities and rail transport were also owned by the state; and the government had at its disposal all the necessary credit and fiscal and other financial tools to steer investment in whichever direction it might choose.

The government treated the prospect of economic planning gingerly, to say the least. To begin with, two of the DC's oldest partners, the Liberals and Republicans, either oppose planning (PLI) or want it very delicately applied (PRI). They doubt that governments can make effective policies to correct imperfections in the market. Along with the DC, they prefer that the activity undertaken by government be referred to as "economic programming" and not "economic planning."

Some new administrative machinery was created to carry forward this activity. It worked pretty well in the conduct of research, the establishment of a data base for policy, and the delineation of specific development objectives. But when it came to nailing down and, more important, executing public policies, the planners and their apparatus were almost utterly without power or influence.

The experiment as a whole was a total failure.[5] It fell afoul of every conceivable obstacle. Socialists and Christian Democrats, the two major partners in this new departure, were at loggerheads over the desirability of directed economic change. Important instruments like the IRI and the ENI, as well as the banks, were in the hands of Christian Democrats or their appointees. Most of these persons, even if politically beholden, opposed policies that invited an even more heavy-handed political presence in the management of public enterprises.

To top it off, none of the administrative bodies that were designed to coordinate the efforts of public ministries involved in economic and industrial matters ever really did so. Despite a lot of flag-waving in favor of the program, each ministry continued to go its own way. This gave unlimited opportunity to interest groups that represented workers, industrialists, or geographic regions to influence policies in directions that were certain to defeat the goal of a coherent, integrated program.

Above all, the experiment failed because there never existed that degree of political commitment—of consensus within the cabinet and political will on the part of the prime minister—without which success in such a difficult and controversial public undertaking is unthinkable. Central planning of a national economy is problematical even when such political will is assured; without it, planning is likely to be the kind of joke it became in the late 1960s. No wonder Italians called the economic program "the book of dreams."

PRIVATE SECTOR POWER

Quite a few Italians believe that the country is really in the hands of and for all practical matters governed by the private financial and industrial sectors. The small scale of society, the astonishing prominence within it of a few leading families, the ubiquity of these selfsame families in banking, industry, the mass media, politics, and wherever else the levers of power are located lend credence to this belief. These interests, for example, would ferociously oppose centralized economic planning, just as they have always opposed essentially any governmental coalition, program, or regulation that might inhibit the unfettered exercise of their rapacious impulses toward the state.

Everywhere among democracies, the private industrial and financial sector enjoys both privileged access to government and, as a result, public policies that further its interests.[6] Italy nevertheless is unusually generous to this group. It is not just that governments, even those headed by socialists, would not dream of making public policy without taking the interests and wishes of this sector carefully into account.[7] Beyond this, the norm seems to be that the fortunes of a relative handful of leading families will be protected and augmented, if necessary at public expense.[8] On a national scale, this is the contemporary rendering of the droit du seigneur.

Typically, private entrepreneurs will try to palm off on the government, at inflated prices, industrial enterprises that are not viable. It is singularly reassuring for the vaunted Italian capitalist to know that when his propensity to risk vanishes, when his managerial intelligence or luck in the market runs out, or when his enterprise is on the brink of bankruptcy, he can turn it over to the state at a nice profit. Safety nets of roughly this type have always been provided in other Western market economies as well—but certainly not on as wide, as guaranteed, or as lucrative a scale as in Italy.

Protected and coddled entrepreneurs who profit so handsomely from this convenient arrangement display neither gratitude toward the state nor embarrassment over their approximate, not to say hypocritical, commitment to free enterprise and the market. Without trace of a blush, those who pull off these coups and enrich themselves at public expense will also publish statistics to "prove" that private-sector industries are much more efficient and profitable than those that are publicly owned.

The private sector's strategy is not limited to palming off losers on the state. It will also use political clout to compel the state to sell at bargain prices public-sector industries that, far from verging on bankruptcy, are in very good shape indeed. This tendency reached a crescendo in the mid-1980s, not only under the nose of a government led by the Socialist Bettino Craxi but with its encouragement and active support.

Margaret Thatcher and Ronald Reagan brought a "new look" to national policy-making that appealed to the Continent's governments. The welfare state became everyone's whipping boy, deregulation and privatization of industry almost everyone's pious desire. Only the intellectually hobbled, it was argued, would not make it to the bandwagon of the free market; only the ideologically blinkered would fail to recognize the superior virtue of private entrepreneurs over the bloated, hackneyed bureaucrats. Keynes was out, and Friedrich von Hayek and Milton Friedman were enthroned in his place. In Italy, the "new look" featured a scramble among private interests, all of them hell bent on acquiring at bargain prices some of the jewels among state-owned economic enterprises.

As it unfolded, this aspect of the private sector's strategy was not without its difficult and eye-opening moments. For example, one small group of operators, on the basis of a secret pact with former public officials, had for some time controlled the policies of Mediobanca, Italy's major investment bank in which three other state-owned banks, operating under the IRI, were the majority stockholders. In practice, this minority control of Mediobanca meant that it served as a clearinghouse for Italy's most powerful families. Through Mediobanca, they could regularly realize for themselves everyone else's fantasy of gaining control of large-scale enterprises without putting up much of one's own money.

In many democracies, the revelation of such a pact and of the improprieties it implied would produce legislative investigations, and perhaps some indictments. In Italy it produced instead a bold campaign by the private interests to compel the IRI (that is, the Italian state) to sell them enough additional stock in Mediobanca to reach a majority share of the equity. This would then render legal, and presumably above moral reproach, their long-standing de facto control of that public instrument. Leading cabinet members applauded this solution.

Maneuvers of this kind are rendered obscure by ideological verbiage, by misleading debates over the relative economic merits of public or private control of financial institutions and capital markets. Behind the salvos of justifications for and against the sale, one could discern a struggle among the leading political parties (especially those inside the governmental coalition), as well as conflict among a relative handful of industrial and financial operators in both the private and the public sectors. The naked issue was simple: who would gain control of this important financial instrument, in favor of which industrial and financial groups and the political parties or party factions associated with them.

In 1985, in what looked like a lightning stroke, the IRI's top managers announced that the SME, a healthy, multibillion dollar holding company in the food, food processing, and agribusiness sectors, would be sold to the Buitoni Company, a holding company controlled by the Olivetti Corporation's Carlo De Benedetti. The latter is a brilliant financial operator who has made as many magazine covers as he has closed spectacular deals. He is as intriguing a figure as one will find in the history of Italian capitalism. His public relations apparatus is so skillful it once persuaded Italians that De Benedetti's sale of a controlling interest in the Olivetti Corporation to AT&T was a giant step taken in the Italian national interest.

The announced sale of the SME created a political uproar. Leading newspapers lined up for or against De Benedetti, not on the merits of the issue but on the basis of the political implications of the attempted sale. The prime minister's office complained that the IRI's managers, without full authority or required prior notice to the prime minister, had signed a highly questionable contract. The price, for example, was said to amount to an outright gift to De Benedetti of two hundred million dollars. IRI managers were additionally accused of acting in haste without having taken competitive bids that would more likely produce an offer closer to the SME's real market value.

Subsequent events included the usual barrages of charges and countercharges, as well as a few newspaper attempts to get behind these to the core of the issue. For many, the real question was not the propriety or legality of the sale but, more fundamentally, which political parties would benefit or lose as a result of this move. The most cynical explanation of the furor created by Palazzo Chigi was that the Socialists were piqued over the fact that De Benedetti, once friendly toward Bettino Craxi and his party, no longer was. As a result, he had opted to promote the SME sale with and through the Christian Democrats who controlled the IRI and the SME itself.

On essentially the same set of considerations and often with almost exactly the same cast of characters, dramas have been played out over the transfer of ownership in large-scale industries in the petrochemical, steel, or textile sectors, the membership and structure of financial holding companies, the sale of major newspapers or television stations, and even the annual salary the RAI agreed to pay one of the country's leading TV personalities.

The scenario will change somewhat when a proposed acquisition emanates from a foreign company. Thus, late in 1986, it appeared that the

Ford Motor Company might gain control of the Alfa Romeo Corporation, owned by a branch of the IRI. Indeed, most of the IRI's top managers seemed favorably disposed toward Ford and openly welcomed the foothold in the Italian automotive market that Ford would garner through the acquisition. It took the Fiat Corporation no time to blow Ford out of the water. Almost everyone in the government concluded that it was not in the national interest that Fiat should be faced with competition in its own backyard. And so Fiat, not Ford, acquired Alfa Romeo, and at a price that many believe to be considerably less favorable to the Italian government than what Ford had offered. Whatever the merits of this last argument, it was highly unlikely that the government would take a step that was so unqualifiedly defined as unfriendly by Fiat's managers and owners.

When the government does accommodate private-sector financial and industrial interests, the latter will sometimes return the favor with praise and support. When it becomes less so inclined, when public policies seem not to favor their material interests, leading industrialists will quickly turn hostile. Indeed, they can be remarkably heavy-handed and even nasty in their attacks. This occurred at Turin late in 1985 at a much-publicized meeting of the Confindustria called to celebrate and to take stock of Italian industry. Having invited members of the government, including the prime minister, to participate as guests, official speakers for the confederation heaped opprobrium on them: for their bigness and inefficiencies, for their alleged mismanagement of the economy, for their lack of success in encouraging higher levels of industrial investment and innovation, even for their alleged mismanagement of foreign policies. Following this barrage, newspapers published headlines like: "Agnelli Gives the Government Failing Grades." The prime minister and others from government were placed on the defensive, and they tried to reply in kind.[9]

This is far from a system of anarchy. Nor is Italy a country where, when the chips are down and the stakes run into the billions of dollars, the issues will remain unclear or the problems will become "ungovernable." These brief examples, which could be many times multiplied, show that the competition for the things people value or covet is very fierce, that it tends to center on politics, that the major players are relatively few in number and well known, and that, even if they do not hold public office, the leaders of the private sector are deeply enmeshed in the game itself, more often than not as almost certain winners.

INSTITUTIONALIZED POWER

Because power is so scarce and the competititon for it is so fierce, rules must be established regarding its allocation and exercise. Especially in democracies, constitutions and laws are written largely with this purpose in mind. If anarchy is to be avoided, if people and groups with economic and other interests to protect are expected to support the polity and to play by its rules, they will want some say in establishing what the rules (formal and informal) are. They will also insist that the political process display some evidence of stability and predictability. All of this requires at least a modicum of "institutionalization."

The institutional side of Italian political power is blurred. Institutions do not seem to work well, and perhaps not as the constitution intends.[10] The constitution does not always delineate with clarity the specific powers, and their limits, that are conferred on each major institution. As the formal institutions of government operate, little suggests a general commitment to well-established rules and procedures that should or will produce un-equivocal outcomes. On the contrary, much of what we have already described about political and governmental practice suggests that rules for setting explicit policy alternatives, for choosing among them, and for assuring that they are in fact implemented are very complex, very vague, very flexible, or simply nonexistent.

This situation is deliberate, not accidental. It was planned that way. Italians will go out of their way to avoid head-on political confrontations. Rather than meet a problem early and directly, they prefer to temporize as long as possible and then to go around it. Political solutions are never considered permanent here. Politicians not only try to avoid painting themselves into a corner; they try to leave today's political opponents, who may be tomorrow's political allies, an escape route as well.

This approach to life and politics is anything but Anglo-American. Italians are not addicted to clear-cut outcomes to conflict; for them the world is not neatly divided into winners and losers. Just as everyone may be said to win, or to lose, elections, so it is with the struggle over public policy: more often than not, most contenders are accommodated. The trick is to put it all together in the right way, and not under the glaring spotlight of public scrutiny.

This approach is sometimes called Byzantine, and aspects of Byzantium are certainly there. How could it be otherwise? But the Byzantine style of politics, like the Italian that followed it, was not only opaque and arcane; it was also highly pragmatic, displaying when necessary a remarkable degree of patience and toleration. There may also be something cynical and fatalistic in the Italian approach, much of it obscured by inflamed political rhetoric and the fire-eating outbursts of political writers and propagandists. Deep down, though, everyone knows that, given the way elections typically come out, decisive victory over one's opponents is really not in the cards.

Appearances notwithstanding, this is not a society of unremitting political conflict. Were it so, the political terrorists would have had a field day in the 1970s instead of the limited success, and then systematic decline, they experienced. And where conflict is fierce, blurred institutional responsibilities and vague rules surely help to blunt its effects. Italians know or sense this, and I imagine that the growth in popular respect for the republic's institutions is an important result of this.

Ask an Italian how things—anything, not just politics—are going, and he or she will likely reply, "si tira avanti," one tries. Ask how problems are solved, and the Italians will reply, "ci arrangiamo," we improvise, make shift, or get along. Expressions of this kind invite interpretation. They are, of course, rooted in an ancient peasant culture, and what peasant would tempt the gods, or the tax authorities, by revealing that things are just great? They suggest that nothing that is desirable in life comes along automatically. They imply, too, that life is a continuing challenge that taps the ingenuity of the individual, whether in his or her effort to get out of the vegetable or fish market unscathed, to drive in traffic, to file an acceptable tax return, or to get sistemato.

Such statements also signal that those who utter them place a high value on improvisation and, by implication, an equally low value on rigid approaches to problem-solving. Taken together, it is easy to see why these implications sometimes lead Italians to believe that what is great about Italy is due to the "real" country and not to the "legal" one. The trait is, after all, cultural, not governmental.

Italians seem to me to be much more gifted than are the English at this muddling-through approach to problems. This is so not just because, as they like to say in Rome, "We have seen politics of every conceivable color"; it is so too because Italians realize that the democratic nation-state is a relatively recent, and still problematical, experiment. To muddle through a problem means that there will not be an all-or-nothing, once-

and-for-all-time resolution of it. On occasion, attacks on problems may also require breathtaking, virtuoso performance. Italians do not mind this at all; indeed, they count on it!

The institutional exercise of power is also blurred by the practice of trasformismo. Trasformismo not only makes improbable a direct connection between electoral outcomes and government. It also erodes the meaning we ordinarily attribute to the executive branch of government, the legislature, and the other key institutions of representative democracy. Trasformismo's message is clear: behind the facade of democracy's formal institutions, there is a substantial and highly structured system of power in operation. If this is true in all democracies, the contrast appears sharper in Italy.

BUREAUCRATIC POWER

On a day-to-day basis, one would easily identify the bureaucracy as the major locus of power, and the bureaucrats as the prime exercisers of it. This is true of all governmental systems, whether or not democratic. As a rule, citizens become aware of government when they make personal contact with one or more of its representatives.

If this sounds trite and benign, in Italy it is neither. Given the scope of government, the bureaucracy is palpably present everywhere." And given the Kafkaesque administrative code and rules, and the bureaucrats' tendency to be insensitive and arrogant toward citizens, one can easily imagine a nightmarish condition where power is exercised arbitrarily, beyond the reach of democratic controls.

Any number of Italians daily experience exactly such nightmares. There is no doubt that Italian bureaucrats constitute formidable wielders of power and that one can find in Italy ludicrous, horrifying, and perhaps extreme cases of power's misuse. These bureaucrats, after all, are not just protected by the trade unions, by life tenure in their jobs, or by a fierce guildlike solidarity that one finds among public bureaucrats everywhere else. In addition, there is law.

In a culture whose fetishlike respect for written law dates back to the Roman Republic, bureaucrats turn to their certain advantage a complicated written administrative code that permits them to interpret almost any situation pretty much as they choose. In the hands of dialectically minded southern Italians, who dominate the bureaucracy, the code becomes an inexhaustible arsenal for their defense. Combined with the military-type hierarchy and jealousy about "turf" that are endemic to the bureaucracy, these norms give senior civil servants considerable power.

In fact, Italy is a lawyer's paradise, and not just because Italians admire forensic skills. A prevailing lawyer's mentality dictates that all possible contingencies regarding public policy must be anticipated and codified. This means that people are forever in search of what nuance The Law will or will not permit. Of course, it will or will not permit anything or everything, or almost, depending on circumstances and on who does the interpreting, and to what end. Anyway, one has the impression that without the *Gazzetta ufficiale*, which publishes weekly updates of the country's many legal codes, the country, or at least most of its institutions and transactions, would simply fall apart.

Note that the system, allegedly governed by the codes, does not make the political process less pragmatic than I have more than once described it. It simply means that the several million members of the public bureaucracy, and especially those who occupy the higher reaches of it, are forces to be reckoned with.

It does not take the average Italian long to learn that, formidable and remote though it may appear on the surface, the bureaucracy is anything but impregnable. The bureaucrats themselves, for all of their arrogance, preening, and bloated numbers, cannot administer law without the collaboration of individuals and organizations. Administrative agencies have their own clients in society, including those persons (like doctors, lawyers, farmers, businesspeople, housewives, teachers, taxpayers, and so on) the bureaucracy is supposed to regulate. In the process of soliciting their "cooperation," the bureaucrats themselves inevitably give up something to the others in the form of influence.[12]

Equally important, these bureaucrats do not operate in a political vacuum, especially in a society as highly politicized as we know Italy to be. Not only do bureaucrats typically owe their jobs and their promotions (and transfers to limbo!) to political contacts; they themselves are often political party activists. Indeed, it takes no time at all to identify not just the political party, not just the party faction, but also the political party "notable" with whom many of the most able senior bureaucrats are allied. The pattern may not be as crass as the *caudillo* system of Latin American countries. It does mean, at a minimum, that bureaucrats respond to political pressures.

Remember that this is a system of patrons and clients, and that patrons who make *raccomandazioni* on behalf of clients are key channels through which ordinary citizens can make their needs and demands felt. The patrons enjoy that status because of a demonstrated capacity to leverage the bureaucracy, that is, to produce results. This occurs either directly or through the agency of one of the political parties or party factions.

The surest way to go when it comes to setting limits to bureaucratic power or to influencing its exercise is either to become one of bureaucracy's clients or to exploit an established kinship, or *parentela*, relationship between a patron, a political party, and a bureaucratic agency. Either method will help to convert the otherwise overbearing power of the bureaucracy to more human proportions and to render the bureaucracy more susceptible to "democratic controls" than might first appear possible.[13]

PARTY GOVERNMENT

This last point brings us to the heart of the matter, and perhaps to the most reliable statement we can make about the Italian democratic state: effective political power is heavily concentrated in the hands of its political parties. This may or may not be a good thing for Italy, and, as we shall see, there are many who flatly state that it is not. Among other things, it seems to encourage not only morally suspect and often corrupt behavior in the management of public administrative, banking, and industrial enterprise. It also tends to immunize public servants and institutions from the type of oversight that democracy would seem to require.

No one can doubt that the political parties are in control of the country. In a somewhat haphazard way, and perhaps much to the surprise of the party leaders themselves, Italy has evolved a remarkable and perhaps unique form of "party government." We need to define this term, in particular because there are so many people in the West who believe that party government is the essence of representative or parliamentary democracy.[14]

Party government does not mean merely government-by-party. The Soviet Union, the Chinese People's Republic, Cuba, and a great many other dictatorial regimes are dominated by single parties. In such countries, if additional parties exist, they are mere instruments of the "official" party. Where a single party governs, and substantive opposition is not permitted, there is little to distinguish such a system from a military dictatorship or a tyranny. No one would mistake such regimes as democracies.

As I am using the term here, party government presupposes the existence of a pluralistic democracy and polyarchy. In a democratic polyarchy, we can say that we have party government when the following conditions obtain:

First, public policy is made, and its execution is overseen, by persons who are elected to governmental office on the basis of their political party identity and affiliation.

Second, decisions about which policy alternatives will be made official are taken not independently by officeholders but either within the political parties of which they are members or in the name of these parties.

Third, public policy makers and supervisors are responsible to the voters, again not as individuals but as representatives of the parties under whose label they were elected. That is, the political party not only fronts for the candidate; it is also responsible to the electorate for the official actions of those of its members who are elected or appointed to public office.

Fourth, the above implies that the party has identifiable organization and leadership, that it has authority over its own members, and that it can effectively compel its elected and appointed officials to behave according to law, as well as according to what the party's leaders themselves prescribe.

This is obviously an idealized description of party government that we would not expect to find full-blown anywhere in the world. Nevertheless, we should be able to say how close to this ideal any given polity comes. The Soviet Union and the Chinese People's Republic, as well as all other forms of dictatorship, including military ones, do not belong in this container. For quite different reasons, we would also have to exclude the American federal system, because truly national political parties are nonexistent in the United States and also because the constitution makes it possible for one party to control the presidency while another controls the Congress. Party government is easier to come by if the political system is "parliamentary" rather than "presidential." It is impossible if more or less disciplined parties, organized nationally, are not around.

Note that party government does not imply efficient or effective government. Party government could, and sometimes does, produce immobilism, wastefulness, drift, poor implementation of public policies, venality, and worse. In limiting cases, such as the ill-fated Weimar Republic, party government can bring about the breakdown of democracy itself. In a less spectacular way, the advent of Italian fascism was also the result of failure of party government.

Of the four necessary conditions just mentioned, Italy today clearly meets only the first. There is little question that public policies in Italy are made by political parties.[15] There is equally no doubt that the political parties have a lot to say about how policies themselves are administered. Indeed, one of the most strident complaints, as we shall see in a moment, is that the country is being suffocated by this particular aspect of party government.

As for the other requisites, the evidence is mixed. As in other democracies, it would be almost impossible to show that the political parties are, in fact, responsible to the electorate for the policies that governments produce or for the manner in which these last are then administered. It is easier to say in theory that the parties should reap rewards or be punished for what their representatives do in office than to show that this is how it actually works out in practice.

The problem is endemic to representative democracies. This is one of the reasons why many consider the referendum (as well as the legislative initiative and the recall of public officials) essential instruments that assure effective mass political participation. In the Italian context, it is worth recalling that the referendum may have been used recklessly by some, like the Radical party, who circulate petitions. The voters, however, have yet to reverse a single act of the legislature submitted to their electoral judgment. No lack of "maturity" there. This record may also be read as evidence that the voters approve of party government itself. It is the parties, after all, at least the major ones, that produce the laws in the first place, and the voters have systematically endorsed them.

What about "party discipline"; does not Italy fall remarkably short where this aspect of party government is concerned? Well, measured against, say, how effectively Britain's parliamentary whips keep members of their respective parties in line, Italy's performance looks ghastly. But lawmakers break ranks in other parliamentary systems, too. The issue is not whether the political parties make policy 100 percent of the time or whether party discipline is iron-clad. It is, rather, whether policy-making by parties is considered legitimate; whether the responsibility for successes or failures in government management is laid at their feet; and whether, most of the time, it is expected that elected officials will vote as their respective parties dictate. Italy meets these criteria reasonably well.

THE ITALIAN TWIST

Italy is a deviant case of party government on the second, or policy-making, requisite. That is, it is not just the party or parties that constitute the government that make public policies, but the parties of the opposition as well.[16] We have alluded several times before to this very important aspect of democracy, Italian style. We must now underscore three particular aspects of it:

First, as noted above, leaders of the political parties go to great trouble to deflect issues away from points of head-on collision among the competing groups. Reflected here is a deep psychological aversion to divisive confrontations that would surely occur if the so-called ideological polarization of the country were more substantial than electoral campaign rhetoric. Even so, the Italian political class's instinct is to avoid direct ideological confrontation wherever possible.

Second, before divisive issues reach parliament they are likely to be settled among the political parties, so to speak, on the outside. This follows from the above: confrontations in parliament are not only public, they are also formal, that is, real in the sense of having authoritative consequences. The formal and official resolution of conflict can readily degenerate into an erosion of the polity itself.[17]

Third, because the process of negotiation and search for compromise is located somewhat outside the formal institutional framework, it requires that the opposition be consulted as well. This consultation involves primarily, but not exclusively, the Communist party. The goal is to obtain the concurrence of the opposition in order to set limits to conflict within the formal areas of policy-making.

Politicians engage in this type of collusion in part because of the aversion toward extreme partisan conflict just noted. In the PCI's case, we have a party that represents almost a third of the electorate; notwithstanding this, there exists an unwritten agreement among the other parties that the PCI cannot validly, or safely, be included in a national coalition government. This situation is often called "blocked democracy." As long as it persists, some other practical or informal means must be found to make the PCI and its voters count. The parliamentary game will not work very well if a third of the players are told in advance that there is absolutely no way they can score points in it.

Thus, when the government prepares budget proposals, tax measures, laws pertaining to economic and industrial development or to regional government, and a host of other issues, you may be sure that leaders of the PCI will be consulted. Similarly, in the often protracted processes of lottizzazione, such as those pertaining to appointments of persons to banks, some public industries, or the RAI television and radio networks, the so-called outsiders will also be consulted.

This informal, party-centered method of bringing the so-called opposition into the policy-making process is not limited to the PCI but involves the smaller parties as well. Of the latter, only the neofascist MSI has suffered discrimination, but even this exclusion is fading as memories of World War II dim and the neo-Fascists themselves learn to be more guarded in their public statements about democratic institutions.

There is much to commend in this type of party government. Superficially, Italian electoral and political struggles look very much like those we find in Latin America. They suggest head-on collisions over ideological points of view that cannot be reconciled. One can easily infer from evidence of this kind that politics there represents continuous mortal combat. We know this to be in part the illusion created by politics-as-spettacolo. More important, centuries of trial and error have solidified the principle that, no matter how severe the apparent conflict, creative leaders will work out some form of mutual accommodation. Beyond the sound and fury of ideological exchanges, especially those that occur around elections, one finds the norm to be a continuous search for peace and reconciliation. Italians are unequivocal realists on this score.

In practice this means that part of the time the "outs" will be very much "in" the rule-making group and not standing on the outside as opponents. Thus, Italy practices political syncretism of the highest order. It manages to produce agreements and cooperation among groups that by right should be at each others' throats and that often create exactly that impression. In fact, whereas the Italian party system looks hopelessly fragmented, it is cohesive enough to provide most sectors of society with a sufficient rationale for lending legitimacy to the system itself.

Some political leaders are not enthusiasts of the informal arrangements just noted. Bettino Craxi, for example, strongly believes that the majority should govern and that the minority should engage, responsibly, in opposition. Opponents of the PCI are particularly incensed on grounds that consultations with that party "under the table," or outside of parliament, provide the Communists with prestige that it in turn exploits on election day. In effect, collusion makes it unlikely that the PCI's electoral base will wither away: the party may not be in the cabinet, but it manifestly has considerable leverage over policy.

There is the additional objection that to engage in this form of policy making is in violation of the procedures outlined by the constitution. This is true, as far as it goes. It is also true that no political democracy known to man has ever slavishly behaved as a piece of paper called a constitution dictates. If nothing else, the constitution never speaks for itself but requires someone's interpretation, or claim, about its meaning. So far, the Italians have displayed a healthy pragmatism in their interpretation of their constitutional norms.

During the prime ministership of Bettino Craxi, some steps were taken to reduce the PCI's de facto influence over policy. But they were hesitant and cautious moves, especially because many Christian Democrats and members of the Socialist party do not believe it healthy to pretend that Italy does have a parliamentary system, with a majority that governs and a minority that loyally opposes, when in fact everyone understands that the present "opposition" will not be permitted to become the country's government.

The PCI itself tacitly accepts and covets the existing arrangement. Indeed, it will complain when it appears that leaders of the PSI but especially of the DC are inclined to cut it out of the informal process. As things stand, the PCI can both have its cake and eat it: it can both participate in the formulation of public policies and attack them when that suits its purposes. Not a bad arrangement. Needless to say, the PCI must avoid the abuse of this privilege.

PARTITOCRAZIA

Obviously the system described is based more on the centrality of parties than of institutions. It both reflects and reinforces the omnipresence of politics. The political parties not only drive the operations of most governmental institutions; their role in the system is actually self-sustaining.[18]

The parties' intrusive presence is now widely referred to as *partitocrazia*, or partyocracy. Coined about thirty years ago, partitocrazia is not a term of admiration but rather of indictment and alarm.[19] The claim is that the penetration of society and government by these organizations has gone much too far, so far indeed that they have replaced the legislature, the executive, the bureaucracy, and even the courts. This state of affairs would be worrisome for any democracy but especially for a relatively young one that should get started on better footing and develop sounder habits.

The other side of it is that blurred responsibility of institutions, vague decision rules, informality in the resolution of conflict is exactly what the shrewd doctor would order if he or she took a hard look at Italy's real condition. The underlying idea is this: If there are serious obstacles that stand in the way of institutions performing as the theory of parliamentary democracy would prescribe, look for a substitute that at a minimum will not destroy the democratic process. The system of party government called partitocrazia seems to provide exactly that kind of solution. The Fourth Republic of France, similarly challenged, failed to find a solution all'italiana, and Charles DeGaulle got rid of it.

The epitome of partitocrazia involves wheeling and dealing by the secretaries general, and a few other notables, of the political parties. Needless to say, their activities are prominently covered by the mass media. One has the impression of a continuing "summit meeting" among men who may or may not be cabinet members but who nevertheless exercise powers of life and death over them, and over public policies as well. These persons now spend almost as much time engaged in the so-called verifica, or checkup to see if the government should continue to live, as the government itself may spend making public policies. Indeed, the verifica may actually come to replace the vote of confidence in parliament, which is the more normal and constitutional way to determine a government's longevity. It is not so much that these men may decide over a weekend dinner that a government will fall. It is that the mass media will communicate this to the public as they tune in the late news or pick up the morning paper and that many members of parliament may learn about their fate in the same way.

This informal system drives the constitutional lawyers and other purists to distraction. What kind of a democracy is this, they ask, where those who head political parties, including parties that are supposed to be in the opposition, get together outside parliament, or away from the cabinet, and decide by themselves which laws will or will not pass, which governments will or will not survive? On this ground alone, some experts demand reforms that would hem in the powers of the party secretaries, while others insist that nothing short of a new, or second, republic will set things straight.[20] We will examine some of the suggestions for reform in the next chapter.

We must note two radical disjunctions here. The first, trasformismo, severs the connection between elections and governments; the second, partitocrazia, severs (or almost) the connection between formal institutions and public policies. Both disjunctions can be and are tolerated because the political parties are tied to subcultures and to organizations through which the interests of differing segments of the electorate are both expressed and pursued.

If this were not materially the case, the disjunctions themselves would truly paralyze and perhaps destroy the system. The point is that the present arrangement persists not because it is pathological but rather because it works. That is, in ways that the major theorists of democracy may not have anticipated, and may not approve, Italy's political parties do constitute the main vehicles through which political conflict is mediated and political democracy unfolds.

If parties govern in this way, they do so far from perfectly. No one can claim, for example, that the parties rule on behalf of the people or that they operate primarily as instruments of the latter. Indeed, the parties are so central in the political process, so pervasive in society, and yet so tightly in the hands of a relatively small group of persons who make political life their only profession, that one might argue they actually do fail to live up to the theoretical requirements of representative democracy. This would no doubt be so were the parties monolithically organized internally or were they the only or even the main channel through which the people are able to register their needs, preferences, demands, and reactions regarding public policy.

The masses, however, are not without other forms of influence.[21] Their desires and indeed their weight can be registered through political "notables," or patrons, through mass movements and the mass media, and, of course, through interest groups like the trade unions and others we have discussed. The omnipresence of political parties does not make them omnipotent. However competent the party leaders may be, they cannot and dare not try to rule Italy alone. These men and women may weigh very heavily in society at large, but they do not even pretend to control any of society's spheres, including the political sphere, by themselves.

Even if parties were monolithic and there were no other channels of access to places where political power is leveraged, it is well to remember that there are several political parties and that they do compete. Indeed, there are party factions as well, and persons in search of political leverage can turn this overall configuration to their advantage. The parties, which means their leaders, are simply not independent of the individuals and organizations, some of them very powerful, that support them and/or with which they maintain close relationships.

Neither the Liberals nor the Republicans, for example, can pretend to be unmindful of what the industrialists and the well-heeled middle-class Italians prefer or need. The Christian Democrats cannot ignore the wishes of the Vatican or of Catholic organizations, even if this were their strongest innermost wish. The Communists, on the other hand, not only use the trade unions to their own purposes and advantage, they are also to some extent used by these same organizations. The same can be said for the trade union confederations associated with the DC and PSI. Political pluralism means, among other things, that there are many different channels through which people can gain access to and perhaps exercise influence over the political process. Italy's democracy is a pluralistic system par excellence. It is also a pluralism in which formal institutions of government weigh somewhat less and political parties weigh somewhat more than may be the case in other democracies. In thinking about democracy, we need to overcome the tendency to believe that only the version of it we happen to be living, or prefer, qualifies for that label.

A CORPORATIST SYSTEM?

It has been suggested that Italy's method for arriving at public policies is really "corporatist." The basis for this claim lies in several assumptions. The most important of these is that the more powerful organized groups in society, like labor and business, exercise a direct, substantial, and often determinant influence over public policies, especially those policies that fall into the "political economy" category. A second assumption is that the official policymakers and, even more, those responsible for the implementation of policy require the cooperation of these groups if the policies themselves are to be successful.

For a corporatist system to exist, key organized groups must be able to gain special access to the nerve centers of the governmental process. Indeed, in a truly corporatist system, there would be one and only one, essentially official, "corporation" or "syndicate" for each major interest or broad professional/occupational category, and the leaders of these would enjoy the privileged access. This privilege, however, would also carry special responsibilities: the group leaders, in exchange for the influence they would exert in setting policies, would be expected by the government to assure that group members would comply with the letter and spirit of the policy agreements reached.[22]

The model corporatist system would also be a highly technocratic one; primary influence and responsibility for the formation and execution of public policies would fall into the hands of specialists. The picture we have is clear: in each of many specialized policy domains, government officials and representatives of the most relevant organized groups get together to make policy—or at least to determine the options to be placed, say, before the legislature. In such a system, the experts become the de facto governors.

It is easy to see why, were such a system to emerge, some liberal democratic institutions, chief among them the legislature, would appear to be superfluous. Once the experts have taken things in hand, the legislature could do little on the lawmaking side, even though it might still retain some important functions, as, for example, the oversight of public administrative activities.

Some of those who write about these supposed developments not only report on corporatism but become its advocates. Among other things, they argue that this form of representation of society's major interests may be superior to the traditional liberal democratic legislature. This was, of course, one of the main claims of the Italian Fascists around Mussolini, from whom the basic corporatist model of representation derives.

The corporatist mode of representation and of policy-making is not necessarily inimical to party government. Nor is it, as many believe, a step in the direction of the dictatorial state. However, the corporatist mode certainly implies a degree of basic consensus, at least among the so-called social partners like business and labor. The consensus would apply not only to the problems that require high-priority attention from government but also to the means (including collaboration by organized groups) to be used in their solution.

Needless to say, consensus of this kind would soon make a relic of older-style conflict among political parties. Some believe such conflict is already on the wane. Where? In highly industrialized societies where welfare-state measures have brought more material benefits than anyone ever dreamed possible. As a result the citizens of these so-called postindustrial societies can turn to the pursuit of postmaterial values.

Many in Italy who anticipated this scenario also welcomed it. Among other things, this form of policy-making would presumably overcome some of the more objectionable aspects of partitocrazia, because policy would emanate more directly from those major groups in society that were most interested in or affected by it.

Predictions about the postmaterial society were premature, just as the observation that the policy-making process had become corporatist was considerably off the mark. Italian political practice is immensely less corporatist than it may once have appeared on the surface. The wrong inferences were drawn from a few episodes that began in the mid-1970s when a somewhat reunited trade union movement seemed disposed to collaborate with business and government in the setting of incomes policies. Later, in the early 1980s, it actually appeared that leading members of the Christian Democratic and Socialist parties, who headed ministries, might bring organized labor and business together in a corporatist mode of policy-making.

It was mostly illusion, and it lasted only a brief moment. Not only do employers feel more comfortable when they are fighting the unions, as opposed to collaborating with them, but the unions feel the same way. As for the latter, despite the generous hopes and hard work of several union leaders who tried to further reunification of organized labor, the unions feel more at home when they are quarreling with each other. It is this older pattern that has now reasserted itself, and it looks anything but corporatist.[23]

Corporatism, in fact, requires very strong trade union and industrial organization, whereas these organizations, especially the trade unions, are quite weak. Indeed, the trade unions today, after about a decade of astonishing growth, appear as weak as they were over thirty years ago. Even if the three major competing confederations were to be reunited, they would face the problem that only a sharply reduced proportion of the labor force belongs to any union at all.

Corporatism presupposes that the basic differing interests in society will tend to crystallize, or be forced into, single organizations in each sphere. But as we have seen in Italy, these organized interests are fragmented. This is true not just of the trade union sphere but of many others as well. In short, corporatism is not easily squared with the existence of powerful political subcultures. Nor is it compatible with equally powerful impulses to bring about more pluralism and experimentation in the forms of political participation. Both impediments, as well as others like the cultural gap between north and south, make corporatist government unlikely.

Things may have gone in a more corporatist direction had the PCI's Berlinguer and the DC's Moro succeeded with the Historic Compromise.[24] I frankly doubt this. The step would have encouraged the reunification of the labor movement. It would also have emanated in a great deal of triangular negotiations among members of the executive and representatives of the unions and organized business. But it is unlikely that this change would have brought anything like a radical modification of the powerful system of party government I have described here.

And this suggests the decisive reason why any description of the government process, and especially of the representation of interests, as bordering on corporatism will be in error:[25] if partitocrazia of the kind we have examined is real, then the corporatist mode of making public policy is simply impossible. You cannot have government by the experts if the party leaders are required to play the role described in order to keep the democratic system together.

The Italians who know this best are the selfsame leaders of organized labor and business. To be sure, some of them may have deluded themselves in the 1970s that a new era of technocratic policy-making had dawned. Especially in the case of trade union leaders, the heady victories of the early 1970s led to the expectation that they could henceforth devote most of their time to the matter of setting the broader goals for society through their immediate, essentially corporatist, participation in the policy process. Having gained the workers a permanent, respectable, and secure place in the sun, they could now turn their attention to matters of higher politics. This false step not only eroded the authority of the unions in the workplace; it also brought on the reassertion of political party efforts to bend the unions to their own instrumental purposes.

In any event, the leaders of the organized groups know very well where power is located and how it is exercised. This means that they pay a good deal of attention to the secretaries general of the political parties, to the party factions and their leaders, and to the local party notables and patrons who constitute the base of the power system. Leaders of industrial and other interest groups know and do the same thing.

That these group representatives actually reach party leaders is made plain by the kind of squabbling and infighting that occurs not just within the parties but within the cabinet itself. Indeed, an additional reason why parties that should constitute the opposition have so much clout over policy lies in the fact that they, too, are entirely integrated into this dynamic system.

This party-centered dynamic that drives governmental institutional processes also assures that the outcomes from these processes will be unstable. The corporatist model, however, not only assumes stability, it requires it. But, with the exception of the PCI and the CGIL, which to some extent the PCI still dominates, no other party or organized group could offer the disciplined behavior that a thriving corporatist system must demonstrate.

If the country seemed to be leaning in a corporatist direction a short while ago, this is no longer true. The policymakers are back at the same old stand, which is a political party stand where party leaders practice the same old form of policy-making that has persisted in Italy for as long as there has been democratic government, indeed, for as long as there have been political parties.

Make no mistake about it: as far as national policies are concerned, it is the parties par excellence that govern the country. The chances that this will change in any significant way is a question I will address in the concluding chapter.

REGIONAL VARIATIONS

Does party government as described also prevail in regional and local governments? Largely, yes, but there are a couple of qualifications that should be noted. To begin with, the regions of Italy now enjoy a certain amount of political and governmental autonomy.[26] Not as much as we find in genuinely federal systems like the United States or West Germany, but more than is found in unitary governmental systems like those of France or the Scandinavian democracies. This autonomy means that the regional governments can make some policies on their own, and to some extent this is also true of the cities and communes.

Now, the coalition of parties that makes up the national government does not necessarily repeat itself locally, for at least three reasons. First, the distribution of the electoral strength of each political party varies considerably from place to place. This being so, parties like the PCI, frozen out of the coalition at the national level, may actually dominate some regional and local governments, as it has and, to a diminished extent, still does. An important implication here is that persons who support parties that are formally excluded from national government may nevertheless experience gratifications because their parties are in power in some of the regions and cities.

Second, several regions have powerful indigenous political parties that are not present nationally. In Sardinia, for example, the Partito Sardo di Azione is fast becoming the dominant party there, and it will in fact dictate what coalition comes into existence. A similar, but ethnically based, party is found in the South Tyrol. In other regions, special interest parties like those organized by pensioners or the "greens" may be quite important as instruments through which their followers achieve some influence over policies.

Third, the regional and local organizations of many of the national parties do not necessarily agree with their official national leaders. Indeed, they may be and often are the local and regional machines that support powerful factional leaders in the national party apparatus. The DC, for example, is a somewhat loose, and often very tense, confederation consisting of local and regional notables who are in effect political warlords. Within their own jurisdictions, these leaders enjoy considerable autonomy to do as they like, to make (within broad limits) their own independent deals and arrangements.

Each of these three conditions means that the pattern of power and influence that may exist nationally is not automatically reproduced in microcosm at all other levels of government.

In the mid-1970s, the surge in PCI electoral appeal that surrounded Eurocommunism brought the party unexpected control of the local governments of all of the major cities. Together with the Socialists, some minor parties on the left, and laical parties like the Republicans, the Communists enjoyed almost a decade of governmental predominance not only in these municipalities but in several of the regional governments as well. That is now in the past, and, under pressure from the DC, the Socialists have withdrawn from the few remaining places where, were they so inclined (which under Craxi they were not), they could still form left-wing juntas with the PCI.

Communists have accused the PSI of betraying the left, although not so vociferously as to preclude the possibility of future collaboration between the two parties. The PCI must also take some responsibility for this turnabout; its own appeal to the voters has certainly declined since the salad days of the mid-1970s.

In the meantime, the Socialists have intelligently and unabashedly pursued their own self-interests. The PSI, in fact, has gained much more control of mayoral and regional presidential offices than its somewhat puny showing at the polls would justify. Because it has been willing and able to move either to the right or to the left in the formation of local and regional coalition governments, it has optimized the price it can demand from others in exchange for its collaboration.

Do these regional and local coalitions imply that there is more effective "popular government," that is, government by the citizenry through elections, at these levels than in national politics? Not really, or at least not everywhere. The process of trasformismo reaches into local government, too, sometimes producing highly unlikely and entirely unexpected coalitions. In some cities, like Naples, working coalitions may fail to materialize for months or years. Byzantine maneuvers, at either the local or national level, may bring about such paralysis.

In addition, despite what the constitution or the laws may say about regional or local autonomy, powerful forces are at play to keep this at an innocuous level. Bureaucratic agencies at Rome, for example, always jealous of their prerogatives, will try to make local and regional autonomy a dead letter. The failure of the national government to devolve to these other governmental authorities the power to tax and independently to raise revenues implies that, at best, autonomy will emerge only from a continual struggle between center and periphery.

The parties themselves, no matter what they may say about the desirability of greater local autonomy, rarely act to turn these high-flown words into effective policy. Local autonomy or self-determination is not easily permitted to interfere with the strategies of the national parties, particularly those like the PSI and the PCI that are run with an iron hand from the center.

This contamination of local and regional politics by the national political forces has gone so far that the so-called administrative electoral campaigns are now conducted as if the life and death of national government depended on their outcome. Just as relatively slight shifts in the votes in national elections will sometimes have greatly magnified consequences, so may be the case with regional or local electoral outcomes. What these consequences will be cannot be established in advance, but we can bet that each party will try to make the most of them. In a recent case, a Communist party leader made the ludicrous claim, which nevertheless frightened some voters, that were the PCI to come first in scattered local elections it would demand entrance into the *national* government!

The average Italian voter may or may not be as poorly informed politically as the pollsters claim. But it would manifestly require an improbable level of political sophistication, and a small computer, to work out in advance all of the possible nuances and permutations that go with these small electoral shifts. By and large, citizens are happy to leave this arcane activity to those who engage in it as a profession. Where elections rarely produce any obvious winners or losers, one can do this in a relaxed way, without much fear that the country will fall into the well of political alienation or violence as a result of it.

We conclude on this point that, whatever may be the level of opportunity to participate politically offered by regional or local governments, the political parties remain at the center of the process. This being so, those who wish to leverage the process of government are best advised to attempt it through the agency of the parties. The optimal approach remains that of working through a party, as well as organizations and political patrons, that are manifestations of one's own political subculture. To be outside any of the major three of these is to invite complete ineffectiveness as a citizen. This will remain the case as long as the subcultures themselves remain in place.

PARTIES AND BUREAUCRACY

The parties may be ubiquitous, but so are the several million Italians who constitute the state's public administrative apparatus. In the final analysis, the exercise of influence and power will be manifested in what these men and women do or do not do, allow or do not allow. The legalistic mentality I mentioned earlier gives these bureaucrats, particularly those at the upper reaches, enormous powers. The citizenry may be entirely justified in expression of criticism, even of disdain, for the ways in which the bureaucracy heaps disservices on the country; but they dare not ignore the reality of things.

Party leaders are well aware of this situation, and the more creative among them take steps to render it more serviceable to their needs. The basic strategy is to anticipate where the key bureaucratic levers are located and to assure that these are staffed by otherwise qualified persons who are friendly toward the party. Parties like the DC that can directly affect the career mobility of the bureaucrats are particularly advantaged in this process. But the Socialists and even the other parties, including the PCI, have also been successful in establishing working parentela, or kinship relationships, with powerful bureaucratic agencies.

In short, if party government is to incorporate the major power wielders within the bureaucracy, the parties must politicize it. They have been remarkably successful in this regard. Lottizzazione, for example, applies not just to the appointment of ministers and undersecretaries, managers of public corporations and banks, or the chiefs of cabinets who are obvious and accepted political appointees. Party considerations will reach even the austere levels of the prestigious Council of State and Court of Accounts. The underlying rationale for these efforts to colonize the bureaucracy politically is not inspired exclusively by considerations of sheer patronage. It also rests on the conviction that if one party does not gain influence or control of a bureaucratic sector, another one will.

Some balance or equilibrium in the system is achieved by the fact that clientist relationships between bureaucrats and interest groups and kinship relationships between bureaucrats and political parties exist side by side. Where these overlap, they create a formidable sector of influence for the groups and political parties involved. Catholic interest groups and DC strongholds in certain ministries (like agriculture, the development of the south, public works) would be good examples. In recent years, the Socialists have made some inroads into certain ministries, like the one that controls state participation in industrial and banking activities, but the old Christian Democratic powerholders are not easily dislodged.[27]

A GOVERNMENT OF LAWS?

To some extent, the third branch of government, the judiciary, has also come under this type of party influence.[28] The national parliament, sitting in joint session, appoints one-third of the members of the Constitutional (or Supreme) Court. These judges have a clear-cut party label, although this does not mean that they are at the beck and call of the party to whom they owe their election. In fact, the tribunal has given every evidence of being no more politicized than is the Supreme Court of the United States. But that comparison is enough to suggest that, like its counterpart in Washington, the Italian court is not free of often deep political coloration in what it does. The fact that a proportion of its membership is elected

on the basis of the most open, sometimes polemical, political considerations makes it even more subject to this interpretation.

The severest degree of politicization of the judiciary is found in the
lower reaches of the judicial system, and particularly in the appointment
and in the activities of "investigating magistrates." There are no district
attorneys here in the Anglo-American sense. Investigating magistrates,
who are judges in their own right, serve that function. They are authorized
by other judges to delve into possible or alleged violations of law. Indeed,
if it comes to a public magistrate's attention that a crime has allegedly
been committed within his or her jurisdiction, official responsibility requires that an investigation be opened.

The investigating magistrate, called the *inquirente*, has remarkable leeway in the conduct of investigations. The inquirente may subpoena persons, take depositions from them and others, order official and private
files sealed and delivered to their custody, and amass evidence, sometimes
over a period of several years. Almost every move they make invites public
speculation, and the media do not miss many opportunities to provide a
surfeit of it.

Once an investigation has been completed, not a grand jury but simply
another magistrate, the public minister, must agree with the investigator
that there are sufficient reasons to arrest persons and to proceed judicially
against them. Many such persons will not be submitted to bail, and, given
crowded court calendars and other procedural complications (some of
which may be deliberately encouraged), the accused may be incarcerated
for long periods without coming to trial. Where habeas corpus is essentially unrecognized and where even bail is a very uncertain right of the
accused, truly enormous powers, which can be easily abused, accrue to
judges.

Add to this picture that the magistrates themselves are organized into
professional associations that have quite distinctive left-wing, center, or
right-wing political coloration, and we reach the conclusion that judicial
power itself is quite consciously, and some would say cynically, guided
by ideology in favor of one political group or party as against others.
Collusion between judges and the political powers that be is a problem
that goes far back into Italian history, and it emerged in the postwar era
shortly after the republic itself got under way.

In the 1970s the problem took an unexpected turn; some of the magistrates decided, so to speak, to take the law into their own hands, without

guidance from the political parties. A number of these magistrates—appropriately dubbed "assault-judges"—turned themselves into a combination of legal Robin Hoods and vigilantes, determined to protect against erosion the hard-won privileges of the workers.

This initial and often entirely generous impulse was soon directed against a broader range of alleged inequities of the capitalist system. For example, some of the magistrates went out of their way to assure that the political terrorists got more than an even break. Others turned their attention to the Mafia and other aspects of organized crime. It was also they who were responsible for uncovering scandalous behavior that involved members of the political and ruling classes at the very highest levels.

As in other democracies, then, Italy is also governed by judges. Whether judicial action takes place on the basis of law or men is a question that from time to time besets all democracies. Italy has not been spared these dilemmas. The operation of the judiciary shows that in this democracy, too, some of the organized groups, directly or through the agency of the political parties, can turn the judicial branch of government to their service, in pursuit of their selfish interests.

In recent months the cry has been raised that the judicial arm, even when turned to the best of causes, is actually in the narrow service of one political party or another. It has also been charged with the flagrant use of the judicial power as a weapon against political opponents. A general alarm has been sounded to the effect that the judiciary has arrogated to itself, unconstitutionally, powers that are not appropriately its own. These accusations, against the background of partitocrazia I have described, would be explanation enough for the growing conviction that some institutional reform of the republic is now in order.

9

PRIMUM VIVERE

Political reform movements often generate their own momentum beyond the control of those who launch them. Something of this sort may now be afoot. A new constitutional convention or a "second republic" may not be in Italy's future; but given the insistent rhetoric of recent years, institutional tinkering seems in the cards. Never mind that the Cassandras may be wrong; that they cannot agree on which of the republic's ailments are major or minor, real or imagined; or that their prescriptions derive from all over the *Manual for the Practice of Political Medicine*. Call their recommendations social engineering, political quackery, or what you will; the mood to indulge in at least a bit of it is quite strong.

Or so it seems on the surface. To judge by what the scholars, the intellectuals, the journalists, and the pollsters say, most Italians are unhappy with things as they are and ready to support institutional changes. The print media report this, and they avidly conduct polls that purport to show a lack of public confidence in key institutions like the judiciary, the legislature, the bureaucracy, and, above all, the political parties.

One way or another, a remarkable number of persons manage to get into the act. This is so perhaps because political institutions are ready targets; they also provide critics an opportunity to make concrete their otherwise abstract references to crises. Things are not going as well as they might? Well, then, reform the state or one of its more obvious institutions. After all, everyone knows that the system is a mess and that the good things in life are there not thanks to the state but in spite of it.

For many, the degeneration of political institutions has gone so far as to suggest that this time around La Crisi, writ large, is real. Can we save this poor wreck of a republic, many ask. Is it really worth saving, some reply. Not to be outdone, the politicians themselves chime in that institutional surgery is now very much in order. QED.

DOUBTFUL PREMISES

The strident campaign for institutional reform is about ten years old. This in itself suggests that, despite the Greek chorus and the claims that there is solid consensus on the need to move ahead, things are not so simple. A broad consensus that something should be done may exist, but it does not survive even well-intentioned efforts to choose the most pressing problems and to specify how they can be effectively attacked.

Given what we have learned so far about Italian society and democracy, it will surprise no one that Italians are wary of political nostrums, especially those peddled by alien political parties or subcultures. Anthropologists keep reminding us that Italian peasants find it difficult "to trust the Lord God himself." That mentality persists into the industrial age and represents the framework within which political leaders must try to make the political process and institutions work.

For more than two millenia Italians have experienced every conceivable vicissitude of politics. Many outsiders mistakenly claim that this history produces only cynics. I believe instead that it creates a people who privilege the political imperative *primum vivere*. This instinct for survival may in some circumstances numb the more noble or heroic human impulses. But it also guarantees skepticism and foot dragging about risky institutional reforms. More than others, Italians are inclined to leave strictly alone things that seem to work well enough, even if not ideally.

The Italian constitution is a monument to this mentality. Like that of the United States, it is rigid, or difficult to amend. The founding fathers wanted it that way. They sensed that, given the peninsula's turbulent political histories, the republic they were about to launch should be protected, even against those who, with the best of intentions, would cripple it before it reached adulthood. The constitution is often also incredibly vague. The founding fathers realized that to be crystal clear about basic laws will as often divide a people as unite them.

Postwar Italy greatly needed instruments that would bring the peninsula back together. From the time of the Risorgimento and national unification, Italy has required institutions, experiences, and, above all, *time* to create Italians, as opposed to Tuscans, Umbrians, Romans, Milanese, Neapolitans, Sardinians, Sicilians, or what have you. It also needs time, as we know, to wear away those aspects of its major subcultures that divide even those people who share a regional or local identity. Where the cleavages are as varied and as deep as we find them here, the political imperatives that guide other democracies may be unthinkable luxuries.[1]

Primum vivere applied to a redemocratized society that has once fallen to fascism is anything but a crass imperative. The commandment reflects the widely shared insight that institutional changes often produce unwanted surprises even in older, well-established, highly stable polities. In young democracies, based as they often are on delicate and improbable equilibriums, institutional tinkering can readily have perverse effects. Sensing this, Italians seem inclined to go slowly in the matter of making more than cosmetic changes in institutions.

Advocates of change naturally argue that the public clamors for it. There are reasons to doubt this. Even pollsters are slowly coming to recognize that, behind surface-level criticisms, there exists considerable public admiration for the system. Possibly this was not so in earlier years when everyone reported Italians as hostile toward politics and institutions. Since then, either public opinion has changed or the quality of research has improved.[2]

Recent polls, of course, continue to show that the cutting edge of public criticism of politics remains very sharp. Despite this evidence, there is scant reason for thinking that the public is interested in either radical change or a sweeping reform of existing arrangements. Were this the case, the Communist party would have come to power a generation ago. Instead, the PCI has failed to make significant electoral gains even when the DC and other ruling parties have been caught red-handed in the most flagrant examples of political corruption and the perversion of political institutions.

It is not that the public is indifferent to such revelations. The advocates of change have simply not clarified for them how much different things would be were their pet schemes to be adopted. Public skepticism on this score is certainly not reduced by the Tower of Babel erected by the proponents of change. How is the average person to interpret the hand-wringing, the claims and counterclaims, the warnings and dire predictions—many of them delivered in the arcane language of the jurists and journalists, the professors and pundits who vie for his attention and support. The more strident, catastrophic, or unfathomable the claim, the greater the average citizen's tendency to discount it or tune it out entirely.

Masters at the art of standing still when the risks are too high, Italians can be expected to do just that about most of the institutional and procedural changes advocated.

The public is also sharp-eyed and self-interested. It will have noticed that, despite continuous references to degeneration and crisis, the country's plight is anything but dismal. Daily reminders by the media that organized crime is coddled by some public officials or that others of them are grossly incompetent or venal admittedly cast dark shadows. But equally arresting, much brighter aspects of the overall picture counterbalance these.

By mid-1986, the government of Bettino Craxi had broken all records for longevity. During Italy's twelve decades as a nation, only a fascist dictator had held executive office longer without interruption. Craxi may have generated much antipathy within the political class. But the general public warmed to his arrogance, his *grinta*, or true grit, and his negative charisma. Craxi's implacable opponents, especially those who are fond of depicting him (even in political cartoons) as a latter-day Mussolini, have actually given him a hand. Many who believe that democracy should be leavened by just a bit of authoritarianism find Craxi ideally suited to that role.

Bettino Craxi, in or out of government, symbolizes Italy's newfound political stability. His unexcelled political skills, the weaknesses of his enemies, and, perhaps, a little help from *Fortuna* combined to make him the most impressive prime minister since Alcide De Gasperi. Even the Reagan administration, in its misplaced attack on the Craxi government because of its refusal to handle the *Achille Lauro* hijacking as Washington dictated, helped make Craxi a national hero and prolong his tenure at Palazzo Chigi. Italians learned from the Craxi premiership that extended tenure there does not place the country in danger of dictatorial political control.

Bettino Craxi's *decisionismo*, or forceful style of executive leadership, his overuse of the executive decree as a substitute for ordinary legislation, and his willingness to take on Communists and Christian Democrats alike in head-on collisions certainly made him the center of controversy. But he demonstrated that, within the existing framework of institutions, the country is eminently governable. As he was fond of replying to the fiercest critics of his stewardship, "e la nave va," and the ship sails on.[3] Italians ate it up. Several years without a cabinet crisis was more than alluring; it was downright addictive.[4]

Equally gratifying were the most recent economic indicators. By 1987 inflation rates, once two or three times the European Community average, were essentially in line with it. Savings rates remained very high, as did profits in industry. Despite an official unemployment level in excess of 10 percent, industrial relations remained unusually quiescent. This occurred in part because more than a few of the officially unemployed were not on breadlines but rather on assembly lines in the hidden economy. By 1987 the most striking economic news was the spectacular increase in the value of common stock and the explosive development of mutual funds and other financial institutions that rushed to help Italians put their money on the line in a massive expression of confidence in the system and its future.

As if they needed reminding. People were told by the media, but especially by the government, that economically speaking the country had never known better times nor had its residents been more affluent. A 1986 survey showed Italian families on average with $18,000 in bank deposits, $15,000 in government bonds and other fixed-income securities, $6,000 in common stock or mutual funds, and with real property (usually a home) worth $85,000. As one newspaper put it, the answer to the question, How rich are the Italians? is "very rich and perhaps too much so."[5] Whatever that means, this is not the kind of news that saps the legitimacy of political institutions and leaders or breeds a groundswell in favor of change.[6]

As evidence continues to pile up that the democratic state is not in decline but remarkably robust, not severely hobbled by its undoubted shortcomings but, despite them, often able to run at full clip, the drumbeat in favor of change may become somewhat muted. Critics who tend to see only the darker side of things, if they wish to remain credible, cannot ignore these realities. This goes in particular for the intellectuals, on whose continuing but responsible and constructive criticisms the viability of democratic society in the long run depends. But intellectuals will fall short here as long as they remain unwilling to acknowledge, except grudgingly on rare occasions, that the republican edifice, even if it did develop largely under Christian Democratic hegemony, is worth preserving largely as it is.

A final reason to doubt that major institutional reforms will materialize involves the political parties and the system of party government discussed in the last chapter. What if the critics are correct, not only about the alleged pathologies of the republic but also in the claim that most of these are the direct consequences of partitocrazia? This would imply that all proposed reforms designed to cut the parties down to size or radically to change their place and role in the system would be viewed with hostility by these same parties. That is, successful reforms would require the co-operation of exactly those organizations that explicitly stand to lose by them. There may be a democracy somewhere whose political parties would behave in this heroic and self-effacing fashion. But it is not the one located in Italy.

RELUCTANT REFORMERS

The best evidence that the parties, despite what their leaders may say, are not committed to institutional reform is the failure so far of reforms to materialize. It is true that Italians do not rush into such actions. Take the still desperate need for bureaucratic reform. Since the beginning of the fascist era, more than twenty different committees have been charged with achieving this. The "solution" eventually chosen in the 1950s was to create a ministry for bureaucratic reform. To no one's surprise, in short order the ministry itself became a grotesque caricature of the ills it was created to alleviate. Its most striking qualification for dealing with bu-reaucratic pathology remains the unexcelled ability to practice it.

One might imagine that each political party has its blueprint for in-stitutional reform and would impose it if it could.[7] The neofascists, for example, are no admirers of liberal democracy but consider it a fool's invention that sooner or later produces mischief. In their view, people require, indeed really want, not liberty but law and order, discipline and direction, from a demanding centralized state. At the other extreme, the smaller left-wing parties, also unfriendly toward liberal democratic insti-tutions, would either fall into an orgy of institutional populism or wind up fashioning a Big Brother of their own invention.

But, as I have noted, Italians remain somewhat immunized against the appeals or the formulas of either political extreme. Before the masses can be mobilized to act against the state or to subject state institutions to a new set of ground rules, much more adversity has to afflict them than has been true of the past several decades. As for political terrorism, it made Italians, if anything, even more distrustful of radical prescriptions. The realities of politics will not permit any of the parties, not even the largest ones, to impose their will on the country.

Furthermore—and this is why the thought is appealing that most of the parties want little or no change—the prevailing rules of the game, in their day-to-day application, do not constitute mortal threats for any of the parties. One way or another, each is able to turn the prevailing system to its advantage. Under the circumstances, the powerful but inarticulated major premise is to leave things pretty much as they are. There may be opponents to this logic, such as some members of the Radical party, unreconstructed Stalinists in the PCI, Socialist "maximalists," or Catholic "integralists," but they do not count for much.

Party leaders know it is safe to pay lip service to reform so long as they can keep matters abstract and so long as they can be sure that, even at that level, they will lack a meeting of the minds about priorities. Thus, on the occasion of President Francesco Cossiga's June 1986 speech in celebration of the republic's fortieth birthday, *Corriere della sera*, Italy's leading newspaper, asked the secretaries or leading exponents of the nine major parties to name the reform of the system they would put at the top of their list.[8] The two largest parties, the DC and PCI, came out in favor of a more streamlined parliamentary process, but without specifying what would be its new rules. The Socialists, as the sometime main targets of the sharpshooters at Montecitorio, forthrightly wanted to abolish secret balloting there, at least on spending bills. The Republicans also gave high priority to limitations on the secret vote. The remaining parties specified priorities that ranged from electoral reform to the direct election of the president, from more decentralization of powers to the regions to greater use of the referendum and the legislative initiative. In short, no clear marching orders emerged from these responses.

Precisely because reform is unlikely, it is difficult to nail down with confidence how each party feels about one form of change or another. On the important question—what should the parliament look like?— parties such as the DC, PCI, PSI, and PRI have suggested extensive changes that, if adopted, would certainly make that body considerably different. Members of such fringe political groups as the Left Independents, elected under the PCI banner, offer even more sweeping suggestions for change. So far, the only characteristic these would-be reformers share is the certain knowledge that their contrasting blueprints will wind up in a stalemate.

THE COMMUNIST CONNECTION

What about the Communist party? Is it not a Marxist party that by definition is against the liberal democratic state and committed to its eradication? This is no idle question; even with the party's recent electoral decline, it still attracts almost one voter in every three. This alone makes democracy, Italian style, quite unusual. The PCI's size, its electoral appeal, its undoubted sway over organized labor, and its salience to the political management of the economy lead all discussions of the "Italian case," and especially discussions about institutional reform, to center on this party.

This practice can be dilatory, as well as boring. It is dilatory whenever even modest reforms are put off or dismissed on grounds that to tinker with the system, or to accept that it has serious imperfections, will give aid and comfort to the Communist party. Even worse, according to those inclined to this logic, reform of the system may give the PCI so much legitimacy it may actually make additional headway on election day. In short, no reforms are to be launched until the PCI disappears as an electoral force or achieves complete legitimacy. According to these same temporizers, the latter event will occur, if ever, only in some distant future. Needless to say, when the Christian Democrats themselves do not produce such arguments, they are happy to reap the benefits of those generated by others.

The pattern is also boring. Virtually all conversations about Italian politics, indeed about Italy, tend toward the reductionism just mentioned.[9] Problems of political process and institutions are automatically transmuted into *Il problema del comunismo,* and everyone is expected to agree that this is the appropriate optic. Is Italy a special case? Is Italian democracy difficult or blocked? Is Italian society eccentric? Is the party system imperfect or polarized? Is Italy a case of uneven development, a republic without government, or a political miracle of surviving without governing? Well, then, much or all of this can be laid at the doorstep of a powerful communist party that refuses to disappear. Truly remarkable attention is paid a party that has not held a cabinet seat since 1947. This has been a boon to the PCI. Until the advent of the terrorists a few years ago, and Bettino Craxi more recently, the Communists easily managed to dominate the main stage of politics.[10]

As I noted in chapter 5, the PCI remains at center stage in part because many Italians still have reservations about its democratic credentials. Some worriers are visceral anticommunists whose blood pressure rises as soon as they encounter the word *left.* Others are ardent Catholics who have heard and repeated for decades that the Communist party is the Antichrist and would menace the Catholic church and religion were it to gain more political influence. There are also those who genuinely believe that the PCI in power would attack their wealth or other established privileges in society. These worriers would export their capital, and perhaps themselves, if they thought the PCI would take over the government. Others still are the crassest of political or intellectual opportunists who find it advantageous to exploit already existing negative images of the PCI and to generate additional ones, sometimes out of whole cloth. They practice a subtle Italian version of McCarthyism.

In this context, any Communist-supported initiative for institutional reform is likely to generate more than a little suspicion. Evidence that for forty years the PCI has been one of the republic's most unflagging defenders will not cut much ice. The PCI's most implacable opponents will find it easy enough to claim that the Communists are decidedly adroit at masking their baser intentions. For many, including those who are not blindly opposed to the Communists, it remains difficult to believe that, in view of its origins in Marxism-Leninism, its Stalinist years, and its ferocious past attacks on the liberal capitalist state and on democratic socialism, the Communist party is really committed to democratic pluralism. In short, many Italians still claim that the PCI's declared willingness to accept democratic polyarchy and the rules of that system is pure eyewash designed to obscure deeper antidemocratic impulses and ambitions.

Understandably, PCI leaders are frustrated, sometimes enraged, by these indictments of their private thoughts. They are aware that where the accusations are opportunistic nothing the party can do will ever persuade the critics that its democratic credentials are finally in order. PCI leaders are particularly galled when they are placed on the defensive by members of the Socialist party, especially the most-faithful-to-Craxi among them who have honed this weapon to a fine cutting edge. Like the Christian Democrats, the Socialists believe they can turn these fears about the PCI to their electoral advantage. That this has not yet happened means only that most of them will redouble their efforts.

The PCI itself has not been entirely astute when it comes to dispelling such fears. The evidence is by now beyond reasonable doubt that the PCI has long since abandoned whatever Leninist, Stalinist, revolutionary, or dictatorial intentions it once may have had. It has also largely buried Karl Marx, although in a relatively private and silent service to which the party militants were not invited. Even so, where one is not blinded by ideology or motivated by opportunism, it requires an act of will not to recognize that the only thing even mildly menacing about the Communist party today is its name. It is neither the Vatican nor the U.S. Sixth Fleet headquartered at Naples that has brought the PCI to accept Western European-type democracy. It is postwar history itself. The Red Brigades knew this, as do the radicals to the PCI's left who believe the party has long since become an integrated part of the Establishment.

Despite this metamorphosis, the party self-destructively continues to deny that it has occurred. It does not want to be labeled a social democratic or reformist party, even though it has now changed its older tune and recognizes that such parties elsewhere in Europe have managed to bring substantial benefits to the working class. Its neurotic ambivalence became poignantly visible in the late 1970s when the PCI (without any hope of gaining a cabinet seat at that time) gave its support to the government of Giulio Andreotti. The PCI then called itself the "party of government and of struggle," a phrase that was designed to placate its own militants but that wound up confusing them and everyone else. Giorgio Napolitano, a distinguished PCI leader,in a rueful reflection on that abortive experience, pointedly noted that the PCI had somehow managed to get halfway across the stream only to mire itself down in the middle of it."

Even in a country as tolerant as is Italy of arcane political language, the PCI somehow manages to create consternation and unwittingly to supply its critics and enemies with ammunition. A few years ago, when the party's march toward a share of power seemed unstoppable, its leaders produced the vague but arresting statement that, when this happened, the PCI would not *administer* the capitalist system but would *change* it. When pressed to specify what this would mean, what changes in society, the economy, or the polity this would imply, the party became coy. The Communists have done no better at making explicit exactly what they mean when they claim that their approach to government would be a "third way" between democratic socialism of the Western European variety and what has been practiced in Italy since the late 1940s. Alessandro Natta, the PCI secretary general, in a recent case of how to make Italians needlessly nervous, boldly asserted that were the PCI to gain more votes than the Christian Democrats in a few scattered *regional* elections, the Communists would demand the opportunity to form a *national* government! The PCI's opponents had a field day with that blooper.

Today the main reason why the PCI's search for legitimacy runs aground is international not domestic. By and large, the survey data show that much larger numbers of Italians than in the past (even if far from all of them) agree that the PCI represents no threat to the country's internal democratic institutions. These same persons, like many others, are never-theless perplexed by the degree of ambiguity that still characterizes the PCI's relationship to the USSR.

To be sure, that relationship is not what it once was, and the PCI has more than once come close to a rupture with the USSR.[12] But it is still naive for the PCI leaders to insist that they should be as free to criticize the United States or the Western Alliance as are other Italian political parties or their counterparts in other Western countries. Unlike the PCI the latter have never been the willing instruments of the Soviets, nor have their commitments to democracy ever been in doubt.

Thus Italy confronts not just the "problem of communism" but, as one writer astutely put it, the "problems of the Communists" as well.[13] As long as the PCI churns out confused and confusing messages about its intentions inside Italy, as long as it remains (even for understandable reasons) in an ambiguous relationship with the Soviet Union, and, above all, as long as it persists in the identity crisis that afflicted it in the mid-1970s, even its innocuous proposals for reform of the system will raise suspicions in many quarters. In short, more than any other party, the PCI must understand that the public will continue to wonder and worry about its ulterior motives.

Communist party leaders, aware of this problem, have treated the issue of reform with kid gloves. How much reform do they want, and how would they change the system? Very little, and gingerly, when all is said and done. This seems as unlikely as it is amazing. After all, among political parties, the PCI has yelled the loudest and longest about what a mess the country is in and how far beyond the point of no return any number of so-called crises have gone. The real change they are after, though, is less of institutions than it is of their own pariah status. The pathos here is that neither the PCI alone, nor any amount of institutional tinkering, can bring that particular transformation to pass.

THE GOVERNMENTAL CONNECTION

What do the other parties want? It depends. Laical parties like the Republicans, Liberals, and Social Democrats are certainly for some re-forms, but not necessarily the same ones. The Liberals and Republicans want a stronger executive, more morality and less lottizzazione in politics, and, above all, a government free of populist pressures in the management of the economy. This last issue places them at loggerheads with a Social Democratic party that takes a backseat to no other when it comes to the demagogic exploitation of any populist opportunity. Segments of the Socialist and Christian Democratic parties would not be far behind. Under recent leadership changes, the Liberal party is reaching for a less conservative image, and the Social Democrats for a less populist and opportunistic one. These leadership changes, however, will be reflected more in what the parties do regarding public policies than in what they recommend by way of institutional change.

The Liberals and Republicans, for good historical reasons, also see themselves as the guardians of the liberal democratic state and as those most knowledgeable regarding the proper operations of its institutions. Against the civil rights of citizens, these parties would counterpose the need to assure the integrity of representative institutions. Against political expediency of the kind that led the Socialist party to waver dangerously when Aldo Moro's kidnappers sought to bring the government to its knees, they would weigh the need to maintain "the sense of the state," that is, the democratic state's integrity. They are vital parties in the liberal democratic scheme of things.

In recent years, the Socialist party beat the drums for *La Grande Riforma*. Once ensconced at Palazzo Chigi, though, the Craxi government did not fan but rather dampened the fervor about innovation. Nor was this the only irony: for a party that made public morality the centerpiece of its rise to prominence, a remarkable number of the PSI's leaders have since wound up accused, convicted, and jailed for egregious acts of public corruption.

In addition to broaching the issue of reform with caution, the Christian Democrats are downright defensive about it. And well they might be. In the eyes of many, what now exists politically is *their* system, fashioned in their image. For good reason, the DC sees attacks on the system, especially those mounted by left-wing intellectuals, as not-so-veiled attacks on its postwar stewardship. The syllogism is elementary: If the republic is indeed on the rocks, one must remember that the DC has been almost uninterruptedly at its helm.

The DC thus hears much more in the chorus that intones reform. From deeper down, overtones come through that echo laical and Marxist reservations about Catholicism and the Catholic subculture. These doubts are rooted in the past. They reach back through the centuries to lay bare once more every aspect of the Catholic church's opposition to the modern

Italian state, and indeed to modernity itself. These older doubts and fears of the church are the filters through which passes every move the DC makes. The basic fear is, politically speaking, primeval: that the Catholic church will be able to reverse history and realize its integralist ambitions through the instrumentality of the DC.

The fact that Pope John Paul II seems less interested in Italy's internal politics than many of his predecessors only mildly allays these fears. They have been rekindled of late by the Vatican's intransigent stand on the "right to life," its fierce initial reactions to Liberation Theology in Latin America and elsewhere, and, closer to home, by aggressive interventions of the Catholic clergy in domestic politics. This is topped off by the emergence of Movimento Popolare and Communione e Liberazione, two aspects of one large evangelical Catholic movement that now appears as a major factor in the political resurgence of the DC.

Images of the DC as a still-confessional party naturally lead its opponents to be hypersuspicious of its proposals for reform. Thus, both the DC and the PCI, which together account for between two-thirds and three-fourths of the electorate, are in an anomalous position: they are, one way or another, major reasons why many reforms are said to be needed. At the same time, they are the cause of diffidence and suspicion expressed about many suggested changes.

Antipathy toward the DC and suspicion about its stand on reforms seem grossly misplaced when either implies that only the country's major ills, and none of its strengths, are of that party's handiwork. Similarly, one must be dubious toward allegations that the Christian Democrats have a special talent to pervert political institutions and to practice political corruption. No political institution invented by man is corruption-proof. As for venality in office, the Socialists have demonstrated, with breathtaking speed, that they can outdistance the Christian Democrats in every dimension of it and add a few twists of their own. If venality in Italy seems out of hand, we should not blame institutions. More important may be the fact that opportunity and temptation there are unchecked by the prospect that today's opposition may become tomorrow's government.[14]

Like everything else about this country, the debate over reform has layered, nuanced, and contradictory meanings. We can say with confidence only that all parties will tend to make self-serving proposals for change, that most of these proposals will not pass, and that those that do turn out to serve the interests of democracy, or the general welfare, will achieve this effect by sheer accident.

I intend this observation neither as an arrogant dismissal of suggested reforms nor as a cynical judgment of those who propose them. I mean it as a reminder that the "reform" of political institutions is invariably a reflection of conflict over power and how it is distributed. If this sounds reasonable, we should take political party self-interest as given and judge reform proposals on such other grounds as whether they have any chance at all of enactment and, if enacted, whether they will lead to the salutary effects desired. We will look at just a few of the proposed changes in this light.

THE COMMITTEE OF FORTY

In the spring of 1983, parliament created the Committee of Forty (twenty members from each house, with parties proportionally represented) to look into reform and report back within a year. The committee held dozens of meetings, opened its proceedings to the public and transmitted them on closed-circuit television, and received extensive coverage by the press. After its deadline was extended, it reported back in late January 1985.

Committee work was tough sledding. Debates were lively and sometimes heated. Its members jostled one another as they reached for the limelight. Two members resigned, allegedly in disgust. Few missed an opportunity to engage in polemics. Even so, it is somewhat surprising, as well as writing on the wall, that only sixteen of the forty members signed the final report. If, as is likely, most of the recommendations go by the board, only crocodile tears will be spilled on the committee's account.

From the beginning, the committee ruled out radical change in the 1948 constitution and, even more, any idea of a "second republic." Its specific brief was to "reinforce republican political democracy, to make it more capable of efficiency and of stable and lasting policies . . . and to endow it with a modern technical apparatus, with the additional end in view of the democratic governance of the country."[5]

The committee intended to skirt "utopistic" recommendations, although these, like beauty, are largely in the eyes of the beholders. Almost as a throwaway line, the committee acknowledged that "institutional revisions are in substance modifications in the rules of the game." Which is of course the rub—as well as the thought to keep in mind for the rest of this chapter.

The report covers the waterfront. It recommends changes, by ordinary law or constitutional amendment, in the parliament, the prime minister-ship and executive office, the presidency of the republic, the bureaucracy (including the system of justice), local and regional government, political parties and electoral systems, trade unions, and regulations pertaining to the government of the economy. Some proposals are radical on their face while others have radical implications. A few are of marginal importance. They add up to a major facelift for the present republic.

Committee members did not work in an intellectual hothouse. Nor were they atop Mount Olympus, hurling bolts of criticism with one hand and inscribing god-given laws with the other. Instead they shopped around quite a bit, and they revealed eclectic tastes. The West German system, perhaps because it has been so stable, was especially attractive. But a German-type chancellor would be too powerful for Italians whose memories of Mussolini are still acute.

The Communists recommended a single-chambered legislature, but this was flatly rejected. It seems curious that the PCI, already notorious for its iron discipline and unparalleled expertise in the present legislature, would make such a proposal. It requires no effort whatsoever to reason that a single-house legislature would be even easier for the PCI to exploit.

True enough, Italy's bicameral system, although similar to that of the United States, does not make as much sense because both the lower and upper Italian chambers are based on population. The committee decided to attack this anomaly by downgrading the powers of the Senate to have it resemble more the British House of Lords or the West German Bun-desrat. In compensation for a mild form of castration, the Senate would be given new powers, especially the potentially significant power of over-sight over the executive branch. However, this power is not worth the paper it is written on unless other changes—most of them unlikely—are made in the national legislature.

Considerable attention is paid the chief executive and the cabinet. The prime minister needs to be strong, it is argued, vis-a-vis the cabinet, the legislature, and the political parties. The tendency of cabinet members to speak publicly and incoherently on matters of public policy or to pursue their own policies as opposed to those of the prime minister needs to be curbed. Greater power to steer the government's legislative program through parliament freer from obstructionism and booby traps is also desirable. A stronger prime minister would reduce the freedom of parties to make deals, including those that topple governments, outside parliament. He would also provide the electorate with a more certain basis to fix responsibility for public policies and to reward and punish on that basis.

Italians, however, are schizophrenic about executive power. How strong can you make the prime minister before he gets delusions of grandeur like Mussolini's? How weak can he get before the narcissistic impulses of cabinet ministers turn national government into a shambles? The committee moved cautiously, but essentially in the direction of making the prime minister more responsible to the legislature and the cabinet members more subject to his direct control than is currently the case. The underlying model is still that of the Federal Republic of Germany.

A moment's reflection reveals that the target of these and other reforms is partitocrazia. The reformers want to bring the parties to heel, and many committee members make no bones about this. In particular, they want to defang the general secretaries whose "summit meetings" make and unmake governments outside the halls of parliament. Thus, one reform would compel the prime minister, were he to resign, to come before the parliament to explain why he takes this step. The idea is that, as is presumably the case in other parliamentary systems, it should be the parliament that installs a government and gets rid of it when it loses the confidence of a majority in that body. The parliament, not the parties and their general secretaries, should create, evaluate, and decide the fate of governments.

Other proposals reflect uneasiness over executive power. As I noted earlier, there is widespread criticism about the tendency of prime ministers, faced with a recalcitrant legislature where sharpshooters lurk, to rule the country through a proliferation of executive decrees. More often than not, the legislature, whose approval these decrees eventually require, is faced with the Hobson's choice of rubber-stamping what the prime minister and cabinet have done or bringing about chaos. The double-barreled solution offered by the committee would severely limit the power to issue decrees but would also streamline the bill-passing process for matters the government defined as urgent.

A final touch to the reforms that pertain to government and legislature involves the secret ballot. Committee members were unable to agree on this issue. The Socialists would opt for an open vote, except when a secret ballot is called for in each house. Needless to say, they oppose the secret ballot on issues that imply nonconfidence. The Communists want to preserve things as they are and to leave it to each chamber to establish, as part of its internal procedures, when votes are to be open or closed. The DC and other parties are somewhere in between. One would imagine some agreement here to be a foregone conclusion since it could be effected by a mere change in the by-laws of parliamentary procedure. But things are never so easy.

EVALUATION

The beneficial effects of these and other proposals are far from self-evident. Take the committee's wish to bring the governmental process back into the legislature, where everyone seems to agree it rightfully belongs. As long as no one party gets a majority at the polls and/or in the legislature, governmental coalitions will have to be formed. To create them implies negotiations, bargains, and compromises *among parties*. The same party leaders, inside or outside the cabinet, who agree to create a coalition can, on the basis of later considerations, decide to have it fall. It is wishful thinking that new written rules, even constitutional ones, can bring back "into parliament" a political process that takes place on the "outside." Indeed, it may be a prior mistake to believe that the problem itself is unique to Italy.[16]

Many of the suggested rules would create the illusion but not the substance of change in a country where the political process is too illusory already. Were the changes adopted, political party secretaries and internal party factions, against whom these reforms are directed, would be challenged to discover new ways to defeat them. In the land of *fatta la legge, trovata l'inganno,* it would be a cinch.

What about the open vote in parliament? Amintore Fanfani and Nilde Jotti, respectively the presiding officers of the Senate and Chamber of Deputies, felt enough pressure to act that, true to form, they appointed a small committee of "wise men" to survey the studies and proposals relating to parliamentary procedures and to report their recommendations. The committee's first suggestion was to curb the secret ballot, at least on all bills involving public revenues and expenditures. This is the Socialist proposal, supported by the Republicans, and seemingly innocuous enough.

Nothing happened. As one of the "wise men" said, "Every time one turns to discuss the secret ballot, it opens a dialogue among the deaf." Giuliano Amato, a political scientist who was then also undersecretary in the prime minister's office, feigned genuine surprise. How could it be, he wondered, that nothing happens to the secret ballot despite the facts that the founding fathers deliberately did not "constitutionalize" it, a majority is apparently committed to its revision, and the proposal of the "wise men" would not abolish the secret ballot entirely but simply curtail it where votes of confidence and money bills are concerned?

The answer is that the present arrangement suits almost everyone, and especially the political party factions. Restrictions on the secret ballot and the requirement of roll-call votes would little change the relationship among the political parties. But *it would change profoundly the relationship among factions*; the rapport between party leaders and backbenchers in the legislature; and, above all, the relationship between factions and parties as well as the organized interest groups found in society.

Transparency of the governmental process is not an unmitigated virtue. It could be quite desirable in democratic societies that are highly consensual but considerably less so in societies that are not. Italy offers much food for thought on this score. Its organized interest groups are not voluntary in the sense that they may be in the United States or Great Britain. Workers and consumers, businesspeople and the barons of the universities, tradespeople and professionals do not organize simply on this basis. They organize instead by subcultures. Their organizations gain access to the policy-making process by the establishment of clientist ties to the bureaucracy. Alternatively, they operate through the political parties or, more precisely, through political party factions. Above all, they try to operate quietly and not in full view of the public. This approach to the political process is not sinister; it is highly realistic and pragmatic. It does not mock democracy; it makes democratic government possible, at least in the Italian context.

The arrangement is admittedly Byzantine. As such, it permits alliances among "grand electors," political patrons, and notables, as well as among the political factions of different parties. Many alliances and agreements would prove impossible were there greater transparency. To avoid either total paralysis of the political process on one side, or total conflict on the other, some degree of opaqueness is required. To put this differently, as long as trasformismo remains a necessary, or a central, aspect of politics, a fish-bowl approach to policy-making is not the best way to keep the system from shattering. A reform here might have perverse effects.

The secret ballot commends itself on other grounds. Since the majority coalitions in parliament are artificial or based on minimal consensus, governments need to fall from time to time to underscore this point. That is, since parties that make up coalitions are known to disagree on many issues, it is better that this fact be registered now and again—but without the dubious benefit of detailed information about exactly who abandoned the majority and brought the government down.

Recall, too, that through this mechanism the PCI, while formally excluded from government, is nevertheless enabled to be a valid, working part of the policy-making process. Insofar as the abolition of the secret ballot were to force Italy to acknowledge that it is not yet, nor can it readily become, a more "normal" parliamentary system of government and opposition, the step would be destabilizing. In short, it is simplistic to insist that democratic government requires open voting.

If a reform like the above is undesirable, others seem unnecessary. A good example is the committee's recommendations to strengthen the prime ministership. The accepted wisdom deems such a step a good idea. In the early 1980s, beginning with the government of Giovanni Spadolini, modest attempts were made to reorganize the executive office. In 1986, one such proposal was accepted by the Chamber of Deputies and now requires approval by the Senate. It remains to be seen whether the plan will overcome the still widespread prejudice among members of parliament that a weak executive is a safe executive.

It is also worth recalling that because politics is about power, little concerning its exercise long remains static. The republic's founding fathers may have set out to make strong executive leadership difficult; they did not make it impossible. Thus some of the committee's desires can be and often are a matter of daily practice.

The past forty years have seen weak and very weak, strong and very strong prime ministers. All operated within essentially the same formal institutional framework and game rules. Personality, intelligence, political skills, and the size of the prime minister's parliamentary party (to say nothing of his party faction!) will affect how much power he wields. So will the quality of his cabinet members, and of course the type and magnitude of the problems he and they confront.

There is more. Offices, including public ones enshrined in constitutions and laws, evolve. They may move forward or backward, flourish or decay, but they never stand still. Offices may become smaller, but typically they become bigger, and not just in the public sector. They can be given, or may usurp, new authority or functions. A skillful prime minister uses his office to full advantage, to make it stronger, and, above all, to get others, especially his cabinet members, to behave as he wishes. Bettino Craxi, without any thought that he needed formal authorization to do so, created a small "inner cabinet," of the kind long in place in Britain, where he concentrated the few ministers with whom he really ran the country. They were troublesome, too, but they were few in number.

Obviously, such things can and do occur without the benefit of new legislation or constitutional surgery. On occasion, it may be necessary to "constitutionalize" these changes—or to curtail them. Nothing, except perhaps the anxieties of lawyers, dictates a close fit between the formal definition of an office and its day-to-day operations. The concern of democracies and of those who wish to maintain or improve them should be the living constitution and not ill-conceived efforts to force practice to conform to a more procrustean idea of the democratic or the efficient state.

Of course, there are problems galore. Prime ministers have become too casual in the use of decree powers whenever things threaten to bog down in the legislature. There are surely too many ministries, and therefore even more of those interministerial committees that are supposed to co-ordinate the public policy process but never do. The national bureaucracy probably has too much power but, even if it does not, power is exercised in a fragmented, anarchical way by senior bureaucrats, too many of whom are southerners who believe the service state is an exotic, not-for-export, northern-European invention.[17]

Nevertheless, it is incorrect to say that Italy is without government or that it is essentially ungovernable. In the midst of apparent chaos there has been considerable stability of leadership. It is reflected in the postwar hegemony of the Christian Democrats and in the handful of national leaders who have held the prime ministership and other key cabinet posts during the four decades of the republic.[18] I mentioned earlier that the 1980s seem to have introduced greater longevity of governments as well as other signs of political stability. These developments do not square with the persistent claim that the country lacks executive leadership.

There is powerful evidence that during the last forty years the consti-tutionally weak president of the council of ministers has become a de facto prime minister.[19] Forty years ago, Alcide De Gasperi was assisted in his office by about fifty persons; today this group exceeds nine hundred. De Gasperi and his earliest successors were helped in their work almost exclusively by prefects, men almost always trained in law. Today, the prefects have been largely replaced by members of the Council of State, a highly respected body that as closely as anything else in Italy constitutes an administrative elite. Beyond this, the prime minister can call on all manner of expert assistance from every conceivable profession or walk of life. A fair number of these men and women are "borrowed" from other ministries or public corporations, because the prime minister's office has little budget of its own. Nevertheless, this staff works for the prime minister, and it plays a major role in directing the country's policies. The system is improvised; those who work in it like to complain about this, but it works. The English, who pride themselves about keeping bureaucratic staffs lean, would be amazed.

The constitution empowers the prime minister to "direct the policy of government." This broad mandate leaves lots of room for initiative and leadership. If some prime ministers have been reticent to become directly involved in the determination of who will head the major banks or public industries, who will be named to manage a vast public communications network, men like Bettino Craxi (Aldo Moro and Giulio Andreotti would be additional examples) have not hesitated a moment.

In addition, a number of important institutions are directly responsible to the prime minister or open to his influence. These include the Council of State, regional administrative tribunals, the attorney general, the superior council for public administration, the advanced school for public administration, all cabinet ministers without portfolio, and the immensely important court of accounts. This latter body can go a long way to determine whether funds authorized and appropriated by the legislature are ever spent! Sensitively used, the prime minister's authority here can add muscle to his operations.

If the present constitution does not encourage a strong prime minister, it leaves ample space to finesse the things that bind. The message seems to be: you can be strong if you want to be, but you have to work at it. The trick is to understand the nature of existing institutions and to turn them to your needs and purposes. Some do this better than others. It is unlikely to differ much if formal constitutional changes are made, and it could easily be worse. If weak men occupy offices that are "strong" only on paper, they either turn out to be paper tigers or erode the legitimacy of the office by injudicious use of its powers. In Bettino Craxi's case, the complaints were certainly not that he was a weak prime minister who lacked the tools to give the country direction. Forattini, Italy's premier political cartoonist, captured the real public image: he typically dressed Craxi in black shirt and boots.

As things now stand, the successful prime minister must be inventive and resolute in his efforts to give the system direction. He must learn to improvise, and to make "transformist" accommodations to the parties. Lawyers may throw up their hands in alarm and claim that this kind of system is written on water. They fail to appreciate, as one Italian scholar nicely put it, that this is not a weakness at all but rather one of the system's main strengths. It is entirely in keeping, I might add, with the penchant to muddle through problems and to applaud the occasional virtuoso performance. If there have been weak prime ministers, unable to keep their cabinet colleagues in check or deeply mystified about how to maintain a tight hold of the reins of leadership, this is no more than they deserve.

NECESSARY REFORMS

A critically important, and potentially explosive, issue involves the system of justice. Italy has many of the same problems here that afflict other democracies: overcrowded courtroom calendars and prisons; too many laws, including contradictory ones that permit judges to become de facto policymakers; and a penal code, dating from the fascist era, whose overhaul is long, long overdue.

Two aspects of the legal system are particularly arresting. Judges are extraordinarily powerful because they enjoy the constitutional right (or have usurped it) to make law. That is, they can set legal norms for society even if there is no existing legislation on which to base their interpretations and sentences. In effect, they can go directly to the constitution and come up with the conclusion, for example, that a medium-sized athletic stadium is not to exceed ten thousand seats, or that psychiatric hospitals are to be closed and their inmates released.

A second feature is the assumption of guilt or innocence of persons arrested and accused of crimes. In Italy, the burden of proof is on the accused to establish his or her innocence. Years ago, an eminent jurist wryly remarked about this approach to justice that were he accused of stealing the Tower of Pisa, he would go into hiding until someone else had established that the tower was still in place. More recently, Ferdinando Imposimato, a fearless magistrate made famous by his investigations of the Mafia and terrorist groups, chimed in that he was terrorized by a system of justice that made it easier to defend oneself when guilty than when innocent.

Problems do not stop here. As I noted earlier, the professional associations of magistrates are deeply politicized. Ideologically motivated "assault magistrates" can use their extraordinary arrest powers, coupled with weak habeas corpus and uncertain rights to bail, as powerful political weapons. It is unclear whether this power is more pernicious when exercised at the behest of the political parties or when the judges take it into their own hands.

Typically, two trials run side by side—one in the courtroom, the other in the press. I know of no other democracy where the mass media are as free as in Italy to destroy with impunity reputations, professional careers, fortunes, and psyches. Far from setting a sober example, leading newspapers and mass circulation magazines are, often as not, among the most reckless practitioners of this ghoulish approach to justice. Needless to add, efforts to curtail these acts of irresponsibility are quickly scored by the press and its defenders as unwarranted attacks on constitutional freedoms.

By now it is clear that change is essential. Perhaps the public does not consider the system of justice to be, as some critics claim, the "black hole" of Italian democracy. In fact, the polls show considerable public confidence in the judicial system and very little fear of judges and the courts. Nevertheless, almost three out of four Italians do not think the system operates well enough; many find its worst defects in the penal system; and too many believe that "money talks" in the citizen's search for justice.

The problem is serious enough that even persons in high places, like Bettino Craxi and Francisco Cossiga, the president of the republic, have criticized judges who use their authority as a political weapon. Predictably, the judges—who have one of the world's oldest experiences in the practice of guildlike solidarity when the going gets rough—close ranks against these provocations. Even so, the Committee of Forty very gingerly recommended reforms that would more neatly separate investigatory and judicial function, more carefully define the limits of judicial powers, and more efficiently treat the enormous case loads that now afflict the courts.[20]

Surely everyone now understands that the extraordinary powers of investigating magistrates, or inquirente, should be redefined and curbed. One direct step in this direction would be the abrogation of the preventive detention laws passed in the 1970s as part of the state's response to the problem of terrorism. Another would be to institute habeas corpus or, in any case, a more severe limitation on the power to hold persons in jail without bail and without bringing specific charges. The accusation that the existing system often rivals the Inquisition in its arbitrariness is not farfetched.

As obvious as is the need for intervention, only a brave or reckless person would bet that it will occur in the short run. The parties are split here, too. For many Communists and others it is enough that Bettino Craxi and some of his *fedelissimi* support certain reforms, like those of the judiciary, to turn them into implacable opponents of change. When the Italians' conservatism toward institutions is combined with their corporatist motivations to protect their turf from outsiders, even marginal reforms seem improbable.[21]

The irony in the debate about reform lies in the failure of Italy to enact beneficial changes that would require neither major legislation nor constitutional amendment. The national legislature, a prime example, is weak because it is starved for material, technical, and professional assistance. Individual members of parliament do not have their own offices or telephones, to say nothing of professional staffs. Committees of the legislature are similarly compelled to operate on a shoestring. Italian lawmakers who visit the U.S. Congress and see at close range the resources available to its members go into shock.

The legislature can be made better able to deal with the complex problems of a modern industrial society, to respond more responsibly to the legislative programs of the cabinet, and to become a watchdog over the executive branch only if it is equipped with the research and reference services, and with the professional staff, that such activities would require. Since this is no secret, the fact that steps have not been taken in that direction in four decades suggests deliberate neglect. As things stand, lawmakers are dependent on their political parties or on interest groups associated with the latter for the "assistance" they get. Sometimes they can get help from the bureaucracy, which is in turn dependent on certain clientist groups. One way or another, the intention seems to be to make the performance of certain legislative functions impossible. Because so many of the would-be reformers are themselves parliamentarians, including academic scholars, the admonition "heal thyself first" seems entirely in order.

Members of parliament are, to say the least, ambivalent. Late in 1986, it appeared that Montecitorio would take the revolutionary step of providing each MP with an "assistant." All hell broke loose. The Senate, led by a Christian Democrat, responded that it would *reduce* the privileges of its members, particularly former members, who can still ride around gratis and first class on the country's trains. The Communist party, which initially backed the lower-house proposal, officially approved by the Communist speaker of the house, later withdrew support. An endless stream of objections, some of them valid, was offered underscoring the wasteful, ludicrous, and perhaps mischievous use to which MPs would put any additional assistance. Change will occur slowly, if at all.

These considerations suggest either that the would-be reformers are not entirely serious about change or that they direct their aim at the wrong, more difficult, or even dangerous targets. An even better interpretation is that much of the rhetoric and the grandstanding about reform is pure spettacolo. It certainly makes good copy and has been a major industry for the press and for many intellectuals. It keeps some people amused and provides others with a sharp focus for directing their anger. It nicely serves the Italians' need to insist that little is safe and nothing is permanent, while at the same time they build quite solid and permanent institutions, at home and in the political sphere.

The Committee of Forty fell right into this mode. Rather than find a least common denominator, it submitted a report that not more than two-fifths of its members would sign. More than one member of the committee had earlier assured me: "Wait and see, nothing, even less than nothing, will happen." If a microcosm of the legislature that worked intensively on the issue of reform for more than a year produced such minimal and uneven consensus, we can imagine what it will look like if and when reform becomes a matter of full-scale parliamentary discussion.[22]

POPULIST IMPULSES

The Committee of Forty's most remarkable recommendations are designed to give the people a more direct voice in government. The proposals are as sweeping as they are certain to be controversial. They include not only such instruments of direct democracy as the legislative initiative and referendum but also devices to compel the political parties and the trade unions to be, internally speaking, more "democratic."

Where the referendum is concerned, the feeling is that it has been overused in recent years, and so the proposal is that more signatures on petitions be required before an existing law can be submitted to the voters for approval or rejection. As we know, the electorate has shown a remarkable unwillingness to reverse legislation. Thus, the new suggestion from the committee is that the "legislative initiative" be introduced. This would give voters an opportunity to turn some of their specific proposals into law if, within a designated period, they were not formally enacted by the legislature.

This hunger after more democracy would affect the trade unions, too. Although the present constitution requires that these organizations be internally democratic, la classe politica has so far wisely steered clear of any effort to implement that provision. For one thing, the unions do not warm to that sort of interference, which would have to come from the state. For another, it would be a nightmare, and potentially quite dangerous, were public authorities to establish criteria for democracy inside the union and then try to enforce them. Not only would such a step probably boomerang. It takes quite a bit of courage or naïveté to believe that large-scale organizations—trade unions or any other kind—can be made to operate according to democratic norms.

The rationale for interference is that the unions, like employers' organizations, exercise considerable de facto political and economic power. Because the unions represent millions of workers, the thought is that they should not be in the hands of oligarchs but rather led by those who are democratically elected and responsible to the membership. It all sounds appealing in theory. In practice it would invite the state to move into areas where, in most democracies, the doors are solidly barred.

Proposals of this sort come more often from disgruntled or sanguine intellectuals than from seasoned politicians. Those who find the corporatist modes of policy-making attractive are particularly inclined to want more democratic unions. If in a brave new corporatist world policy is to be made by a few cabinet ministers who hammer out deals with leaders of organized labor and business, it would seem all the more important to democratize the unions and similar organizations.

In a corporatist world that gives labor and business organizations modes of representation constitutional status, effective worker participation in the unions' internal affairs would be a basic necessity. Once this were achieved, the national legislature would presumably fall by the wayside, a dessicated remnant of a liberal democratic system that many of the would-be reformers do not admire in the first place. In theory, the unions, now largely outside the decision-making system, should welcome this turn of events. Few of them will. The degree of official interference in their internal affairs that this kind of "democratization" would imply is too high a price.[23]

Other suggested changes are open attacks on partitocrazia. As with union members, card-carrying party members would also to be given more effective control over political party affairs, and especially over leaders and candidates. The populist impulse is to cut the parties down to size, to make them more directly and inescapably the instruments of their members. Similarly, other reform would give voters greater influence over what follows from the way their balloting in elections works out. One thought is that voters should know in advance for which government coalition they can cast ballots. Another is that they should have more to say about who are named to run for office.

All manner of schemes have been offered.[24] The Christian Democrats, for example, seem to favor a preelectoral "pact" whereby, in advance of election day, the parties that intend to form a majority coalition, put the public on notice to this effect. An interesting twist is that the pre-announced coalition that gets the most votes be given a premium, or bonus, of extra seats, in order to fatten its legislative majority. This would presumably make it easier to govern, with less fear that the government will be done in by sharpshooters.

The Christian Democrats pushed through such a scheme far back in 1953. It was immediately dubbed "the swindle law" by the left, and the hoped-for electoral majority failed to materialize, but only by a hair. Now the idea is back, this time curiously supported by elements of the same left wing that once claimed to abominate it.

Some who support this kind of change recognize that it is not likely to work very well so long as the PCI, the MSI, and the fringe parties on the left are not considered legitimate players in the electoral/governmental game. Others claim that, once such a reform is enacted, it would accelerate the PCI's legitimation and force the Socialists to say in advance where they stand regarding left-wing, center, or right-wing policies.

These suggestions, however, seem more appropriate for almost any democratic system except the Italian. Among the practitioners of trasformismo, the opposition to this reform will be universal. But even in other countries where coalition governments are the rule, not many politicians would wish to expose their negotiating strategies or to make basic coalition decisions *before* the votes are counted.

In order to give party members more control, a few reformers would introduce some form of the direct primary election. This idea is obviously imported from the United States, where disciplined national parties in the European sense have never existed. It is difficult to see how the introduction of this device would do anything other than weaken the Italian parties and make them even more subject to the maneuvers within them of factions and organized groups.

My sense of the direct primary in Italy is that it would diminish what little stability and predictability the republic has so far achieved. This has been based, as we know, on an amazing continuity of political leadership. These leaders, that "super elite" who constitute la classe politica, have been able to operate a transformist system in part because they are somewhat protected from public scrutiny and in part because they bring in new leaders by cooptation. The direct primary, as its advocates know, would fundamentally change this pattern. To my mind, it would not be for the better.

Even in the United States, it is worth adding, many now view the direct primary as the mixed blessing it so obviously is. It weakens the parties, encourages single-issue political intervention that leads the better lawmakers to retire in droves, and gives organized groups, especially the well-heeled, formidable control over policies. In Italy a modification of this kind whose declared intention is to augment effective democracy would very easily wind up producing less of it.

The Committee of Forty also made some interesting recommendations to produce more "government by the people" through the decentralization of governmental authority to the regions and cities. Once again, there is visible in these suggestions an underlying and idealized notion that derives from American practice: that local government provides wonderful and unlimited opportunities to experiment with the tools of democracy. But, whatever the truth of that claim, the American system is federal, and, unlike in Italy, states and cities have the power to tax. Without this governmental power, local autonomy is not likely to amount to much.

In many ways, the committee's report and other reform proposals add up to a generous wish list for Italian democracy. Some reforms are very much in order and others are overdue; some will be easier to come by than others, and most will never materialize. It would help if the preparation, and now the paring, of the wish list were guided by a greater sense of priorities and feasibility. For example, more transparency in the governmental process is desirable. But one might try to require it first in

corporate balance sheets, stock-market and other major financial transactions, tax audits, and so on.

The general morale would no doubt be helped if even modest steps
were taken to bring the public bureaucracy under insistent official public
scrutiny. A modest step in that direction might be taken through the
adoption of the ombudsman system recommended by the committee. It
would certainly raise everyone's spirits to learn that someone means to
keep the bureaucracy on the straight and narrow, in the service of citizens
and taxpayers. It will not be easy.

The problem is not so much the identification of major and minor
problems, or where and how one might want to intervene in their solution. It is, rather, that the grandiose schemes to remake the republic
tend to blunt the edge of a more pragmatic problem-by-problem approach. As things stand, too much is on the agenda, and most of it is on
the main stage—where the risk is high that it all will turn out to be an
illusion.

A real threat to the present republic might well occur were a momentum
for sweeping changes to take hold. It would lead, in my view, to a
substantial crisis precisely because so many of the suggested changes are
imports from elsewhere, where they may or may not work as the reformers
believe. If these institutional rules and processes are not entirely alien to
Italian culture, they would certainly not fit the pattern of democratic
government that has evolved in the past four decades.

It is time to say something about this in synthesis, and in conclusion.

10

DEMOCRACY, ITALIAN STYLE

Prince Metternich, a state builder par excellence, once dismissed Italy as nothing more than the territory occupied by quarrelsome Italians. Since Metternich's time, many others have doubted the likelihood of a viable Italian nation, to say nothing of a democratic one. What can we conclude about democracy in Italy?

Here we have a highly differentiated people caught up in a plural, somewhat segmented, small-scale society that is saturated by politics. Its principal subcultures—Catholic, Marxist-leftist, and laical—define the lines of political cleavage. For most Italians, the only political identity, organization, and communication they really understand and trust are located within these same subcultural spheres. If they move around at all as voters, from one party to another, this behavior, too, takes place within these subcultural confines.

If this condition does not polarize politics, it does appear to separate it into mutually suspicious and somewhat hostile enclaves. Forty years after the birth of the republic, its citizens still line up politically and electorally pretty much as they did at the beginning.[1] This suggests political stasis, or an armed truce. How can democracy thrive in that kind of setting?

It turns out that these conditions are not necessarily inimical to democratic development and that, in the case at hand, they have actually contributed to the gradual tilt toward democracy. Italian citizens, their postwar political parties and leaders, and certain historical and cultural legacies have combined to give democracy a better lease on life than it has found in many other places, including Italy itself the first time around.

CITIZENS

Political subcultures may produce parochial citizens but not alienated ones. They may channel political participation, but they neither discourage nor prevent it. On the contrary, the subcultures mobilize their respective members and bring them coherently into the political process. Thus, if political alienation means emotional isolation and physical withdrawal from the polity, Italians must number among the least alienated citizens in the history of democracy. In any case, within the electorate there is no reservoir of chronic nonparticipants who might suddenly be mobilized to vote, or to do anything else that would be perilous to democracy.

Perhaps heavy electoral turnouts are largely ritualistic and criticisms of political leaders and institutions are reflexive actions, or a form of role-playing. Or perhaps this form of participation is both an emotional outlet for the citizen and an admonition to party leaders and officeholders not to take citizens for granted. In either case, the net effect on the polity of the always-voting, much-demanding, and never-satisfied citizen is probably positive.

To many this assertion will appear unlikely, especially in light of information about public attitudes regularly furnished by survey groups like the European Economic Community's Eurobarometre. Over the years, Italians are invariably reported to be somewhat less satisfied than are other Europeans with their democracy—and much more distrustful of their national government. It is time to ask about these and similar public opinion data—so what?

I mean by this that, even if the surveys themselves are technically reliable, and even if the questions asked in ten different languages in as many European countries accurately tap the same feelings, no one has yet shown what difference it makes that Italy's distrust-of-government index is 3.4 while the average for the European Community as a whole is 2.8. We should pay more than passing attention to such attitudes only if they can be demonstrated to have a significant impact on the polity.

For example, it might be argued that some aspect of democratic government flourishes or deteriorates depending on the average degree of trust the people place in their government. In my opinion, no one has ever done this persuasively—not even the historians of democracy, who have the benefit of hindsight. In the case of Italy, postwar history suggests that distrust of government (as it is typically defined and measured) is either unrelated to anything else or, if it relates to politics at all, has positive, not negative, effects.

Actually, the most thought-provoking aspect of the Eurobarometre surveys is not the differences between and among countries where satisfaction-with-democracy or trust-in-government indexes are concerned. It is, rather, that over periods of a decade or more there is almost no change in the attitudes of the British, the French, the Italians, or anyone else. On its face, this fact is puzzling.

Does this mean that attitudes are immune from any of the economic, social, and political changes that each country experiences over the years? Or is it the way questions are worded that monotonously produces essentially the same average result in each country, regardless of what may be happening there? Or might it be that people's attitudes shift about a lot but the shifts cancel each other out, creating the illusion in global terms that nothing has changed? Any of these questions would caution us not to leap to conclusions when another poll shows that Italians are a little bit more unhappy than others with their democracy and more than a little bit more distrustful of their government.

The message is clear: First judge the behavior of citizens within the political space they occupy. Generalize much later, cautiously. For example, absenteeism from the polls on election day will not mean the same thing in France, Britain, and the United States. Or, if not as many Americans as Italians invalidate their ballots by writing angry or uncomplimentary messages on them, this may be because Americans use voting machines and Italians do not. Et cetera.

I have my own (untested) theory about Italian nonvoters, an explanation that reflects simultaneously the stability of electoral outcomes and the relatively low level of vote switching. The proposition is that most nonvoters fall into two categories, one of which is always transient, the other of which is almost always variable in membership. The transient category consists of the youngest voters who have not yet learned to participate as regularly as do the older voters. Eventually they will, only to be replaced by other first voters who will go through a similar process.

The variable category consists of those voters who at a given moment are unhappy with their party. But because such unhappy voters also tend to be the party's most rabid supporters, they are loath to switch parties. Rather than "give testimony" for another party, particularly one that represents another subculture, these voters prefer to sit at home. Ardent supporters of the Communist and Christian Democratic parties are likely to behave this way.[2]

If this explanation makes any sense, it would fit nicely with my earlier surmise that, relatively speaking, few citizens are politically alienated. Like the Italians' unusual inclination to keep political leaders under continuous fire, this basis for nonvoting is not necessarily a minus for the democratic process. It is apparent how important it is to examine nonvoting, spoiled ballots, distrust of government, or anything else in context before we make sweeping generalizations that presumably apply to all democracies.

We saw in earlier chapters how easily we can be misled by the fact that certain forms of political participation found in one democracy are not present in another. Compared with Italians, for example, Americans say they have a lot of direct contact with elected and appointed public officials. Italians avoid such contacts, and they make their approaches indirectly, often through influential individuals or organizations who are their patrons, or sponsors.

These two styles reflect diverse Anglo-American and Continental European philosophies about the state and citizenship. The stress placed by the first on the centrality of the individual and his or her natural rights makes it a foregone conclusion that direct approaches to those who pretend to govern him or her are entirely legitimate. Even organized lobbies are acceptable, as long as they register and operate within the law.

The Continental tradition centers on the collectivity, as embodied in the state. The state grants or denies privileges on behalf of that collectivity. The *Rechtstaat, Stato di Diritto,* or state based on law can be counted on to do the right thing.[3] In this tradition, individual demands are suspect because they are considered self-serving. Thus the Italian may be as much "in contact with" government as the American, but not necessarily in the same way. This being so, direct forms of contact with public officials does not make American citizens more "participant" or "civic-minded," and certainly not any more effective, than their Italian counterparts. It just makes them different.

The New Pluralism in Italy may produce new patterns closer to those we find in the United States, but this transformation will be slow. Furthermore, nothing about citizen representation or participation through powerful interest groups makes such an arrangement any more democratic than the Italian pattern I have described.

In the meantime, we should recall that Italians have at their disposal the national referendum, an instrument of direct democracy with which few other nations have ever experimented. However, the outcome of referendum elections, like other electoral results at every level and in every part of the country, underscore another noteworthy characteristic of the average Italian: conservatism. Typically, upwards of five hundred thousand qualified voters sign petitions that submit something the legislature has enacted to the verdict of the electorate. Just as typically, the latter hand the lawmakers a vote of confidence.

The simple truth is that Italians resist change. This is apparent not just in politics but in every other aspect of culture and society: eating habits, recreational activities, savings and spending patterns, hierarchy of values—all these and more turn out to be very stable. Italians are conformists in their dress, in the fads they generate, and even in their individualism! This may well be inevitable in a small-scale society. It means, though, that in politics, too, change will be incremental and that it will occur without shock or fanfare primarily at the margins of the system.

Given the seeming turmoil and chaos of the political process, this basic fact may not be easy to see. One can put it in better focus by following this guideline: the more the mass media, or the world of scholars, ballyhoo some alleged radical change in the Italians, the more we should suspect that the analysis is wrong or the change only a fleeting one. The sweeping assertions made (not just in Italy) about the implications of the protest movements of the late 1960s would be a prime example.

One might object that many of the changes I discussed in an earlier chapter were indeed radical and that today's Italy is a far cry from what prevailed a generation ago. The changes are no doubt as important as many of them were painful. But they were slow in evolving. Also, they were cushioned by some of the same conservative mechanisms that served Italian migrants to the United States and other countries. Just as these latter, most of them from the Mezzogiorno, early in the century created Little Italies in cities like Philadelphia, New York, and Chicago, so in more recent years southern migrants created Little Mezzogiornos in cities like Turin and Milan, where, by the way, they ran into just as much bigotry. In all of these places, powerful forces of conservatism (like the family, the *paesani* from one's village or province, the church, the *patrone*, and the Mafia) were at work to ease the transition.

What about the feelings of Italians toward each other? Are these citizens as mutually suspicious and hostile as the pollsters still claim? It follows from what I have said in this book that the answer is yes. Were this not so, the boundaries of the subcultures would be more permeable, and the language of politics would be modified, as would the relationship among political parties. Italians are immensely less parochial than they were thirty or more years ago. And they believe as they never have before that it is good to be informed about politics and to participate in the political process. Furthermore, their commitment to democracy has never been more firmly rooted.

But they remain considerably more distant from each other politically, and more distrustful of their political opponents than the other changes in society might lead one to believe. My sense of this is not that the society is polarized, with armed camps facing each other across an ideological abyss. Nor do I believe that mutual distrust is a simple or automatic consequence of the persistence of the subcultures.

Anthropologists and others have served us well in delineating the roots and contours of feelings of distrust, as well as the practices and experiences that reinforce them.[*] The subcultures encapsulate the distrust and, in the process, harness it to assure that it finds strong but essentially benign political expression. In effect, one can be tolerant of opponents and live at peace with them precisely because patrons and organizations and political parties exist that provide protection. To be distrustful does not imply war or, for that matter, make cooperation impossible. To my mind, the mutual distrust persists also because it serves the needs as well as the interests of the political elite to keep things that way. Given its deep roots, mutual distrust is a condition that will guide, as well as set limits to, the form and pattern that Italian democracy takes on.

If Italy and Italians are in so many noteworthy ways different today, this results not from sharp changes in viewpoints but rather from slow generational turnover. Furthermore, whatever may be the degree of change in different aspects of society, we should not assume that these inevitably or even necessarily affect politics. Terms like silent revolution, or postindustrial or postmodern society, when applied to politics, do little more than add jargon to a language already overloaded with it.

The average Italian may be politically more open and tolerant than in the past, and perhaps less encapsulated and isolated by his ideology and subculture. This does not mean that Torinesi and Palermitani interact with ease, or that members of each of the subcultures easily cross over to share with each other experiences outside the sphere of work. Politically speaking, Italians are suspicious of each other's motives. It is not just those on the left who distrust the "bourgeoisie," or Catholics who distrust Communists, and laics who distrust both of the latter, or northerners who distrust southerners, and vice versa. The history of how these and related groups have treated each other has placed most Italians on the *chi vive*. If you do not distrust the other person's motives, you will be judged naive at best and, even worse, fesso. Much that is of consequence about politics, including the "operational code" worked out by key members of la classe politica, reflects this baseline condition.

POLITICAL LEADERS

Political leaders, not just on the left but across the board, are not just mutually suspicious; they are very partisan and ideological as well.[5] Indeed the language of politics is often so inflammatory and uncompromising, one wonders why the system does not go up in flames. Some would say it was doing just that during the years of terrorism and that nothing guarantees that it will not in the future. More than one analyst of terrorism has laid the responsibility for its outbreak at the feet of those who have been Italy's most outspoken firebrands, the idea being that words have consequences, especially when, for decades, they have urged the need for violent change.

As we saw earlier, there are almost as many explanations of terrorism as there are persons who have written about it. It may be that those who preached violence must share some moral responsibility for its outbreak. Nevertheless, the years of terrorism also brought up short both the general public and members of the political class. When the moment of truth occurred, they demonstrated that the democratic system they had jointly fashioned had greater resilience and staying power than many had believed or dared imagine.

The evidence is equally clear that political leaders are extremely tolerant toward each other. It may be, as someone has claimed, that their tolerance is more a matter of necessity than of moral principal, but its effect on the democratic system is no less positive for this reason. What if it were true that not just the Communists but also the Christian Democrats and many of the others have treated each other with tolerance and respect because alternatives were unavailable to them? The fact is that they have now played only that game for almost a half-century. Its rules have been passed along to a younger generation of leaders who have lacked the antidemocratic ideological commitments of some who went before. It would be silly to deny that the overall effect of this conditioning has been constructive for Italian democracy.

Recall that political leaders do not always operate in a fish bowl. When they are prominently before the public, leaders seem to be engaged in perpetual, unrelenting warfare. If the words spoken and the actions taken in such places represented all or even most of the political process, Italy would long since have degenerated into civil war. But if the more public side of politics always approaches pure spettacolo, it is also the less transparent side of the governmental process that keeps democracies on an even keel. In those less transparent places, where public policies are actually forged, political elites collaborate. They may or may not do this as optimally as elsewhere; but they certainly do it with unusual finesse and, I believe, with greater gusto. Given how rare are stable and enduring systems of problem-solving, Italy's leaders take understandable pride in having fashioned one that works remarkably well.

Their framework for action and their rules for reaching decisions call for tolerance of opponents and for a pragmatic, muddling-through, incremental attack on problems. The fiercest verbal exchanges are tolerated—but not to the point where the *institutions* of the republic, and the delicate balance among them, are placed in jeopardy. On this score, the amount of attention paid the need to protect the "integrity" of republican institutions is extraordinary.

Bettino Craxi initially sought to overcome the limits of this system by emphasizing the need for crisp and sometimes brutal decisions. But when his *decisionismo* upset some of the above norms, he got into trouble with everyone else, including members of his own party. As I will argue below, neither the country nor its political class is ready to accept the full implications of Craxi's approach to the prime ministership and, indeed, to government.

Although the less visible and more informal aspects of politics are found in all democracies, we take special note of it in Italy because politics looks so unremittingly strife ridden there. In truth, the style of politics is more Machiavellian than it is Hobbesian. The reality of things invites, indeed it forces, political leaders to find solutions to problems that appear to be absolutely intractable or beyond hope. These seemingly virtuoso performances are sometimes nothing of the kind, in the sense that the crises themselves are greatly exaggerated, sometimes even constructed of *panna montata*, or whipped cream, in order to create the illusion that the politicians are really earning their pay. Everyone in Italy except the Milanesi seems to appreciate both the substantive and the more frothy side of this role of the politicians.

Things can also go wrong here. Baroque constructions are only deceptively symmetrical or precise. Their management in the political sphere requires a subtle admixture of fantasy and iron discipline. Thus the rhetoric of politics is a dangerous entrapment for those leaders who, in the less visible spheres of the governmental process, believe they must practice what they preach. Political ideologues fall into this category, and Italy may have a larger share of these than other democracies. Fortunately, they do not drive the process of government, although they may shake it up from time to time.

To my mind, the most eye-catching characteristic of la classe politica is its overwhelming public endorsement of democracy. I refer not just to political behavior by the democratic rules, but to public, continuous, and insistent declarations that these are the only acceptable rules and that a better democracy is the only legitimate goal toward which everyone in politics and society should strive.

I know it is tricky to interpret the meaning of all of this. Protestations of democracy are often used as a weapon. Typically, one party will accuse another of violating the rules of democracy, of overstepping its bounds. Alternatively, the accusation will be that a party impedes democratic development. Whether or not well motivated, these are serious charges in a country that once saw nascent democracy snuffed out because of the blind spots and egoisms of its political leaders. Even when such exchanges are self-serving, they concentrate everyone's attention on the issue of democracy and underscore that no other system is acceptable. In short, one way to reinforce the legitimacy of democracy is to claim that there is not enough of it around. Another is to accuse the political opposition of ignoring democratic norms or riding roughshod over them.

The question, How much does the political elite actually support democracy? is also complicated by its lack of agreement on what democracy or the democratic state means. For centuries, entirely reasonable men and women have expressed widely varying views on this score. It is no small matter that for some the matrix of the democratic state is found in the writings of Jean-Jacques Rousseau while, for others, the right works to consult are those of Edmund Burke or Joseph Schumpeter. Some Italians, concentrated on the left, are closer to Rousseau or are strong advocates of direct or classical democracy. Others, like the laical parties and, to some extent, the Christian Democrats are much more committed to a pluralist and representative conception of democracy. Recall that the debate over institutional reform reflects this age-old dichotomy.

My impression is that a majority of the political elite share a schizophrenic conception of democracy. On one side, there is an underlying authoritarian belief that the state should govern uninhibited by intervening institutions and organizations that get in the way of the "proper" relationship between the nation and the individual. On the other, there is the fear that the state, through governmental institutions, can easily degenerate into a Leviathan. For some, the appropriate counterweight to a too-strong state would be more direct popular participation in the governmental process. For others, the only effective protection against this, in the Italian context, is the kind of representative democracy that the parties and partitocrazia provide.

The two basic conceptions of democracy, direct or representative, Rousseauean or Schumpeterian, live side by side in a state of tension. The tension is evident not only between or among the different political parties, but within each of them and their leaders. Some of the latter, for example, will simultaneously endorse more direct popular participation in the political process and more hierarchy and elitism in policy-making. The same leaders who distrust political pluralism because of the prominence it gives organized groups will endorse corporatist forms of representation (which favors interest groups) or, alternatively, the type of government-by-party Italy has evolved.

Whatever may be the nuances that separate their conceptions of democracy, political leaders are unanimous in their declared support of the constitution and the institutions created under its aegis. Some make a fetish of the constitution. It was no accident that the Committee of Forty set as a premise for its work the maintenance of the integrity of the constitutional system established in 1948. Even so, much of the opposition to the committee's recommended reforms is based on the argument that before the existing constitution is amended it should be more assiduously implemented.

Universal suffrage and mass-based political parties have democratized politics in general but not the composition of the political class. Its most distinguished members continue to derive disproportionately from the uppermost reaches of the social and economic hierarchies.[6] It can come as a shock to learn that a radically inclined party leader, intellectual, newspaper editor, or what have you is a count, marquis, or baron or, in any event, a member of a prominent family whose weight in Italian economic, political, and cultural life has been felt for centuries. Italy remains not only a small-scale society but also a country whose basic wealth and economic institutions are in the hands of an astonishingly small number of families—the members of the so-called nice living rooms, primarily located from Rome north.

An unspoken plot exists among many of these persons to make it appear that members of the political class are universally derided and never held in public esteem. Wealthy, prominent newspaper editors assure their readers that everyone in the country thinks that officeholders are laughable at best and at worst the enemies of good sense and collective well-being. Many officeholders, equally prominent and well-heeled, lament that this is indeed their sorry plight. You could easily believe that elective office is one of the more unfortunate ills to befall the unwary.

Nothing could be farther from the truth in this highly deferential society where anyone with even the mildest claim to a title, and many without any claim at all, will insist on being addressed as *avvocato, geometra, ragioniere, direttore, maestro, commendatore, ingegnere, professore*, and so on. Everyone here who graduates from college gets the coveted title *dottore*. Do not believe it when you hear or read that the member of parliament— who is addressed as "Mr." in England's system of reverse snobbery and as "Onorevole" in Italy's more honest one—has little or no status. Politics being about power, its distribution among relatively few persons, and its all-too-inevitable use for purposes of helping one's own, those who make politics a profession are unlikely to be shunned.

Relative common social origin and educational background, an arcane language that derives from the Curia, and the prominent (if often hostile) attention it attracts from the mass media help to assure the political elite its high status. These factors also contribute to the maintenance of that invisible but very palpable line that separates the elite from the masses. Being the object of so much criticism also creates in the elite, if not an esprit de corps then without doubt considerable homogeneity of thought and behavior. In this sense, members of la classe politica, over time, come to resemble each other more than they do members of the subcultures from which they derive. This, too, helps them to carry out the political process without placing its more democratic aspects in a state of jeopardy.

I do not wish to overstate this point. Italy's political elite is perhaps less narrowly based than that of Spain or Greece. Its public administrative elite is without question not as narrowly circumscribed in social origin and educational experience as is its counterpart in France, the United

Kingdom, or Japan. In fact, Italy has interesting sectoral and segmented elites. Northerners may dominate the private industrial sector all over the peninsula. But it is southerners who run the national bureaucracy from the southern tip of Sicily to the French, Swiss, and Austrian borders. One can find a little evidence of "family dynasties" in some bureaucratic sectors, like foreign affairs, and in parliament itself. The military, on the other hand, has probably experienced more democratization since the war (in part because of how the war went for Italy) than other elite sectors. As for the priesthood, Pope John XXIII was clearly an exception: not many talented young men of peasant origin are likely to make it even halfway as far up that particular mobility ladder.

Each of these elite sectors—parliamentary, administrative, industrial, military, intellectual, mass media, and clerical—bring a different point of view to the process of government. Each also has its own experience and reason for understanding how apt today remains Massimo d'Adzeglio's admonition of over a century ago: "Having made Italy, we must now create Italians!" This is easier said than done. In the meantime, Italy's status as a democratic state turns largely on how its elites, politically speaking, manage to live with each other.

INSTITUTIONS AND PROCESSES

This last comment raises questions about where, or in what institutional context, these elites actually interact. If, as we know, much of this interaction is both invisible and informal, it is fair to wonder what this might mean for the formal institutions of government. To put this bluntly, if the formal institutions are not being used as the constitution intends, what good are they anyway?

On reflection it is easy enough to see why so many critics of Italian institutions and processes compare them unfavorably with a presidential system such as that of the United States, a parliamentary system such as Britain's or West Germany's, and many others in between. Major Italian governmental institutions do not seem to work very well. This remains true even after we discount some criticisms because they may be self-serving or simply wrong.

The *caso italiano,* or Italian case, is not one person's fantasy or another's nightmare. One can read about its more or less arresting aspects in any newspaper on any day. To many, the arrangement definitely looks not just deviant but, from a democratic point of view, pathological. Those who share this view quickly add that what little democracy Italy has achieved cannot endure unless pathology is attenuated.

My answer has been that the extent of pathology is greatly overstated, in part because of the love–hate views about democracy the Italians themselves entertain and in part because democracy is very much on almost everyone's mind. One can also overestimate pathology because Italians are (verbally at least) hypercritical of their institutions and too much inclined to judge things against some idealized standard.

It is necessary to add, however, that Italy is sui generis in an additional sense. It somehow manages to carry on a democratic process of government in a set of institutional patterns that fly in the face of almost any theory of the democratic state. Only some very special Italian circumstances will help us to place these apparent contradictions in better perspective.

The three most singular characteristics of the Italian democratic system are these: Trasformismo, or the particular way in which the linkages between elections, governments, and public policies are either uncoupled or never come into existence; the particular and deliberate separation of the policy process into its less- and more-visible aspects; and, above all, partitocrazia, or the special type of party government that has evolved.

These three aspects of government will to some extent be found in any other democracy. It is the specific way they are combined in Italy and the circumstances that led to this configuration that are important. Many Italians would deny this uniqueness, and many more would now argue that it need no longer stand in the way of institutional performance that is more "normal" among democracies. That is, despite the special conditions I will discuss in a moment, reform-minded Italians believe that the parliamentary system no longer needs to be as strikingly different from others as it so obviously remains.

Many Italians abominate partitocrazia on grounds that it will cause the institutions of a liberal democracy created by the 1948 constitution to fall into disuse and atrophy. Even those who are not high on liberal democracy and who might prefer their democracy more popular and direct worry that a weak or atrophied legislature will eventually be discredited or that a prime minister who cannot govern through the legislature will increasingly do so by executive decree. Others fear that if representative institutions do not work well, organized groups, like business and labor, will combine with some bureaucrats and ministers to create a de facto corporatist system of the kind that existed under fascism.

Another objection to partitocrazia is worth some thought. "Life as politics," dominated as it is by the political parties, creates in Italy a singular relationship between civil society and its institutions, on one side, and the state and its institutions, on the other.[7] In effect, neither the state nor civil society is independent or autonomous. It is not so much that the line between these two sectors is blurred. It is that the line itself is irrelevant because both sectors are dominated by the parties. This makes Italy a *parties-centered* democracy. We could think of it as an established multiparty government, meaning that the political parties are not just the prime instruments of representation but also the major institutions of policy-making, policy implementation, and much more that transpires in society. In practice, they relate to society as I have described in an earlier chapter.[8]

One way to see this is by analogy to the established single-party governments one finds in Soviet-type countries.[9] This similarity understandably distresses those Italians who notice it. They are in any case disturbed that most of the important processes in society proceed through some sort of mediation by the political parties. The Italian version of party-centered government differs from an established one-party system in that many parties, and not just one, run the system.

This is, of course, no small matter. At one level it spells the difference between democracy and dictatorship. The maintenance of polyarchy in a pluralistic democracy turns on the freedom of political parties to organize, to oppose or collaborate with each other, and to work, alone or in collaboration with other parties, to gain control of the institutions of government through legal means.

At another level, established multiparty government brings Italy some special problems that pertain to the operation of its formal governmental institutions. The parties directly intervene in all of these processes. This obviously does not please those who would rather have a liberal representative democratic system steer much more closely to what writers like Schumpeter had in mind. And the existing arrangement pleases even less those who favor more direct forms of democracy. Indeed, they have become perhaps the most vociferous critics of partitocrazia.

The Italian arrangement seems exceptional then, largely in the sense of how salient are the parties and how deeply they have penetrated the apparatus of both government and society. But the established multiparty government is not for that reason alone less democratic than other arrangements. Yet this is exactly what many of the critics and reformers would have everyone else believe. Nor, as I see it, is it tenable to argue that because the Italian system is I have described, democracy there is in a more parlous condition than it might be elsewhere, including those democratic countries with which Italy is often compared so unfavorably.

In some ways, Italian democracy seems to resemble the Japanese variant more than any other. Unlike the Anglo-Americans, the Japanese find Italy neither bemusing nor baffling. They see a curious combination, much like their own postwar society, of fierce commitment to democracy against a background of deference and hierarchy. They find a powerful underlying religious ethic and impulse side by side with a propensity of the extremely disaffected among the true believers to turn to violence against the state. They see that politics is still based on political party notables whose factions are geographically based. They note, too, that for almost all of the years since World War II, Italy, like Japan, has been dominated by a single hegemonic political party.

The resemblances are deceptive. I do not mean by this only that Christian Democratic hegemony has now been somewhat attenuated, whereas that of Japan's Liberal Democratic party has not. Nor would I stress that Italy and Japan have quite different ancient and recent histories and that each came to democratic government by very dissimilar philosophical and political routes. I mean above all else that Italy's postwar elite not only confronted its own special legacies; it fashioned certain modes of accommodation and ad hoc solutions to existential problems that will distinguish Italian democracy from other democracies for some time into the future. Let us see why this is so.

FASCISM AND ITS LEGACIES

The world's political graveyards tell us that the only thing more improbable than the birth of a democratic state is its survival to old age. History's admonitions are laconic on this score: democracies are rare. They reach maturity against great odds. More often than not, they will degenerate, or be violently transformed, into nondemocratic states. Ironically, history might add, those who interrupt democratic development, be they populists or praetorians, Jacobins or Bolsheviks, do so in the name of a "superior" or "perfected" democracy.

Not so with Italy's Fascists. They took dead aim at liberal democracy and its institutions. It was not just popular sovereignty, even when exercised through representative institutions, that repelled them. More objectionable still was pluralism, the idea that other social aggregates and organizations—like trade unions, fraternal associations, the church, or social classes—could pretend to compete with the state for the individual's loyalty. This antipathy to an individual-centered democracy was also shared by the Marxist and Catholic parties in the prefascist Italian legislature who, with the Republican and Liberal parties, also became fascism's victims. The Liberals, who should have known better, initially welcomed fascism as a bulwark against populism, little realizing that the Fascists would wind up dismantling the liberal democratic state crafted by Cavour and the others.

In place of liberty, fascism offered paternalistic guidance; in place of freedom, it promised law, order, and discipline but extracted abject obedience in return; in place of individual rights it imposed those of the collectivity, whose supreme expression was the state. The new categorical imperatives easily followed: Nothing without the state! Nothing outside the state! Nothing against the state! In this context, the institutions of both civil society and the state disappear in that they are engulfed by the party and there then emerges the party-state. This being fascism's ambition, Benito Mussolini was right to claim: "A party holding 'totalitarian' rule over a nation is a new departure in history. There are no points of reference or comparison."

Fascism left its legacies and lessons. An important legacy, already noted, is the relationship between the political parties, on the one hand, and the state and civil society, on the other. Three of the more striking and enduring aspects of Italian politics—the politicization of society, weak formal governmental institutions, and partitocrazia—began in earnest during the fascist era or were greatly reinforced then. In organizational terms, totalitarianism means the erection of a political party structure in every place and at every level where government is found. This was the Fascists' goal in Italy, even though their system never reached the hair-raising heights of efficiency displayed by the Nazis or Stalinists who applied this formula.

In Berlin or Moscow, Mussolini's political Goliath must have appeared ludicrous. Over and again, the Fascist party failed to get the degree of compliance it demanded. The industrialists frustrated the party's intention to hold economic development under tight rein and to direct it from the center. The military not only resisted the Fascist Grand Council's direct orders; it hoodwinked the Fascist Hierarchs, and Il Duce himself, into believing that they had a formidable war machine at their disposal.[10] Even the regime's effort to keep the industrial workers in a supine state ran afoul of highly successful Communist party efforts to establish a network of factory cells and the nucleus of a postwar labor organization it would later dominate.

But the Fascist party did politicize society! It became the chief mechanism through which people were recruited and promoted to coveted positions. It colonized the universities and gained tight control over the mass media. It controlled the arts, and it awarded or denied lucrative contracts in industry. It funneled public funds to some local jurisdictions and not to others for exquisitely political considerations. Even if it did not entirely succeed in having its way with them, the party did bend to some of its purposes industrial and other organizations, including the Vatican itself. It also tried to keep close enough tab on citizens in order to reward its supporters and to treat its enemies badly, sometimes with extreme prejudice. In effect, fascism was a political party machine that operated on a national scale.

People pay attention to this kind of a political party. It left in its twenty-three year wake at least the idea that it does not hurt the average person to join such an organization, especially an important one. Barring such a step, one could think about getting close to a party notable or patron who has influence. There would be more of a tendency in this direction south rather than north of Rome, but it would be felt everywhere.

Fascism also influenced the Italian Communist party, in more ways than one. The organization of the Fascist party must have suggested to Antonio Gramsci, writing in a fascist prison, the importance of *presenza*, if a political party was ever to achieve a condition of "hegemony" in various sectors of society. It could not have escaped Gramsci's sharp eye that, once an ambitious party like the Fascist party establishes its authoritative "presence" in the occupational, professional, artistic, and other cultural spheres of society, political power would come as an automatic consequence, without the need of recourse to violence. And so presenza did indeed become prominent in the PCI's postfascist strategy and remains an important basis for its influence.[11]

The PCI not only inherited the Fascist party's organizational model, it also picked up some of its apparatus. Without it, a party of three or four thousand members at war's end could scarcely have become one of over two million members in four or five years. Almost overnight, the PCI became a national party, articulated at the local level not just through its party cells and sections but also through its youth, trade union, women's, cooperative, and similar auxiliaries. Assisted by the Catholic church and its own capillary organizational network, the Christian Democratic party simply followed suit. It could do no less, given the nature of the political and electoral challenge the PCI represented. Thus the Fascist party left its organizational stamp on both of the major postwar political parties.

The party-state, of course, is an extreme form of party government. In creating it, the Fascists were able to show that the country could be governed despite, and indeed because of, the weakness of certain formal institutions. The Fascists not only outlawed their political competition; they also abolished the legislature and replaced it with the Chamber of Corporations. Based on occupational categories, it was supposed to be the supreme policy-making body, but no one ever believed this to be the case. The basic understanding grew that a determined political party could indeed fashion the machinery to bring the political process largely under its control. In this sense, too, the Fascist experience was instructive for the parties of the republic.

Where there exists only one party we think of such arrangements as dictatorship. Where there are several parties that dominate the political process we may call this partitocrazia, or an established multiparty government. There is obviously a risk in such an arrangement that the formal institutions of government may not be taken seriously. That is, everyone will understand that the institutions have little to do with the real exercise of power. Insofar as the current plight of the national legislature reflects this weakness, it appears to many as uncomfortably similar to what had gone before. Would it not be better, one might well ask, to overcome this fascist legacy and place the present democratic system on a firmer institutional footing?

No doubt it would. But neither the powerful incentives nor, more to the point, the necessary conditions for effecting this transformation are yet present. To understand why this is so, we need to consider Italy's transition from fascism to democracy and to note the extent to which it, too, left the country with significant legacies.

Before we do that, though, we should consider one of the most striking lessons registered during the fascist era: the Italian people have a remarkable capacity to resist government, even when its ostensible credentials are totalitarian. It is possible that Mussolini, a true megalomaniac, believed that the fascist state could impose its will and that he, in Orwellian fashion, would become Big Brother. His well-known disdain for the Italian masses might well have led him and his henchmen to such a gross miscalculation, but I doubt it.

It is true that Italians made their peace with the fascist state. Millions happily sang Il Duce's praises in the piazzas. Legions were ready to follow him along the road to a glorious Third Roman Empire as long as this did not prove too costly or painful. However, even as the novels of writers like Ignazio Silone underscore fascism's irrationalities and brutalities, even as they depict the dehumanizing effects produced by opportunistic support for dictatorship, they etch just as deeply the Italians' remarkable supply of evasive strategems when they do not wish to be governed.

Mussolini knew this. He may have terminated work stoppages and compelled the railroads to keep better schedules. He may have cajoled some and brutalized others into submission. His thugs may have murdered heroes like Giacomo Matteotti or sent thousands of others to prison or exile. And the millions who returned his Roman salute may have caused his ego to soar. Deep down, though, he knew that totalitarian control of the peninsula was a chimera. And so he raged in envy over the knowledge that the formula he considered his personal invention worked so much better for the Hitler he feared and the Stalin he despised.

The lesson here is that Italy is indeed a plural society whose social institutions and those who compose them have a marked capacity to resist control from the center, no matter what kind of government, democratic or otherwise, may be in place there. It is equally true that these same institutions, in part because of the fascist interlude but not only for that reason, are unable to cohere well and to form the framework for a stronger civil society. This is so because the country remains differentiated on a geographic, religious, cultural, and ideological basis and grouped into the three political subcultures I have described. It is also because during the period of redemocratization agreements were reached and structural conditions were created that, as long as they persist, imply that Italian democracy will either remain what it has become or not be a democracy at all.

REDEMOCRATIZATION

The Italian republic is neither an old democracy nor a new one. It is a born-again democracy that managed to emerge from the trauma of fascism and defeat in war. Postwar Germany, the western half anyway, is also a born-again democracy, whereas the third member of the Axis powers, Japan, at the United States's insistence, has tried democracy for the first time. Indeed, the Allies imposed democracy on a defeated Germany as well. Italy differs from the other two in that, relatively speaking, it had considerable leeway to shape the postwar political system to its own tastes.

Whatever may have motivated the Allies' decision to allow postwar Italy considerable powers of self-determination, it was a step in the right direction. As I have said, governmental schemes arbitrarily imposed from the center do not fare well in Italy. Also, it was important to the Italians that their totalitarian interlude be differentiated from the German. The Nazi regime, after all, was responsible for the Holocaust, as well as for material and human devastation that extended from Stalingrad to London, from Oslo to the sands of the Sahara. The Fascists, by way of contrast, were much less destructive.

Self-determination's most felicitous aspect is that it left the Italians themselves with a number of the hardest choices.[12] How were they to treat major and minor Fascist leaders? What were they to do with or about the monarchy? Were they really interested in the radical political changes advocated by the National Committee for Liberation? What would be the appropriate way to pursue postwar relations with the Vatican? Should the country fully reactivate the governmental system of the still-valid constitution of 1848, or should they write a new one and in the process create several new governmental institutions?

Italy launched a "defascistization" program, but it was nothing like the "denazification" activities that were pursued in Germany under Allied pressure and supervision. There were also none of the agonies that the Germans and Japanese underwent when many of their wartime leaders were tried, jailed, and in some cases executed for "war crimes." There were plenty of Italian hard-liners around prepared to be ferocious with the Fascists, but, on the whole, wiser and milder temperaments prevailed.

It was a foregone conclusion that postwar Italy would not return to dictatorship. The Allies would not have countenanced any such tendency.

The Italians themselves had made a few moves in a democratic direction in the last months of the war. The Armed Resistance against Fascism was a major force, especially from Rome north. It was committed to democracy, even if its components were split about what this would mean. The Italian military, along with the monarchy, took significant steps against the fascist regime before the war ended in defeat. The Republic of Salò, Mussolini's last-ditch effort, with Nazi help, to rescue fascism, was defeated by the Italians themselves. Unlike the other Axis powers, the Italians could say that they were already moving under their own power toward the restoration of democracy.

The miraculous aspect of this transition is the extent to which the redemocratization of the country was dominated by good sense. Much of the moderation, the sensitive treatment of explosive issues, the willingness to compromise I have delineated in earlier chapters was apparent from the beginning. Indeed, the miracle itself was given more than one boost by startling events that few expected and no one would have dared predict.

Take the famous Svolta di Salerno of 1943, when Palmiro Togliatti, fresh from his years in Moscow and his guru status in the Comintern, returned to Italy to say that his "new" Communist party would accept the Badoglio government, appointed by the king after the fall of Mussolini. Whatever else may have been on Togliatti's mind, this bombshell signaled that it was not violent revolution or even, for that matter, a knockdown confrontation with the other political parties.

Equally unexpected was the peaceful, deliberate manner in which the Italians sent the monarchy packing. The vote was close, and some of the monarchist die-hards tried to discredit or nullify the first free election held in twenty years, but King Umberto thought it better to leave the country than to encourage civil war. As postwar elections were soon to show, few Italians would shed real tears over the monarchy's eclipse.

By far the most surprising aspect of redemocratization is that it took place on the basis of a fundamental agreement among political parties that had little in common except their hatred of fascism. The leaders of these parties were able to acknowledge that fascism itself would never have destroyed democracy in the first place but for the failure of the parties to unite against the threat. Before the war itself ended, and within the National Committee for Liberation, these leaders agreed that whatever might later be their differences, they would assure that the country would become and remain democratic, even if this implied sacrifices on their part.

This initial consensus among the antifascist parties, important as it was in the restoration of democracy, would have been insufficient were it not for the fact that impulses for revenge were held in check and leading persons, institutions, and social classes that may have collaborated with the fascist state were not severely threatened. Nevertheless, no one was fooled regarding the extent of ideological conflict among the nascent postwar parties or the contrasting preferences for postwar Italy that most of the party leaders harbored.

These differences and the predictable clashes they would introduce were well known to the political leaders. The poignant problem for these restorers of democracy was the one that always besets those who would construct a democratic state: How can it be shown that the democratic process is better than any other method for attacking long-standing issues that divide a territory, its inhabitants, and their major institutions? Given the nature of the Italian peninsula, this was no small challenge for the would-be redemocratizers.

I believe with most interpreters that the left initially went along with the basic agreement to restore democracy, and later with a liberal democratic constitution, because the Communists and most of the Socialists thought that whatever form of democracy emerged would represent and in fact facilitate a transition to a left-dominated political system. Given the armed resistance against fascism, the organizational strength of the Communist party (with a Socialist party as its willing captive), the aura of left-wing revolution that seemed to permeate postwar Europe, and the expectation that the United States would soon take its troops and its warships home, the Italian left could easily believe that time was on its side.

This turned out not to be the case, but for reasons that had little to do with Italy as such. International politics and the Cold War intervened to force a rupture in the coalition that the antifascist parties and restorers of democracy had forged. The Communist party, fully accepted as a member of the national governmental coalition at war's end, was excluded from the cabinet by the Christian Democrats. But it was not, nor was it thinkable that it might be, excluded as a legitimate competitor for electoral support and, by implication, as a party that might well come to power, alone or with its Socialist party satellite, through the ballot box in a free election.

It was at this moment as well as on this specific issue that Italy's political class had to decide how to handle "the problem of communism." If the magnitude of this chore was vague in 1947 when De Gasperi pushed the PCI out of the cabinet, it was clearly less so after the elections of 1948. True, the left did not come to power. But the PCI came out of those elections as the strongest party on the left, a status that it was destined to improve with each succeeding election until it became typical that about one out in three electors support the PCI.

It is also true that in 1948 the Christian Democrats wound up with a small but clear majority in the Chamber of Deputies. Rather than try to govern alone, De Gasperi insisted on forming a broad coalition. That act served both to presage and to underscore that the Italian republic would be quite different from any other democratic system.

ESTABLISHED MULTIPARTY GOVERNMENT

Italy's most recent constitution-makers were faced with severe dilemmas. They did not anticipate, for example, that on the left there would be an electoral shift in the direction of a party, the PCI, that, even if one were to trust its willingness to play by the democratic method, initially and for some years raised great doubts about its commitment to Western democracy in any form. During the early years of the Cold War, the PCI itself gave even those outsiders most favorably disposed toward it ample reason to doubt its democratic intentions. Only the foolhardy would have been willing to entrust that party with the major responsibility to form a coalition government. Even today, several million Italians would consider such a step too risky.

Finding a common ground on what a republican government would actually look like in constitutional and institutional terms was another problem. For obvious reasons, the Christian Democrats and laical parties believed it would be better to divide powers among several institutions and between the national and local governments. For similar reasons, the left preferred that powers be concentrated.

Two important compromises were reached. The first involved the constitution itself and, by implication, the institutions created under its authority. It was agreed that many of the constitution's features would not be self-executing but would require later legislation—and that the leaders would take their time before enacting these laws. As a formula for democratic government, many aspects of the 1948 constitution make it look revolutionary. But the revolution took place on paper, its weapons were ink, and its realization was delayed to some unspecified future time.

The political left would later complain about these delays, and the Christian Democrats would be accused of using the "menace of communism" as an excuse for its own constitutional excesses. Much evidence suggests that this is the case. But the additional truth is that the left acquiesced in this foot-dragging, even as it publicly condemned it. The reason for this lies in the second compromise.

I have alluded to the second compromise many times in this book. It is that whereas the left as a whole at first, and the PCI later, would be denied certain rights to occupy the formal institutions of government, it would not in practice be cut off from substantive participation in the governmental or policy-making process. That is, from the outset there was an implicit understanding that the left would not be an opposition in the normal sense, just as the majority would not be a government in the sense usually associated with majoritarian democratic parliamentary systems. This kind of concession may have appeared unnecessary in the late 1940s or early 1950s, when the PCI had two million members but under one-fourth of the votes. It appeared remarkably less so when party membership more or less held its own but the PCI's electoral support grew to over one-third.

Let us recall that the decision to restore democracy was an agreement reached *among parties*. As we have seen, these parties represent broad subcultures that manage to live productively in peace in large measure because of the parties and the nature of party leadership. It is through the mechanism of these same parties—and not through any particular set of institutions—that consensus in support of the democratic method was reached. Democracy, like other forms of the polity, is in essence a set of basic rules about how binding decisions are to be reached. Regardless of how differently democratic systems are defined, they cannot be maintained if a substantial proportion of the electorate is denied effective participation in the system. In particular, the diverse interests, and the party organizations that represent them, cannot be expected to make the sacrifices democracy always implies if they conclude that the cake is not worth the candle.

It is one thing, therefore, for those who form the convention to exclude the PCI to say that it may not legitimately form a government even were it to win a plurality of votes in a free election. It may even be understandable and, more important, acceptable to the party that it be denied formal membership in a national coalition government, with one or more places on the cabinet. It is quite another story to add that it will be denied influence over public policy and never have its way where policies of particular interest to its constituents are concerned.

So far, the *conventio ad escludendum* has implied the first of these exclusions but not the last and most extreme one. Because of this, the system has worked. To make it work as well as it has, however, has implied, and to my mind has actually required, that the system called partitocrazia come into being. Established multiparty government makes it possible to bring the formally excluded back into the process and thereby to avoid the rupture that would occur were one to communicate in so many words that the PCI on the left, and the MSI on the right, with about 40 percent of the electorate lined up behind them, were not going to play a substantial role in the determination of public policy.

Many who claim that the republic's institutions do not work well are fully aware of the convention to exclude the PCI and MSI, but they would deny that the agreement itself carries the implications I have just suggested. Fortunately for Italy, that point of view has not held sway, although there is now some feeling that the time is ripe to give it a real test.

My sense is that the test is both premature and, for that reason, potentially destabilizing. If democracy is to work at all, its elite must be convinced that from its point of view democracy is superior to any alternative. The alternative to the established multiparty government is not, as some have claimed, a parliamentary system that more nearly approximates the Westminster or the West German model. The alternative would be a highly majoritarian system based on the simplistic assumption that majority and minority are essentially permanent and that the latter will have to live with what the former enacts unless and until it becomes an electoral majority itself.

It is a dangerous fiction that such an arrangement is possible in a divided society like Italy's. Majority rule, where it exists at all, works because it does not deny the minority access to power. One alternative in its more classic multiparty form is consociational democracy, which somehow manages to bring the elites of several divisions (but all of them legitimate) together to govern in a formal institutional framework. But, as I have already explained, this is not in the cards in Italy. Another alternative is corporatism, which is also out in Italy, in part because it would imply what is least likely: more direct power for the trade unions and possible replacement of political parties as the center of policy-making.

To be sure, the picture might change dramatically were either one of two events to occur. First, Italy's political elite might accelerate the tempo at which it comes to accept the PCI as legitimate and thereby fully integrate it into the democratic process. For many reasons, this is an unlikely turn of events in the near or medium term. Second, the Communist party might go the electoral way of its French counterpart. As a weaker party, it would be more easily cut out of the real political action. By the same token, it might then be included in a cabinet coalition because it would not create as much nervousness as it now does. This line of development, while also not obviously in the cards, is more likely than the first alternative.

Until something changes about this kind of formal exclusion, parties must remain the center of Italy's democracy. The compromises noted above imply that parties constitute the only effective mechanism through which representative democracy can operate. That prefascist Italy already had a tradition of trasformismo was a piece of good luck; it served to legitimate the existing system of partitocrazia as well as to provide those who manage it with some historical guidelines about both its mechanisms and its entrapments.

Partitocrazia, or established multiparty government, has its shortcomings. The first reaction to a severe political problem is to temporize. The process of government is inordinately slow. Protracted delays in the legislative process then encourage the exponential growth in the use of the executive decree powers, which in turn lead to alarmed warnings about potential dictatorship. For those not adept at how the system works, the process will look hopelessly confused, and its practitioners will appear wholly incompetent.

Many opposed to partitocrazia argue that it inhibits the development of both a strong state and a strong civil society. Well, so what? It is true that Italy's democracy, as currently fashioned, inhibits the growth of strong, autonomous organizations. But in such other democracies as the United States, these organizations work to lock in existing levels of inequality and to assure uneven access to the levers of power. To my mind, the essence of a strong civil society is, in fact, corporatism. Corporatism may not imply fascism, but it surely implies that effective power shifts away from representative governmental institutions. In the long run, it will also tend to make parties marginal. Alternatively, it will turn party leaders into technocrats. What kind of a democracy would that be!

Many critics of the present system will accuse it of being confused, but I believe this to be a misreading. Democracy, Italian style, is no doubt confusing to outsiders. In its earlier years it was disorienting for many Italians as well, given the kinds of accommodations it required and the adaptations of citizens, political parties, leaders, and governmental institutions its evolution and maintenance have extracted along the way.

Yet it is obvious that there are rules here, that the members of the political class understand them well, and that, by many of the common tests of how things are going politically, economically, or otherwise, Italy seems to be doing quite well. These results are not lost on the larger public, which, in a basic sense, is also committed to play by those rules. This is the critical, perhaps somewhat metaphysical, level at which an otherwise highly variegated, individualistic, litigious, even anarchical people are united.

Democracy, after all, is nothing more than a method of government and agreement among the people involved to use it. As a method, it will have to be adapted to the mores, as well as the quirks and peculiarities, of this same people. Italians may be different on many dimensions and politically divided on even more. They seem united in their willingness to push ahead with a method and system of governance that looks highly unlikely and unstable at one level but is nothing of the kind at another.

A MATURE DEMOCRACY?

Democracies grow to maturity not in a continuous or linear way but through cycles. Their rate of growth is always uneven, and sometimes interrupted by retrograde steps, some of which may suspend or terminate democracy itself. For most young democracies, the trick is to avoid sharp swings of the pendulum toward popular government in order to avoid equally sharp reactions in the other direction.

The United States itself, as with all other democracies, has experienced notable ebbs and flows in its democratic development. The process whereby the democratic method becomes widely accepted has aptly been described as the struggle of "interests versus numbers." That has surely been the underlying impulse and tension of democratic development from Magna

Charta to the seventeenth-century debates with the Levellers at Putney, England; from the movements for universal suffrage to demands for the welfare state; from yesterday's Supreme Court decisions on the rights of homosexuals to tomorrow's new struggles over the relative status of human life and property.

Italy, since its relatively recent rebirth as an aspiring democracy, has had its share of ups and downs. Since 1945, when it shed its fascist past, it has experienced the many economic and social transformations reviewed in these pages. More often than not, some of the jolts looked to the outsider to be so destabilizing it appeared impossible that the commitment to democracy would persevere.

Instead, postwar Italian democracy has in many ways appeared to be at the cutting edge of political innovation. The late 1960s ushered in a period of sharp democratic expansion. Legislation like the Workers' Statute, the laws on abortion, the use of the national popular referendum, experiments with new modes of popular government in the workplace and the neighborhoods seem to place Italy at the vanguard of the modern democratic state. This has not been an immobilist democracy, stagnating because of the incapacity of its political leadership or institutions. If the idea of a living constitution implies creative adaptation to gnawing or unexpected challenges, without the sacrifice of democracy itself in the process, I frankly know of no postwar democracy with a better record than Italy's.

If this sounds like excessive praise, I would add that it is not enough. The real miracle of Italian democracy is this: whereas Italy represents a plural, divided society with a high potential for exaggerated conflict, those same individuals and institutions that might be expected to promote or to exacerbate conflict have worked to dampen it. If not at the verbal or rhetorical level, where so much is sound and fury, then without doubt at the level of making and implementing policies, where it really counts. This astonishing achievement is largely the work of a much maligned political class, but it is a credit that goes to the Italians as well. As Barzini might say, they may pretend to love anarchy and practice forms of it when it is safe. But they have little inborn taste for dangerous adventures, political or otherwise.

If Italian democracy faces a serious challenge today it may be that neither its intellectuals nor important sectors of the mass media seem willing to judge Italian democracy in its particular existential context. Because they insist on holding Italy up to a much idealized standard, they inevitably find it wanting. Why would that kind of criticism not erode the foundations of any democracy, anywhere?

The answer lies in how well Italians, intellectuals included, recognize the meaning of politics-as-spettacolo and the role that each individual and group is expected to play if the democratic method is to endure. The constant harping over crisis or complaints about the shortcomings of la classe politica may never produce in Italy political virtue, as Aristotle would have intended that term. But it does seem to have the transcendental effect of encouraging a type of political virtuosity that is, at bottom, every Italian's secret pride.

NOTES

These notes are intended for those readers who may welcome or require some documentation along the way. I have favored English-language materials, except where it would have been outlandish not to include some Italian-language citations.

CHAPTER 1

1. Naples may be the most extreme case on this score. See the searing but sympathetic account of its politics by Percy Allum, *Politics and Society in Postwar Naples,* Cambridge: Cambridge University Press, 1973. Naples is not alone, as seen in the comparisons drawn between it and Palermo in Judith Chubb, *Patronage, Power and Poverty in Southern Italy,* Cambridge: Cambridge University Press, 1982.

2. There are quite different ways to assess how well a democracy may be doing. For evidence, see Peter Lange and Hudson Meadwell, "Typologies of Democratic Systems: From Political Inputs to Political Economy," in Howard Wiarda, ed., *New Directions in Comparative Politics,* Boulder, Colo.: Westview Press, 1985, pp. 80–112.

3. On why democracies break down, in theory and practice, see Juan J. Linz and Alfred Stepan, eds., *The Breakdown of Democratic Regimes,* Baltimore: Johns Hopkins University Press, 1978.

4. These historical observations are brutally condensed. More probing insights into this fascinating national history are provided by Denis Mack Smith, *Italy: A Modern History,* rev. ed., Ann Arbor: University of Michigan Press, 1969, and Luigi Salvatorelli, *A Concise History of Italy,* trans. Bernard Miall, New York: Oxford University Press, 1939.

5. The evolution of the Catholic church's involvement in Italian national politics is nicely traced by Richard Webster, *Christian Democracy in Italy, 1860–1960,* London: Hollis and Carter, 1961. The most authoritative Italian author on this subject is Arturo C. Jemolo, *Church and State in Italy,* Oxford: Blackwell, 1960.

6. The fascist state benefited, too. See the stinging comments in Gaetano Salvemini and George La Piana, *What to Do with Italy,* New York: Duell, Sloan, and Pearce, 1943, pp. 80–165, and Daniel A. Binchy, *Church and State in Fascist Italy,* New York: Oxford University Press, 1940.

7. This seems to be the judgment of Benedetto Croce, *A History of Italy, 1871–*

1915, trans. C. M. Ady, Oxford: Clarendon Press, 1929. There are obviously dissenters from this view. See René Albrecht-Carrie, *Italy from Napoleon to Mussolini,* New York: Columbia University Press, 1950, chap. 1; Arthur J. Whyte, *The Evolution of Modern Italy, 1715–1920,* Oxford: Blackwell, 1950, pp. 190ff.; and Chubb, *Patronage, Power, and Poverty,* pp. 19ff.

8. Varied but always sobering interpretations on the rise of Italian fascism are found in essays collected in A. William Salamone, ed., *Italy from the Risorgimento to Fascism,* New York: Doubleday Anchor Books, 1970. Readers who want a pleasurable shortcut through readings already cited can do worse than spend an evening with this paperback.

9. The basic English-language reference on Italy's postwar international orientation is Norman Kogan, *The Politics of Italian Foreign Policy,* New York: Praeger, 1963. See especially chap. 3 and the author's bibliographical references.

10. For details on the economic magnitude of fascism's debacle, see Shepard B. Clough, *The Economic History of Modern Italy,* New York: Columbia University Press, 1964, chaps. 7–8. An interesting composite picture that encompasses key political and economic events from the fall of Mussolini in 1943 to the birth of the republic is found in Giuseppe Mammarella, *Italy after Fascism: A Political History,* Notre Dame, Ind.: University of Notre Dame Press, 1966, pp. 3–133. Cogent essays on the same period are included in Stuart J. Woolf, ed., *The Rebirth of Italy, 1943–1950,* London: Longmans, 1972. On the longer-term effects of the fascist interlude, see Giuseppe Di Palma, "Italy: Is There a Legacy and Is It Fascist?" in John H. Herz, ed., *From Dictatorship to Democracy,* Westport, Conn.: Greenwood Press, 1982, pp. 107–34.

11. My usage of *polyarchy* here derives from Robert A. Dahl, *Polyarchy: Participation and Opposition,* New Haven: Yale University Press, 1971, and Dahl, *Dilemmas of Pluralist Democracies,* New Haven: Yale University Press, 1982.

I will make many observations along the way about the "performance" of the Italian democratic system. I mean by performance a combination of citizen participation in the political process, the degree of stability of the political system, and the kinds of outputs, especially material ones, it produces. See discussions of performance in Lange and Meadwell, "Typologies of Democratic Systems," and G. Bingham Powell, Jr., *Contemporary Democracies: Participation, Stability, and Violence,* Cambridge, Mass.: Harvard University Press, 1982, esp. chaps. 3, 6–9.

CHAPTER 2

1. The essay, written in 1828, is entitled "Discorso sopra lo stato presente dei costumi degl'italiani," and is included in Francesco Flora, ed., *Tutte le opere di Giacomo Leopardi,* 2 vols., Milan: Mondadori, 1940, 2:550–89.

2. Giuseppe Borgese, *Goliath: The March of Fascism,* New York: Viking, 1937, takes the contrary view that Italians, in part because of the authoritarian institutions that surround them, are inclined to be sheepishly passive toward public authority, especially if it is tyrannical. I think he is wrong.

3. Luigi Barzini, in his famous book, *The Italians: A Full-Length Portrait Featuring Their Manners and Morals,* New York: Atheneum, 1964, is often more out of hand than Leopardi in describing his countrymen. The author provides an amusing discussion of the difference between being *fesso,* stupid, and *furbo,* sly or foxy (pp. 166–74).

4. A convenient, reliable guide to some of the more important transformations in

Italian society are the annual volumes published by Fondazione CENSIS. See, e.g., *XVIII rapporto 1984 sulla situazione sociale del paese*, Milan: Franco Angeli, 1984. Additionally, some recent over-time statistical information is contained in CENSIS, *A metà decennio: Riflessioni e dati sull'Italia dall'80 all'85*, Milan: Franco Angeli, 1986. A highly useful English-language summary of some of this latter information is CENSIS, *Italy Today: Social Picture and Trends, 1985*, Milan: Franco Angeli, 1986.

5. The information summarized in the next several paragraphs derives from national surveys conducted by DOXA, one of Italy's premier polling organizations, and reported in CENSIS, *Rapporto, 1984*, pp. 76–86.

6. See ibid., pp. 41–45, 437–54, for some statistical information on the Italian family's economic status.

7. The Central Institute of Statistics at Rome set off a bombshell in late fall 1986 when it reported that, whereas Denmark's birthrate for the first five months of the year was −1.8 persons per thousand of population and West Germany's was −1.1, Italy's rate had also fallen into the negative column −0.9. Uniquely in Europe, these three countries are no longer maintaining their populations. See the amusing comments, pro and con, in Rome's largest circulation daily newspaper, *Il messaggero*, October 29, 1986, p. 3.

8. For an overview of women in some aspects of politics, see Karen Beckwith, "Women and Parliamentary Politics in Italy, 1946–1979," in Howard R. Penniman, ed., *Italy at the Polls, 1979: A Study of the Parliamentary Elections*, Washington, D.C.: American Enterprise Institute, 1981, pp. 230–53. Ann Cornelisen, *Women of the Shadows*, Boston: Little, Brown, 1976, is worth a look. An important study is Lucia Chiavola Birnbaum, *Liberazione della donna: A Cultural History of the Contemporary Italian Women's Movement*, Middletown, Conn.: Wesleyan University Press, 1985. For readers of Italian: do not miss Maria Antonietta Macciocchi, *Le donne e i loro padroni*, Milan: Mondadori, 1980.

9. An earlier elaboration of the meaning of these subcultures is found in my "Italy: Fragmentation, Isolation, Alienation," in Lucian Pye and Sidney Verba, eds., *Political Culture and Political Development*, Princeton: Princeton University Press, 1965, pp. 282–329. Two statements on the same subject by a leading Italian scholar are those of Alessandro Pizzorno, "Introduzione allo studio della partecipazione politica," *Quaderni di sociologia* 15 (1966): 235–87, and Pizzorno, "Elementi di uno schema teorico," in Giordano Sivini, ed., *Partiti e partecipazione politica in Italia*, Milan: Giuffrè, 1969.

10. For more on this subject, see Gianfranco Poggi, *Catholic Action in Italy*, Stanford: Stanford University Press, 1967.

11. The term means that Catholicism and its norms would come to permeate life. Catholic principles would both inform and limit behavior in all spheres—from the home and workplace to political, cultural, and recreational life. One can readily see why those who worry about the ambitions of the Vatican would take a dim view of any evidence of integralist impulses or maneuvers.

12. Basic information is provided by Daniel Horowitz, *The Italian Labor Movement*, Cambridge, Mass.: Harvard University Press, 1963, and Joseph LaPalombara, *The Italian Labor Movement: Problems and Prospects*, Ithaca: Cornell University Press, 1957.

13. A useful overview of the postwar vicissitudes of Italian organized labor is provided by Carol Mershon, "Unions and Politics in Italy," in Howard R. Penniman, ed., *Italy at the Polls, 1983: A Study of the National Elections*, Durham, N.C.: Duke

University Press, 1987. The classic statement of postwar labor's place in the Italian social system is found in Alessandro Pizzorno, *I soggetti del pluralismo: Classi, partiti, sindacati,* Bologna: Il Mulino, 1980, pp. 99–154.

14. The year-to-year conditions of the labor force, labor market, and industrial relations are traced by CENSIS. See, e.g., *XVIII rapporto,* pp. 235–77.

15. See Tiziano Treu, ed., *L'uso politico del Statuto dei Lavoratori,* Bologna: Il Mulino, 1975.

16. Problems for the unions associated with efforts to develop a common and coherent approach to politics are discussed in Peter Lange, George Ross, and Maurizio Vannicelli, *Unions, Change, and Crisis: French and Italian Union Strategy and Political Economy, 1945–1980,* Winchester: Allen & Unwin, 1982.

17. A fascinating in-depth treatment of the workers' councils is found in Carol Mershon, *The Micropolitics of Union Action: Industrial Conflict in Italian Factories,* Ph.D. diss., Yale University, 1986.

18. Tensions within the trade unions over austerity policies accepted by union leaders and worker compliance with such policies often sharply divided the majority of workers from radical minorities. See Miriam Golden, "Austerity and Its Opposition: Persistent Radicalism in the Italian Labor Movement," manuscript, Wesleyan University, 1986. Also Marino Regini, *I dilemmi del sindacato: Conflitto e partecipazione negli anni Settanta e Ottanta,* Bologna: Il Mulino, 1981, and Regini, "Labor Unions, Industrial Action, and Politics," in Peter Lange and Sidney Tarrow, eds., *Italy in Transition,* London: Frank Cass, 1980, pp. 49–66.

19. The CENSIS annual reports constitute a major source of the idea that Italians are radically revising their attitudes toward parties, politics, and traditional interest groups. A comparison of basic attitudes on these and related matters expressed by younger Italians today and a generation ago is found in Percy Allum and Ilvo Diamanti, *'50 / '80, Vent'anni: Due generazioni di giovani a confronto,* Rome: Edizioni Lavoro, 1986. The best over-time analysis of survey data of this kind is Giovanna Guidorossi, *Gli italiani e la politica,* Milan: Franco Angeli, 1984. For more information, consult Guidorossi's rich bibliography. See also CENSIS, *Italy Today,* pp. 131–46.

20. Allum and Diamanti, *'50 / '80, Vent'anni,* provide a balanced interpretation of the implications for politics and political life of certain transformations in the value systems of Italians.

21. Two important statements on this issue by eminent economists are Giorgio Fuà and Emilio Rosini, *Troppe tasse sui redditi,* Bari: Laterza, 1985, and Antonio Pedone, *Evasori e tartassati,* Bologna: Il Mulino, 1979.

22. General theoretical issues pertaining to the referendum, as well as discussions of Italy's form and use of it, are found in "Forme della democrazia ed uso del referendum," *Quaderni costituzionali* 5 (August 1985).

CHAPTER 3

1. This is as good a place as any to record a mea culpa for my own past contributions to this image of Italy, an image that I trust this book will modify. Although I do not renounce it entirely, I would today make radical changes in my "Italy: Fragmentation, Isolation, Alienation," in Lucian Pye and Sidney Verba, eds., *Political Culture and Political Development,* Princeton: Princeton University Press, 1965, pp. 282–329.

2. Not everyone will be as sanguine as I sound about patrons and clients. For other views, see Luigi Graziano, *Clientelismo e sistema politico: Il caso dell'Italia,* Milan:

Franco Angeli, 1980, and, earlier, Graziano, ed., *Clientelismo e mutamenti politici,* Milan: Franco Angeli, 1974. Acute insights into the clientist patterns of the Italian south are found in Sidney Tarrow, *Peasant Communism in Southern Italy,* New Haven: Yale University Press, 1967. For broader reading: Steffen W. Schmidt et al., eds., *Friends, Followers and Factions: A Reader in Political Clientelism,* Berkeley: University of California Press, 1977, and Peter Blau, *Exchange Power in Social Life,* New York: Wiley, 1964.

3. I wrote about some of this in my *Interest Groups in Italian Politics,* Princeton: Princeton University Press, 1964.

4. On the history of this matter, see Arturo C. Jemolo, *Church and State in Italy,* Oxford: Blackwell, 1960. Aspects of the postwar experience are treated by P. Vincent Bucci, *Chiesa e stato: Church-State Relations in Italy within the Contemporary Constitutional Framework,* The Hague: Martinus Nijhoff, 1969.

5. For a glimpse of the magnitude of this public support, see Carla Bodo, *Rapporto sulla politica culturale delle regioni,* Milan: Franco Angeli, 1982.

6. For example, Giovanni Bechelloni, *Modelli di cultura e classe politica,* Rome: Officini Edizioni, 1979, and Bechelloni, *La macchina culturale in Italia,* Bologna: Il Mulino, 1974.

7. On this important subject, see William E. Porter, *The Italian Journalist,* Ann Arbor: University of Michigan Press, 1983, esp. chap. 5. A leading Italian journalist, Gianpaolo Pansa, provides an eye-opening look at the structure of newspaper ownership in *Comprati e venduti: I giornali e il potere negli anni '70,* Milan: Bompiani, 1978. He published an even more explosive, controversial, updated indictment in *Carte false,* Milan: Rizzoli, 1986.

8. Porter, *Italian Journalist,* chap. 9, provides interesting comparisons of American and Italian journalists. A revealing comparison of American and Italian television news reporting, especially about politics, is provided by Paolo Mancini, *Videopolitics: Telegiornali in Italia e in USA,* Turin: ERI, 1985. Also: Graziella Priulla, *La realtà confezionata,* Catania: CUIC, 1984.

9. Survey data on this structure of power is provided by Pier Paolo Giglioli, *Baroni e burocrati: Il ceto accademico italiano,* Bologna: Il Mulino, 1979. Burton R. Clark, *Academic Power in Italy,* Chicago: University of Chicago Press, 1977, is an American sociologist's interpretation of it.

10. There is a vast Italian literature on the subject. Two relatively recent works worth consulting: A. Caracciolo, ed., *La formazione dell'Italia industriale,* Bari: Laterza, 1969; Giorgio Fuà, ed., *Lo sviluppo economico in Italia,* 3 vols., Milan: Franco Angeli, 1969, 1981. Note that the historical and sectoral materials were published on the later date. In English: Shepard B. Clough, *The Economic History of Modern Italy,* New York: Columbia University Press, 1964.

11. See M. V. Posner and S. J. Woolf, *Italian Public Enterprise,* Cambridge, Mass.: Harvard University Press, 1967.

12. Stuart Holland, ed., *The State as Entrepreneur: New Dimension for Public Enterprise, the* IRI *State Shareholding Formula,* London: Weidenfield and Nicolson, 1972.

13. Charles R. Dechert, *Ente Nazionale Idrocarburi: Profile of a State Corporation,* Leiden: E. J. Brill, 1963.

14. One of Italy's most striking postwar economic and political swashbucklers, and rightly considered a national hero. For some of the reasons why, see Dow Votaw, *The Six-Legged Dog: Mattei and ENI,* Berkeley: University of California Press, 1964.

15. Late in 1986, in the midst of widespread acid commentary, the parties reached

a division of the spoils in the television and banking sectors. Some sense of the magnitude of what they divided among themselves is provided by Tullio Fazzolari and Guido Quaranta, "La grande spartizione," *L'espresso,* March 23, 1986, pp. 7–13.

16. All this and more happened in connection with a mass meeting of industrialists organized by the Confindustria at the Fiat Company's famous Lingotto plant. See the newspaper coverage for the period November 30–December 1, 1985.

17. Obviously, many consider this degree of politicization highly pathological. See, for example, Antonio Baldassarre, "Partiti e società: Una crisi di legittimazione," in Giovanni Gozzini and Luigi Anderlini, eds., *I partiti e lo stato,* Bari: De Donato, 1982, pp. 23–36.

18. I use this term as suggested in G. and M. Wilson, *The Analysis of Social Change,* Cambridge: Cambridge University Press, 1945.

CHAPTER 4

1. Giovanna Guidorossi, *Gli italiani e la politica,* Milan: Franco Angeli, 1984, p. 45, hits the nail squarely when she notes that a highly participatory political culture does not have to be a consensual one and that Italians can be critical of government without necessarily falling into a state of political alienation. Most survey research misses this nuance.

2. Guidorossi, *Gli italiani,* esp. pp. 191ff., is worth a careful read on this score. It appears, for example, that over the last several decades Italians have come more and more to understand that they are, in fact, an integral part of the political process. These Italians are anything but "outsiders."

3. Note, though, that some Italians describe this particular kind of exploitation as the "Americanization" of the mass media. See, for example, Carlo Marletti, *Media e politica,* Milan: Franco Angeli, 1984, pp. 41ff. See also Marcello Fedele, *La deriva del potere: Trasformazioni e tendenze del sistema politico americano,* Bari: De Donato, 1981.

4. For all of its interesting insights into the Italian "soul" and "national character," this is the trouble with Luigi Barzini, *The Italians: A Full-Length Portrait Featuring Their Manners and Morals,* New York: Atheneum, 1964.

5. Edward Banfield, *The Moral Basis of a Backward Society,* Glencoe, Ill.: The Free Press, 1958. Most of this book's claims about Italy have long since been recast or refuted. The gratuitous title of the volume, noted by many critics, did not discourage others from following suit. Thus: Gian Enrico Rusconi and Sergio Scamuzzi, *Italy Today: An Eccentric Society,* London: Sage, 1981.

6. In a now classic study, these characteristics of Italians led to the conclusion that Italian democracy was in a parlous state. In fact, heavy turnouts at elections were considered fundamentally pathological for the system. See Gabriel A. Almond and Sidney Verba, *The Civic Culture: Political Attitudes and Democracy in Five Nations,* Princeton: Princeton University Press, 1963.

7. The problem with most survey research is that Italians are not asked whether they pursue their own interests by asking a patron to intervene in the political process on their behalf. See some evidence for this judgment in the tables found in Guidorossi, *Gli italiani,* pp. 163–90.

8. The structure of the media's role is nicely laid out by Marletti, *Media e politica,* chaps. 2–5. In particular, the author suggests a striking symbiotic relationship between the media (which tend to become "political parties") and the parties (which turn into "mass media").

9. I confess that I too suggested that the inflated language of Italian politics and other aspects of the country's political culture boded ill for democracy's future there. See my "Italy: Fragmentation, Isolation, Alienation," in Lucian W. Pye and Sidney Verba, eds., *Political Culture and Political Development*, Princeton: Princeton University Press, 1965, esp. pp. 284–97.

10. Insights into the legislative process as a form of spettacolo are provided by Antonio Baldassarre, "Le 'performances' del parlamento italiano nell'ultimo quindicennio," in Gianfranco Pasquino, ed., *Il sistema politico italiano*, Bari: Laterza, 1985, pp. 304–44.

11. Standard works on the legislature are Alberto Predieri, *Il Parlamento nel sistema politico italiano*, Milan: Edizioni di Comunità, 1975, and Andrea Manzella, *Il Parlamento*, Bologna: Il Mulino, 1977. By far the best thing around in English is Giuseppe Di Palma, *Surviving Without Governing: The Italian Parties in Parliament*, Berkeley: University of California Press, 1977. On the point at issue here, see chap. 5 of this work. On relationships between majority and minority in parliament, see Franco Cazzola, *Governo e opposizione nel Parlamento italiano*, Milan: Giuffrè, 1974.

CHAPTER 5

1. For obvious reasons, scholars in and of democracies write much about public opinion, political parties, and elections. Italians are no exception. Their output on this subject is sensitively reviewed by Silvano Belligni, Angelo Panebianco, Piergiorgio Corbetta, Renato Mannheimer, Alberto Marradi, and Giacomo Sani in Antonella Arculea et al., *La scienza politica in Italia: Materiali per un bilancio*, Milan: Franco Angeli, 1984, pp. 155–350. The bibliographic items at pp. 189–92, 284–89, 329–32, and 348–50 represent a fine array of Italian scholarly writing in this area.

Equally important are chapters by Gianfranco Pasquino, Piergiorgio Corbetta and Arturo Parisi, Mario Caciagli, and Franco Cazzola in G. Pasquino, ed., *Il sistema politico italiano*, Bari: Laterza, 1985, pp. 1–207.

For English-language readers, the best bibliographic resource from World War II to the mid-1970s is Peter Lange, *Studies on Italy, 1943–1975*, Turin: Fondazione Agnelli, 1977, esp. pp. 10–25.

2. Political factions are in many ways another face of a patron and client system. See Ernest Gellner and John Waterbury, eds., *Patrons and Clients*, London: Duckworth, 1977, for comparisons. For Italy, Alan Zuckerman, *The Politics of Faction: Christian Democratic Rule in Italy*, New Haven: Yale University Press, 1979; Giovanni Sartori, ed., *Correnti, frazioni, e fazioni nei partiti politici italiani*, special issue of the *Quaderni della rivista italiana di scienza politica*, Bologna: Il Mulino, 1973.

3. It is this single-mindedness of factions that makes them highly objectionable to some writers. A striking example: Giovanni Sartori, *Parties and Party Systems*, Cambridge: Cambridge University Press, 1976, chaps. 1, 4.

4. On this point, see Zuckerman, *Politics of Faction*, pp. 183–206, in which he draws comparisons to factional politics in countries like India and Japan. The danger of this is that it makes factional politics look exotic and a sign of "underdevelopment." We need to look closer at places like Stockholm, Manchester, Frankfurt, Philadelphia, Marseilles, and Sydney, too!

5. The results and many aspects of the 1983 elections are analyzed in Howard R. Penniman, ed., *Italy at the Polls, 1983: A Study of the National Elections*, Durham, N.C.: Duke University Press, 1987.

6. Interpretations, including some of my own, of earlier elections, are found in

Howard R. Penniman, ed., *Italy at the Polls, 1976*, Washington, D.C.: American Enterprise Institute, 1977, and Penniman, ed., *Italy at the Polls, 1979*, Washington, D.C.: American Enterprise Institute, 1981. See also Angelo Panebianco, "Ipotesi di ricerca sui partiti politici italiani," and Piergiorgio Corbetta and Arturo Parisi, "Struttura e tipologia delle elezioni in Italia, 1946–1983," in Antonella Arculea et al., *La scienza politica in Italia*, pp. 195–215, 217–61.

7. The real losers were the pollsters, who did not come remotely close to predicting the outcome. It is an old problem. See the pertinent remarks of Samuel H. Barnes, "Secular Trends and Partisan Realignment," in R. J. Dalton and P. H. Beck, eds., *Electoral Change in Advanced Industrial Democracies: Realignment or Dealignment?* Princeton: Princeton University Press, 1985. Cf. Giorgio Galli and Alfonso Prandi, *Patterns of Political Participation in Italy*, New Haven: Yale University Press, 1970, Alberto Spreafico, "Le previsioni elettorali," in M. Dogan and O. Petracca, eds., *Partiti politici e strutture sociali in Italia*, Milan: Comunità, 1968, pp. 124–64; and G. Sani, "Gli studi sugli atteggiamenti politici di massa: Bilanci e prospettive," in Arculea, *Scienza politica*, pp. 333–50.

8. Craxi's, as well as De Mita's, comments are reported in *La repubblica*, June 29, 1983, pp. 1, 3, 5.

9. This comment is by the much-respected journalist Leo Valliani and appears in *Corriere della sera*, June 29, 1983, p. 1. The construction of the so-called third party consisting of nonvoters, invalid ballots, etc., is by Eugenio Scalfari, editor of *La repubblica*, June 29, 1983, pp. 1, 4.

10. See Barnes, "Secular Trends," for a cogent discussion.

11. See Paolo Mastropaolo, *Partiti e famiglie politiche nel l'Italia repubblicana*, Turin: n.p., 1983. Cf. G. Sani, "The Italian Electorate in the 1970s: Beyond Tradition," in Penniman, ed., *Italy at the Polls, 1979*, pp. 81–122.

12. The comment is by Antonio Cavallari, *La repubblica*, May 17, 1985, p. 1.

13. What follows in the next several pages is not entirely in tune with the dominant interpretations of Italy's electoral puzzles. To measure the degree of deviation, see the chapters by Belligni, Panebianco, Corbetta, Parisi, and Mannheimer in Arculea et al., *Scienza politica*, pp. 159–89.

14. On the limited utility of the "party ID" concept outside the U.S., see I. Budge and D. Fairlie, *Voting and Party Competition*, London: Wiley, 1972.

15. Important statements on voter motivations, types of votes, and shifts of voting support among parties are A. Parisi and G. Pasquino, *Continuità e mutamento elettorale in Italia*, Bologna: Il Mulino, 1977; A. Parisi, ed., *Mobilità senza movimento*, Bologna: Il Mulino, 1980; Renato Mannheimer, "Gli studi sul comportamento elettorale in Italia," in Arculea, *Scienza politica*, pp. 263–89; and Mannheimer, "Come spiegare la mobilità elettorale in Italia," *Rassegna italiana di scienza politica* 16 (April 1980): 45–80.

16. By far the most authoritative scholar on this general subject is Giacomo Sani; see his "The Ambiguous Verdict," in Penniman, ed., *Italy at the Polls, 1983*, as well as the bibliographical references there to others of his articles. Cf. Sani, "The Political Culture of Italy: Continuity and Change," in G. A. Almond and S. Verba, eds., *The Civic Culture Revisited*, Boston: Little, Brown, 1980, pp. 273–324.

17. The description of Italy as a system of "polarized pluralism" is by Giovanni Sartori and is not to be lightly dismissed, precisely because it has generated many objections and controversies. Much of the literature involved in these exchanges is cited in Giovanni Sartori, *Teoria dei partiti e caso italiano*, Milan: SugarCo, 1982.

CHAPTER 6

1. It is important, of course, that so many Italians believe the country to be in crisis, even if it is not. Moreover, some problems are certainly not figments of overactive imaginations. Two striking books that provide food for thought: Giuliano Amato, *Una repubblica da riformare*, Bologna: Il Mulino, 1980, and Gianfranco Pasquino, *Crisi dei partiti e ingovernabilità*, Bologna: Il Mulino, 1980.

Additional evidence for the view that all is not well with the Italian system can be gleaned from Paolo Farneti, *Il sistema politico italiano:* Bologna: Il Mulino, 1973; Fabio Luca Cavazza and Stephen R. Graubard, eds., *Il caso italiano: Italia anni '70,* Milan: Garzanti, 1974; and Luigi Graziano and Sidney Tarrow, eds., *La crisi italiana*, Turin: Einaudi, 1979.

2. The relationship between political class and a generalized, worldwide "crisis" of democracy is reviewed by Paolo Farneti, *La democrazia in Italia tra crisi e innovazione*, Turin: Fondazione Agnelli, 1978, pp. 13–98.

3. These concepts are rooted in the thought of major writers like Gaetano Mosca and Vilfredo Pareto, particularly the former. See Ettore A. Albertoni, ed., *Studies on the Political Thought of Gaetano Mosca*, Milan and Montreal: Giuffrè Editore, 1982. An international group worked on problems of definition, as reported in Associazione Italiana di Scienze Sociali, *Le elites politiche: Atti del IV Congresso mondiale di Sociologia*, Bari: Laterza, 1961. Applications of the concepts are treated by Robert Putnam, *The Political Study of Political Elites*, Englewood Cliffs, N.J.: Prentice-Hall, 1976.

4. It is not intended as a term of endearment, or even as a neutral label. See Eugenio Scalfari and G. Turani, *Razza padrona*, Milan: Feltrinelli, 1974.

5. I cannot repeat this point too often, especially because many still purport to assess the health of democracies by asking people to answer questions that produce, at best, misleading answers. Inevitably, these surveys find the Italian "case" to be quaint, deviant, paradoxical, or pathological, when in fact it is nothing of the kind. Italian scholars now call many of these surveys by the right word: absurd. See, for example, Alberto Marradi and Antonella Arculea, "Rassegna dei sondaggi sui valori degli italiani," in Antonella Arculea et al., *La scienza politica in Italia: Materiali per un bilancio*, Milan: Franco Angeli, 1984, pp. 291–327.

6. For as long as public opinion polls have been conducted, there has been the problem, often egregious, of the researcher who confuses verbal behavior with other forms of human action. This is particularly the case with so-called unconventional political behavior, of which protest demonstrations, civil disobedience, riots, sabotage, destruction of property, violence against persons, and other acts of terrorism would be examples. The fact that a person expresses "approval" of any such acts does not mean he or she would commit them. If more people in society A than in B tell the pollsters that they approve political violence or are in favor of curbing certain political freedoms, this does not make A more "violent" or more "repressive" than B. See, e.g., Samuel H. Barnes and Max Kasse, *Political Action: Mass Participation in Five Western Democracies*, Beverly Hills, Calif.: Sage Publications, 1979. See also the survey data reported in Giovanna Guidorossi, *Gli italiani e la politica*, Milan: Franco Angeli, 1984, pp. 211–65.

7. The impulses and implications of this type of trend are discussed by Alfio Mastropaolo, *Saggio sul professionismo politico*, Milan: Franco Angeli, 1984, esp. chaps. 5–6.

8. I am measuring Italy against the contours of a plural society and consociational democratic system provided by Arend Lijphart, *Democracy in Plural Societies*, New Haven: Yale University Press, 1977, chaps. 1–2.

9. Some of the magnitude and quality of the transformations I have in mind can be gleaned from sources like the following: annual reports of the ISTAT, or Central Institute of Statistics at Rome; annual reports of the CENSIS, noted in earlier chapters; Sabino Acquaviva and Mario Santucci, *Social Structure in Italy: Crisis of a System,* London: Robertson, 1976; Joseph Lo Preato, *Peasants No More,* San Francisco: Chandler, 1967; and Gian Enrico Rusconi and Sergio Scamuzzi, *Italy Today: An Eccentric Society,* London: Sage, 1981. For readers of Italian, do not miss: Paolo Sylos Labini, *Saggio sulle classi sociali,* Bari: Laterza, 1974, and Labini, *Le classi sociali negli anni '80,* Bari: Laterza, 1986. The earlier volume is especially useful for those interested in measures of the magnitude of change in Italy.

CHAPTER 7

1. English-language accounts of this key event: David Moss, "The Kidnapping and Murder of Aldo Moro," *Archives europeènnes di sociologie,* 22, no. 2 (1981): 265–95, which underscores the critical role of ritual and communication in the whole affair, and Robert Katz, *Days of Wrath: The Public Agony of Aldo Moro,* London: Granada, 1980, an ideologically loaded and somewhat wrathful account, but useful nonetheless. R. E. Wagner-Pacifici, *The Moro Morality Play,* Chicago: University of Chicago Press, 1986, is a fascinating treatment of the case within an anthropological framework.

2. Moss, "Kidnapping of Aldo Moro," pp. 267–72, provides some statistics. For more details, Donatella della Porta and M. Rossi, "I terrorismi in Italia tra 1969 e 1982," *Cattaneo* (Bologna) 3 (1983): 1–44.

3. I treated this significant episode in "The Achille Lauro Affair: A Note on Italy and the United States," *Yale Review* 75 (1986): 542–63.

4. See the chapters by Rosario Minna, Franco Ferraresi, and Nando dalla Chiesa, in Donatella della Porta, ed., *Terrorismi in Italia,* Bologna: Il Mulino, 1984, pp. 21–74, 227–330.

5. On the Mafia, see Michele Pantaleone, *The Mafia and Politics,* London: Chatto and Windus, 1966, and Anton Blok, *The Mafia of a Sicilian Village, 1860–1960,* New York: Harper and Row, 1975. For some of the history of political violence, see Nicola Tranfaglia, "La crisi italiana e il problema storico del terrorismo," in Mauro Galleni, ed., *Rapporto sul terrorismo italiano,* Milan: Rizzoli, 1981, pp. 477–544.

6. The classic reference: Eric Hobsbawm, *Primitive Rebels,* New York: Norton, 1975.

7. This is a sore and still somewhat controversial issue in Italy. For openers, see Angelo Ventura, "Il problema delle origini del terrorismo di sinistra," in Donatella della Porta, ed., *Terrorismi in Italia,* pp. 75–149; Domenico Settembrini, "Il PCI e la violenza rivoluzionaria," in Renato Mieli, ed., *Il PCI allo specchio: Venticinque anni di storia del comunismo italiano,* Milan: Rizzoli, 1983, pp. 345–409. In the same volume, see the "Relazione di ricerca" in support of Settembrini's essay prepared by Giuseppe Mazzei, pp. 410–517.

8. Some of the flavor of these years and episodes is found in Gianpaolo Pansa, *Storie italiane di violenza e terrorismo,* Bari: Laterza, 1980.

9. A valuable set of biographic insights into some of the leaders of Italy's terrorist groups is found in Alessandro Silj, *Never Again without a Rifle,* New York: Karg, 1979.

10. A rare treatment of this critical aspect of terrorism is Angelo Ventura, "La responsabilità degli intellettuali e le radici culturali del terrorismo di sinistra," in Carlo Ceolin, ed., *Università, cultura, terrorismo,* Milan: Franco Angeli, 1984, pp. 32–53; for similar evidence, see pp. 74ff.

11. The most blatant example of this line of interpretation is Mimmo Scarano and Maurizio De Luca, *Il mandarino è marcio: Terrorismo e cospirazione nel caso Moro,* Rome: Editori Riuniti, 1985. The obvious bias mars an otherwise gripping account.

12. See the caustic comments of Severino Galante, "Intellettuali e terrorismo: Un caso di 'irresponsibilità'?" in Ceolin, ed., *Università, cultura, terrorismo,* pp. 284–89; cf. Federico Mancini, *Terroristi e riformisti,* Bologna: Il Mulino, 1981.

13. For a striking English-language example, see Paul Wilkinson, *Terrorism and the Liberal State,* New York: Wiley, 1977. Also: Peter Merkl, ed., *Political Violence in Contemporary Society,* New York: Free Press, 1983.

14. I offer just a few examples of Italian efforts to explain terrorism; many others could be added: Renzo Villa, ed., *La violenza interpretata,* Bologna: Il Mulino, 1979; Gianni Statera, ed., *Violenza sociale e violenza politica nell'Italia degli anni '70,* Milan: Franco Angeli, 1983; Sabino S. Acquaviva, *Guerriglia e guerra rivoluzionaria in Italia,* Milan: Rizzoli, 1979; and Luigi Bonanate, ed., *Dimensioni del terrorismo politico,* Milan: Franco Angeli, 1979. An interesting theory on the cyclical aspects of terrorism is suggested by D. Della Porta and Sidney Tarrow, "Unwanted Children: Political Violence and the Cycle of Protest in Italy, 1966–1973," *European Journal of Political Research,* 14, nos. 5–6 (1986): 607–32.

15. See Ceolin, ed., *Università, cultura, terrorismo,* part 3.

16. Scarano and De Luca, *Il mandarino è marcio,* provide an often terrifying day-by-day description of how effectively and effortlessly the Red Brigades instrumentalized the Italian mass media during the Moro affair.

17. They are now also on the U.S. agenda where international terrorism is concerned. See the telling remarks of Antonio Gambino, "Terrorismo e spettacolo," *La repubblica,* July 16, 1985, p. 6.

18. This was the unhappy fate of Alessandro Silj, *Brigate Rosse-Stato: Lo scontro spettacolo nella regia della stampa quotidiana,* Florence: Valecchi, 1978. Nothing approaches this book in laying bare the perplexing aspect of the role of the mass media in a free society that I address here.

19. Quoted in Giorgio Bocca, *Noi terroristi,* Milan: Garzanti, 1985, p. 55. This volume contains a wealth of information extracted by the author directly from conversations with the terrorists.

20. See the shattering details of this aspect of the Moro affair, as reported in Scarano and De Luca, *Il mandarino è marcio,* pp. 183–224.

21. See Luciano Violante, "Pentiti e dissociati," in Ceolin, ed., *Università, cultura, terrorismo,* pp. 257–61.

CHAPTER 8

1. On the implication of this state of affairs for the theory and practice of democracy, see Norberto Bobbio, *Il futuro della democrazia,* Turin: Einaudi, 1984, pp. 75–100.

2. How "big" is Italy? See, e.g., Michael S. Lewis-Beck, "The Growth of the Contemporary Italian State," paper presented to the conference on *The State and Social Regulation in Italy,* Bellagio, Italy: Conference Center of the Rockefeller Foundation, April 1986. For statistical data, see Giorgio Petroni, "La pubblica amministrazione: Analisi delle disfunzioni e indirizzi di riforma," in Gianfranco Miglio et al., *Verso una nuova costituzione,* 2 vols., Milan: Giuffrè, 1983, pp. 794–824.

3. P. Guzzetti, *Lo stato padrone,* Milan: Mondadori, 1978; P. Saraceno, *Il sistema delle imprese a partecipazione statale nell'esperienza italiana,* Milan: Giuffrè, 1975; M.

Toniolo, ed., *Lo sviluppo economico italiano, 1861–1940*, Bologna: Il Mulino, 1973; M. V. Posner and S. J. Woolf, *Italian Public Enterprise*, Cambridge, Mass.: Harvard University Press, 1967.

4. See, e.g., Jack Hayward and Michael Watson, eds., *Planning, Politics and Public Policy: The British, French, and Italian Experience*, London: Cambridge University Press, 1975.

5. I treat this abortive experience in *Italy: The Politics of Planning*, Syracuse: Syracuse University Press, 1966. For reflections by one of the leading Italians involved, see Giorgio Ruffolo, *Rapporto sulla programmazione*, Bari: Laterza, 1973.

6. For a most impressive treatment of this basic matter, see Charles E. Lindblom, *Politics and Markets*, New York: Basic Books, 1977.

7. I examine the political role of organized business in *Interest Groups in Italian Politics*, Princeton: Princeton University Press, 1964. See also Alberto Martinelli, "Organized Business and Italian Politics," in P. Lange and S. Tarrow, eds., *Italy in Transition: Conflict and Consensus*, London: Frank Cass, 1980.

8. By and large, this subject is not treated much in Italy, except polemically by some and, needless to say, gingerly by others. An important earlier exception: Ernesto Rossi, *Lo stato industriale*, Bari: Laterza, 1953, and Rossi, *I padroni del vapore*, Bari: Laterza, 1955. Rossi, in many other books as well, had no doubt about who governed Italy.

9. See the leading newspapers, November 30–December 1, 1985.

10. Examples of what the analysts have in mind: P. Allum, *Italy: Republic without Government*, New York: Norton, 1973; Frederic Spotts and Theodor Wieser, *Italy: A Difficult Democracy*, Cambridge: Cambridge University Press, 1986; G. Di Palma, *Surviving without Governing: The Italian Parties in Parliament*, Berkeley: University of California Press, 1977; and Robert Putnam et al., "Il rendimento dei governi regionali," in G. Pasquino, ed., *Il sistema politico italiano*, Bari: Laterza, 1985, pp. 345–83.

11. A basic work on the public administrative system is Sabino Cassese, *Il sistema amministrativo italiano*, Bologna: Il Mulino, 1977. See also his *Esiste un governo in Italia?* Rome: Officina Edizioni, 1980, esp. pp. 21–180. Cf. Alberto Spreafico, *L'amministrazione e il cittadino*, Milan: Comunità, 1965.

12. On the relationship of bureaucracy to interest groups, see my *Interest Groups in Italian Politics*, chaps. 6–8.

13. Evidence about the mediating role of bureaucracy and its relationship to interest groups and citizens is provided by J. D. Aberbach, R. D. Putnam, and B. A. Rockman, *Bureaucrats and Politicians in Western Democracies*, Cambridge, Mass.: Harvard University Press, 1981.

14. Problems of definition are sensitively treated by Giovanni Sartori, *Parties and Party Systems*, Cambridge: Cambridge University Press, 1976. I should add that Sartori would not go along with the point of view I express about parties here and elsewhere in this book. For a classic statement, see E. E. Schattschneider, *Party Government*, New York: Holt, Rinehart, and Winston, 1942. On the somewhat less powerful role of parties in representative democracies, see J. Schumpeter, *Capitalism, Socialism, and Democracy*, New York: Harper and Row, 1950. The most interesting and arresting work on this topic is Richard S. Katz, ed., *Party Governments: European and American Experience*, Berlin: de Gruyter, 1987, esp. pp. 1–26.

15. Not alone, obviously, as Aberbach, Putnam, and Rockman, *Bureaucrats and Politicians*, will attest. Furthermore, for obvious reasons, each party's influence over

policy will weigh differently. For example, it makes a difference whether your parentela connections are with the DC or the Liberals or the Fascists!

16. Although his interpretation differs somewhat from my own, I cannot recommend too highly P. Farneti, *Il sistema dei partiti in Italia, 1946–1979*, Bologna: Il Mulino, 1983. It is nevertheless Farneti's important insight that the Italian system is at bottom centripetal and not centrifugal. Cf. Sartori, *Teoria dei partiti e caso italiano*, Milan: SugarCo, 1982. For an intelligent review of the literature on the nature and effects of Italy's political parties, see S. Belligni, "Italia: Il puzzle del 'sistema politico'; Cosa dicono i politologi," in Antonella Arculea, et al., *La scienza politica in Italia: Materiali per un bilancio*, Milan: Franco Angeli, 1984, pp. 155–97.

17. This aspect of the political process is illuminated by F. Cazzola, *Governo e opposizione nel parlamento italiano*, Milan: Giuffrè, 1978.

18. Telling observations on the working of the system are provided by Giuliano Amato, *Economia, politica, e istituzioni in Italia*, Bologna: Il Mulino, 1979.

19. Attributed to G. Maranini. See his *Miti e realtà della democrazia*, Milan: Comunità, 1958.

20. See the sweeping, highly controversial report by the so-called *Gruppo di Milano* in G. Miglio et al., *Nuova costituzione*.

21. Consult the bibliography in Belligni, "Italia," 191–95, 197.

22. The writing on this topic has appropriately been called a growth industry. For minimal reading, consult the essays in the following: P. Schmitter and G. Lehmbruch, eds., *Trends toward Corporatist Intermediation*, Beverly Hills, Calif.: Sage, 1979; S. D. Berger, ed., *Organizing Interests in Western Europe*, Cambridge: Cambridge University Press, 1981.

23. M. Regini, "Sindacati e sistema politico: Un bilancio critico dei contributi italiani nell'ultimo decennio," in Arculea et al., *Scienza Politica*, pp. 139–54, includes a rich bibliography.

24. S. Tarrow, "Historic Compromise or Bourgeois Majority: Eurocommunism in Italy," in H. Machin, ed., *National Communism in Western Europe: A Third Way for Socialism?* London: Methuen, 1983.

25. M. Golden, "Interest Representation, Party Systems, and the State: Italy in Comparative Perspective," *Comparative Politics* 18 (1986): 279–301.

26. See S. Tarrow, *Between Center and Periphery: Grassroots Politicians in Italy and France*, New Haven: Yale University Press, 1977; P. Allum and G. Amyot, "Regionalism in Italy: Old Wine in New Bottles," *Parliamentary Affairs* 24, (Winter 1970–71): 53–77; and R. D. Putnam, R. Leonardi, and R. Y. Nanetti, "Explaining Institutional Success: The Case of Italian Regional Government," *American Political Science Review* 77 (March 1983): 55–74.

27. Franco Cazzola, ed., *Anatomia del potere DC: Enti pubblici e centralità democristiana*, Bari: De Donato, 1979.

28. M. Cappelletti, J. Merryman, and J. M. Perillo, *The Italian Legal System: An Introduction*, Stanford: Stanford University Press, 1967; G. Di Federico, "The Italian Judicial Profession and Its Bureaucratic Setting," *Judicial Review* 1 (1976): 40–57; G. Freddi, *Tensioni e conflitti nella magistratura*, Bari: Laterza, 1977.

CHAPTER 9

1. Fierce advocates of institutional reform understandably allege that the country is much more homogeneous than I suggest. See, e.g., Gianfranco Pasquino, "Il Partito

Comunista nel sistema politico italiano," in G. Pasquino, ed., *Il sistema politico italiano,* Bari: Laterza, 1985, pp. 128–68, esp. pp. 144–45. Pasquino's more extensive argument for reform is found in his *Degenerazione dei partiti e riforme istituzionali,* Rome and Bari: Laterza, 1982, and his *Restituire lo spettro al principe: Proposte di riforma istituzionale,* Bari: Laterza, 1985.

2. Important evidence regarding changed public attitudes toward the political system is found in Giovanna Guidorossi, *Gli italiani e la politica,* Milan: Franco Angeli, 1984, esp. pp. 191–208. Note in particular the evidence on the remarkable staying power of the political subcultures. Cf. Giuliano Urbani and Maria Weber, *Cosa pensano gli operai,* Milan: Franco Angeli, 1984, and Weber, *Italia: Paese europeo,* Milan: Franco Angeli, 1986.

3. See the prime minister's account of the *Achille Lauro* affair in Bettino Craxi, *E la nave va,* Rome: Edizioni del Garofano, 1985.

4. Some of Craxi's political opponents also believe that his style of leadership is dangerous to democracy. See G. Pasquino, "Modernity and Reforms: The PSI between Political Entrepreneurs and Gamblers," *West European Politics* 9 (January 1986): 120–41.

5. See *La repubblica,* June 3, 1986, pp. 3, 5.

6. This is so even if, as some claim, the management of the economy leaves much to be desired. See Michele Salvati, "Muddling Through: Economics and Politics in Italy, 1969–1979," in P. Lange and S. Tarrow, eds., *Italy in Transition: Conflict and Consensus,* London: Frank Cass, 1980, pp. 31–48.

7. The PCI came up with a broad formula for institutional change two decades ago. See Autori Vari [Various authors], *La riforma dello stato,* Rome: Editori Riuniti, 1968.

8. *Corriere della sera,* June 6, 1986, p. 2.

9. A Columbia University conference on "Italy 1985" quickly degenerated into another boring litany of Italy's parlous state and the role of the PCI in bringing this condition about. The tone of the Italian contributions is contained in conference papers reproduced in *Mondo operaio* 7 (July 1985): 24–46.

10. Indications of the PCI's centrality and how the party is treated can be sampled in A. Ranney and G. Sartori, eds., *Eurocommunism: The Italian Case,* Washington, D.C.: American Enterprise Institute, 1978; D. L. M. Blackmer and S. Tarrow, eds., *Communism in Italy and France,* Princeton: Princeton University Press, 1975; D. Sassoon, *The Strategy of the Italian Communist Party: From the Resistance to the Historic Compromise,* New York: St. Martin's Press, 1981; D. I. Kertzer, *Comrades and Christians: Religion and Political Struggle in Communist Italy,* Cambridge: Cambridge University Press, 1980; F. L. Cavazza and S. Graubard, eds., *Il caso italiano,* Milan: Garzanti, 1974; and R. Mieli, ed., *Il PCI allo specchio: Venticinque anni di storia del comunismo italiano,* Milan: Rizzoli, 1983.

11. Readers of Italian should not miss Napolitan's much noticed book, *In mezzo al guado,* Rome: Editori Riuniti, 1979.

12. See the very good treatment of this topic by Joan Barth Urban, *Moscow and the Italian Communist Party,* Ithaca: Cornell University Press, 1986.

13. Sidney Tarrow has insisted on this important aspect of Italian politics. See, for example, his "Three Years of Italian Democracy," in H. R. Penniman, ed., *Italy at the Polls, 1979,* Washington, D.C.: American Enterprise Institute, 1981, pp. 1–33.

14. Aspects of this theme are treated by Leonardo Morlino, "The Changing Re-

lationship between Parties and Society in Italy," *West European Politics* 7 (October 1984): 46–66.

15. References to the committee's report are taken from Commissione Parlamentare per la Riforma Istituzionale, *Relazione conclusiva*, Rome: Camera dei Deputati and Senato della Repubblica, January 29, 1985. The committee's brief and its general approach are described at pp. 5–15.

16. See Giuliano Amato, *Una repubblica da riformare*, Bologna: Il Mulino, 1980, esp. chap. 6.

17. However, do not assume that Italy's bureaucracy is in every sense "worse off" than its counterparts elsewhere in Western Europe. For some comparisons, see Istituto Centrale di Statistica, *Statistiche sulla pubblica amministrazione*, Rome: ISTAT, 1986. See the commentary on this volume in *Il messaggero*, August 2, 1986, p. 3.

18. For an eye-opener regarding the nature of Italy's "super elite," see Mauro Calise and Renato Mannheimer, *Governanti in Italia*, Bologna: Il Mulino, 1982, esp. pp. 147ff.

19. I am leaning heavily here on Sabino Cassese, "Esiste un governo in Italia?" in G. Pasquino, ed., *Il sistema politico italiano*, Bari: Laterza, 1985, pp. 269–303.

20. See Commissione Parlamentare, *Relazione conclusiva*, pp. 72–82.

21. The process of reform is, of course, deeply political. See, for example, Stefano Bartolini, "The Politics of Institutional Reform in Italy," *West European Politics* 5 (July 1982): 203–21. For why reform will not easily emerge, see Giuseppe Di Palma, "The Available State: Problems of Reform," in Lange and Tarrow, *Italy in Transition*, pp. 149–65.

22. For two examples of reactions of Italian authorities to the committee's proposals, see Gianni Ferrara, "Le risultanze della Commissione Bozzi: Un giudizio," *Democrazia e diritto* 25 (March–April 1985): 7–19, and Stefano Rodotà, "Istituzioni e società: Tra riforma e restaurazione," *Laboratorio politico* 2 (1983): 50–70. Cf. Franco Pizzetti, "Riforme istituzionali e prospettive di bicameralismo in Italia: Riflessioni e interrogativi," *Quaderni costituzionali* 4 (August 1984): 243–67.

23. Commissione Parlamentare, *Relazione conclusiva*, pp. 109–14.

24. Ibid., pp. 114–21.

CHAPTER 10

1. The best restatement of an earlier, exaggerated picture of Italy's internal political setting, as well as a discussion of changes that have occurred over the years, is Giacomo Sani, "The Political Culture of Italy: Continuity and Change," in G. A. Almond and S. Verba, eds., *The Civic Culture Revisited*, Boston: Little, Brown, 1980, pp. 273–324. Note, however, the cogent remarks of Maria Weber, *Italia: Paese europeo*, Milan: Franco Angeli, 1986, pp. 131–40.

2. For empirical evidence on the nature of ardent adherents to the DC and PCI, see Marcello Fedele, *Classi e partiti negli anni '70*, Rome: Editori Riuniti, 1979. Cf. S. Barnes, *Representation in Italy: Institutionalized Tradition and Electoral Choice*, Chicago: University of Chicago Press, 1977; A. Parisi, *Mobilità senza movimento*, Bologna: Il Mulino, 1980; and A. Parisi and G. Pasquino, "Changes in Electoral Behavior: The Relationship between Parties and Voters," in P. Lange and S. Tarrow, eds., *Italy in Transition: Consensus and Conflict*, London: Frank Cass, 1980, pp. 6–30.

3. See Giovanni Sartori, *Democratic Theory*, Detroit: Wayne State University Press, 1962, pp. 288–91, and Sartori, "Nota sul rapporto tra stato di diritto e stato di

giustizia," *Rivista internazionale di filosofia e diritto* 41 (January–April 1964): 310–16.

4. An English-language sampling: S. Silverman, *Three Bells of Civilization,* New York: Columbia University Press, 1975; J. Lopreato, *Peasants No More,* San Francisco: Chandler, 1967; A. Cornelisen, *Torregreca: Life, Death and Miracles,* Boston: Little, Brown, 1969; and R. Sarti, *Long Live the Strong,* Amherst: University of Massachusetts Press, 1985.

5. The best work around on this subject is R. D. Putnam, *The Beliefs of Politicians,* New Haven: Yale University Press, 1973.

6. See the impressive evidence arrayed by M. Calise and R. Mannheimer, *I governanti in Italia,* Bologna: Il Mulino, 1982.

7. For two other descriptions of the relationship, see Giuseppe Di Palma, "The Available State: Problems of Reform," in Lange and Tarrow, *Italy in Transition,* pp. 149–65, and Peter Lange, "Semiphery and Core in the European Context: Reflections on the Postwar Italian Experience," in G. Arrighi, ed., *Semiperipheral Development,* London: Sage, 1985, pp. 179–212.

8. See G. Guarino, *Quale costituzione: Saggio sulla classe politica,* Milan: Rizzoli, 1980, for a striking depiction of the role of parties. Cf. G. Gozzini and L. Anderlini, eds., *I partiti e lo stato,* Bari: De Donato, 1982. For a view that does not come down hard on party government as I have described it, see F. D'Onofrio, "I partiti, il parlamento, il governo," in Gozzini and Anderlini, *I partiti e lo stato,* pp. 87–102.

9. S. P. Huntington, "Social and Institutional Dynamics of One-Party Systems," in S. P. Huntington and C. M. Moore, eds., *Authoritarian Politics in Modern Society,* New York: Basic Books, 1970, pp. 3–47.

10. Insights into this folly are provided by Denis Mack Smith, *Mussolini,* New York: Knopf, 1982, and by Macgregor Knox, *Mussolini Unleashed, 1939–1941,* Cambridge: Cambridge University Press, 1982.

11. See Sidney Tarrow, *Peasant Communism in Southern Italy,* New Haven: Yale University Press, 1967.

12. A thoughtful analysis of this critical moment of transition is found in G. Di Palma, "Italy: Is There a Legacy and Is It Fascist?" in J. Herz, ed., *From Dictatorship to Democracy,* Westport, Conn.: Greenwood Press, 1982, pp. 107–34.

INDEX

Achille Lauro, 168, 195, 232
AGIP, defined, 76–77
Agnelli, Gianni, 1, 41, 80, 185
Andreotti, Giulio, 238, 249
Anticlericalism, conditions for, 63–64
Art and artists: role of, 65; patronage of, 65–66; political penetration of, 66–68
Autonomia Operaia Organizzata, 175, 180
Azzione Cattolica Italiana. *See* Catholic Action

Bakunin, Mikhail, 171
Berlinguer, Enrico, 37, 108–9, 131, 221
Bicycle Thief, The, 16
Brigate Rosse. *See* Red Brigades
Bureaucracy: political pressure on, 209; and patron-and-client system, 209–10; and *parentela*, 210

Cagol, Mara, 192
Calogero, Pietro, 174
Camorra, 111, 170; and the state, 84. *See also* Mafia; Organized crime
Campanilismo, defined, 86
Cardinale, Claudia, 66
Catholic Action, 36, 61, 63, 176
Catholic church, 36, 52, 58, 218; role of, in politics, 60; history of political involvement, 60–61; and Liberation Theology, 61–62, 241; power of, in politics, 62–63; and Christian Democratic party, 63; involvement in politics of, 63–65; and the Italian left, 176–77. *See also* Christian Democratic party; Vatican
Cavour, Count Camillo di, 8
Christian Democratic party (DC), 11, 34, 35–36, 61, 84, 118–19, 121–22, 201, 204, 218, 235; and industry, 77–78; and the IRI, 78; Communist party view of, 122; factions of, 123–24; and June *1983* election, 131; decline of, 142–43; and the Italian left, 176–

77; political resurgence of, 241; antipathy toward, 241; and the "swindle law," 255–56; and postwar Italy, 279–80. *See also* Catholic church; Vatican; *and individual parties*
Churchill, Winston, 15
Classe dirigente, la: defined, 147; members of, 147; and *la classe politica*, compared, 146–47
Classe politica, la, 87, 143, 197, 286; defined, 146; members of, 146–48; and the *razza padrona*, 147; and political parties, 148; as scapegoat, 148–49, 152, 154–55; criticism of, and fate of democracy, 149; criticism of, and the Mafia, 150; criticism of, and terrorism, 150; criticism of, and tax evasion, 150–51; criticism of, and communism, 151–52; reactions to, 152; effects of, 152–54; as abstraction, 153; as government surrogate, 153–54; as profession, 155–56; stability within, 156–57; expansion of, 157; as "professional performers," 157; homogeneity of, 158; accomplishments of, 160–65; and institutional reform, 254; characteristics of, 266–69. See also *Classe dirigente, la*; Government, national
Committee of Forty, 251, 253; activity of, 242–43; *partitocrazia* exhibited by, 244; findings of, 245–50; recommendations of, 253–57
Communione e Liberazione (Communion and Liberation; CL), 36
Communist party (PCI), 2, 35, 53, 55, 63, 67, 84, 118–19, 174, 175, 214–15, 218, 222, 253; and Federation of Young Italian Communists (FGCI), 35; and the Catholic church, 63; impact on society of, 83–84; function of, 118–19; and party factions, 122–23; and June *1983* election, 130; and status of Ital-